An Introduction to International Capital Markets

For other titles in the Wiley Finance Series
please see www.wiley.com/finance

An Introduction to International Capital Markets

Products, Strategies, Participants

Second Edition

Andrew M. Chisholm

A John Wiley and Sons, Ltd., Publication

This edition first published 2009
© 2009 John Wiley & Sons, Ltd

Registered office

John Wiley & Sons Ltd, The Atrium, Southern Gate, Chichester, West Sussex, PO19 8SQ, United Kingdom

For details of our global editorial offices, for customer services and for information about how to apply for permission to reuse the copyright material in this book please see our website at www.wiley.com.

Library of Congress Cataloging-in-Publication Data

Chisholm, Andrew, 1959-
  An introduction to international capital markets : products, strategies, participants / Andrew M. Chisholm. – 2nd ed.
    p. cm. – (Wiley finance series)
  Rev. ed. of: An introduction to capital markets : products, strategies, participants. 2002.
  Includes bibliographical references and index.
  ISBN 978-0-470-75898-4 (cloth : alk. paper)
  1. Capital market. 2. International finance. I. Chisholm, Andrew, 1959- Introduction to capital markets. II. Title.
  HG4523.C485 2009
  332′.041–dc22

                                                                                                    2009013327

ISBN 978-0-470-75898-4 (H/B)

A catalogue record for this book is available from the British Library.

Typeset in 10/12pt Times by Laserwords Private Limited, Chennai, India
Printed in Great Britain by CPI Antony Rowe, Chippenham, Wiltshire

For Sheila

Wipe your glosses with what you know.
James Joyce.

Contents

Acknowledgements

This book owes a great deal to the late Paul Roth, a very brilliant man who had the uncommon ability to explain complex ideas in a simple way. We all miss him. My thanks to Sam Whittaker at John Wiley who commissioned the first edition and to Sir George Mathewson who somehow found the time to read the original manuscript. Jonathan Shaw's kind remarks about the first edition and suggestions that a new version would be valuable started me off on this second edition. I am also grateful to Neil Schofield who commented on the new chapter on credit markets, and to Pete Baker and Aimee Dibbens for keeping me on track. Finally, I would like to thank all of those I have worked with over the years in the financial markets, too numerous to mention individually, who have given their time and patience to help improve my understanding of the industry. It is a competitive business but I have experienced a lot of kindness and support along the way.

1
Introduction: The Market Context

1.1 CAPITAL AND THE CAPITAL MARKETS

Financial capital can be defined as accumulated wealth that is available to create further wealth. The **capital markets** are places where those who require additional funds seek out others who wish to invest their excess. They are also places where participants can manage and spread their risks. Originally, capital markets were physical spaces such as coffee houses and then purpose-built exchanges. In our day, capital markets participants may be located in different continents and conduct deals using advanced information technology.

Who are the users of capital? In a broad sense we all are, at least part of the time. We borrow money to buy a house or a car so that we can live our lives, do our jobs, and make our own small contribution to the growing wealth of nations. We save to pay school and university tuition fees, investing in the 'human capital' that will sustain the economic health of the country. More narrowly, though, financial capital is used by corporations, governments, state and municipal authorities, and international agencies to make investments in productive resources. When a company builds a new factory it is engaged in capital expenditure – using funds provided by shareholders or lenders or set aside from past profits to purchase assets used to generate future revenues. Governments use tax revenues to invest in infrastructure projects such as roads. Agencies such as the World Bank inject funds into developing countries to create a basis for economic growth and future prosperity.

Who are the suppliers of capital? Again, the answer is that we all are. Sometimes we do this directly by buying shares issued by corporations and debt securities issued by governments and their agencies. Sometimes we employ brokers to invest funds on our behalf. We deposit cash in bank accounts, invest in mutual funds, and set aside money in pension plans for our retirement. We pay taxes to the government and local authorities. We pay premiums to insurance companies who invest the proceeds against their future liabilities. Companies too become sources of capital when they reinvest their profits rather than paying cash dividends to shareholders.

This book is about the operation of the capital markets, the market participants, the roles of the main financial intermediaries, and the products and techniques used to bring together the suppliers and users of financial capital in the modern world. It is also to a large extent about the management of risk. Risk takes many forms in the capital markets, and financial institutions play a critical role in assessing, managing, and distributing risk. For example, a bank that lends money assumes a **credit risk** – the risk that the borrower may default on its payments. Bankers try to analyse and mitigate such exposures to minimize losses. As the global 'credit crisis' which started in 2007 revealed, when they fail it has major repercussions not only for bank shareholders and depositors but also for taxpayers and for individuals working in the 'real economy' outside the banking system.

In recent years banks have increasingly used their position as financial intermediaries to originate loans and then 'package' them up and sell them off in the form of bond issues. This process is called **securitization**. The bond investors assume the credit risk on the loan book in return for a rate of interest greater than they could earn on safe government securities. The banks recycle the capital they were originally provided with by their shareholders and depositors, so that they have funds available to create new loans. They analyse risk, manage risk, and then distribute risk through the public bond markets.

This so-called 'originate and distribute' business model received a setback in the credit crisis starting in 2007, when bonds backed by US mortgage loans suffered major losses and became difficult to trade. It seems highly likely that securitization will remain a standard technique in the capital markets for the foreseeable future. However it also seems likely that the practice will be subject to closer supervision by the regulatory authorities.

The boundaries between different types of financial institutions have been becoming increasingly blurred in the modern financial markets. Earlier in the previous century the demarcation lines seemed more rigid. In the US the 1933 Glass-Steagall Act created a firm distinction between what became known as **commercial banking** and **investment banking**. Commercial banks took in deposits and made loans to businesses. They assumed credit or default risk and contained this risk by evaluating the creditworthiness of borrowers and by managing a diversified portfolio of loans. Investment banks underwrote new issues of securities and dealt in shares and bonds. They took **underwriting risk**. This arises when a bank or a syndicate buys an issue of securities from the issuer at a fixed price and assumes responsibility for selling or 'placing' the stock into the capital markets.

At the time of Glass-Steagall, the US Congress believed that a financial institution faced a conflict of interest if it operated as both an investment and a commercial bank. As a consequence, the great banking house of Morgan split into two separate organizations. The commercial banking business later became part of JP Morgan Chase. The investment banking business was formed into Morgan Stanley.

In the UK similar divisions of responsibility used to apply until the barriers were progressively removed. After the Second World War and until the 1980s the new issue business in London was largely the province of so-called **merchant banks**. Retail and corporate banking was dominated by the major clearing or 'money centre' banks such as Barclays and National Westminster Bank (now part of the Royal Bank of Scotland group). Trading and broking in UK and European shares and in UK government bonds in London was conducted by a number of small partnership-businesses with evocative names such as James Capel and Wedd Durlacher. The insurance companies were separate from the banks, and the world insurance market was dominated by Lloyds of London. These segregations have all since been swept away. Nowadays large UK financial institutions offer a very wide range of banking and investment products and services to corporate, institutional, and retail clients.

In the US the constraints of Glass-Steagall were gradually lifted towards the end of the twentieth century. US commercial banks started to move back into the new issuance business both inside the US and through their overseas operations. One factor that spurred this development is called **disintermediation**. In the last decades of the twentieth century more and more corporate borrowers chose to raise funds directly from investors by issuing bonds (tradable debt securities) rather than by borrowing from commercial banks. The development was particularly marked amongst top-quality US borrowers with excellent credit ratings. In part the incentive was to cut out the margin charged by the commercial banks for their role as intermediaries between the ultimate suppliers of financial capital (depositors) and the ultimate users. In part it reflected the overall decline in the credit quality of the commercial banks themselves. Prime quality borrowers discovered that they could issue debt securities and fund their capital requirements at keener rates than many commercial banks.

Disintermediation (cutting out the intermediation of the lending banks) developed apace in the US and then spread to other financial markets. Later even lower credit quality borrowers found that in favourable circumstances they could raise funds through the public bond markets.

The advent of the new single European currency, the euro, encouraged the same sort of process in continental Europe. Before the single currency was created, Europe developed as a collection of small and fragmented financial markets with many regional and local banks. Banks and corporations had strong mutual relationships, cemented by cross-shareholdings. In Germany the major banks and insurance companies owned large slices of the top industrial companies. Most corporate borrowing was conducted with the relationship bank. Shares and bonds were issued and traded primarily in domestic markets and in a range of different currencies. There were restrictions on the extent to which institutional investors such as pension funds could hold foreign currency assets. There was a general lack of understanding amongst investors of other European markets.

All this has been changing in recent decades, and at great speed. For example, Deutsche Bank has grown to be a major international presence in the global capital markets, with substantial operations in centres such as New York and London as well as in Frankfurt. Although cross-border mergers are still complicated by the actions of governments and regulators, banks across Europe have been consolidating. For example, in 2005 the Uncredit group of Italy merged with the Munich-based HVB group, which was itself formed from the merger of two Bavarian banks. In 2007 the Dutch bank ABN-Amro was taken over by a consortium led by the Royal Bank of Scotland. On their side, European borrowers are increasingly looking to the new issue markets to raise funds. Investors in Europe can now buy shares and bonds and other securities denominated in a single currency that are freely and actively traded across an entire continent. Stock and derivative exchanges that originated in national markets have been merging and re-inventing themselves as cross-border trading platforms.

One of the most dynamic influences on the international capital markets in recent years has been the growth of **hedge funds**. Essentially, hedge funds are investment vehicles aimed at wealthier investors and run by professional managers. Traditionally they were largely unregulated, but this is now set to change in the aftermath of the global credit crisis. Often hedge funds use leverage (borrowing) in an attempt to magnify the returns to the investors. Unlike a traditional mutual fund, which buys and holds stocks for a period of time and therefore tends to profit when markets rise and lose when they fall, hedge funds aim to achieve an absolute return – that is to say, to make money in all market conditions. This comes at a price however. Typically a hedge fund manager takes '2 and 20': a 2 % annual management fee plus 20 % of the profits. Investors also tend to be 'locked in' for agreed time periods and so cannot quickly redeem their investments.

Hedge funds can pursue a wide range of different strategies, some of which are highly risky, though others are actually designed to contain risk. One classic approach is the **long-short fund**. As well as buying ('going long') shares, it can also take short positions. This involves betting that the price of a security (or an entire market index) will fall over a given period of time. Sometimes a hedge fund constructs a 'spread' trade, which involves betting that the price difference between two stocks or markets will increase or reduce over a given period.

However, the activities of hedge funds have greatly diversified in recent years. Some buy shares of companies that are potential takeover targets. Others speculate on commodity prices and currency rates, analysing macroeconomic trends in the global economy. Some use complex mathematical models to exploit pricing anomalies; while others bet on the levels of volatility in the market by using derivative products. There are also hedge funds which take direct stakes in unlisted companies, which is the traditional business of private equity houses. Some hedge funds invest in so-called 'distressed' securities, such as bonds issued by companies in severe financial difficulties. They can profit if the amount recovered by selling off the company's assets exceeds the price paid for the bonds.

One of the major growth areas for investment banks in recent years is the **prime brokerage** business, which involves providing high-value services to hedge funds. This includes stock lending, research advice, trading and settlement services, administrative support, providing loans against collateral, and tailoring advanced structured products to help a hedge fund implement a particular investment strategy.

Outside Europe and the US, a recent key trend in the capital markets is the rise of China, India, Brazil, and other emerging countries. With its huge trade surpluses, China has amassed capital that is no longer invested only in US government bonds. For example, in 2007 it took a $3 billion stake in US private equity firm Blackstone in an initial public offering of shares.

The power of so-called **sovereign wealth funds** (SWFs) is now felt everywhere in global markets. SWFs make international investments using wealth derived from the sale of natural resources and other export activities. According to forecasts published by the *Economist* in May 2007, based on research from Morgan Stanley, SWFs could have assets of $12 trillion under management by 2015. The largest SWF as at March 2007 was run by the United Allied Emirates with assets of $875 billion. At that time China had around $300 billion under management. In 2008 US banks such as Citigroup and Merrill Lynch sought major cash injections from SWFs to re-build their balance sheets following losses in the sub-prime mortgage lending market.

1.2   THE EUROMARKETS (INTERNATIONAL CAPITAL MARKETS)

The modern capital markets have become truly global in their scale and scope. Although New York is the biggest financial centre in the world by many measures, some of the developments that led to today's international marketplace for money originated in London. In the years immediately following the Second World War London had lost its traditional role as a place where financial capital could be raised for large-scale overseas investment projects. It shrank to a small domestic market centred around the issuance and trading of UK shares and government bonds. It rediscovered its global focus through the growth of the so-called **Euromarkets** starting in the 1950s and 1960s. (The prefix 'Euro' here is historical and does not relate to the single European currency, which was created later.)

It all started with **Eurodollars**. These are dollars held in international accounts outside the direct regulatory control of the US central bank, the Federal Reserve. The largest Eurodollar market is based in London, and from the 1950s banks from the US and around the world set up operations in London to capture a share of this lucrative business. These dollars were recycled as loans to corporate and sovereign borrowers, and through the creation of

Eurodollar bonds sold to international investors searching for an attractive return on their surplus dollars. The first Eurobond was issued by Autostrade as far back as 1963.

The oil crisis of the early 1970s gave a tremendous boost to the Euromarkets. Huge quantities of so-called petrodollars from wealthy Arab countries found a home with London-based banks. The Eurobond market boomed in 1975, and the international market for securities has never looked back. The banks became ever more innovative in the financial instruments they created. A market developed in other Eurocurrencies – Euromarks, Euroyen, and so forth. The watchwords of the Euromarkets are innovation and self-regulation. The UK government allowed the market to develop largely unhindered, and kept its main focus on the domestic sterling markets and the UK banking system. To avoid confusion with the new single European currency, Eurobonds are now often referred to as 'international bonds'. They can be denominated in a range of different currencies, though the US dollar is still the most popular.

Although London is the home of the Euromarkets, there are other centres such as in Asia. The London market has been compared to the Wimbledon tennis tournament – it is staged in the UK but the most successful players are foreigners. This is not entirely fair, given the presence of firms such as Barclays Capital and Royal Bank of Scotland. However it is true that the large US, German, and Swiss banks are strong competitors. The trade association for Eurobond dealers is the International Capital Market Association (ICMA). It provides the self-regulatory code of rules and practices which govern the issuance and trading of securities.

1.3 MODERN INVESTMENT BANKING

The term 'investment banking' tends to be used nowadays as something of an umbrella expression for a set of more-or-less related activities in the world of finance. Firms such as Goldman Sachs and Morgan Stanley were up until very recently classified as 'pure play' investment banks because of their focus on debt and equity (share) issuance and trading as well as on mergers and acquisitions advisory work. Other organizations such as Citigroup and JP Morgan Chase have actually developed as highly diversified 'universal' banks which have commercial and investment banking divisions as well as other businesses such as retail banking, credit cards, mortgage lending, and asset management.

In the wake of the credit crisis, however, it is not clear what the future holds for the concept of a 'pure play' investment bank, except for smaller niche businesses which focus on specific areas such as corporate finance. In March 2008, in the wake of the crisis which began over write-downs on the value of sub-prime loans, Wall Street's fifth largest investment bank Bear Stearns was taken over by JP Morgan Chase. In September 2008, Lehman Brothers filed for bankruptcy, and Merrill Lynch was taken over by Bank of America for around $ 50 billion. In the same month the two remaining major US investment banking giants, Morgan Stanley and Goldman Sachs, asked the US Federal Reserve to change their status to bank holding companies. This means that they are now subject to tighter regulation, including requirements on holding capital against potential losses. However it also allows them to act as deposit-taking institutions and to borrow directly from the Federal Reserve.

In some ways it is easier to explain what does *not* happen inside an investment banking operation these days than what does. For example, it will *not* operate a mass-market retail banking business, which demands a completely different skill set. If an investment bank is a division of a large universal bank then retail banking will be located elsewhere in the group.

An investment banking operation *will* handle activities in the international wholesale capital markets and will also house the corporate advisory function. It will manage new issues of securities for corporations and governments, distributing the stock amongst investors; conduct research on financial markets; trade shares, bonds, commodities, currencies, and other assets; advise institutional investors on which assets to buy and sell and execute orders on their behalf; and structure complex risk management and investment products for clients.

There is a more detailed list below of the activities typically carried out in an investment banking operation, with a brief description of what happens in each business area. The next section also sets out some profiles of clients of investment banks. Some large banking groups have also folded in with their investment banking division that part of the operation which makes loans to major corporate customers. The view taken here is that large clients expect their relationship bank to 'put its balance sheet at their disposal' and that corporate lending, while not in itself particularly profitable, will lead to lucrative investment banking mandates.

- **Corporate Finance or Advisory.**
  Advising corporations on mergers, takeovers, and acquisitions.
  Advising corporations on strategic and financial restructurings.
  Advising governments on the privatization of state assets.
- **Debt Markets.**
  Debt capital markets (DCM): managing or 'originating' new bond issues and underwriting issues for corporate and sovereign borrowers, often operating as a member of a syndicate of banks.
  Government bonds ('govies'): research, trading, sales.
  Corporate and emerging markets bonds: sales, trading, credit research (researching into the risk of changes in the credit quality of bonds, which will affect their market value).
  Credit derivatives (products that manage and redistribute credit risk): research, trading, sales.
  'Flow' derivative products (standardized derivatives dealt in volumes): research, trading, sales.
  Foreign exchange: research, trading, sales, and currency risk management solutions for corporations and investors.
  Structured derivative products (complex structures often devised with the needs of specific corporate or investment clients).
- **Equity Capital Markets (ECM).**
  Advising companies on initial public offerings (IPOs) of shares and subsequent offerings of new shares to investors.
  Underwriting and syndicating new equity issues.
  (Note that in some banks DCM and ECM have been combined into a single entity responsible for helping clients raise either debt or equity capital.)
- **Equities and Equity Derivatives.**
  Cash equities (known as common stock in the US and ordinary shares in the UK): research, trading, sales to institutional investors.
  Equity derivatives: equity swaps, options, and structured products. Trading, sales and research, dealing with investors and corporations.

An investment banking business or division *may* also include:

- a custody business which holds securities on behalf of clients and manages cash;
- a private banking and wealth management operation aimed at high net-worth individuals;
- a private equity business which invests the bank's own capital and that of its clients in unlisted companies and in the shares of companies listed on smaller stockmarkets;

- a structured finance operation which creates complex and tailored funding structures;
- a prime brokerage team which provides value-added services aimed at hedge funds.

It *will* include:

- operational staff who settle trades and handle payments (the so-called 'back office');
- risk management specialists and auditors and 'middle office' staff who monitor and measure risks and exposures and profits;
- information technology professionals who develop and manage the bank's computer systems;
- human resources and other support functions.

One of the most distinctive features of investment banking is the **trading function**. Essentially, traders buy and sell assets to make a profit. A trader who has bought more of a particular security (such as a share or bond) than he or she has sold is said to have a 'long position' in that security. A trader who has sold more of a security than he or she has bought is said to hold a 'short position'. In share trading, short positions are managed by borrowing stock from investors on a temporary basis, and providing collateral in the form of cash or bonds to protect the lender. Some deals are made on organized exchanges, such as the New York Stock Exchange. Other deals are conducted on an **over-the-counter** (OTC) basis, which means that they are arranged directly between two parties, one of which is normally a bank. Most corporate bonds are traded OTC. In the past bond trades were conducted over the telephone, though now the transactions may be made through electronic networks.

Traders are given **risk limits** so that there is a limit to the amount that the bank is exposed to by their activities. One technique developed in recent years is called **value-at-risk (VaR)**. This uses statistical methods to forecast the maximum loss likely to be made on a particular trading position over a given time period to a given level of confidence. At an aggregate level, it is also possible to assess the benefits that arise from the fact that a bank tends to hold a diversified portfolio of assets, so that losses on one trading position may be offset by gains on another.

Statistical tools such as value-at-risk can be effective in managing risk in normal market conditions. However, banks tend to augment such models by using what is known as **stress testing**. This involves investigating the losses the bank would be likely to make in extreme circumstances, when asset prices become highly volatile or when 'liquidity' dries up in the market – that is, when it becomes difficult to trade at all without having a major impact on prices. For example, a bank might explore what would happen to its current trading positions if a scenario as extreme as the 1987 stock market crash were to happen now.

In theory, there are two different types of traders, although in reality the distinction is far less clear-cut. Some traders act as **market makers**. They make two-way prices consisting of bid (buy) and ask or offer (sell) prices in particular assets, such as shares or bonds. This helps to ensure that there is an active and liquid market in those securities. The difference between the two prices is known as the **bid-ask spread**. It tends to widen in volatile markets.

Sometimes market makers operating in particularly active markets are known as 'flow traders'. Their role is essentially about facilitating the needs of the clients of the bank, which can be assured of obtaining a price for assets even in difficult circumstances. A market maker buys and sells securities on his or her trading book, and takes **market risk** – the risk of losing money because of changes in the market value of those securities. It may sometimes be necessary to manage or hedge market risk by using products such as financial futures.

In volatile markets it may be very difficult to avoid taking losses. On the other hand, 'flow traders' can acquire useful information about what is happening in the markets which they can use to manage their positions.

The other type of trader is a **proprietary** trader, who takes positions using the bank's own capital rather than facilitating client business. For example, a 'prop' trader may decide to 'go short' by selling US dollars, anticipating a fall in the value of the currency. In practice, though, market makers are normally also allowed to take market views, within defined limits.

1.4   THE CLIENTS OF INVESTMENT BANKS

Investment banks deal with corporations, investing institutions such as pension funds, governments, hedge funds, municipal authorities, and supranational bodies. They also deal with other commercial and investment banks. For example, the bulk of international currency trading takes place between banks. The larger international investment banking operations also provide services for smaller regional and local banks. For instance, if a small bank wishes to construct a deal to help a corporate client solve a complex risk management problem, perhaps hedging against changes in currency rates or commodity prices, then it may turn to a global investment bank for help and advice. It may have a long-standing relationship with the investment bank.

One of the key roles of an investment banking operation is to act as an intermediary between corporations that need to raise financial capital through share or bond issues, and the large investors that ultimately purchase such assets. For example, in an **initial public offering** (IPO) a company sells its shares to the public and obtains a listing on a regulated stock exchange. It is assisted in the process by an investment bank acting as **lead manager** (sometimes more than one is involved). The lead manager helps to set the offer price for the stock and typically underwrites the issue, operating with a syndicate of other banks. In effect, the syndicate agrees to take up any unsold stock at the offer price. The sales people help to 'place' or distribute the shares amongst investors, and the traders will normally make a market in the stock after it is issued to provide liquidity.

In the capital markets institutional investors such as pension funds and insurance companies are sometimes referred to as the 'buy side'. Investment banks and securities houses are called the 'sell side' because they advise institutional investors on suitable assets to purchase. In effect, what the analysts and the sales people in investment banking operations are selling is investment ideas. Their traders then execute the resulting customer orders. The bank earns brokerage commissions on orders, and also gains from the fact that the traders charge a bid-offer spread. In practice, there can be tensions between the sales staff and the traders in a dealing room because the former are seeking to maintain a good relationship with key clients, which involves making attractive prices, while the latter are trying to run a profitable trading book.

The remaining paragraphs of this section outline the main institutional investors and their investment objectives.

Pension schemes are sponsored by companies and other organizations to help their employees provide for their retirement. There are two main kinds. A **defined benefit** (or final salary) scheme promises to make certain payments to pensioners, such as a percentage of their final salary on retirement, in some cases rising in line with inflation. By contrast, in a **defined contribution** scheme the sponsor and the employee make regular payments which are invested in assets such as shares and bonds. The pension received by an individual depends on the level of contributions and the performance of the assets in which those contributions are invested. The management of the money is normally outsourced to a professional asset management firm. Sometimes individuals have a right to choose between different funds which have stated investment strategies. In the US employees are allowed to contribute a proportion of their salary to a defined contribution scheme known as a participant-directed 401(k) plan. Normally cash can be reallocated between funds at any time.

Defined benefit schemes have to generate sufficient returns so that the sponsor can discharge its obligations to the pensioners. The sponsor will be advised by actuaries who establish the future liabilities, taking into account forecasts of salary growth, mortality rates, changes in the workforce, and early retirement rates. A **fully funded** plan is one in which the assets match the liabilities. The managers of the fund will also have to take into account cash inflows and outflows, and ensure that there is sufficient cash and liquid assets available to make payments.

The investment strategy of a defined benefit plan is influenced by a wide range of factors. The key considerations include workforce demographics, the extent of provision for early retirement, whether the fund is currently in surplus or deficit, and constraints imposed by government regulations on what are considered to be suitable investments for pension schemes. A scheme run for a company with a younger workforce will have a longer investment time horizon than one in which the majority of members are already retired, and the fund managers may be prepared to be more risk-seeking. However, the investment strategy will also be influenced by market forecasts. For example, if the sponsor or fund manager believes that inflation is set to increase in the future it may prefer to invest in securities which offer some level of protection, such as shares or alternatively bonds that pay a variable rate of interest.

Some banks are now prepared to take over complete pension obligations from companies. For example, in February 2008 it was announced that a subsidiary of Goldman Sachs would acquire the defined benefits pension scheme of UK gaming operator Rank Group after taking part in a bidding process. In this deal, Goldman Sachs assumed the risks and the liabilities of the scheme, which had approximately 19,000 members. In arrangements of this kind the acquiring bank can gain if it is able to manage the assets effectively so that it can honour the pension commitments and still return a profit. It can also benefit if the payments to pensioners are less than originally forecast.

Unlike pension funds, which are aimed at individuals, an **endowment fund** is designed to generate income for an entity such as a university, hospital, school, or charitable institution. They are particularly important in the US. The managers typically invest in long-term assets, and the protection of the value of the capital is an important consideration. Investments may be in government bonds, shares of 'blue chip' companies, and low risk corporate bonds.

The job of the insurance industry is to help protect against personal and business risks. The premiums collected from policy holders are invested in assets such as shares and bonds. **Life insurance** companies provide a benefit that is linked to the survival or death of the policy holder. A whole life policy provides a payment on the event of death to a beneficiary, which may be a fixed sum of money or based on the performance of a given fund. In an annuity contract an individual uses an accumulated pension fund to purchase an annuity from a life insurance company, which pays a regular sum of money until death. Some annuities rise in line with inflation.

The main investment objective of a life insurance company is to provide for the benefits and claims of the policy holders, as forecast by the actuaries. Life insurance companies are long-term investors and may hold investment assets for 20 and more years. They tend to invest in long-dated corporate and government bonds. In some countries, life funds may also invest in equities to achieve capital growth and also to hedge against inflation. However the industry tends to be heavily regulated by governments and only certain authorized investments are permitted.

Non-life insurance companies provide a wide range of policies including health and property insurance and insurance against claims for negligence and occupational injuries. The liabilities of non-life companies tend to be shorter-term compared to life companies, though there is more uncertainty over the timing and the size of payments that will have to be made to policy holders. As a result, non-life companies are concerned about liquidity and tend to hold a percentage of their portfolio in short-term securities such as Treasury bills, as well as investing in longer-dated securities and equities. The longer-dated bonds may be chosen with maturities that match anticipated obligations, or to ensure a rate of return that generates sufficient cash to match those obligations. Switching from government bonds into corporate bonds may increase investment returns, though at the expense of taking on a higher risk of default. In general, non-life companies may be prepared to purchase a certain proportion of riskier assets in pursuit of higher returns. They tend to be less highly regulated than life companies and have greater investment flexibility.

As well as pension funds and insurance companies, investment banks also deal with **investment companies**. These are vehicles which pool money from investors and invest in assets such as shares, bonds, and commodities. The assets are managed by professional money managers. The precise legal structure varies between countries, but broadly speaking there are two main types of investment companies: closed-ended and open-ended. A **closed-ended** fund is a limited company which has a set number of ordinary shares (common stock) currently on issue. The shares are listed on a stock exchange or traded over-the-counter by dealers. The company can actually create new shares through periodic secondary offerings, though this is a relatively cumbersome procedure.

The net asset value per share (NAV) of a closed-ended fund equals its assets less its liabilities divided by the number of shares. The shares can trade at a discount or premium to the NAV. For example, the shares of a fund which holds attractive assets which investors find hard to access directly may be in considerable demand. Because there is limited supply, this can create a premium to NAV. However, if the fund holds more standard assets which are widely available it may find that its shares trade at a discount to NAV. In some countries so-called 'vulture funds' have bought such shares as a cheap way of gaining exposure to the underlying assets held by the fund. In theory, a 'vulture' can push for a vote to liquidate the fund, though liquidation can be costly. In practice, it may take a shorter-term view and seek to force the fund's management to take steps to reduce the discount to NAV, such as share buy-backs.

In an **open-ended** fund (known in the US as a mutual fund) the fund manager has the ability to create and sell new shares to investors on a regular basis. Investors buy and sell the shares directly from the fund manager or a broker operating on its behalf rather than on a stock exchange. In a no-load mutual fund shares are sold to investors at NAV. In a load fund investors have to pay an additional commission to the manager. Even in a no-load fund, however, investors may have to pay a charge when they redeem shares. Sometimes this decreases the longer the shares are held.

In the UK closed-ended funds are traditionally called **investment trusts**. As discussed above, they sometimes purchase and cancel their own shares in an attempt to reduce a discount to NAV. They can also borrow money to enhance the returns to the shareholders. The traditional open-ended investment vehicle in the UK is known as a **unit trust**. Here, investors buy and sell 'units' from the fund manager, which earns a commission by quoting a bid-ask spread. It also charges an annual management fee, which is typically around 1–2 %. In 1997 UK legislators introduced a new hybrid structure called an **open-ended investment company** (OEIC). This is set up as a limited company, but with the flexibility to issue or cancel shares in response to investor demand, so that the share price reflects the NAV. A further attraction is that OEIC shares are normally bought and sold at one price, with commission charged on top at an agreed rate.

The objectives of investment companies are many and varied. Some are set up to invest only in major 'blue chip' shares or in safe government bonds. However, others are designed to invest in emerging markets or ·commodities or lower credit quality corporate bonds, seeking higher returns from taking higher risks. Some funds aim to generate capital gains, reinvesting any earnings; whilst others focus on producing high levels of income from share dividends and from the interest received from cash and bonds.

One investment vehicle that has become popular in recent years is the **exchange-traded fund** (ETF). This has the aim of tracking a stockmarket index such as the S&P 500, or the price of a commodity such as gold. The advantage of an ETF is that shares in the fund can be bought and sold on an organized stock exchange via brokers. The expenses incurred in running the fund can also be relatively low.

1.5   ABOUT THIS BOOK

This book is intended to provide a convenient one-volume introduction to the capital markets. The subject is of course a massive one and there will necessarily be topics that individual readers will wish to explore later in more detail. There are many excellent titles in the Wiley Finance Series that perform this function. The aim of the current volume is to provide sufficient depth of explanation so that it is of practical use to people who are entering or planning to enter the capital markets business, or who are already working in the industry and who wish to improve their knowledge of specific areas of the markets.

Chapters 2 and 3 are concerned with two areas of the business that are intimately related, the market for short-term interest rate (STIR) products and the foreign exchange (FX) markets. In the past a bank dealing room handling such instruments would have been segregated into separate desks handling 'cash market' products and 'derivatives'. The cash or spot market is the underlying market, in this instance for short-term loans and deposits and for spot foreign exchange transactions. A derivative is anything whose value is derived from prices in the underlying cash market. Examples include options on interest rates and on currencies.

Nowadays the cash and derivatives businesses are closely aligned, and sales and marketing staff are expected to have a wide knowledge of a range of products that provide solutions to the problems of a bank's corporate and institutional clients. The traders are also expected to have an understanding of the impact of events in other aspects of the business on the particular instruments they deal in. Chapter 3 explores the links between the short-term interest rate market and the foreign exchange market and between spot trades and forward

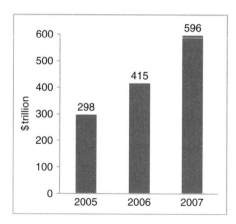

Figure 1.1 Notional amounts outstanding OTC derivative contracts at year-end.
Source: Bank for International Settlements.

foreign exchange deals. Later chapters continue the theme of linking events in the underlying and the derivatives markets.

Figure 1.1 above gives an idea of the size of modern derivatives markets and the tremendous growth rate. It shows the notional amounts outstanding for 'over-the-counter' contracts, which are bilateral deals agreed between two parties. The amounts are stated in trillions of US dollars.

Corporations and governments raise funds through the issuance of longer-term debt. Chapters 4–7 look at the markets for government and corporate bonds, the issuers and the investors, and the role of the banks in bringing issues to the market and in trading bonds. Investors and traders in bonds have to understand how securities are priced and how the returns and risks are evaluated. These chapters consider a range of measures including yield-to-maturity (internal rate of return), duration, convexity, and their practical applications and limitations.

The value of a financial asset such as a bond or a share (or indeed an entire company) is the present value of the expected future cash flows. The key to valuation is therefore an assessment of the likely future cash flows, and the application of the correct rate of discount with which to establish present value. Chapter 5 looks at the sensitivity of bonds to changes in market interest rates. Chapter 6 shows how to derive and apply discount rates and forward interest rates, absolutely essential tools in modern finance. Chapter 7 extends the discussion by exploring credit risk on debt securities as well as credit default swaps and securitization. It considers the relationship between the probability that a company will default on its debt obligations and the returns on its debt.

Corporations also raise funds through the issuance of shares (known as common stock in the US). Chapter 8 describes the role of equity capital markets specialists within investment banks in the process of issuing new shares. The majority of shares in modern developed markets are held by institutional investors. Chapters 8–10 explore equity investment styles and the markets for trading shares once they are issued. They also consider how shares are valued using multiples such as the price/earnings ratio and also using discounted cash flow methods.

As noted previously, in the modern capital markets banks and securities houses not only bring together investors with corporations and governments looking to raise funds. They also play a critical role in the evaluation and management of risk. Chapters 11–14 explain key products that are used to manage interest rate exposures and exposures to changes in bond values: forward rate agreements, interest rate futures, bond futures, and interest rate swaps. Through a series of examples and case studies these chapters show how these instruments are used in practice and how they can be priced using tools introduced in earlier chapters. Chapter 15 extends the discussion by exploring listed equity futures contracts and equity swap transactions.

One of the most remarkable features of the modern financial markets is the growth of financial options and structured products based on options. Sometimes the options are so deeply embedded in the structure of a financial product that it is not obvious to the untutored eye that they are there. Chapter 16 introduces fundamental option concepts and Chapter 17 describes the principles underlying the pricing of options, including an explanation of how the famous Black-Scholes option pricing model can be set up on a spreadsheet.

Chapter 18 considers the application of the pricing model in more detail. It looks at how the risks on option positions are measured and managed. Chapter 19 explores some of the many applications of options in hedging and trading. Chapter 20 applies option concepts to currency and interest rate options, with a set of risk management cases and examples. It considers how the standard pricing methodology can be adapted to value currency options and key interest rate option products such as caps, floors, and swaptions. Finally Chapter 20 discusses convertible bonds and their use in investment and in constructing arbitrage trades.

2
The Money Markets

2.1 CHAPTER OVERVIEW

This chapter explores the markets for borrowing and lending funds over the short term, traditionally known as the money markets. Borrowers include corporations, banks, and governments. Investors include pension funds, insurance companies, corporations, governments, and some retail investors. Money dealers working for major banks provide liquidity to the market by taking in deposits and making loans. Borrowers can also raise funds directly from investors by issuing short-term debt securities which are tradable in secondary markets. A domestic money market is one in which funds are borrowed and lent in the home currency, subject to the authority of the central bank. The largest is for deals made in US dollars contracted inside the United States. This chapter considers the role of central banks such as the US Federal Reserve, the European Central Bank, the Bank of England, and the Bank of Japan in the day-to-day operations of domestic money markets and in setting interest rates. It looks at how governments borrow on a short-term basis by issuing Treasury bills, and at their repo operations. In addition to domestic money markets there is an international wholesale market for borrowing and lending funds traditionally called the Eurocurrency market. It is based in global financial centres such as London. The prefix 'Euro' here is historical and is not related to the new European single currency. The chapter reviews the growth of the Eurocurrency market. It considers the major types of financial instruments used, including Eurocurrency loans and deposits, certificates of deposit, and Euro-commercial paper.

2.2 DOMESTIC MONEY MARKETS

The money markets are markets for borrowing and lending funds over the short term. 'Short term' is usually taken to mean a maturity of one year or less, although in practice some money maket deals have maturities greater than one year. Major economies such as the US, Germany, France, the UK, and Japan have highly developed domestic money markets in which short-term funds are borrowed and lent in the local currency, subject to the control of the regulatory authority of the central bank. These domestic money markets are quite distinct from the so-called **Eurocurrency market** which is an international market in which banks take deposits and make loans in a range of currencies outside the home country for those currencies, and outside the direct regulatory control of the central banks responsible for those currencies.

2.2.1 Market Participants

Borrowers using the money markets include:

- financial institutions such as commercial and investment banks;
- companies (often known as 'corporates' in the banking world);
- governments, their agencies, state and regional authorities.

The main investors are organizations (and some individuals) with surplus cash to invest, including:

- insurance companies, pension funds, mutual funds;
- the treasury departments of large multinational corporations;
- governments, their agencies, state and regional authorities.

Money dealers working for banks and securities houses around the world bring borrowers and investors together by helping to create an active and liquid market for money market instruments. Business is conducted by telephone and through computer screens rather than on a physical marketplace. At the simplest level, money dealers take in short-term deposits and make short-term loans (sometimes known as 'placements'). They may also trade a range of short-term interest rate ('STIR') products such as Treasury bills, commercial paper, and certificates of deposit. These are described in detail in the current chapter.

Basis Points

Market participants often refer to interest rates in terms of **basis points**. One basis point is 0.01 % p.a. Therefore 100 basis points is 1 % p.a. If a central bank increases or lowers interest rates by 25 basis points this represents a change of 0.25 % p.a.

2.3   US DOMESTIC MARKETS

Activities in the US domestic money markets are dominated by the operations of the Federal Reserve System, the US central bank. The 'Fed' has been used as a model for central banks around the world, and many of its features appear in the new European System of Central Banks.

The Federal Reserve System was set up by Congress in 1913 and consists of 12 District Federal Reserve Banks and a Board of Governors appointed by the US President and confirmed by the Senate. Major policy decisions affecting the supply of credit and the cost of money in the US are taken by the Federal Open Market Committee (FOMC) which includes the Governors, the President of the New York Reserve Bank, and the Presidents of four of the 11 other District Banks. Since 1981 the FOMC has held eight regularly scheduled meetings each year at intervals of five to eight weeks. At its meetings the FOMC considers:

- the current and prospective business situation;
- conditions in the financial markets;
- economic trends such as income, spending, money supply, the business investment;
- the prospects for inflation in the United States.

2.3.1   FOMC Directives

The FOMC issues a directive at the end of a meeting to the Federal Reserve Bank of New York which carries out day-to-day open market operations. The Fed can inject cash into the banking system by buying back Treasury bills (short-term government debt securities) thereby increasing the supply of credit in the economy. Or it can seek to tighten credit and

Release Date: September 16, 2008

For immediate release

The Federal Open Market Committee decided today to keep its target for the federal funds rate at 2 percent.

Strains in financial markets have increased significantly and labor markets have weakened further. Economic growth appears to have slowed recently, partly reflecting a softening of household spending. Tight credit conditions, the ongoing housing contraction, and some slowing in export growth are likely to weigh on economic growth over the next few quarters. Over time, the substantial easing of monetary policy, combined with ongoing measures to foster market liquidity, should help to promote moderate economic growth.

Inflation has been high, spurred by the earlier increases in the prices of energy and some other commodities. The Committee expects inflation to moderate later this year and next year, but the inflation outlook remains highly uncertain.

The downside risks to growth and the upside risks to inflation are both of significant concern to the Committee. The Committee will monitor economic and financial developments carefully and will act as needed to promote sustainable economic growth and price stability.

Voting for the FOMC monetary policy action were: Ben S. Bernanke, Chairman; Christine M. Cumming; Elizabeth A. Duke; Richard W. Fisher; Donald L. Kohn; Randall S. Kroszner; Sandra Pianalto; Charles I. Plosser; Gary H. Stern; and Kevin M. Warsh. Ms. Cumming voted as the alternate for Timothy F. Geithner.

Figure 2.1   FOMC announcement 16 September 2008.
Source: US Federal Reserve, reproduced with permission.

slow down economic growth by selling Treasury securities to the banking system, which reduces the supply of funds available for lending to companies and to individuals. Figure 2.1 shows an FOMC announcement.

In practice nowadays the Fed normally tends to perform its open market operations through so-called **repo transactions** rather than outright sales and purchases of Treasury securities. When the Fed conducts repo transactions it supplies funds to the banking system on a temporary basis and accepts Treasuries as collateral against loans. Repos are explained in more detail in the final sections of this chapter.

2.3.2   Federal Funds and the Discount Window

The FOMC directives to the New York Federal Reserve Bank are designed to maintain the Federal funds rate at a certain target level. The Federal funds market is a market for interbank dollar lending inside the US and therefore operates under the supervision and control of the Fed in its capacity as central bank. The Fed funds market arises because depository institutions in the US have to maintain minimum **reserves** in cash or on deposit with the Federal Reserve in order to sustain the stability of the banking system. A bank that has excess reserves can lend via the Fed funds market to another bank which is temporarily short of funds. The bulk of lending is for overnight maturity, on an uncollateralized basis, although longer-term loans are also contracted.

Eligible US deposit-taking institutions can also borrow directly from the Fed through the so-called **discount window**. This is a lending facility secured against approved collateral, and the lending rate is known as the **discount rate**. Normally the level of borrowing is small but in turbulent times it can become a key source of liquidity for banks. Exceptionally, in March 2008 during the 'credit crisis', the Fed created a new type of facility providing direct funding to major dealers in securities in the US market. Loans were made on an overnight basis and could be secured using a range of collateral, including mortgage-backed securities. The objective was to stem widespread concerns over liquidity in the financial markets – the fear that some institutions might not be able to raise sufficient funds in the interbank market to sustain their operations.

2.4   THE EUROPEAN CENTRAL BANK (ECB)

The ECB is the central bank for the euro, the European single currency. From a statutory point of view it forms part of the European System of Central Banks (ESCB) which also includes the national central banks (NCBs) of the European Union countries. However because some EU countries such as Sweden and the UK have not (as yet) adopted the euro, the tasks of the ESCB are at present carried out by an institution called the **Eurosystem**. The Eurosystem comprises the ECB and the NCBs of those countries that have adopted the euro. The member countries at the start of 2009 are listed in Table 2.1.

The primary goal of the ESCB was defined at its outset as the maintenance of price stability, that is, the control of inflation across the euro area. To this effect, the Eurosystem is responsible for monetary policy and for operations in the foreign exchange markets. To ensure independence, members of the ECB and of NCBs are forbidden from taking instructions from any external body, and member states may not seek to influence members of the ECB or NCBs in the performance of their duties. Indeed since the system was established by international treaty in one sense it is more independent than the central bank of a sovereign state – the system can only be changed by common agreement of all the member countries rather than by a single national legislature.

The Governors of the NCBs and the members of the Executive Board of the ECB are guaranteed security of tenure, except in extreme cases where matters are subject to adjudication by the European Court of Justice. The main decision-making body of the ECB is the Governing Council. It consists of:

- the six members of the Executive Board;
- the governors of the NCBs of the 15 euro area countries.

The Governing Council usually meets twice a month, in Frankfurt. At its first meeting it assesses monetary and economic developments and takes its monthly monetary policy decision. At its second meeting, the Council discusses mainly issues related to other tasks and responsibilities of the ECB and the Eurosystem.

Table 2.1   The eurozone countries at start 2009

Austria	Belgium	Cyprus	Finland	France
Germany	Greece	Ireland	Italy	Luxembourg
Malta	the Netherlands	Portugal	Slovakia	Slovenia
Spain				

While the Fed has a 'dual mandate' to maintain both price stability and economic growth, the primary objective of the ECB is to maintain price stability and only 'without prejudice' to this goal to support the general economic policies of the European Union. Some commentators argue that this means that inflation rates are likely to run at higher levels in the US than in the eurozone.

2.4.1 Eurosystem Regulation

Like the Fed, the Eurosystem imposes regulatory constraints on banks operating in its territory, which are required to maintain funds on reserve with the NCBs in proportion to their deposit base. The system of minimum reserve requirements is designed to prevent excessive lending by the banks and to stabilize money market interest rates. Compliance with the requirement is based on average reserves over a defined maintenance period.

The Eurosystem has taken the decision to pay interest on reserves, perhaps to ensure that money market activities in the euro do not move offshore where reserve requirements would not apply. It provides short-term borrowing and lending facilities to banks in the system, and these rates establish minimum levels of interest rates throughout the euro area. Finally, the Eurosystem conducts regular open market operations through the NCBs by which it provides funds to the markets, taking in return securities such as government bills and bonds as collateral.

2.5 STERLING MONEY MARKETS

The Bank of England (BoE) has set monetary policy in the UK since 1997. Decisions on interest rates are made by the Bank's Monetary Policy Committee (MPC). The Bank's primary monetary policy objective is to deliver price stability as defined by an inflation target set by the UK government. Like the ECB, it is only required to support the government's efforts to maintain high and stable growth and employment subject to achieving its primary goal of price stability. The inflation target is expressed in terms of an annual rate of inflation based on the Consumer Prices Index (CPI). In 2008 the target was 2 % p.a.

The MPC sets the short-term interest rate in pounds sterling and implements this rate through open market operations in the sterling money market. The Bank of England is therefore functionally independent of the UK central government. (Although there is provision in the Bank of England Act 1998 for the UK Treasury, in consultation with the Governor of the Bank of England, to issue directives on interest rates in an emergency.) Transactions between banks in the UK are settled through accounts held with the Bank of England. The open market operations of the Bank of England help to ensure that the commercial banks have enough funds available to settle transactions. The intention is that the interest rate at which the Bank supplies these funds is quickly passed through the financial system, affecting the rates charged by commercial banks.

The Bank of England normally lends funds against very safe collateral such as:

- UK Treasury bills;
- gilts (UK government bonds);
- certain high-quality securities issued by major financial institutions in sterling or euros;
- securities issued by EU governments.

In December 2007 during the 'credit crisis' the Bank of England widened the range of assets used as collateral in its lending operations to include mortgage-backed securities. In April 2008 it allowed banks to swap illiquid asset-backed securities on a temporary basis for Treasury bills which they could then use as collateral to raise funds.

Open market operations are conducted electronically, using the Bank's own tendering system. In addition, if the Bank believes that there are surplus funds in the banking system and wishes to reduce the amount of money available for lending, it can mop these up through outright sales of UK Treasury bills. Eligible UK banks and building societies are required to hold target reserves at the Bank of England over maintenance periods running from one MPC decision date until the next. Interest is paid on reserves if an average balance is within a range around the target level.

2.6   THE BANK OF JAPAN

The role of the Bank of Japan (BoJ) is to carry out currency and monetary control aimed at achieving price stability, to ensure smooth settlement between banks and other financial institutions, and to issue banknotes. It influences interest rates by conducting operations in the money markets including buying and selling government securities.

The nine-member Policy Board which determines monetary policy consists of the Governor, the two Deputy Governors and six outside experts. The key interest rate targeted by the BOJ is that for **overnight call money**. This is the rate charged on overnight uncollateralized loans in the interbank market. At its Monetary Policy Meetings (MPMs) the BoJ Policy Board discusses the economic and financial situation in Japan and sets guidelines for money market operations which are designed to provide additional funds or to absorb funds available in the financial markets. Figure 2.2 shows a recent announcement.

2.7   SYSTEMIC RISKS AND MORAL HAZARDS

The BOJ is the lender of last resort to banks in Japan. However it is careful to clarify its role by saying that it will only consider lending to a financial institution facing a temporary liquidity problem when the problem poses a threat to the stability of the financial system. All central banks have to balance two concerns. One is that a bank failure may pose a **systemic risk**, the threat of a collapse in confidence in the whole financial system. However, a blanket guarantee of central bank support might create a **moral hazard**: banks may be tempted to take on ever greater risks in the expectation that the central bank will bail them out.

October 14, 2008

Bank of Japan

At the Monetary Policy Meeting held today, the Bank of Japan decided, by a unanimous vote, to set the following guideline for money market operations for the intermeeting period:

The Bank of Japan will encourage the uncollateralized overnight call rate to remain at around 0.5 percent.

Figure 2.2   Bank of Japan monetary policy meeting announcement.
Source: Bank of Japan, reproduced with permission.

The Bank of England drew a line in 1995 when it declined to rescue Barings Bank from collapse as the result of speculative trading by Nick Leeson. However in 2007 and in 2008 the Bank and the UK government *did* decide to rescue two mortgage banks, Northern Rock and Bradford and Bingley, because of fears for the overall health of the UK financial system. In particular, the authorities were keen to reassure bank depositors that their savings were secure.

In March 2008 as part of the same 'credit crisis', resulting from losses in the mortgage lending market and the subsequent drying up of interbank lending, the Federal Reserve orchestrated a rescue of Bear Stearns, then the fifth largest investment bank in the US. Bear Stearns was soon after acquired by JP Morgan Chase. However in September 2008 the US authorities *declined* to fund a rescue of the investment bank Lehman Brothers. Many market observers felt that the Fed wanted to make a firm statement on the moral hazard issue – that not all ailing financial institutions would be bailed out. Following its bankruptcy, units of Lehman Brothers were acquired by Barclays Capital and by Nomura.

2.8   TREASURY BILLS

Treasury bills are short-term negotiable securities issued in their domestic money markets by governments such as the US, the UK, France, and Germany. They are fully backed by the governments concerned and used as short-term funding instruments, in part to help smooth out the flow of cash from tax receipts but also as instruments to control the supply of money in the banking system and hence the economy at large. The US Treasury regularly sells bills at auction with maturities ranging from four to 52 weeks. The auction cycle as at 2008 is as follows:

- **Shorter-Term Paper.** Four-week, 13-week, and 26-week bills are offered each week.
- **52-week Paper.** These are auctioned every four weeks.

The participants in the auction are banks, securities houses, institutional investors, and private investors. There are two types of bid that can be submitted: competitive and non-competitive. In a non-competitive bid the investor agrees to accept the rate determined by the auction. Most retail investors make non-competitive bids which can be submitted via the Internet and are currently limited to $5 million each. Since 2004, prices for awarded securities have been calculated to six decimal places per $100 face or par value. In the current system all successful bidders are awarded securities at the same rate, although a number of alternative systems have been tried over the years.

2.9   DISCOUNTING TREASURY BILLS

US Treasury bills, also known as 'T-bills', do not pay interest as such. Instead they are issued and trade at a discount to their face or par value, the amount repayable by the US government at maturity. The discount method, also used with UK T-bills, goes back to the early days of commercial banking and is sometimes known as the **bank discount method**, to differentiate it from modern discounted cash flow calculations. Financial instruments traded using the bank discount method are quoted in terms of a percentage discount from their face value rather than at their yield or rate of return on investment.

Simple Example: Discounting Commercial Bills

An exporter agrees an export transaction with an importer and submits a bill for $1 million for the goods, payable in one year. The exporter needs to raise cash today and approaches a bank. The bank agrees to discount the bill at a rate of 10 % and pays the exporter upfront $1 million less 10 % of $1 million, which is $900,000. In one year the bank will collect the $1 million payment due from the importer for the goods.

In the above example the 10 % discount from the $1 million par or face value of the bill charged by the bank is not in fact the yield or investment return it earns by discounting the bill. The bank pays out $900,000 today and will receive $1 million in one year. Its return on the original investment is calculated as follows:

$$\left(\frac{\$1,000,000 - \$900,000}{\$900,000}\right) \times 100 = 11.11\%$$

Clearly the bank must be earning more than 10 % on the deal. If it invested $900,000 at 10 % for one year it would only have $990,000 at the end of the period. This is very satisfactory for the bank but not so pleasant for the exporter in the story. The exporter is effectively paying an interest rate of 11.11 % to obtain money today rather than in one year, as opposed to what looks at first glance like a 10 % charge.

2.9.1 Discount Formula

Of course not all discount securities mature in exactly one year. The general formula for calculating the settlement amount (dollar purchase price) of a US Treasury bill is as follows:

$$\text{Settlement Amount} = \text{Face Value} \times \left[1 - \left(\frac{\text{Discount Rate}}{100} \times \frac{\text{Days to Maturity}}{360}\right)\right]$$

The formula takes into account cases where there is less than one full year to the maturity of the instrument. It also uses the traditional US money market day-counting convention known as actual/360. The discount rate is pro-rated by the actual number of calendar days to the maturity of the bill divided by a fixed 360-day year basis. The actual/360 convention has been adopted for Treasury bills issued in euros, the new European currency, by eurozone countries such as Germany, France, and Italy and is widely used in money markets around the world. A notable exception is the case of UK Treasury bills where an actual/365 day-count convention applies.

US Treasury Bill Calculation

A dealer purchases US Treasury bills with 40 days to maturity at a quoted discount rate of 2.5 % per $100 par value. The total face value of the bills is $100,000.

$$\text{Settlement Amount} = \$100,000 \times \left[1 - \left(\frac{2.5}{100} \times \frac{40}{360}\right)\right] = \$99,722$$

2.9.2 Yield or Return

The yield or investment return on an instrument such as a US Treasury bill using the bank discount method is always understated by the quoted discount rate. It can be calculated from the actual cash flows involved in buying the bill and holding it until maturity. In the above example the purchase price of the bill is $99,722. From this we can work out the percentage return on holding the paper until maturity and then annualize this figure to calculate a yield or return, on the assumption that the bill is held until maturity.

$$\text{Yield} = \left(\frac{\$100,000 - \$99,722}{\$99,722} \right) \times \frac{360}{40} = 0.0251 = 2.51\% \text{ p.a.}$$

The rate of 2.51% can now be directly compared with money market instruments such as short-term bank deposits which are quoted in terms of the simple annualized rate of return on the investment, i.e. without compounding. The following explicit formula will calculate the yield on a Treasury bill directly. For UK Treasury bills substitute 365 for 360 in the formula. Insert the discount rate in the formula as a decimal, i.e. as the percentage rate divided by 100. Multiply the calculated yield by 100 to obtain the percentage value.

$$\text{Yield} = \frac{\dfrac{\text{Quoted Discount Rate}}{100}}{1 - \left(\dfrac{\text{Days to Maturity}}{360} \times \dfrac{\text{Quoted Discount Rate}}{100} \right)}$$

In the example:

$$\text{Yield} = \frac{0.025}{1 - \left(\dfrac{40}{360} \times 0.025 \right)} = 0.0251 = 2.51\% \text{ p.a.}$$

2.9.3 UK Treasury Bills

The UK government also issues Treasury bills on a discount basis. These are fully backed by the UK government and effectively by the tax revenues of the country. The typical maturity is around three months and the maximum maturity is one year. On 3 April 2000 the Debt Management Office (DMO), an agency of the UK government, took over full responsibility for the weekly tender of T-bills from the Bank of England. The formula for calculating the settlement amount (sterling purchase price) of a UK Treasury bill is as follows. The day-count method used is called actual/365.

$$\text{Settlement Amount} = \text{Face Value} \times \left[1 - \left(\frac{\text{Discount Rate}}{100} \times \frac{\text{Days of Maturity}}{365} \right) \right]$$

2.9.4 The 'Risk-free Rate'

The yield or return on Treasury bills issued by major economies such as the US, the UK, France, and Germany is sometimes taken to establish the so-called **risk-free** rate available in that currency. The return is 'risk-free' in the sense that the market assumes that these governments are extremely unlikely to default on their short-term debt. If this is the case then a purchaser of a T-bill can effectively lock into a known and (effectively) guaranteed rate of return until the maturity of the paper. It is a discount instrument so there are no interim interest payments to reinvest during the lifetime of the paper and therefore no uncertainty about future reinvestment rates.

In developed economies money market instruments issued by companies and banks normally offer an additional return over the return on T-bills. This **spread**, or additional yield over the T-bill rate, reflects the risk that the issuer might default on payments – in other words it represents additional return for taking on the additional credit risk. Note that not all short-term government debt is risk-free. For example Russia defaulted on its Treasury bills in August 1998.

2.10 US COMMERCIAL PAPER

Commercial paper (CP) is an unsecured promissory note (effectively an IOU) issued by:

- corporates;
- financial institutions;
- governments;
- supranational agencies.

Commercial paper originated in the US in the nineteenth century and the US commercial paper (USCP) market is the largest such market in the world. Originally CP offered a means by which large business enterprises such as the railroads could tap into sources of capital across the US continent and internationally, at a time when US banks were confined to single states and relatively small in terms of their capital base.

Classic commercial paper is unsecured and does not carry a bank guarantee. As a result (except in times of economic boom) it tends to be primarily a market for 'name' issuers with strong cash flows and a good credit rating. The average maturity of USCP is around 30 days, normally with a maximum of 270 days. The limit arises from the fact that paper issued with a maturity of more than 270 days requires registration with the US Securities and Exchange Commission (SEC) and this adds to issuance costs. In the case of a corporate borrower the funds are typically used to finance operating costs and working capital requirements.

USCP Quotation

USCP is quoted on a bank discount basis in the same way as US Treasury bills, so that the yield or return is understated by the quoted rate.

2.10.1 Settlement and Dealers

Settlement in the USCP market is normally the same day as purchase. Issuers often **roll over** USCP on maturity. That is, they issue new paper to redeem the maturing instruments. There is a risk that the new paper may not find enough buyers, so issuers can arrange a standby credit line with a bank so that the funds will always be available.

Large CP issuers such as General Electric Capital Corporation (GECC) can place their paper directly with investors and employ teams of salespeople for this purpose. Issuance fees can be very low for a large and frequent borrower, as little as one or two basis points. However many issuers still operate through dealers who work for major investment banks and securities houses. The dealers may agree to buy up and then resell the paper at a fixed price, or alternatively may agree simply to use their 'best endeavours' to find investors (the latter type of arrangement carries a lower fee). The denominations of bills are normally $ 100,000 and above.

Many top European names have set up USCP programmes, starting with Electricité de France in 1974, which used the proceeds to pay for its oil requirements in US dollars. Part of the reason for issuance in the USCP market is that domestic commercial paper markets in Europe were relatively underdeveloped before the advent of the euro.

2.11   CREDIT RISK ON USCP

Investors in USCP include:

- insurance companies;
- pension funds;
- governments;
- municipal authorities;
- corporates.

Generally speaking, investors buy commercial paper because they are looking for higher returns than they can achieve on Treasury bills. The spread over the risk-free rate is the number of basis points an issue of commercial paper pays above the rate on the Treasury bill with the nearest maturity. The spread will depend on the credit rating of the issuer – the greater the risk of default, the higher the spread over Treasuries. It will also depend on the market's general appetite for risk.

The major US rating agencies, Standard & Poor's (S&P) and Moody's, use the rating scales set out in Table 2.2 for assessing default risk on short-term money market securities such as US commercial paper. These are for investment grade paper.

The highest rated paper is at the top of the list, the lowest at the bottom. Because of the short-term nature of the securities being evaluated the agencies focus on assessing the cash flow-generating ability of the issuer: how likely or otherwise it is that the paper will be repaid at maturity in 30 or so days' time. The concern is normally not so much with the risk of outright insolvency as with the danger that the issuer may not have enough cash to redeem all the paper at maturity. However when there is an economic downturn investors do start to have concerns about default, particularly about less well-rated paper.

Table 2.2   Ratings for investment grade money market paper

S&P	Moody's
A1+	P1
A1	
A2	P2
A3	P3

Sources: Ratings agencies.

A Flight to Quality

A US building materials company called Armstrong World Industries defaulted on its commercial paper in November 2000. In the aftermath the spread between Al/P1 paper and the riskier A2/P2 paper widened to over 100 basis points. The spread stood at only 15 basis points in the late 1990s. The market for lower-rated paper started to dry up as investors moved their money into lower risk, higher credit quality investments. Banks became reluctant to extend standby credit facilities. Some issuers switched to other sources of funds including asset-backed commercial paper which is secured or backed by specific revenue streams.

2.11.1 Advantages of USCP

For companies and institutions with a good credit rating USCP is an extremely cost-effective means of borrowing short-term funds, cheaper than the traditional European method of borrowing short-term via a bank on an overdraft facility. Top name Al/P1 borrowers can raise funds at a rate that is higher than the rate on US T-bills, but below the London Interbank Offered Rate and the rate payable on certificates of deposit issued in the Eurodollar market. In favourable market conditions lower quality A2/P2 issuers can also achieve keen funding rates. The secondary market for USCP is far less liquid than that for US Treasury bills and most paper is held by investors until maturity.

2.12 BANKERS' ACCEPTANCES

Bankers' acceptances (BAs) are trade-related negotiable bills issued by companies but **accepted** or guaranteed by a bank in return for a fee. They can be freely traded in the secondary market. In the US and UK BAs are issued at a discount to face value. The accepting bank guarantees that the face value of the bill will be paid at maturity. The goods involved in the underlying commercial trade also serve as collateral backing up the paper. BAs have declined in importance since the growth of the commercial paper market. Most BAs are backed by documentation such as invoices held by the accepting bank. The instrument traded in the secondary market may simply be a note briefly describing the underlying commercial trade and specifying the name of the accepting bank.

2.12.1 Eligible Bills

In some domestic money markets a distinction has been made between **eligible** and **ineligible** BAs. An eligible acceptance is essentially one which can be used by banks as collateral to borrow short-term funds from the central bank. The distinction grew up in the 1960s and 1970s when BAs were issued in the US and the UK as a means of avoiding tight credit restrictions rather than in support of trade-related activities. In an attempt to control the rising money supply the Fed and the Bank of England made such bills ineligible for rediscount with the central bank.

2.13 THE EUROCURRENCY MARKETS

The Eurocurrency markets have their origins in the 1950s and 1960s when substantial pools of US dollars were deposited with banks outside the US, mainly in London. The market received a major boost after the 1973–4 oil crisis when oil-producing states decided to place the bulk of their substantially increased dollar receipts in foreign centres such as London rather than in New York.

London's main competitive advantage was that US dollar accounts held there were not subject to the regulatory regime of the Federal Reserve, in particular to reserve requirements and other laws in place at the time restricting the rate of interest that could be paid on dollar deposits in the US domestic market. The London-based banks recycled the money by making loans to major corporations and governments, and the so-called Eurodollar market was born. The prefix 'Euro' in this context is an historical accident and is not related to the new European currency called 'the euro' (symbol €).

Eurocurrency Definition

A Eurocurrency is essentially a currency borrowed and lent outside the domestic money market for that currency and therefore outside the direct regulatory control of the domestic central bank. A dollar borrowed or lent inside the US and subject to reserve requirements imposed by the Federal Reserve is a domestic money market transaction. A dollar borrowed or lent outside the US is a Eurodollar (the transaction does not have to take place in Europe). Following the lead set by the dollar, international markets later developed in other currencies such as Euroyen.

2.14 EUROCURRENCY LOANS AND DEPOSITS

The Eurocurrency markets are primarily wholesale markets in which the main participants are international corporations, institutional investors, commercial banks, and global investment banks. In London the main players include the major American, German, UK, and Swiss banks, names such as Citigroup, Deutsche Bank, and Union Bank of Switzerland. Most Eurocurrency money market deals are term deposits and loans with a maturity of one year or less, with the majority of deals around the three to six-month maturity range. Money dealers at the major banks stand ready to quote their offer (lending) rates and bid (borrowing) rates for a range of Eurocurrencies and a range of maturities from overnight out to one year and beyond.

2.14.1 Term or Time Deposits

In the case of overnight deals the funds are delivered on the day the deal is arranged and repaid with interest on the next business day. In the case of a **term** or time deposit for longer periods such as three months the funds are normally delivered two business days after the deal is arranged. This is called **spot delivery**, or a deal agreed 'for value spot'. The funds are then repaid with interest at maturity three calendar months (or whatever the agreed term of the deal is) after the spot value date. This aligns the Eurocurrency market with the foreign exchange (FX) market in which the bulk of trades is for value spot, i.e. two currencies are exchanged two business days after a deal is agreed. (See Chapter 3 for details on the currency markets.)

2.14.2 LIBOR

The key reference rate in London, the largest Eurocurrency market in the world, is the London Interbank Offered Rate (LIBOR). LIBOR is compiled by the British Bankers'

Table 2.3 BBA LIBOR rates 26 February 2008

Period	USD	GBP	CHF	JPY	EUR
1 week	3.14125	5.34625	2.57167	0.59688	4.12750
1 month	3.12500	5.56000	2.62167	0.63750	4.18563
3 months	3.09000	5.68125	2.78833	0.89750	4.38563
6 months	3.05750	5.64500	2.80917	0.95750	4.39125
12 months	2.92500	5.52625	2.83917	1.04875	4.39500

Source: British Bankers' Association.

Association in conjunction with Reuters and released shortly after 11:00 a.m. London time. It is an average based on data provided by a panel of major banks on offer (lending) rates for short-term interbank funds available in the London market. A panel consists of at least eight banks. There is a separate LIBOR rate for each currency listed by the BBA and for a range of maturities. Table 2.3 shows a selection of LIBOR rates for 26 February 2008 for one-week, one-month, three-month, six-month, and 12-month loans. The currencies shown are US dollars, pounds sterling, Swiss francs, Japanese yen, and euros.

For example, in Table 2.3 the three-month dollar LIBOR rate is 3.09 % per annum. This is a rate for spot delivery of funds (in two business days' time). This is normally called the **value date**. Principal plus interest is then paid at the maturity of the loan three months after spot. Sterling is the exception in Table 2.3 in that the rates are quoted for value 'same day'. For instance, the three-month sterling LIBOR rate of 5.68125 % quoted in the Table is for a loan that starts on 26 February 2008 and matures three months after that date.

If a loan matures on a non-business day the **modified following** rule is used. This means that the maturity date is moved forward to the next business day, unless that is a new month, in which case it is moved back to the previous business day. (Different rules apply for deals lasting less than one month.) The modified following rule is widely used in the international capital markets, such as with interest rate swaps.

2.14.3 Applications of LIBOR

LIBOR is frequently used in the financial markets as a benchmark or reference point for establishing payments. In the syndicated loan market the rate of interest paid by a borrower to a syndicate of lending banks is often reset every three or six months according to the LIBOR rate fixed for the period, plus a spread in basis points based on the relative creditworthiness of the borrower. For instance, the rate might be set at the three-month dollar LIBOR for an interest period plus 80 basis points (0.8 %). In the interest rate derivatives markets, also, the payments due on many products are based on LIBOR.

Less frequently mentioned are LIBID – the rate top banks in London bid to take in deposits from other banks – and LIMEAN which is mid-way between LIBOR and LIBID. Section 2.3 discussed the Fed Funds rate. It is an interbank lending rate for dollar loans inside the US and is therefore the domestic US equivalent of the international dollar interbank lending rate established by dollar LIBOR.

2.14.4 The TED Spread

The Treasury Eurodollar (TED) spread measures the difference between the three-month dollar LIBOR rate and the rate on 'risk-free' three-month US Treasury bills. The TED spread reflects market perceptions about the credit risk on banks and is an indication of their willingness to lend to each other. In September 2008, during the midst of the credit crisis and pervasive worries about the solvency of banking institutions, the TED spread ballooned to almost 500 basis points. Chapter 13 discusses a related measure of credit risk on banks called the LIBOR OIS spread.

2.15 EUROCURRENCY INTEREST AND DAY-COUNT

Interest on Eurocurrency deposits and loans up to one year is normally paid at maturity along with the repayment of the principal. This type of repayment structure is sometimes called a **bullet**. Deposits with more than one year to maturity usually pay interest on an annual or six-monthly basis.

Example Interest Calculation

Interest on Eurodollar and most other Eurocurrency deals is calculated using the actual/360 day-count convention. Suppose a bank borrows $ 10 million for three months at 4 % p.a. from a money dealer. The value date, when the funds are actually received, is spot, two working days after the deal is agreed. The actual calendar number of days from spot to maturity is calculated as 93 days. The interest due at the maturity of the loan is $ 10 million × 0.04 × 93/360 = $ 103,333.

The actual/360 convention has some interesting side effects. For example, suppose a bank decides to borrow $ 10 million for a full year (365 days) at a rate of (say) 5 %. The interest due at maturity would be more than $ 500,000.

$$\text{Interest Due} = \$\,10 \text{ million} \times 0.05 \times \frac{365}{360} = \$\,506,944$$

The borrower has to pay an extra five days in interest ($ 6944) because of the day-count convention. Put another way, the *effective* rate of interest is actually higher than the rate quoted by the dealer.

$$\text{Effective Rate} = 5\,\% \times \frac{365}{360} = 5.0694\,\%$$

The key formulae for Eurodollar deposits and loans with one year or less to maturity are as follows.

$$\text{Interest Accrued} = \text{Principal} \times \frac{\text{Interest Rate}}{100} \times \frac{\text{Actual Days}}{360}$$

$$\text{Principal} + \text{Interest} = \text{Principal} \times \left[1 + \left(\frac{\text{Interest Rate}}{100} \times \frac{\text{Actual Days}}{360} \right) \right]$$

Interest in all the above formulae is calculated on a simple interest basis i.e. without compounding.

2.16   EUROCURRENCY CERTIFICATES OF DEPOSIT

A Eurocurrency certificate of deposit (CD) is created when funds are deposited with a bank. Unlike a regular term deposit, however, the CD can be freely traded and the holder can sell the paper for cash in the secondary market. In practice, the liquidity of CDs in the secondary market will depend on the credit standing of the issuing bank. In the Eurocurrency market CDs are traditionally issued in **bearer** form, which means that the holder has sole title to the principal and interest on the underlying bank deposit due to be paid at maturity.

Nowadays CDs and other money market instruments can be issued and held in 'demateri-alized' form – i.e. as electronic book entries – rather than in the form of physical documents. In London the book entry system is operated by CRESTCo, a subsidiary of Euroclear. Securities are transferred using a 'delivery versus payment' mechanism and changes of ownership are recorded electronically.

2.16.1   CD Cash Flow

A CD is simply a title to a known future cash flow of principal plus interest. The rate of interest is sometimes called the **coupon rate**. The future value (FV) of a Eurodollar CD at maturity is calculated using the same formula used for Eurodollar deposits. It is the principal amount deposited, also known as the present value (PV), plus interest at maturity.

$$\text{Future Value at Maturity} = \text{PV} \times \left[1 + \left(\frac{\text{Coupon Rate}}{100} \times \frac{\text{Actual Days}}{360} \right) \right]$$

2.16.2   Eurodollar CD Example

A Eurodollar CD is issued for settlement on 3 March 2008. This is the day it starts to accrue interest. It matures on 3 June 2008. There are 92 actual days between these two dates. The principal invested is $1 million and the coupon (fixed interest rate) on the CD is 3.25 % p.a. Therefore:

$$\text{Future Value at Maturity} = \$1 \text{ million} \times \left[1 + \left(\frac{3.25}{100} \times \frac{92}{360} \right) \right] = \$1,008,306$$

Suppose an investor buys the CD not when it was first issued but for settlement (delivery) on 3 April 2008. What is the fair value of the instrument – in other words, how much should the investor pay for it for delivery on that date? There are now only 61 days remaining until maturity. Suppose the money market rates screen says that the rate for two-month money is currently 3 % p.a. By rearranging the formula for calculating future value it is possible to work out the value today of a sum of money to be received in the future – its present value. The formula becomes:

$$\text{Present Value} = \frac{\text{Future Value}}{1 + \left(\frac{\text{Interest Rate}}{100} \times \frac{\text{Actual Days}}{360} \right)}$$

$$\text{Present Value} = \frac{\$1,008,306}{1 + \left(\frac{3}{100} \times \frac{61}{360} \right)} = \$1,003,206$$

2.17   CD YIELD-TO-MATURITY

Dealers normally quote CDs not in money terms but in terms of the rate of discount used to calculate present value. This rate is also known as the CD's **yield-to-maturity**. In the previous example if the investor buys the CD for $ 1,003,206, holds it to maturity, and receives from the issuer principal plus interest of $ 1,008,306 the total annualized return on the initial investment is 3 %. This is exactly the yield or return achieved by placing the funds on a two-month Eurodollar money market deposit. Quoting CDs in terms of the discount rate allows traders and investors to compare the returns available on these negotiable instruments with those available on Eurocurrency deposits.

  Suppose the investor can buy the CD more cheaply in the market from another dealer, at a dollar price of only $ 1,003,000. By rearranging the formula for calculating the present value of the CD we can calculate the yield-to-maturity the investor would achieve by buying the paper at that price. The formula becomes:

$$\text{Yield-to-Maturity} = \frac{FV - PV}{PV} \times \frac{360}{\text{Days to Maturity}} \times 100$$

In the example the values to insert into the formula are:

Future value = $ 1,008,306

Present value = $1,003,000

Days to maturity = 61 (actual days)

Therefore:

$$\text{Yield} = \frac{\$1,008,306 - \$1,003,000}{\$1,003,000} \times \frac{360}{61} \times 100 = 3.12\,\%$$

If the investor can buy the CD for only $ 1,003,000 the annualized return from holding the instrument until maturity is 3.12 %. Effectively the formula works out the percentage return on the initial investment then annualizes the result based on the number of days from purchase to maturity. Again, this is a simple interest calculation with no compounding. To compare the return on the CD with the return on an instrument which uses a simple interest calculation but an actual year basis rather than a 360-day year multiply 3.12 % by 365/360, or in a leap year 366/360.

2.18   EURO-COMMERCIAL PAPER

Euro-commercial paper (ECP) is issued in the international Euromarkets (primarily in London) rather than in a domestic money market such as the US. ECP issues are short-term, unsecured, bearer securities sold by major corporations with maturities ranging from one week to one year. The market took off in London in the 1980s. The main buyers are institutional investors seeking higher returns than they can achieve on Treasury bills, through a flexible investment that is available with a variety of maturities.

  For a well-known borrower a Euro-CP issue permits access to a global pool of investors; and an issuance programme is fairly inexpensive to set up. Unlike USCP, Euro-CP can be actively traded in the secondary market. The key difference between Euro-CP and USCP is that Euro-CP is normally quoted on a yield basis and not using the traditional bank discount method employed for US T-bills and USCP. Deals are also typically for spot rather than same-day settlement.

Euro-CP Calculation

A dealer buys a Euro-CP maturing in 30 days. The face value is $1 million and the yield quoted by the dealer is 3.5 % p.a.

$$\text{Purchase Price} = \frac{\text{Face Value}}{1 + \left(\dfrac{\text{Yield}}{100} \times \dfrac{\text{Days to Maturity}}{360} \right)}$$

$$\text{Purchase Price} = \frac{\$1,000,000}{1 + \left(\dfrac{3.5}{100} \times \dfrac{30}{360} \right)} = \$997,092$$

2.19   REPOS AND REVERSES

The expression 'repo' is shorthand for **sale and repurchase agreement**. In a classic repo transaction:

- a security is sold for cash to a counterparty;
- with a simultaneous agreement that it will be repurchased on an agreed date in the future at the same price.

A classic repo deal involves drawing up a legal contract signed by both parties, although in developed markets the terms and conditions are often highly standardized. The repo market developed in the US but repos have become extremely common in financial markets around the world. They are used by traders and investors holding positions in securities who wish to raise short-term funds by using the securities as collateral.

The securities are often safe investments such as Treasury bills or Treasury bonds (longer-dated government debt securities; see Chapter 4). This makes repo a cheaper form of borrowing compared to borrowing without collateral. Repos are widely used by fixed-income operations to fund their trading activities. In addition, investors such as pension fund managers can put their securities out on repo and reinvest the funds raised at higher returns.

2.19.1   The Repo Rate

The repo rate is the rate of interest charged by the lender of funds to the borrower, who supplies collateral. A classic repo transaction has two legs. In leg one the collateral (the securities) is sold by the borrower to the supplier of funds. In leg two the sum borrowed against the collateral is returned to the supplier of funds plus interest calculated according to the agreed repo rate, and the collateral is sold back to the original owner.

2.20   REPO: CASE STUDY

A trader holds a $1 million nominal or face value position in US Treasury bonds. This is the principal amount repaid on the bonds at maturity. The bonds can be sold in the market for a total settlement price of $101.9796 per $100 nominal. (The total settlement amount is called the **dirty price** in the bond market; see Chapter 4 for more information on bond quotations.) On a $1 million nominal holding the bonds are therefore worth $1,019,796. The trader decides to repo the bonds out to a repo dealer for three days. The repo rate is 3.13 % p.a. The transaction has two legs.

- **Leg 1: Settlement date.** In the first leg of the repo the trader sells the bonds to the repo dealer and receives the current settlement value of $1,019,796. This is sometimes called the **wired amount**.
- **Leg 2: Termination date.** In the second leg of the repo in three days the repo dealer returns the bonds to the trader (the original owner) who pays back $1,019,796 plus interest at 3.13 % p.a. The total amount repaid is sometimes called the **termination money**.

$$\text{Repo Interest} = \$1,019,796 \times 0.0313 \times \frac{3}{360} = \$266$$

$$\text{Total Repayment (Termination Money)} = \$1,019,796 + \$266 = \$1,020,062$$

The cash flows on the repo transaction are illustrated in Figure 2.3.

2.21   OTHER FEATURES OF REPOS

In a classic repo if there is a coupon payment due on the securities during the term of the deal this is paid over to the original owner, on the payment date. In effect the party 'repo-ing' out the collateral maintains the same economic exposure to the securities as if it

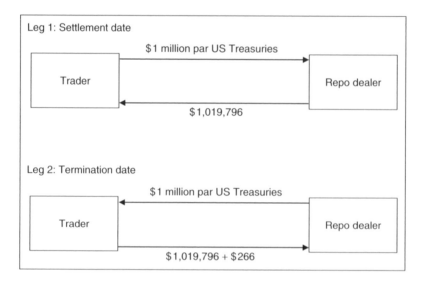

Figure 2.3   Repo transaction.

retained ownership. The lender or supplier of funds in a classic repo transaction is sometimes described as having carried out a **reverse** or reverse repo transaction.

Reverses are often used by short sellers or 'shorts' who need to borrow securities temporarily to cover a position in which they have sold stock they do not own, in anticipation of a price fall. In leg 1 of the repo the short acquires the securities and can then sell them into the market at their current market value. In leg 2 of the repo the short has to return the securities and will receive back the original amount lent against them, plus interest at the repo rate. The short will make a profit if the securities can be bought back cheaply in the cash market in order to return them to the original owner.

In the US market at any given time there is a **general collateral** rate for borrowing funds using US Treasuries as collateral in repo transactions. However sometimes a particular Treasury security goes 'on special' which means that it is sought after and a holder can borrow funds using that issue as collateral at a rate that is lower than the general collateral rate.

As discussed, many central banks use repo as a tool to inject or to drain liquidity on a short-term basis from the market. In their open market operations they take in T-bills or quality commercial bills in return for cash, or sell bills to take cash out of the banking system.

Haircuts

In a repo the sum borrowed against the collateral is typically less than its current market value. The discount is commonly known as a **haircut**. This protects the lender of funds against changes in the market value of the collateral. For example, in the above case study the repo dealer may only be prepared to lend $ 999,800 against the Treasuries put up by the trader as collateral. Since the bonds are worth $ 1,019,796 this means that the trader is actually putting up collateral worth 102 % of the amount borrowed. The haircut will depend on how much the collateral fluctuates in value in the market. In practice repo transactions are usually conducted using safe securities such as US Treasuries and it may be difficult to use riskier assets as collateral.

2.21.1 Sell/Buy-backs

A sell/buy-back agreement is very similar to a classic repo except that it is structured in a slightly different way. It is a cash sale of bonds with a separate agreement to buy the bonds back on a forward (i.e. later) date at a higher price. The rate of interest charged on the loan is not explicitly stated; it is implied in the fact that the repurchase price on the forward date is higher than the cash sale price. Any coupon payments due on the collateral are not paid over separately; they are incorporated into the forward repurchase price and therefore paid at the termination of the agreement rather than on the actual coupon dates.

2.22 CHAPTER SUMMARY

The money markets are markets for short-term borrowing and lending of funds for maturities up to one year. Domestic markets are regulated by central banks such as the Federal Reserve in the US, the European Central Bank in the eurozone, and the Bank of England in the UK. Governments issue short-term funding instruments called Treasury bills in their domestic money markets. The central banks act to control the amount of credit in the banking system by setting short-term interest rates and by conducting open market operations such as lending funds against collateral to commercial banks. In the US many large corporations and financial institutions raise short-term funds by issuing US commercial paper, which carries default or credit risk.

The Eurocurrency market is an international market for funds, based in major global centres such as London. The majority of deals are in US dollars and the banks can borrow and lend Eurocurrencies without being subject to direct regulation by the central bank of the currency in question. The main participants are commercial banks, investment banks and securities houses, international corporations, and investing institutions such as pension funds and insurance companies. Eurocurrency deposits and loans are made for a specific term such as three months or six months. Investors can also buy a range of negotiable (freely tradable) money market securities such as Eurocurrency certificates of deposit and Euro-commercial paper.

3
The Foreign Exchange Market

3.1 CHAPTER OVERVIEW

The foreign exchange market is a global, technology-based marketplace in which banks, corporations, governments, and institutional investors trade currencies around the clock. This chapter explores the structure of the market and the role of foreign exchange (FX) dealers in sustaining liquidity. It considers the changing role of central banks in a world largely based on freely floating exchange rates. It looks at how a spot FX dealer makes two-way quotations and assesses the profitability of deals. The chapter explores the different types of risks that have to be managed in the FX dealing room, such as market risk and settlement risk, and the factors that determine FX rates between currencies. Although the bulk of FX deals are still settled two business days after the deal is agreed (spot transactions) there is also a highly active market in forward FX transactions. The chapter looks at the application of products such as outright forward FX deals and FX swaps in managing currency risks, in matching expected future cash flows, and in switching investments into foreign currency assets.

3.2 MARKET STRUCTURE

In the millennium year 2000 average daily volumes in FX trading around the world exceeded $ 1.5 trillion for the first time. However import and export transactions between countries accounted for only about 3 % of these trades. The bulk of FX deals are made by commercial banks including giants such as JP Morgan Chase, Citigroup, and Deutsche Bank. The banks facilitate the trading and investment activities of their corporate and institutional clients by standing ready to lend or exchange a wide range of currencies, and in turn make markets in currencies amongst themselves.

Activities of the Banks

Some of the FX deals made by banks are purely speculative. Others are contracted as a means of 'laying off' risk acquired through transactions made with their clients and with FX dealers at other banks. As well as transacting standardized or 'flow' trades, increasingly banks assemble and market complex FX derivative products that provide currency risk management solutions for clients.

Traditionally, flows of money between currencies were largely determined by import and export transactions. As currency restrictions were gradually lifted in the decades after the Second World War, and especially in the era of floating exchange rates between major currencies that opened in 1973, speculative currency trading began to assume considerable importance in the FX markets. In recent years the effects of investment flows between countries have become increasingly apparent. Institutional investors such as pension funds, insurance companies and mutual funds invest in shares, bonds and money market securities on a global basis and have to enter the FX markets to buy and sell currencies. Sovereign wealth funds have become significant investors in foreign currency assets. In addition, major international corporations making direct investments in their foreign subsidiaries or completing cross-border takeovers generate substantial requirements for foreign exchange.

3.2.1 The Central Banks

In developed economies such as the US, the eurozone, the UK, and Japan there is no longer an official rate of exchange, and the national currency floats freely against other currencies in response to supply and demand factors in the international markets. In such cases the central banks and associated agencies play two main roles:

- they supervise the market;
- they maintain control over domestic interest rates, which will influence the attractiveness of the currency to foreign investors as well as the level of inflation in the economy.

The central bank may seek to smooth out fluctuations in currency movements by buying and selling currency in the markets, often working in consort with other central banks around the world. However the UK learned a hard lesson in 1992 about the power of market forces in the modern international FX markets when it attempted to peg the pound sterling (within bands) against what was then the strongest currency in Europe, the German Deutschemark. The system was known as the Exchange Rate Mechanism (ERM). In practice, it proved impossible to sustain the targeted exchange rate against the activities of traders and speculators such as George Soros. Despite the UK government increasing base interest rates on 16 September 1992 from 10 % to 12 % and finally to 15 %, a tidal wave of selling hit sterling, and the UK government was forced to capitulate and to leave the ERM. Soros is reputed to have made over $ 1 billion.

In developing countries where there are still exchange controls the central bank fixes the official rate of exchange and may also act as the central counterparty in all FX transactions. For example, until July 2005 the Chinese currency the renminbi (the unit is the yuan, currency code CNY) was pegged against the US dollar. Critics argued that the rate was set at a level which seriously undervalued the yuan. This promoted Chinese exports to the US. However it also caused political tensions between the two countries because of the rising trade imbalance and the potential effects on manufacturing jobs inside the US. Since 2005 the Chinese central bank has fixed the exchange rate against the US dollar on a daily basis, with some minor fluctuations allowed, depending on the yuan's relationship to a basket of currencies of China's major trading partners. The pegged rate at July 2005 was USD/CNY 8.28. By end-July 2008 the yuan had appreciated to just under seven per dollar.

3.3 FX DEALERS AND BROKERS

FX dealers and brokers working for banks tend to specialize in one or more of a small group of closely related currency groups. The most actively traded markets in the world are for deals in major currencies such as the US dollar, the euro, the Swiss franc, the Japanese yen, and the pound sterling. Because of the advent of the euro, trading in formerly active currency pairs such as the Deutschemark against the French franc has ended. Some of the slack has been taken up by trading in emerging markets currencies such as the South African rand (currency code ZAR).

The professional FX market is a predominantly over-the-counter market. In other words, most deals are made directly between market participants over the telephone or using electronic networks such as the Reuters system, without the intermediation of an organized exchange. This means that the currencies involved, deal sizes, value (settlement) dates, and the rates of exchange are all negotiable. However FX dealers post rates for standard deal types on information services such as Reuters and on their bank's own proprietary dealing systems supplied to clients. In a highly developed FX market such as London traders are linked by brokers who relay the best quotes currently available. Traditional brokers send prices through voice systems but increasingly brokers are connected to banks through electronic networks.

Role of the Inter-dealer Brokers

Broking firms do not quote FX rates on their own account or take positions in currencies. They operate on a commission basis and the commission is normally related to the amount, size, and complexity of the deal required. Brokers do not discuss the name of the banks quoting or accepting rates until the deal has been agreed. This can be valuable when a dealer wants to make a trade without revealing his or her current position to the market.

3.4 SPOT FOREIGN EXCHANGE DEALS

A spot FX transaction is a deal in which one currency is exchanged for another for spot delivery. In the case of most major currency pairs this is two business days after the trade is agreed. The details of the trade – currencies, amounts, exchange rate, payment instructions – are agreed by the counterparties to the trade on the trade date and the two currencies are exchanged on the spot date. In the FX markets the day when the currencies are actually exchanged is normally called the **value date** and so a spot deal is said to be 'for value spot'. In the interbank FX market the currencies are normally exchanged by funds transfer through the SWIFT system (Society for Worldwide Interbank Financial Telecommunications.)

On request via the telephone or the Reuters networks, a spot FX dealer will quote a two-way rate to fellow market professionals. This is a bid (buy) rate followed by an ask or offer (sell) rate. The first step in interpreting an interbank FX quote is to determine which is the base currency and which is the counter-currency (the other currency involved). The quote is expressed in terms of so many units of the counter-currency per single unit of the base currency. The dealer making the quote buys the base currency at his or her bid rate, the lower of the two numbers; and sells the base currency at the offer rate, the higher of the two numbers.

Example Spot FX Quotation

A spot FX trader quotes the following rates:

$$USD/CHF\ 1.1122/27$$

The base currency is the US dollar and the counter-currency is the Swiss franc. The dealer buys one unit of the base currency, the US dollar, at the left-hand (bid) rate and pays 1.1122 Swiss francs. The dealer sells one unit of the base currency at the right-hand (ask or offer) rate and asks in return 1.1127 Swiss francs.

The currency pair in the example, USD/CHF, is quoted to four decimal places. The first part of the rate, in this case 1.11, is sometimes known as the **big figure**. The last two digits are the points or **pips**. Notice that in the above example the dealer has quoted only the pips on the offer side of the quotation. The full rate is 1.1127. Professional dealers sometimes quote rates to each other using just the pips – for example '22/27'. However at the end of the conversation the two parties must confirm the trade details using the full exchange rate.

3.4.1   The Dealer's Spread

The dealer's spread in the example quotation is CHF 0.0005 or five pips. The spread represents the risk the dealer takes in pricing the exchange of two currencies at a given moment in time. Suppose a counterparty 'hits' the dealer's bid rate and the trade amount is $ 10 million. In two business days' time the dealer will receive $ 10 million from the counterparty and will have to pay in return a fixed amount of Swiss francs.

- Receive $ 10 million
- Pay 10,000,000 × 1.1122 = CHF 11,122,000

The dealer has acquired a long position in dollars, and at the same time a short position in Swiss francs. If the dollar weakens the dealer will lose out on the position, since to unwind the original trade the dealer will have to sell dollars and buy Swiss francs. For example, suppose that later in the same trading day the spot rate falls to USD/CHF 1.1000. The trader enters into a second offsetting spot deal at that rate. On the second deal the cash flows due on the spot value date are as follows:

- Pay $ 10 million
- Receive 10,000,000 × 1.1000 = CHF 11,000,000

The loss on the two deals combined is CHF 122,000, equivalent to $ 110,909 at a rate of USD/CHF 1.1000.

3.5   STERLING AND EURO QUOTATIONS

In the interbank FX market the dollar is normally used as the base currency. The main exceptions are where the dollar is traded against the euro and the British pound. In these cases the dollar becomes the counter-currency. A two-way quotation of EUR/USD 1.3595/98 means that:

- the dealer bids for one euro and pays $ 1.3595 in return;
- the dealer offers one euro and charges $ 1.3598.

A two-way quotation of GBP/USD 1.7514/18 means that:

- the dealer bids for one pound and pays $ 1.7514 in return;
- the dealer offers one pound and charges $ 1.7518.

Of course if a client of the bank wishes to have the quotation expressed with the dollar as the base currency it is easy to make the conversion. If one euro is worth $ 1.3598 on the offer side of the quote then one dollar is worth 1/1.3598 or 0.7354 euros.

3.6 FACTORS AFFECTING SPOT FX RATES

At any given time some market participants wish to buy a currency and others wish to sell. The rate of exchange is the price of the base currency expressed in units of counter-currency that matches supply and demand. However behind this truism lies a range of economic factors, or **fundamentals** as they are sometimes known in the capital markets industry.

Some Key Economic Fundamentals

- Trade balance
- Interest rates
- Money supply
- Inflation
- Government fiscal policy – its spending and tax policy

3.6.1 The Trade Balance

The trade balance represents the difference between a country's exports and imports of goods and services. Importers are buyers and exporters are sellers of foreign currency. In recent years the United States has run a substantial balance of trade deficit, as illustrated in Figure 3.1. This means that US importers have to sell dollars to buy foreign currency such as the Chinese yuan, Japanese yen, and euros. This exerts a downward pressure on the domestic currency, in this case the US dollar.

However, this effect is balanced to some extent by the fact that in modern global markets currency flows are also strongly influenced by international investment, both direct (buying foreign companies) and indirect (buying financial assets such as bonds and shares denominated in foreign currencies).

Figure 3.2 shows the foreign holdings of US securities as at 30 June in each year between 2005 and 2007. The figures include equities (common and preference stock) and short-term and long-term debt securities issued by the US Treasury, US agencies, and corporations. The graph shows the huge extent of foreign indirect investment in US financial assets. They also indicate that if investment in US assets becomes a less attractive option for foreigners this could have a significant effect on the dollar. This could be brought about by lower yields on dollar-denominated assets compared to alternatives, or investor perceptions that such assets are becoming more risky.

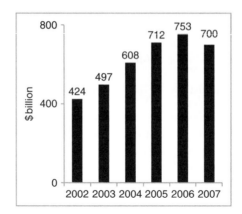

Figure 3.1 US annual trade deficit in goods and services 2002–2007 BOP basis. Figures as at 10 June 2008.
Source: US Census Bureau, reproduced with permission.

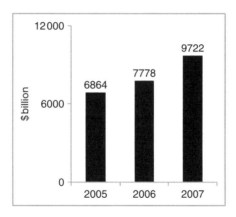

Figure 3.2 Foreign holdings of US securities as at 30 June each year.
Source: US Department of the Treasury.

The effect of international trade flows on foreign exchange rates can also be observed on countries such as Brazil and Australia which export commodities. Other things being equal, when the demand for commodities such as metals or oil or foodstuffs is strong, and the prices are rising in the world markets, this tends to boost exports and so strengthen the domestic currencies of the key producer countries.

One longer-term concern for the US dollar is the risk that foreign countries will hold less of their reserves in dollar-denominated assets and more in other major international currencies such as the euro. According to figures from the International Monetary Fund, the dollar's share of allocated global foreign exchange reserves fell to 64 % at the end of 2007 compared to 72 % at the end of 2001. Meantime over the same period the euro's share had risen to almost 26.5 %. Figure 3.3 illustrates the trend.

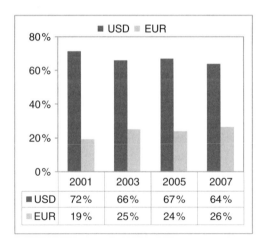

	2001	2003	2005	2007
USD	72%	66%	67%	64%
EUR	19%	25%	24%	26%

Figure 3.3 Percentage of foreign exchange reserves in US dollars and in euros at fourth quarter. Based on allocated reserves.
Source: International Monetary Fund.

3.6.2 Interest Rates and Fiscal Policy

Higher interest rates can make a currency more attractive to international investors, at least over the short term, and increase demand for the currency. One popular trade in FX is known as the **carry trade**. This consists in borrowing or shorting a low yield currency (such as the Japanese yen) and investing in a high yield currency. In practice, however, the relationship between interest rates and currency rates is complex. High rates of interest tend to occur at times of inflation. Accelerating inflation and money supply growth may be signs that a currency could lose its value relative to other currencies. If this happens in a carry trade then the losses from the depreciation of the high yield currency may exceed the gains from the higher interest rate in that currency.

Finally, the government's fiscal stance will have a significant effect on the international standing of the currency. If the government runs a budget deficit by spending more than it collects in tax revenues the difference is made good by borrowing on the domestic or international capital markets. Too much spending can lead to excess growth in the money supply and inflation, which erodes the value of the currency. Too much borrowing can lead to rising interest rates, which slows down economic growth and tends to adversely affect the market values of investment assets such as fixed income bonds and equities, making the currency less attractive as an investment vehicle. Figure 3.4 shows a six-month period during which low and falling US interest rates combined with concerns over the overall health of the US economy conspired to weaken the dollar against the euro, though with some modest recovery towards the end of the period.

3.6.3 Release of Statistics

Statistics on the trade balance, money supply growth, Gross Domestic Product (GDP), business confidence, and other **economic indicators** are reported on a regular basis. The dates

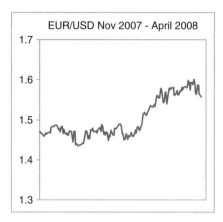

Figure 3.4 Period of general US dollar weakness against the euro.

and times of the key numbers are well known to the market and are avidly followed. Many of the indicators are influenced directly or indirectly by the activities of the central bank and government agencies. Currency analysts, dealers, economists, investment strategy advisors, and corporate treasurers use the indicators to assess the next moves of the authorities. If for example the growth rate in the economy slows down sharply this may be taken as a sign that the central bank will cut interest rates to stimulate growth and to avert a recession.

3.7 SPOT FX TRADING

Spot FX traders may adjust or **shade** their two-way quotations according to their current position and their future expectations on where currency rates are moving. For example, suppose that a trader has the position shown in Table 3.1 in a EUR/USD spot trading book (the base currency is the euro and the counter-currency the US dollar).

The trader has made FX deals which result in a 13.5 million short position in US dollars and a 10 million long position in euros for spot delivery. The deals will be settled in two business days' time, and the dealer will have to pay a net \$ 13.5 million and receive in return a net 10 million euros. If the euro weakens against the dollar the dealer will make a loss on the position. The trader could take that risk and wait for the deals to settle, although it will be important to ensure that adequate funds are available to cover the USD payment. Alternatively, the dealer might decide to **close the position** through an offsetting spot FX trade (or a number of trades).

3.7.1 Shading the Rates

The trader in the example could call another dealer for a quotation. The disadvantage is that the counterparty would gain the benefit of the bid/ask spread. Instead, the trader could

Table 3.1 A trader's spot position in EUR/USD

USD bought (+) sold (−)	Rate	EUR bought (+) sold (−)
−13,500,000	1.3500	+10,000,000

quote a two-way rate into the market that makes it attractive for counterparties to sell US dollars in return for euros. Assume that the current market rates are now 1.3508/1.3511. The trader could quote 1.3507/10.

- **Bid Rate.** The trader is bidding to buy one euro and pay only 1.3507 dollars, so this is unattractive.
- **Ask Rate.** The trader is offering to sell one euro and asks in return only 1.3510 dollars, a better rate than the current market level of 1.3511.

Suppose the trader contracts a spot deal to sell EUR 10 million at a rate of 1.3510 and receive in return $13.51 million. In two business days' time the net cash flows in euros will now be zero but the trader will be left with a net surplus of $10,000. The net profit in dollars is the difference between the rates at which the euros were sold and bought applied to the EUR 10 million position.

$$\text{Net Profit in USD} = (1.3510 - 1.3500) \times 10,000,000 = \text{USD } 10,000$$

Rules for Shading Spot FX Rates

A trader wishing to make a competitive quotation to sell the base currency should lower the ask or offer rate. A trader wishing to make a competitive quotation to buy the base currency should raise the bid rate.

Suppose the market rate is EUR/USD 1.3508/1.3511. A trader wishes to buy euros. An appropriate two-way quotation to make might be EUR/USD 1.3509/12:

- The trader buys one euro and pays 1.3509 dollars, more than the market.
- The trader sells one euro and charges 1.3512 dollars, a less attractive rate than the market, which will discourage buyers of euros.

3.8   SPOT POSITION KEEPING

A spot FX trader keeps a **deal blotter** which lists:

- all the trades that have been made;
- the amounts;
- the rates;
- the counterparties.

Table 3.2 shows a blotter for a spot GBP/USD trader. (This currency pair is often called **cable** in the market, after the trans-Atlantic cable historically used to conduct and settle trades.) The first column shows the deal counterparty. The second shows the counter-currency (US dollar) amount in full. The third column gives the deal rate; the fourth the base currency amount in British pounds. The final column shows the trader's net sterling position for spot delivery, a running total of the numbers in column four. The first trade was with Deutsche Bank. The details are as follows:

- The trader bought GBP 10 million ('10 pounds' in the market jargon) for value spot.
- The exchange rate is 1.7523.
- The dealer will pay in return $17.523 million.

Table 3.2   Spot GBP/USD deal blotter

(1) CPTY	(2) USD bought (+) sold (−)	(3) Deal rate	(4) GBP bought (+) sold (−)	(5) Net GBP position
Deutsche	−17,523,000	1.7523	10,000,000	10,000,000
Citibank	−8,762,500	1.7525	5,000,000	15,000,000
Barclays	17,527,000	1.7527	−10,000,000	5,000,000
JP Morgan	17,524,000	1.7524	−10,000,000	−5,000,000

In the second trade the dealer bought five million pounds at a rate of 1.7525. By the third trade the dealer was starting to unwind the long sterling position by selling pounds. By the fourth trade the pound had started to fall and the dealer had established a net short position of minus five million pounds, possibly in anticipation of a further weakening. To close out the overall position the trader would have to enter into a spot GBP/USD deal buying five million pounds and selling dollars.

3.8.1   Revaluation

How profitable has the cable dealer's trading campaign been so far? One way to work this out is to match off all the deals in which the dealer bought and sold pounds and check the rates at which they were entered into. If the trader buys pounds at a lower rate and sells them at a higher rate the trading campaign is profitable. In practice this can be a laborious way to calculate profits and losses when many deals have been made. In addition, the trader will often have a net open position at the end. This is the case in the example in Table 3.2 – the trader has made purchases totalling GBP 15 million but has sold a total of GBP 20 million, leaving a short position of GBP 5 million.

A common methodology is to take a revaluation or **mark-to-market** rate from the market (often the mid-rate between the bid and ask rates) and apply this to each trade individually to calculate the P&L on that trade. For illustration we will take a rate of 1.7490 and apply this to the trader's blotter, as shown in Table 3.3.

In the first deal in Table 3.3 the trader bought GBP 10 million at 1.7523. The 'reval' rate is 1.7490. This is a loss:

$$\text{Loss (in dollars)} = 10{,}000{,}000 \times (1.7490 - 1.7523) = -33{,}000$$

If this is translated into sterling at the revaluation rate the loss in pounds is as follows:

$$\text{Loss (in pounds)} = \frac{-33{,}000}{1.7490} = -18{,}868$$

Table 3.3   Revaluation profits and losses

CPTY	USD bought (+) sold (−)	Deal rate	GBP bought (+) sold (−)	P&L USD	P&L GBP
Deutsche	−17,523,000	1.7523	10,000,000	−33,000	−18,868
Citibank	−8,762,500	1.7525	5,000,000	−17,500	−10,006
Barclays	17,527,000	1.7527	−10,000,000	37,000	21,155
JP Morgan	17,524,000	1.7524	−10,000,000	34,000	19,440
Totals	8,765,500		−5,000,000	20,500	11,721

In the final deal the trader sold GBP 10 million at 1.7524. At the revaluation rate of 1.7490 this represents a profit of 34 'pips' on a 10 million deal size.

$$\text{Profit (in dollars)} = -10,000,000 \times (1.7490 - 1.7524) = 34,000$$
$$\text{Profit (in pounds)} = \frac{34,000}{1.7490} = 19,440$$

The rule is simple. If the trader has bought above the 'reval' rate, mark in a loss. If the trader sold above the revaluation rate, mark in a profit.

3.8.2   Net Open Position

The total P&L from all four trades in Table 3.3 is a profit of USD 20,500, which is equivalent to GBP 11,721 at the revaluation rate. The result can be cross-checked by calculating the overall position after the four trades have been completed and what it would cost to close this position out. The overall short position in sterling is GBP 5 million. The overall long position in dollars is $8,765,500. If the GBP 5 million was repurchased at the revaluation rate of 1.7490 the cost would be only $8,745,000. This would leave $8,765,500 − $8,745,000 = $20,500 profit in the trader's dollar account.

3.9   FX RISK CONTROL

In a modern dealing room FX traders can enter trades directly into electronic deal capture systems which will maintain the blotter and calculate the revaluation profit or loss based on the current market exchange rate. In addition, periodic checks will be made on the trader's book by the middle office or risk control department to assess the trader's position and to carry out an independent revaluation of the trading book based on current market rates. This shows not only how much realized profit or loss has been made but also the profit or loss that would result from closing any open position. If it appears that the risks are too high the positions may be reduced or cut altogether.

3.9.1   Market Risk

The main risk in an FX dealing room is **market risk**, which arises from running long (short) positions in currencies that might weaken (strengthen). To control market risk traders are set limits on the sizes of the positions they can maintain. Also, as noted above, traders' positions are revalued or marked-to-market to assess the level of risk.

FX trading is carried out in international centres such as London, New York, and Hong Kong and nowadays is a 24-hour business. A spot trader in London running an FX book with an open position overnight in (say) dollar/yen could find that the rate has moved adversely by the time he or she returns to monitor the position on the next morning. One solution to this problem of overnight risk is to close the position at the end of the London trading day. Another is to place an order with a New York bank or with a colleague based in New York to make a deal on the trader's behalf, closing the position if the dollar/yen rate moves adversely beyond a certain level. This is known as a **stop-loss** order.

> **Global Trading**
>
> In the modern global markets the solution to overnight risk in a large bank is for the FX trading book to be passed around the world, from London, to New York, to the bank's Far Eastern centre, and then back to London. The book is traded 24 hours aday.

3.9.2 Settlement Risk

FX deals also give rise to settlement risk of three main types:

- operational failure;
- replacement risk;
- Herstatt risk.

The first type of problem results from what are known as 'trade fails'. It arises, for example, when payment instructions are incorrectly made and the currency that should be credited to a counterparty's account is sent to the wrong place. The bank may have to pay interest to its counterparty if this happens. Simple trade 'fails' of this kind can add up to significant losses over time.

The second type of risk is that a counterparty may cease to trade before the deal is actually settled. The bank may have agreed the trade at an advantageous rate, and replacing the trade with a new counterparty may result in a loss or a reduced level of profit. This is often referred to as **replacement risk**. The third and most dangerous type of settlement problem goes under the title of **Herstatt risk**. It is the risk that a bank dutifully makes the payment for its side of a transaction but the counterparty fails to reciprocate.

> **Herstatt Bank**
>
> Herstatt Bank was a German bank that failed in 1974 as a result of over-trading. Because of time differences, payments on a large number of FX deals in Deutschemarks were made to Herstatt Bank, but it closed operations and never made the return dollar payments to New York. The resulting legal actions spent many years in the German courts.

To reduce the risk of settlement problems and to cut back-office costs, banks have increasingly turned to technology-based solutions. The focus is on electronic deal capture and straight-through deal processing by computer. Human intervention is made on an exceptional basis, to rectify problems, to make sure that trade details are properly set up before the value date, and to handle more complex trades that will not settle automatically. Some financial institutions have decided to outsource back-office arrangements to specialist firms who can invest in advanced technology and spread the investment cost across a range of clients.

Banks also manage general settlement risk problems by entering into 'netting' agreements with their trading counterparties. This means that trades are not settled individually and only the net payments due to either side are made. In addition, a bank may demand **collateral** when it enters into a transaction with a given counterparty. This is held in reserve against the possibility that the counterparty may be unable (or unwilling) to discharge its obligations. Some economists describe the holding of collateral as a 'hostage-taking' arrangement, and a way of reducing uncertainty in conditions where complete trust cannot be placed on the actions of others. In some cases the collateral is held by a third party such as a clearing house. The downside of all such arrangements is that they add to transaction costs because collateral has to be collected and managed.

Nostro and Vostro

A bank's payment account with another bank is called a **Nostro account**, from the Latin word for 'our'. For example, if the Royal Bank of Scotland has a dollar account with the Bank of America in New York for dollar receipts on FX transactions this is a Nostro account for the Royal Bank. If Bank of America has a sterling account with the Royal Bank of Scotland then for the Royal Bank this would be a **Vostro account**, meaning 'your account with us'.

3.10   CROSS-CURRENCY RATES

A cross rate is an FX rate established between two currencies using their exchange rate against a common currency, typically the US dollar. The method of calculation depends on whether the common currency is the base in both cases.

3.10.1   Common Base Currency

Suppose that a corporate client wants a quotation from a bank to sell Swiss francs to the bank for value spot and to buy in return Japanese yen. The bank's spot rates against the US dollar are as follows.

$$USD/CHF\ 1.1120/25$$

$$USD/JPY\ 105.66/71$$

The bank's task is to quote a spot rate CHF/JPY to the client by 'going through the dollar'.

- The bank would sell one dollar to the client and ask in return CHF 1.1125.
- The bank would buy that dollar back and give in return JPY 105.66.

The bank's spot rate CHF/JPY is therefore:

$$\frac{105.66}{1.1125} = 94.975$$

In practice the bank may decide to 'shade' or adjust this theoretical rate. Note that this is the bank's **bid rate** – the rate at which it buys the base currency CHF. Using the same logic we can calculate an ask or offer rate of CHF/JPY 95.063. In this example the two cross-currencies share the same base currency, the US dollar.

Rule: Common Base Currency

To calculate a two-way cross rate divide bid/ask and then ask/bid.

$$Bid/Ask = 105.66/1.1125 = 94.975(Bid)$$

$$Ask/Bid = 105.71/1.1120 = 95.063(Ask)$$

3.10.2 Different Base Currency

Suppose that a UK fund manager wishes to shift funds to the Japanese market to take advantage of rising equity prices. She wishes to buy yen and sell pounds and contacts a bank. Its rates against the dollar are as follows.

$$GBP/USD\ 1.7554/58$$

$$USD/JPY\ 105.66/71$$

The bank is asked to quote a cross-rate GBP/JPY and calculates a theoretical rate 'going through the dollar'.

- The bank would sell 1.7554 dollars to the client and ask in return one pound sterling.
- The bank would buy 1.7554 dollars back from the client and give in return $1.7554 \times 105.66 = 185.48$ yen.

Therefore the theoretical GBP/JPY rate is 185.48. Note that this is the bank's **bid rate** for buying pounds (selling yen). Its ask rate calculated using the same logic would be 185.61.

Rule: Different Base Currency

To calculate a two-way cross rate multiply the two bid rates and then the two ask rates.

$$Bid \times Bid = 1.7554 \times 105.66 = 185.48(Bid)$$
$$Ask \times Ask = 1.7558 \times 105.71 = 185.61(Ask)$$

3.11 OUTRIGHT FORWARD FX RATES

An outright forward foreign exchange deal is:

- a firm and binding commitment between two parties;
- to exchange two currency amounts;
- at an agreed rate;
- on a future value date that is later than spot.

The two currencies are not exchanged until the value date is reached, but the rate is agreed on the trade date. Outright forwards are commonly used by companies that have known cash flows in foreign currencies which are due on specific future dates. They can lock into a known exchange rate and eliminate the risk of losses resulting from adverse foreign exchange rate movements. The other side of the coin is that a contract must be honoured even if a better rate subsequently becomes available on the spot market. A company that enters into an outright forward surrenders any potential gains resulting from favourable movements in FX rates in return for certainty.

3.11.1 Hedging with FX Forwards

The outright forward rates quoted by banks are closely linked to the relative interest rates in the two currencies. Traders sometimes talk about this in terms of the relative **carry cost** of holding positions in the two currencies. In effect, as the following example illustrates, a fair forward FX rate can be established through a hedging or arbitrage argument – what it would cost a bank to hedge against the risks involved in entering into an outright forward FX deal. If a bank quotes a rate that is out of alignment with the fair or theoretical rate then it may create opportunities for other traders to achieve arbitrage or 'risk-free' profits. (In practice though arbitrageurs also have to take into account the transaction costs involved in setting up the necessary trades.)

3.12 OUTRIGHT FORWARD FX HEDGE: CASE STUDY

A Swiss company has exported goods to the US. The payment due is $ 10 million. The current spot rate USD/CHF is 1.2000. If the invoice was due for immediate settlement then the exporter would receive CHF 12 million in exchange for selling the dollars. However the payment is actually due in one year (360 days after spot). If the dollar weakens over that time then the company will find itself receiving fewer Swiss francs for its dollars, perhaps eliminating its profit margin from the export transaction.

Instead, the exporter approaches BIGBANK to enter into an outright forward FX deal. In this deal it will pay over the $ 10 million in one year to BIGBANK in return for a fixed amount of Swiss francs. But how can BIGBANK establish a fair rate for the deal? It could guess what it *thinks* the USD/CHF rate will be in a year's time. But unless it puts some kind of hedge in place this could be risky – the bank could make money on the deal, but it could also lose if it guesses wrongly. An alternative is to base the forward FX rate on the cost of hedging the rate quoted to the exporter. In fact the simplest hedge in this case is to use borrowing and lending in the money markets, as shown below.

3.12.1 Hedging the Bank's Risks

If it enters a forward FX deal with the exporter then BIGBANK will agree to receive $ 10 million in one year's time (360 days after spot) and pay in return a fixed amount of Swiss francs. BIGBANK could manage this exposure through the following market transactions for value spot.

- Borrow the present value of $ 10 million and agree to repay this with interest in a year.
- Sell the dollars that are borrowed for Swiss francs.
- Deposit these Swiss francs for a year.

In one year BIGBANK will have to repay $ 10 million on the loan. However this will be covered by the receipt of $ 10 million from the exporter on the outright forward FX contract. Meantime, the Swiss francs deposited (plus interest) will be available to make a return payment to the exporter.

3.12.2 Calculating the Payments

Suppose that BIGBANK can borrow dollars for a year at 3 % p.a. The present value of $ 10 million is:

$$\frac{10,000,000}{1.03} = \$9,708,738$$

BIGBANK then converts this into Swiss francs at a spot rate of USD/CHF 1.2000. This produces CHF 11,650,485. Suppose that the CHF can be deposited for a year at 2 % p.a. Then BIGBANK will have CHF 11,883,495 on its maturing deposit in one year. This is calculated as follows:

$$11,650,485 \times 1.02 = CHF\ 11,883,495$$

If the bank agrees to pay over exactly CHF 11,883,495 to the exporter in a year it will have covered the cash flows on the forward FX deal without taking risks on FX movements. Suppose that to make a profit on the deal and to cover its settlement risks and operational costs it agrees to pay over only CHF 11,883,000 to the exporter. Then the one year outright forward rate USD/CHF achieved by the exporter is calculated as follows:

$$\text{Outright Forward Rate} = \frac{11,883,000}{10,000,000} = 1.1883$$

3.13 FORWARD FX FORMULA

A forward rate can be calculated directly as follows. Note that the interest rates are entered as decimals p.a.

$$\text{Forward FX Rate} = \text{Spot Rate} \times \left[\frac{1 + \left(\text{Counter-currency Interest Rate} \times \dfrac{\text{Actual Days}}{\text{Year Base}}\right)}{1 + \left(\text{Base Currency Interest Rate} \times \dfrac{\text{Actual Days}}{\text{year Base}}\right)}\right]$$

In the above example:

Spot rate = 1.2000

Counter-currency (CHF) interest rate = 2 % p.a. = 0.02 as a decimal

Base currency (USD) interest rate = 3 % p.a. = 0.03 as a decimal

Actual days = 360

Year base for both currencies = 360 (i.e. the convention for calculating interest is actual/360)

Therefore:

$$\text{Forward FX Rate} = 1.2000 \times \left[\frac{1 + \left(0.02 \times \dfrac{360}{360}\right)}{1 + \left(0.03 \times \dfrac{360}{360}\right)} \right] = 1.1883$$

In the formula the spot rate is adjusted by a factor (in the large square brackets) that is determined by the relative interest rates in the two currencies. In the above example the base currency USD interest rate is higher than the counter-currency CHF interest rate. The adjustment factor is therefore less than one (it is 0.9903) so the dollar buys fewer Swiss francs for forward compared to spot delivery. The USD/CHF forward rate is at a discount. If the counter-currency interest rate is higher than the base currency interest rate then the base currency buys more units of the counter-currency for forward compared to spot delivery. The forward rate is at a premium.

3.14 FX OR FORWARD SWAPS

A forward FX dealer will have numbers of deals on the book and some of the FX risks will cancel out. If there are residual exposures on forward dates the trader could cover this by borrowing and lending in the money markets as outlined in Section 3.12. In practice, however, this is a little messy since it involves using the bank's balance sheet to borrow and lend money and it could involve substantial credit risk.

Returning to the case study, suppose that BIGBANK agrees to enter into a one-year forward FX deal with the exporter at a rate of exactly USD/CHF 1.1883. The bank's cash flows from the deal are set out in Figure 3.5. As it stands it is exposed to a weakening US dollar – if this happens the $10 million it receives from the exporter will be worth less in terms of Swiss francs.

As an alternative to hedging in the money markets, BIGBANK could hedge at least part of its risks by entering into a spot FX deal in which it sells dollars and buys Swiss francs. Then if the dollar weakens it will be losing on the outright forward deal but making a profit on the spot deal (in which it is short dollars). The spot rate USD/EUR is 1.2000 so the combination for BIGBANK (outright forward plus the covering spot FX deal) is shown in Figure 3.6.

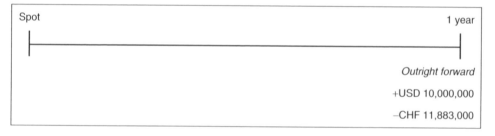

Figure 3.5 BIGBANK'S cash flows from the outright forward FX deal.

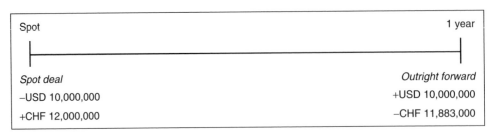

Figure 3.6   BIGBANK'S cash flows covering with a spot deal.

The problem of course is that the spot deal will settle in two business days' time, while the outright forward is for value one year (in fact 360 days) after spot. There is a time lag between the two deals. This can be handled using a product called an FX swap.

FX or Forward Swap: Definition

An exchange of one currency for another on one date (normally spot) combined with a reverse exchange of the two currencies at a later date. Normally one currency amount is kept constant over the two legs.

To manage the time gap, as shown in Figure 3.7, BIGBANK can enter into an FX swap deal to buy dollars (sell Swiss francs) spot. The forward leg of the swap would consist of selling dollars (buying Swiss francs) for value one year after spot. The rate used in Figure 3.7 for the forward leg is again 1.1883.

Looked at another way, the FX swap could be considered as a means by which BIGBANK borrows dollars for a year, combined with depositing CHF 12 million for the same time period. However the deal is structured as an exchange of two currencies for value spot combined with an agreement to re-exchange on a forward date. This has the advantage that the deal is **off-balance sheet** – legally it is a contract which combines a spot with a forward FX deal.

Figure 3.7   BIGBANK'S cash flows covering with a spot deal and with an FX swap.

3.15   FX SWAP TWO-WAY QUOTATIONS

Forward FX traders tend to quote FX swap rates in terms of **forward points** rather than outright rates. These are subtracted from or added to the agreed rate for the spot leg of the deal to establish the rate for the forward leg of the swap. Suppose that in the above example BIGBANK receives a two-way quotation from a dealer for the FX swap of 117/107, and the rate agreed for the spot leg is 1.2000. The left-hand rate here is 117 points or CHF 0.0117 per dollar. The right-hand rate is 107 points or CHF 0.0107 per dollar. The rules for interpreting a two-way FX swap quotation are as follows.

- **High-Low.** If the points are quoted with the numerically larger number first then they are subtracted from the rate for the spot leg to establish the rate for the forward leg. In fact the points are **negative**, although the sign is not normally shown.
- **Low-High.** If the points are quoted with the numerically smaller number first then they are added to the rate for the spot leg to establish the rate for the forward leg. In fact the points are **positive**, although the sign is not usually shown.
- **Left-hand Rate.** The trader making the quotation sells the base currency spot and buys it back forward at the left-hand number.
- **Right-hand Rate.** The trader making the quotation buys the base currency spot and sells it back forward at the right-hand number.

In the BIGBANK case USD is the base currency and the agreed rate for the spot leg is 1.2000. BIGBANK needs to buy dollars in the spot leg and sell dollars in the forward leg of the swap. So the swap trader making the quote to BIGBANK will be selling dollars for value spot and buying dollars back from BIGBANK in one year. The trader will do this at the left-hand number in his two-way quotation of 117/107. But what does this mean?

- **Spot Leg.** The FX swap dealer will sell one dollar for value spot and asks in return the agreed spot rate CHF 1.2000.
- **Forward Leg.** The FX swap dealer will receive back one dollar in one year and pay in return CHF 1.2000 − 0.0117 = CHF 1.1883.

On a $ 10 million trade the swap dealer will sell $ 10 million spot to BIGBANK and receive CHF 12 million. Then on the forward leg the dealer will receive back the $ 10 million from BIGBANK and pay only CHF 11,883,000 in return. This represents a gain to the dealer of 117 points, or CHF 0.0117 per dollar, or CHF 117,000 on $ 10 million. The reason for the gain is related to the relative interest rates in the two currencies. In the swap the dealer is moving out of the higher interest rate currency (USD) and into a lower interest rate currency (CHF).

The dealer is compensated for this by paying back fewer Swiss francs on the forward leg of the swap than are received on the spot leg. In effect the 117 points represent the interest rate differential between the two currencies expressed in currency terms. The dealer is paid 117 points to enter into the FX swap, or in the jargon of the market, receives 117 points 'in his favour'.

3.15.1   Base Currency Interest Rate is Lower

Of course it is not always the case that the base currency interest rate is higher than that of the counter-currency. For example, an FX swap dealer might quote a rate for a one year

EUR/GBP deal of 82/88. The rates here are quoted low-high, which means that they are **added** to the rate for the spot leg of a swap to establish the rate for the forward leg. This tells us that the euro is a lower interest rate currency than sterling and buys more pounds for forward than for spot delivery.

Suppose the spot rate EUR/GBP is 0.8000. Then the dealer sells one euro spot in return for GBP 0.8000. In one year the dealer will buy back one euro and repay:

$$GBP\ 0.8000 + 0.0082 = GBP\ 0.8082$$

The dealer pays 82 points to move into the higher yielding currency GBP and out of euros. On the other side of the quotation the dealer buys one euro spot and pays GBP 0.8000. In one year the dealer will return the euro and receive back:

$$GBP\ 0.8000 + 0.0088 = GBP\ 0.8088$$

In other words, the dealer earns 88 points or GBP 0.0088 per euro to move into the lower yield currency EUR and out of pounds. In practice FX swap dealers may transact the spot leg of a swap at a rate mid-way between the bid and offer spot rate, although there is a certain amount of flexibility in this because whatever rate is chosen for the spot leg is applied to the forward points to calculate the rate for the forward leg of the deal.

FX Swap Dealer's Quotes

In an FX swap you will pay points to move into a higher yielding currency, and receive points to move into a lower yielding currency. If you are paying points to a dealer you will pay the bigger of the two numbers quoted by the dealer. If you are receiving points from a dealer you will earn the lower of the two numbers quoted.

3.15.2   Covered Foreign Currency Investments

It can very often appear attractive to an investor to switch funds into a foreign currency that offers higher interest rates. However the investor also acquires foreign exchange risk in the process, if the foreign currency proceeds have to be converted back into the home currency at some future date. An FX swap can be used to manage the currency risk. The investor uses the spot leg to transfer funds into the foreign currency to buy assets denominated in that currency. The forward leg ensures that funds are translated back into the home currency at a known exchange rate.

3.16   CHAPTER SUMMARY

Foreign exchange trading is dominated by interbank deals, although underpinning such deals are currency transactions made by importers and exporters and by institutional investors such as mutual funds and insurance companies. In developed countries nowadays currencies are freely floating and FX rates are largely driven by demand and supply factors. The central banks in these countries influence FX markets through regulation, monetary policy, and occasional direct intervention. The FX market is a 24-hour global marketplace in which dealers working for major banks are connected by telephones and computer screens. Most deals are for value spot, which for most currency pairs means that the currencies are exchanged two business days after the trade is agreed. Settlement in the interbank market is normally made through the SWIFT system. Spot FX dealers maintain a list of deals on a blotter and also assess the revaluation profit and loss on their positions in order to measure returns and to contain risks. An outright forward FX transaction is one in which two currency amounts are exchanged at an agreed rate for a value date later than spot. Corporates and institutional investors use outright forward FX deals to manage currency risk. In the interbank market most forward deals are made in the form of FX or forward swaps. A FX swap is an agreement to exchange one currency for another and to re-exchange the currencies on a later date. Dealers normally quote the rates in terms of forward points which are subtracted from or added to the rate for the spot leg of the swap to establish the rate for the forward leg. FX swaps are used to manage the risk on outright forward deals, to manage time gaps between currency cash flows, and generally to switch from one currency to another for a specific period of time.

4
Major Government Bond Markets

4.1 CHAPTER OVERVIEW

This chapter explores the market for major government bonds, in particular those issued by G7 countries such as the US, the UK, Japan, and countries in the eurozone. It considers issuance procedures and trading methods in the secondary markets. The most active government bond market is the market for US government debt, and many of the conventions used there have been exported around the world. For example, UK government bonds (gilts) and government bonds issued in the eurozone now use the day-counting convention developed in the US market. The chapter looks at how bonds are quoted and valued using discounted cash flow techniques. Two measures of bond yield or return are introduced: current or running yield, and yield-to-maturity. Finally, investors in government bonds cannot ignore the possibility that governments may default on debt obligations, or at least seek to reschedule payments. The risk of default is very low in the case of US debt but can be substantial with bonds issued by developing countries. The chapter explores sovereign risk and the credit rating of sovereign debt by the major agencies.

4.2 INTRODUCTION TO GOVERNMENT BONDS

Bonds are long-term negotiable debt securities issued by governments, government agencies, financial institutions, and corporations to raise debt capital. The majority are **straight** or 'plain vanilla' bonds which:

- pay fixed interest amounts – known as **coupons** – on regular dates;
- have a fixed maturity or **redemption** date, at which point the bond's par or face value is repaid to the investor.

Governments around the world raise long-term debt by issuing bonds to finance **budget deficits**, the difference between government spending and the money raised by taxation. On the other hand if a government runs a budget *surplus* (as happened in the US in the early 2000s) it may buy its bonds back through outright purchases in the open market or via 'reverse auctions' in which it bids for securities held by dealers and investors.

4.2.1 Primary and Secondary Markets

Larger sovereign states such as the US and the UK hold regular auctions of government bonds. Most are bought by large financial institutions known as **primary dealers** which then distribute the securities around the market, though some are purchased directly by retail investors. The other main issuance method is for a government to sell a bond issue outright to an underwriting syndicate of banks at an agreed price. The syndicate then assumes the risks involved in attempting to sell the securities on to other investors at a profit. The syndication technique is often used by smaller countries which are not able to mount regular auctions.

Once bonds are issued they trade on **secondary markets**. In some cases, such as the UK, government bonds are listed on the local stock exchange. However in the UK and in most countries including the US bonds are mainly traded on **over-the-counter** (OTC) markets through dealers working in large banks and securities houses. Dealers support the liquidity of the market by making bid and ask prices. The prices are displayed on screen-based services such as Bloomberg and deals are transacted over the telephone or by electronic communication. An OTC deal is one which is conducted directly between two parties. The contrast is with a trade conducted via an organized exchange.

In advanced government bond markets such as the US there is a system of **inter-dealer brokers** who further enhance the liquidity of the market by acting as intermediaries between traders and helping them find the best prices currently available.

4.3   SOVEREIGN RISK

In major industrial countries government bonds issued in the domestic currency normally represent the lowest credit risk of any borrower in that currency and set the reference or **benchmark** interest rate for any given maturity. In the US the return or yield on US Treasuries normally establishes a minimum rate of return that any other dollar borrower, whether sovereign, corporate, or financial, will have to match and exceed to attract investors. The benchmark for borrowing in euros is usually set by German government bonds, although sometimes French government bonds are used for certain maturities where they are particularly liquid. By contrast, in a developing country it is not uncommon for a major corporation owning significant assets – particularly natural resources – to borrow more cheaply than the government of that country.

4.3.1   Sovereign Debt Ratings

Nevertheless governments can and do default or seek to restructure their debt liabilities. The default risk on US Treasuries or on bonds issued by the Federal Republic of Germany may be very small but even in such cases it is not zero. The default risk with debt issued in foreign currencies by developing countries can be substantial. This has led the rating agencies such as Fitch, Standard & Poor's, and Moody's to institute **sovereign debt ratings**. The agencies combine an analysis of economic factors such as per capita GDP and government fiscal policy with judgements on more qualitative matters such as the stability and openness of a country's political system.

One of the economic factors that analysts can look at in assessing the level of sovereign risk is government debt as a percentage of GDP. Other things being equal, the higher the figure the more difficulties a country may encounter in sustaining its debt repayments. Table 4.1 shows estimates for 2007 for a range of countries. The rankings in the third column are based on a set of 126 countries for which data were available. Note that public debt is measured here as the total of all government borrowings less repayments denominated in a country's home currency. It is distinct from *foreign currency* liabilities which have to be met from foreign currency reserves. These may be substantial in the case of developing countries, which often borrow funds in US dollars in international markets.

Table 4.1 Estimated home currency public debt in 2007

Country	Public debt (% of GDP)	Ranking
Japan	170.0	3
Italy	104.0	7
Germany	64.9	20
France	63.9	23
United States	60.8	27
India	58.2	31
Brazil	45.1	47
United Kingdom	43.6	50
China	18.4	100

Source: The World Factbook. Estimates as at October 2008.

Although Germany and Italy are both key members of the European Union (they were both signatories to the original 1957 Treaty of Rome) and have both adopted the euro as their currency, the level of government debt in Italy is substantially higher. In addition, Italy has historically achieved a lower rate of economic growth and has suffered from political instability resulting from a succession of short-lasting minority governments. As at November 2008 Standard & Poor's awarded the top AAA sovereign rating to Germany and a rating of A+ to Italy.

As another example, by early 2005 the three major ratings agencies had all raised Russia's sovereign long-term sovereign debt rating to **investment grade**, which removed the restrictions on many large international funds on investing in Russian government debt. The background to the upgrading of Russia was a budget surplus of $25 billion and currency reserves of $120 billion in 2004, driven by booming oil production. Russia is the largest country in the world by geographical area, and owns the greatest mineral resources of any country. However political risks remain, as illustrated by Russia's disputes with the US over Georgia and missile defences in 2008.

One of the non-economic factors that analysts may consider in assessing sovereign risk is the level of **corruption** in a country. Corruption adversely affects economic development because it increases the costs and risks associated with doing business. It can also damage the political and judicial processes in a country. One source of data on this question is the non-political organization Transparency International which publishes a ranking of countries by their perceived levels of corruption, as determined by expert assessments and opinion surveys. In the 2007 table the least and the most corrupt countries listed were respectively Denmark and Somalia. The website http://www.transparency.org/ has further details.

Banks and securities firms tend to have separate dealing desks or business units responsible for trading government bonds issued by major industrial nations such as the G7 or G10 countries. The dealers focus primarily on the effects on bond prices of changes in interest rates and currency rates, driven largely by inflation expectations (although in cases such as Italy periodic concerns are raised over its ability to sustain its high level of public debt). Bonds issued by less well-developed emerging nations are traded by dealers who are particularly alert to the dangers of sovereign default and debt restructuring programmes. They can also take a positive view of a country if it seems likely to improve its economic performance. Other things being equal, the less likely it is that a country will default or restructure, the more valuable its debt will become to investors.

The G10 and BRICs

The G10 nations are those that in 1962 agreed to lend money to the International Monetary Fund (IMF). They are Belgium, Canada, France, Italy, Japan, the Netherlands, Sweden, Germany, the UK, and the USA. Some commentators forecast that Brazil, Russia, India and, China (collectively known as BRICs) will overtake most of the existing developed nations in economic importance as the 21st century progresses. Over the shorter term, though, they are vulnerable to changes in demand for their products in the developed world.

As well as the ratings produced by the agencies it is also possible to assess sovereign default risk by looking at the premiums dealers are quoting for **credit default swaps** (CDS) on sovereign borrowers. The CDS is explained in Chapter 7. Essentially it is a product that allows an investor to insure against the risk that a borrower will default on its debt. Normally the CDS premium on longer-dated US government debt is very low but in the panic over the credit crisis in mid-September 2008 it rose to 0.25 % p.a. for 10-year protection. This means that the cost of insuring $ 10 million in US Treasury bonds against default for 10 years was approximately $ 25,000 p.a. The cost of protecting German government bonds for the same period was lower at around 0.14 % p.a.

4.4   US GOVERNMENT NOTES AND BONDS

US government debt securities are obligations of the US government issued by the US Department of Treasury and backed, ultimately, by the tax-raising powers of the US government. The market for US Treasury securities is one of the largest and most active in the world. There are four main types of marketable securities issued: Treasury bills, Treasury notes, Treasury bonds and Treasury Inflation-Protected Securities or TIPS (Table 4.2). The total amounts outstanding on 30 September 2008 are shown in Figure 4.1. Treasury bills are covered in Chapter 2 above.

Table 4.2   Main marketable US government securities

Treasury bills	Short-term paper with maturities at issue of up to and including one year, issued at a discount to face value. T-bills are quoted in terms of the discount rate (see Chapter 2).
Treasury notes	Medium-term debt securities with maturities at issue of greater than one year and up to 10 years. Interest is paid semi-annually and the securities are redeemed at par. Notes are quoted per $ 100 nominal or par value.
Treasury bonds	Long-term debt securities with maturities at issue of over 10 years. Interest is paid semi-annually and the securities are redeemed at par. Bonds are quoted per $ 100 nominal or par value.
TIPS	Securities with maturities at issue ranging from five to 20 years. The principal amount repayable at maturity is adjusted according to the Consumer Price Index (CPI). Interest is paid semi-annually at a fixed rate which is applied to the adjusted principal so that interest payments rise in line with inflation.

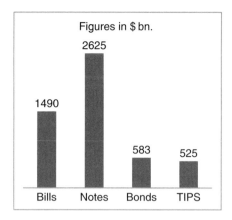

Figures in $ bn.

Figure 4.1   US Treasury securities outstanding at end-September 2008.
Source: US Department of Treasury.

4.4.1   Primary Market: Auction and Issuance Procedures

US Treasury notes and bonds are sold at auction in regular cycles. The system was automated in 1993. The arrangements (as at end-2008) are as follows:

- **Two-Year Notes.** Auctions are usually announced on the third or fourth Monday of each month. The notes are generally auctioned two days later and issued on the last day of the month.
- **Five-Year Notes.** Auctions are usually announced on the third or fourth Monday of each month. The notes are generally auctioned three days later and issued on the last day of the month.
- **10-Year Notes.** Auctions are usually announced on the first Wednesday in February, May, August, and November. The notes are generally auctioned on the second week of the month and issued on the 15th day.
- **30-Year Bonds.** Auctions are usually announced on the first Wednesday in February and August. The bonds are generally auctioned on the second week of the month and issued on the 15th day.

Two types of bid can be submitted. In a **non-competitive** bid the investor agrees to accept the rate determined by the auction and is guaranteed securities. In a **competitive** bid the investor submits a yield and if the bid falls within the range accepted the investor will receive securities. Most Treasuries are bought at auction by the **primary dealers** and then distributed into the markets. The primary dealers are large financial institutions that are selected by the Federal Reserve Bank of New York as counterparties for its open market operations. As discussed below, the primary dealers also provide liquidity in the secondary markets for US Treasuries by quoting two-way prices to other market participants.

Auction Maximum Bid Size

A bid cannot exceed 35 % of the issue size. This rule was instituted mainly in response to an auction in 1991 in which the broker-dealer Salomon Brothers submitted unauthorized orders on behalf of clients and took control of almost 90 % of the issue. Further rules state that the maximum non-competitive bid is for $ 5 million and that it is not permitted to bid competitively in an auction in which a non-competitive bid is made.

4.4.2   The When-Issued Market

Initially only the size of the issue and the maturity is announced. The notes or bonds are traded for a time in the **when-issued** market on an estimated yield for a bond of that maturity. Effectively, this is a forward market in which deals are settled after the issue of the bonds (although in practice many deals are unwound before settlement takes place). The when-issued market provides useful information about the prices likely to be bid at the forthcoming auction.

The most recently issued Treasury note or bond with a coupon that is representative of the current interest rate environment becomes the benchmark or **on-the-run** security for that maturity. Many investors and traders focus on the on-the-run instrument, which becomes highly liquid and often pays a somewhat lower return or yield when compared with other US Treasuries with a similar maturity.

4.4.3   The Secondary Market

The secondary market for US Treasuries operates on a global basis, with centres in Tokyo and London, though the bulk of business is still conducted in New York. Securities are held in electronic book-entry form rather than as physical certificates, which facilitates settlement and transfer. Settlement (the exchange of securities for funds) is normally '$T + 1$' which means that it occurs one business day after the trade is agreed.

As discussed above, the secondary market in US Treasuries is an over-the-counter (OTC) market. The key market participants are the **primary dealers** which include many of the largest banks and brokerage houses in the world. Although the primary dealers are no longer required to do so, in practice they remain the main market makers in US Treasuries, buying and selling securities on their own account at their quoted bid and ask (offer) prices. This provides liquidity to the market and encourages investors to participate. Primary dealers also trade with each other, either directly or through **inter-dealer brokers** who charge a fee for acting as an agent matching the two counterparties to a transaction.

As at September 2008 there were 19 primary dealers in the US market, including names such as Barclays Capital, Citigroup, Goldman Sachs, HSBC, and JP Morgan. The daily average trading volume of the primary dealers in US Government securities during 2007 was approximately $ 570 billion. Primary dealers also provide information to the Federal Reserve Bank of New York that assists it in conducting its open market operations.

4.5   US TREASURY QUOTATIONS

US Treasury notes and bonds pay fixed coupons or interest payments on regular dates throughout their life. In addition the par or face or redemption value (these terms all mean the same thing) is payable at maturity. There are no 'call' features which would allow the securities to be redeemed early by the government. The coupon on a US Treasury note or bond is paid in two semi-annual instalments.

Coupon Payments

$ 100 par value of a Treasury with a coupon rate of 5 % would pay two six-monthly instalments of $ 2.5 each year.

US Treasury notes and bonds are quoted by dealers as a percentage of their face or par value (i.e. per $100 par) on a **clean price** basis, that is, net of coupon interest that has accrued but has not been paid out by the US government since the last coupon date. A bond trading at par is trading at exactly $100. Quotes are in dollars and fractions of a dollar, normally to the nearest 1/32 %, although sometimes to the nearest 1/64 %. The sign '+' or sometimes 'H' is used to indicate 1/64 %.

US Treasury Bond Quotation

On 25 July 2001 the 5 % coupon US Treasury bond maturing on 15 February 2011 was trading at an offer or ask price of 99-6+. Dealers were selling the bond at 99 6/32 % plus 1/64 %. This is equivalent to $99 13/64 or $99.203125 per $100 par value. The settlement date – when the bonds are delivered and cash payment made – is one day after the trade date (known as '$T + 1$'). In this case the price was for settlement 26 July 2001.

4.5.1 Accrued Interest and Dirty Price

The 99-6+ price quoted in the above example is a **clean price**. It is net of interest that has accrued but not yet been paid on the settlement date. The bond's coupon rate is 5 % payable semi-annually. The day-count convention for calculating accrued interest on US Treasury notes and bonds is called **actual/actual**. To calculate the accrued interest in this system we need to know how many days there are in the current semi-annual coupon period and how many days have elapsed from the last coupon date to the settlement date.

The relevant dates in the example are as follows:

Last coupon date:	15 February 2001
Settlement date:	26 July 2001
Next coupon date:	15 August 2001

The calendar says that there are 181 actual calendar days in the current semi-annual coupon period (from 15 February to 15 August 2001) and 161 days have elapsed from the last coupon date to the settlement date. The accrued interest per $100 par value is calculated as follows.

$$\text{Accrued Interest} = \frac{\text{Annual Coupon}}{2} \times \frac{\text{Days Elapsed Since Last Coupon}}{\text{Days in Current Coupon Period}}$$

$$\text{Accrued Interest} = \frac{\$5}{2} \times \frac{161}{181} = \$2.223757$$

The accrued interest calculation is based on the actual number of days that have elapsed since the last coupon period divided by the actual number of days in the semi-annual period. This ratio is multiplied by the semi-annual coupon due in that period. The actual **settlement price** for a US Treasury note or bond is based on the clean price plus interest accrued to the settlement date. This is also known as the bond's **dirty price**. In the above example:

$$\text{Dirty Price per } \$100 \text{ par} = 99.203125 + 2.223757 = \$101.426882$$

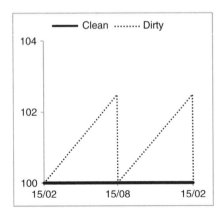

Figure 4.2   Clean and dirty prices during the coupon cycle.

4.5.2 The Coupon Cycle

Given that the actual price paid for a Treasury bond is based on the dirty price, why is it that traders quote the prices on a clean price basis? In fact the standard bond pricing model (discussed later in this chapter) calculates the bond's dirty price. Dealers have to calculate the accrued, then subtract it from the dirty price to establish the clean price. Then when the deal is done the accrued has to be added back again! It seems that it would save time and effort if prices were simply quoted on a dirty price basis in the first place.

To see why prices are quoted clean, Figure 4.2 shows the clean and dirty price of a semi-annual bond during two complete coupon cycles. The coupon dates are 15 February and 15 August. The bond has a 5 % coupon and is priced to yield 5 % on a range of dates over the course of the year. The clean price throughout is at or around par.

The graph shows that the dirty price increases in a straight-line fashion as interest accrues, but when the coupon is paid out the dirty price falls back to the clean price (in this case to par). This phenomenon makes it difficult to see how a bond is being affected by factors such as changes in market interest rates. In effect the clean price is the underlying value of the bond, with the 'noise' factor caused by the daily accrual of interest removed. Using dirty prices also makes it very difficult to compare the relative values of different bonds that have different coupon cycles – a bond that has just paid a coupon will have very little accrued interest compared with a bond that is a long way into its coupon cycle.

4.6 US TREASURY STRIPS

STRIPS stands for Separate Trading of Registered Interest and Principal of Securities. They are zero coupon debt obligations of the US Treasury. They differ from straight notes and bonds in that they do not pay any interest and therefore always trade below par. STRIPS are created by financial institutions which sell off the titles to the individual cash flows on straight coupon-paying bonds in the form of zero coupon securities.

The concept originated in 1982 when a number of US banks started stripping US Treasuries and found they could earn more from the constituent parts than they paid for the bonds. The resulting instruments were given acronyms based on animal names, such as

Merrill Lynch's TIGRs, Salomon Brothers' CATS, and Lehman Brothers' LIONs. (As an aside, it is a sign of how quickly things can change in the capital markets that none of these firms now exists as an independent entity. Salomon Brothers was eventually absorbed by Citigroup. Bank of America agreed to buy Merrill Lynch in September 2008. In the same month Lehman Brothers filed for bankruptcy.)

There is a ready market for STRIPS amongst institutional investors because STRIPs pay a fixed and known cash flow on future dates. By contrast, the return on coupon-paying investments depends to some extent on the rate at which coupon income can be reinvested on future dates. Some financial institutions are also permitted to reconstitute a coupon-paying bond from the individual STRIPS. The 'stripping' technique is explained in Chapter 6.

4.7 BOND PRICING

Notes and bonds are priced by applying discounted cash flow techniques. However since they have maturities of more than a year when issued, the calculations are a little different to those used in Chapter 2 when exploring the money markets. They take into account the effects of compounding, or interest on interest.

Compound Interest Calculation

An investor deposits $\$100$ for two years at 10% p.a. Interest is compounded at the end of each year. Call the $\$100$ the present value, or PV. At the end of year one there is $100 \times 1.1 = \$110$ in the account. To work out the principal plus interest at the end of year two multiply this by 1.1 again. Call this the future value, or FV:

$$FV = 100 \times 1.1 \times 1.1 = \$121$$

The effect of compounding means that in the example there is interest of $\$21$ at the end of two years. The first year's interest is $\$10$. The second year's interest is $\$11$. In addition to interest on the original principal of $\$100$, the investor has earned $\$1$ interest on interest. The general formula is:

$$FV = PV \times (1 + r)^n$$

where:

$n =$ number of compounding periods

$r =$ interest rate as a decimal for each compounding period

In the example interest is compounded only once a year and it is a two-year deposit, so $n = 2$. The interest rate is the rate per annum, so $r = 0.1$. The present value of a future cash flow discounted using this method is calculated by solving for PV in the formula:

$$PV = \frac{FV}{(1 + r)^n}$$

Table 4.3   Cash flows on a straight bond

Time period	1	2	...	n
Cash flow	C	C	...	$C + R$

4.7.1   The Standard Bond Pricing Model

In essence a straight bond is simply a title to a series of future cash flows – the coupons plus the par or redemption value payable at maturity. This is illustrated in Table 4.3. In the table C is a coupon payment, R is the par value, and n is the time to maturity in coupon periods.

The fair value of a bond is simply the sum of the present values of all its cash flows. In the traditional bond pricing model each of the bond's cash flows is discounted at exactly the same discount rate r. The present value (PV) of the bond is therefore given by the following formula:

$$PV = \frac{C}{(1+r)^1} + \frac{C}{(1+r)^2} + \cdots + \frac{C+R}{(1+r)^n}$$

where:

$r =$ discount rate for each coupon period as a decimal

$C =$ regular coupon payment

$R =$ par or redemption value

$n =$ number of coupon periods to the maturity of the bond

4.8   PRICING COUPON BONDS: EXAMPLES

A bond pays an annual coupon rate of 5 % and has exactly four years to maturity. The discount rate – the required rate of return on the bond – is 6 %. In practice the discount rate can be established from the return currently available on investments with a similar risk profile. The present values of the bond's individual cash flows per $ 100 par value are shown in Table 4.4.

The total present value of $ 96.53 is the **dirty price** of the bond, which in this case is the same as the clean price since the bond is exactly one (annual) coupon period away from the next coupon date.

Note that the value of the bond is *less* than its par value of $ 100. This illustrates a basic law of fixed income securities such as bonds – the value of such instruments moves *inversely* with current market interest rates. The bond in the example was issued with a

Table 4.4   PV calculation for an annual coupon bond

Time (coupon periods)	1	2	3	4
Cash flow	$ 5	$ 5	$ 5	$ 105
PV calculation	$ 5/1.06^1	$ 5/1.06^2	$ 5/1.06^3	$ 105/1.06^4
PV	$ 4.72	$ 4.45	$ 4.20	$ 83.17
			Sum of PVs $=$	$ 96.53

coupon rate of 5 %, the going rate for investments of this kind at the time of issue. However time has passed and the current going rate of return for such an investment is now 6 %. The coupon rate on the bond is fixed at an unfavourable 5 % so its price adjusts downwards.

Supply and Demand

Considered in terms of supply and demand, a 5 % fixed coupon bond is less attractive to investors when they can achieve 6 % elsewhere on similar investments, and its price falls to compensate.

4.8.1 Pricing a Semi-annual Coupon Bond

The standard pricing model applied to a semi-annual bond discounts each six-monthly cash flow at half the annual discount rate. The dirty price of the bond is the sum of the present values. Consider the case of a semi-annual bond with exactly two years to maturity and a coupon rate of 6 % p.a. The discount rate is 5 % p.a. The present values of the individual cash flows are shown in Table 4.5. The sum $ 101.88 is the bond's dirty price per $ 100 par value. This is the same as the clean price because the bond is exactly one (semi-annual) coupon period away from the next coupon date.

Table 4.5 PV calculation for a semi-annual coupon bond

Time (coupon periods)	1	2	3	4
Cash flow	$ 3	$ 3	$ 3	$ 103
PV calculation	$ 3/1.025^1	$ 3/1.025^2	$ 3/1.025^3	$ 103/1.025^4
PV	$ 2.93	$ 2.86	$ 2.79	$ 93.31
			Sum of PVs =	$ 101.88

Note that in this calculation the life of the bond is cut into four semi-annual coupon periods.

- The cash flows consist in a series of $ 3 semi-annual coupons plus the $ 100 par value at redemption.
- Each cash flow is discounted at half the annual discount rate. The first $ 3 coupon is discounted back at 2.5 % for one semi-annual period, the second $ 3 coupon at 2.5 % for two semi-annual periods and so on.

This bond is trading above par because the discount rate (the required rate of return in current market circumstances) is less than the fixed coupon rate. In other words, the bond pays an attractive coupon in current market circumstances and so trades at a premium to its par value.

4.9 DETAILED BOND VALUATION: US TREASURY

The last section looked at somewhat simplified applications of the traditional bond pricing model. This is because the bonds were priced at the very start of a coupon period. Some adjustments are required where this is not the case, as the following example shows. This uses the appropriate market conventions for US Treasury notes and bonds. The day-count method (now also used for UK and eurozone government bonds) is called **actual/actual**.

> **Example**
>
> The task is to price a US Treasury bond for settlement 3 July 2006 that matures on 15 November 2007. The coupon rate is 6 % p.a. paid semi-annually. The coupons are paid each year on 15 May and 15 November. The discount rate for valuing the bond is 5 % p.a.

- **Step 1.** Calculate the number of days in the current semi-annual coupon period. The last coupon was paid on 15 May 2006 and the next is due on 15 November 2006. So the current coupon period has 184 days.
- **Step 2.** Calculate the number of days from the settlement date 3 July 2006 to the next coupon date 15 November 2006. It is 135 days.
- **Step 3.** Divide the answer to Step 2 by the answer to Step 1 to get the number of days remaining to the next coupon as a fraction of the current coupon period. It is 135/184 or 0.7337. In other words the next cash flow is due in 0.7337 of a coupon period, the one after that in 1.7337 coupon periods, and so on.
- **Step 4.** Discount the cash flows on the bond as illustrated in Table 4.6.

There are some key features in Table 4.6.

- The semi-annual coupon payment per $ 100 par is $ 3, or half of 6 % applied to $ 100.
- The six-monthly cash flows are present valued by discounting at 2.5 % which is half the annual 5 % discount rate
- The first $ 3 cash flow would be divided by 1.025^1 if it were due in exactly one coupon period's time. In this example it is divided by $1.025^{0.7337}$ to take into account the fact that only a proportion of the coupon period remains.

4.9.1 The Clean Price

The bond's total present value of $ 102.10 is a dirty price, which differs from the clean price in this example because settlement is part way through a coupon period. The accrued interest and hence the clean price can be calculated as follows. The current coupon period has 184 days and 49 days have elapsed since the last coupon was paid (on 15 May 2006) up to the settlement date of 3 July 2006. The semi-annual coupon payment is $ 3.

$$\text{Accrued Interest} = \$ 3 \times \frac{49}{184} = \$ 0.8$$

$$\text{Clean Price} = \$ 102.10 - \$ 0.8 = \$ 101.30$$

Table 4.6 PV calculation for a US Treasury bond

Coupon date	15 Nov 06	15 May 07	15 Nov 07
Time (coupon periods)	0.7337	1.7337	2.7337
Cash flow	$ 3	$ 3	$ 103
PV calculation	$ 3/1.025^{0.7337}	$ 3/1.025^{1.7337}	$ 103/1.025^{2.7337}
PV	$ 2.95	$ 2.87	$ 96.28
		Sum of PVs =	$ 102.10

4.10   BOND YIELD

The discount rate used to price a bond is equivalent to the required return on the bond given the riskiness of the cash flows. In the case of US Treasuries we can assume that there is virtually no risk of default, which is why the return on US Treasuries forms a benchmark or reference rate for dollar investors and borrowers. Normally a corporate or an emerging market country issuing a dollar bond will pay the return on Treasuries plus a **spread** (an additional return) which represents the additional risk of default (see Chapter 7 on credit spreads).

It is also possible to measure the return that would be achieved on a bond if it was purchased at a given price. We saw before that the value of a four-year 5 % annual coupon bond at a 6 % discount rate can be established through a present value calculation:

$$PV = \frac{\$5}{1.06^1} + \frac{\$5}{1.06^2} + \frac{\$5}{1.06^3} + \frac{\$105}{1.06^4} = \$96.53$$

Equivalently, if the bond is bought for $96.53 and held to maturity the annualized yield or return on this investment is 6 % p.a. But what if the bond is bought at a different price, say $96? What is the yield in this case? A simple approximation is to calculate the bond's so-called **current** or running yield (also known in the market as flat or interest yield). This is calculated as follows:

$$\text{Current Yield} = \frac{\text{Annual Coupon}}{\text{Clean Price}} \times 100 = \frac{5}{96} \times 100 = 5.21\%$$

Intuitively, the formula says that the lower the purchase price of the bond the higher the yield or effective return on that investment. If the bond was trading at par the current yield would be 5 %, exactly the same as the coupon rate. Since it is trading below par the current yield is higher than the coupon rate.

4.10.1   Limitations of Current Yield

Current yield is very easy to calculate but unfortunately does not capture all the returns on a bond investment. In the above example if the bond is held until maturity the principal repayment is the par value of $100, whereas the bond can be purchased below par. The bond will 'pull to par' as it approaches maturity and a capital gain will result which is not captured in the current yield calculation. If the bond was trading at a premium to par there would be a capital loss to take into account in measuring the total return on the investment.

Secondly, the current yield calculation does not take into account the time value of money: 'a dollar today is worth more than a dollar in the future'. The cash outflow on the bond today cannot be directly compared with the future inflows of coupons and the redemption payment. Finally, the current yield number also ignores a further source of income from buying a bond, the income that results from reinvesting coupons as they are received.

4.10.2   Yield-to-Maturity (YTM)

The bond market commonly uses a measure of bond return known as **yield-to-maturity** (YTM) or redemption yield. Mathematically, YTM is the single discount rate that equates

Table 4.7 YTM as a constant discount rate that equates market price with present value

Time (coupon periods)	1	2	3	4
Cash flow	$5	$5	$5	$105
PV calculation	$5/1.0616^1	$5/1.0616^2	$5/1.0616^3	$105/1.0616^4
PV	$4.71	$4.44	$4.18	$82.67
			Sum of PVs =	$96.00

the market's dirty price of a bond with its present value. It is an internal rate of return (IRR) calculation. Yield-to-maturity is the total annualized return earned on a bond assuming that:

- the bond is bought at its current market dirty price;
- it is held until maturity and all the future cash flows are received;
- the coupons are reinvested at a constant rate in the market – in fact at a rate equivalent to the calculated yield-to-maturity.

What is the yield-to-maturity on the 5 % annual coupon bond in the previous section if purchased at a total settlement price of $ 96 with exactly four years remaining to maturity? The answer is established through iteration (trial and error) by searching for a single discount rate that generates a total PV for the bond of exactly $ 96. To achieve this in Table 4.7 the cash flows are all discounted at a rate of 6.16 % p.a.

At a 6.16 % discount rate the total PV of the bond is the same as the dirty price of $ 96. The yield-to-maturity therefore is 6.16 %. The YTM is higher than the 5.21 % current yield previously calculated, primarily because of the capital gain that would result from buying the bond below par and holding it until maturity. Note that when market participants in the US talk about 'bond yield' they usually mean the YTM measurement.

4.11 REINVESTMENT ASSUMPTIONS

Unfortunately YTM on a coupon bond is a rather tricky measure, since it makes the simplifying assumption that all the coupons are reinvested at a constant rate – in fact at the yield-to-maturity! This assumption is integral to the standard bond pricing model which uses a constant discount rate to price a bond, or which calculates YTM as the single discount rate that equates the present value with the bond's market dirty price. In practice of course this is just a simplifying assumption, which means that the *actual* return on a coupon bond may turn out to be higher or lower than the calculated YTM, depending on what happens to reinvestment rates in the future.

4.11.1 Horizon Return

Yield-to-maturity also assumes that the bond is held to maturity and that all the expected future cash flows are received. If the issuer defaults on the bond or if it is called back early by the issuer then the actual returns achieved may be significantly lower than those forecast by YTM. In addition, if the instrument is sold before maturity the actual annualized return on the investment will depend on the sale price. It is possible to calculate a **horizon return** based on three assumptions:

- an assumption about how long the bond will be held;

- the price (or yield) at which it will be sold in the future;
- the rate at which intervening coupons can be reinvested.

4.12   ANNUAL AND SEMI-ANNUAL BOND YIELDS

There is a further practical difficulty with the traditional yield-to-maturity measure used in the bond market. Consider two bonds A and B both paying a 10% p.a. coupon. Each has exactly two years to maturity and each is trading at par. Assume that the issuers of the bonds are identical in terms of credit quality. The key difference is that bond A pays the $10 coupon annually in arrears i.e. at the end of the year. Meanwhile bond B pays the coupon in two semi-annual instalments in arrears i.e. $5 is paid at the end of six months and the remaining $5 at the end of the year.

Most people would quickly opt for bond B. Both instruments are trading at par but in the case of bond B half the annual coupon will be received half-way through the year. Basic time value of money precepts tell us that it is better to receive money sooner rather than later, since it can be reinvested in the market. So what is the yield-to-maturity of bond A and of bond B?

In the case of bond A it is fairly obvious that YTM must be 10% – the same as the annual coupon rate – since the bond is trading at par. How do we calculate the yield of bond B? YTM is simply the single annualized discount rate that equates the market dirty price of a bond with the total PV of the bond at that discount rate. As Table 4.8 shows, the discount rate that calculates a PV of exactly $100 is 5% on a six-monthly basis.

Note that in this calculation the life of the bond is divided into four semi-annual coupon periods and the coupon payment in each period is $5. The single discount rate that produces a total PV of $100 is, as noted above, 5%. But this is a rate for each *six-monthly* period. The convention in the market to annualize it is simply to double this number, which means that the annual return on bond B comes out at exactly 10%. In many ways this seems an odd result since the return on bond A was also 10% p.a. and yet most people would prefer bond B to bond A as an investment.

4.12.1   Annual Equivalent Yield (AER)

This result tells us that the traditional YTM calculation is rather crude in that it fails to discriminate properly between bonds with different coupon frequencies. Put another way, it is not possible to directly compare the calculated YTM on an annual coupon bond such as bond A with the calculated yield on a semi-annual bond such as bond B. The problem arises from the fact that the six-monthly discount rate of 5% in bond B was annualized by simply doubling it to obtain a per annum figure of 10%.

In fact if we assume that interim cash flows can be reinvested at a constant rate then a return of 10% p.a. with semi-annual compounding is actually equivalent to 10.25% p.a.

Table 4.8   PV calculation for bond B

Time (coupon periods)	1	2	3	4
Cash flow	$5	$5	$5	$105
PV calculation	$5/1.05^1	$5/1.05^2	$5/1.05^3	$105/1.05^4
PV	$4.76	$4.54	$4.32	$86.38
			Sum of PVs $=$	$100.00

with annual compounding. This is known as the **annual equivalent** rate or AER. (This topic is discussed in more detail in Chapter 6 below.) The AER for bond B is calculated as follows. Note that rates are inserted as decimals in the formula.

$$\text{AER} = \left(1 + \frac{0.10}{2}\right)^2 - 1 = 0.1025 = 10.25\%$$

Although bond B pays a 10% p.a. yield this is a return expressed with semi-annual compounding. It equates to 10.25% p.a. expressed with annual compounding. So effectively bond B *is* a higher return investment than bond A although it does not look like it at first glance! Note that if market participants talk about a 'semi-annual' yield of 10% this does *not* normally mean 10% every six months. It normally means 10% p.a. expressed with semi-annual compounding, which as we have seen is actually equivalent to 10.25% p.a. expressed with annual compounding (the AER). In the capital markets interest rates are usually quoted on a per annum basis, though as the above examples illustrate it is very important to check how frequently the interest is to be compounded.

4.12.2 Yield Conversions

To compare the return on a dollar corporate bond that pays annual coupons with the return on a US Treasury note or bond it is necessary first to convert the semi-annual yield on Treasuries to an annually compounded basis or (this is more common) to convert the annual yield on the corporate bond to a semi-annual equivalent. The semi-annual equivalent of a yield expressed with annual compounding is always lower – for example, the semi-annual equivalent of an annually compounded rate of 10.25% p.a. is 10% p.a. The semi-annual equivalent (r_{sa}) of an annually compounded rate of 5% p.a. is 4.94% p.a. This result can be derived by rearranging the formula for calculating AER.

$$\text{AER} = \left(1 + \frac{r_{sa}}{2}\right)^2 - 1$$

Therefore:

$$r_{sa} = \left[\sqrt[2]{(1 + \text{AER}} - 1\right] \times 2 = \left[\sqrt[2]{1.05} - 1\right] \times 2 = 0.0494 = 4.94\%$$

4.13 UK GOVERNMENT BONDS

UK government bonds (known as gilts or gilt-edged securities) are issued via the Debt Management Office (DMO), an agency of the British government. The DMO took over this responsibility from the Bank of England in 1998 and manages the gilt auctions, which are announced according to a calendar published at the start of the financial year. Primary dealers in gilts are known as **gilt-edged market makers** (GEMMs). They participate in the auctions and also make markets in gilts in the secondary market, posting bid and offer prices. GEMMs are linked by **inter-dealer broking** firms which act as intermediaries allowing the market makers to trade between themselves on an anonymous basis. As at late 2008 there were 15 GEMMs and five inter-dealer brokers.

Most gilts are **conventional** or 'straight' bonds which pay regular semi-annual coupons and have a fixed maturity date. (In the UK the coupon payments are sometimes called **dividends**.) The day-count convention for calculating accrued interest is actual/actual as with US Treasury notes and bonds. Settlement is normally on the next business day after the trade date. Prices are quoted on a clean price basis per GBP 100 nominal or par value and in decimal format, to the nearest penny or GBP 0.01. (Formerly fractions in 32nds were used, as is still the case with US Treasury notes and bonds.) Settlement is based on the clean price plus accrued interest up to the settlement date.

In recent years most conventional gilts have been issued with five, 10, or 30-year maturities, though in May 2005 the DMO issued a new 50-year maturity conventional gilt. As well as conventional gilts there are a number of non-standard bonds currently on issue.

- **Undated Gilts.** There is no fixed maturity date so they could pay coupons in perpetuity. They *can* be redeemed at the discretion of the UK government, but they have low coupons because they were issued many years ago (some date back to the nineteenth century) so there is little likelihood of this happening. Most undated gilts pay semi-annual coupons though some pay interest four times a year. One example of an undated gilt is 3.5 % War Loan, which has GBP 1.9 billion in issue. A yield-to-maturity on an undated gilt can be calculated by making an assumption about the redemption date. Otherwise it can be treated as a perpetual bond. The return on a perpetual bond is simply its current or running yield. For example, if 3.5 % War Loan is offered at GBP 77.24 then the current yield is 3.5/77.24 = 4.53 %.
- **Index-Linked Gilts.** Bonds whose payments are linked to the Retail Prices Index (RPI), a measure of retail inflation in the UK. Both the coupons and the principal amount paid on redemption are adjusted to take into account accrued inflation since the bond was first issued. The first index-linked gilt was issued in 1981.
- **Double-dated Gilts.** There is a range of possible maturity dates, at the option of the UK government. The few remaining double-dated gilt issues are small and illiquid.
- **Gilt Strips.** Zero coupon bonds which pay no coupons during their life, only the face value at maturity, and which always trade at a discount. Zero coupon bonds are very popular with investment managers in institutions such as insurance companies and pension funds since the one-off cash flows from the bonds can be accurately matched with future liabilities. Gilt strips are created by breaking a conventional coupon-paying gilt into its constituent cash flows. For example, a five-year conventional gilt can be broken down into 10 semi-annual coupon payments plus the final par value payment due at maturity. The gilt strip market started in December 1997.

Figure 4.3 shows the total nominal amounts outstanding on all gilts at the end of March in each of the years between 2004 and 2008. Figure 4.4 shows the relative proportions of conventional and index-linked gilts at the end of March 2008 based on nominal amounts outstanding.

4.13.1 Ex-dividend Dates

A key difference between conventional gilts and the US market is that US Treasury notes and bonds are always traded on a **cum-dividend** basis, that is, the buyer of a bond will always receive the next coupon from the US Treasury regardless of the settlement date. Gilts trade cum-dividend except for a short period of time leading up to a coupon payment when they trade **ex-dividend (xd)**. During the ex-dividend period the seller of the bond retains the right to receive the next coupon. The buyer is compensated for the loss of accrued interest

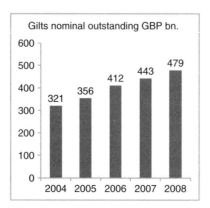

Figure 4.3 Nominal value of gilts outstanding at end-March 2004–8.
Source: UK Debt Management Office, reproduced with permission.

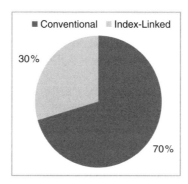

Figure 4.4 Proportions of conventional and index-linked gilts at end-March 2008.
Source: UK Debt Management Office, reproduced with permission.

from the settlement date up to the coupon date. This is sometimes called 'negative accrued'. For all conventional gilts the 'xd' date is seven days before the coupon payment date.

Conventional Gilt Quotation

The 5 % coupon gilt maturing 7 March 2018 has coupon dates on 7 March and 7 September each year. On Friday 16 May 2008 dealers were offering the bond at GBP 101.78 per 100 par. This is a clean price for settlement on the next business day which is Monday 19 May 2008.

The price quoted in the above example is a clean price. There were 184 days in the coupon period and 73 days had elapsed from the last coupon date to the settlement date. The semi-annual coupon payment is GBP 2.50 per 100 nominal. Therefore:

$$\text{Accrued Interest} = 2.50 \times \frac{73}{184} = \text{GBP } 0.99$$

$$\text{Dirty Price} = 101.78 + 0.99 = \text{GBP } 102.77$$

If the bond is purchased for settlement 19 May 2008 at a dirty price of GBP 102.77 the yield-to-maturity (redemption yield) is approximately 4.77 % p.a. with semi-annual compounding. This is calculated by finding a single discount rate such that if the bond's cash flows are discounted at that rate this produces a PV equal to the dirty price. In this case the YTM is less than the coupon rate of 5 % because the bond is trading above par.

4.14   JAPANESE GOVERNMENT BONDS (JGBS)

JGBs are debt obligations of the Japanese government. As at 2008 there were five main types of instrument in issue.

- **Treasury Bills.** Maturities of six months and one year. These are issued at a discount to face value.
- **Medium-term Bonds.** Fixed coupon securities with two and five-year maturities.
- **Long-term Bonds.** Fixed coupon securities with a 10-year maturity.
- **Super Long-term Bonds.** Coupon bonds with maturities of more than 10 years. Most have a fixed coupon though there is a 15-year floating rate note in issue whose coupon is reset periodically.
- **Inflation-Indexed Bonds.** The coupon rate is fixed but the principal amount is linked to the consumer price index, so that interest payments and the redemption value payable at maturity rise with inflation. The maturity is 10 years.

There are also JGBs that are specifically targeted at the Japanese retail investment market. Households accounted for about 6 % of all investors in JGBs as at the fourth quarter of 2007. By contrast, international investors owned just 6.6 % of JGBs, compared to 44 % foreign ownership of US Treasuries and 30 % of UK gilts. During 2007–8 the Japanese Ministry of Finance launched a series of investor roadshows in major centres overseas to stimulate foreign interest in JGBs. At the end of March 2007 outstanding JGBs totalled around JPY 671,000 bn.

JGBs are mainly issued in public auctions, although the auction method varies. In some cases the purchaser buys the security at the actual price that was bid, while some auctions are 'Dutch-style' in which all the winning bidders pay the same lowest price which sells the planned issue amount. In some issues smaller investors are also offered bonds on a non-competitive basis. There is also a 'when-issued' market in JGBs similar to that in US Treasuries. In 2004 a new primary dealer system was introduced in Japan in which financial institutions known as 'JGB Market Special Participants' are required to actively participate in JGB auctions and to help to ensure liquidity in the secondary market. They are also permitted to create zero coupon STRIPS.

Most JGBs are traded on an OTC basis in the secondary market, though some are listed on the Tokyo Stock Exchange and other exchanges. Delivery of JGBs and settlement of funds is based on a book-entry transfer system run by the Bank of Japan. Paper certificates are no longer issued. Fixed coupon JGBs are semi-annual and the yield or return is traditionally quoted on a **simple yield** basis rather than the yield-to-maturity (internal rate of return) measure used with US and UK Treasuries. The simple yield is the current yield (annual coupon payment as a percentage of the clean price) adjusted by a measure of the annual percentage capital gain or loss on the bond based on the difference between its clean price and its par value at maturity.

4.15   EUROZONE GOVERNMENT BONDS

The German Federal government issues bonds with a range of maturities, including those listed below. These are issued via an auction. A set of banks and securities firms called the

Bund Issues Auction Group are entitled to bid at the auctions. They then resell the securities to investors. Since 1997 certain 10-year and 30-year bonds have been strippable, so that the title to the interest and principal cash flows are separately tradable.

- **Treasury Discount Paper ('Bubills').** Issued at a discount to face value with a six-month maturity. The discount amount is calculated using the actual/360 day-count method.
- **Federal Treasury Notes ('Schätze').** Two-year notes with annual coupon payments and redeemed at par. Accrued interest is calculated using the actual/actual day-count method.
- **Five-year Federal Notes ('Bobls').** Annual coupon notes redeemed at par. Accrued interest is calculated using the actual/actual day-count method.
- **Federal bonds ('Bunds').** 10-year and 30-year bonds with annual coupons and redeemed at par. Accrued interest is calculated using the actual/actual method.

Since 2001 the management of public debt in France is the responsibility of Agence France Trésor (AFT). It auctions three different types of instrument.

- **BTFs.** Treasury bills with a maturity of less than one year issued at a discount to face value.
- **BTANs.** Fixed-rate medium-term Treasury notes with annual coupon payments issued with maturities of two years and five years.
- **OATs.** Long-term debt Treasury securities issued with maturities ranging from seven to 50 years. Most are fixed-coupon but some issues have floating coupons or make payments linked to the rate of inflation.

The primary dealers in OATs commit to making prices in the secondary markets. This is an OTC market and settlement is based on an electronic delivery-versus-payment system.

The Italian government bond market is one of the largest in the world. As at the end of 2007 total central government debt stood at EUR 1597 billion, over 100 % of Italy's GDP. Government bonds accounted for about 79 % of this debt.

There are three main types of Italian government securities. **BTPs** are fixed-interest bonds paying semi-annual coupons with maturities of three, five, 10, 15, and 30 years. Accrued interest is calculated using the actual/actual convention. The Italian government also regularly auctions Treasury bills called **BOTs** at a discount to face value. In recent years it has introduced the **BTP€I** note which is a security whose coupon and redemption payments vary according to an index of inflation in the eurozone calculated by Eurostat.

In addition, the public authorities in Italy have shown considerable ingenuity in raising funds through one-off bond issues which are repaid from the cash flows generated by specific assets. This has included bonds paid from the revenue streams produced by ticket sales at tourist attractions such as museums and art galleries, as well as bonds secured on the cash flows due on unpaid tax.

4.16   CHAPTER SUMMARY

Governments around the world issue medium and long-term debt securities. The most active government bond market in the world is in US Treasuries, which are traded around the clock. US Treasury notes and bonds are auctioned according to regular schedules. Large financial institutions act as primary dealers in the market which means that they participate in the auctions and distribute bonds to investors. The secondary market in US Treasuries is an over-the-counter market in which dealers make bid and offer (ask) prices. The dealers are connected by a network of inter-dealer brokers who act as intermediaries matching trades. US Treasury notes and bonds are quoted as a percentage of par on a clean price basis. Settlement is based on the dirty price, i.e. the clean price plus interest that has accrued since the last coupon date. Accrued interest is calculated using a day-count convention called actual/actual which is now widely used in other bond markets around the world.

The ratings agencies use sovereign ratings to assess the likelihood of default on government bonds. The traditional way to price a bond is to present value the cash flows at a single discount rate. This is convenient but makes the simplifying assumption that coupons are reinvested at a constant rate. The current yield on a bond is simply the annual coupon payment as a percentage of the clean price. The yield-to-maturity is the single discount rate that equates the bond's present value at that discount rate with its market dirty price.

UK government bonds are called gilts. Like US Treasury bonds, conventional gilts pay semi-annual coupons and redeem at par at maturity. However the UK government also issues non-conventional bonds whose payments are linked to inflation. Primary dealers in gilts are called Gilt-Edged Market Makers (GEMMs). As well as participating in gilt auctions and sustaining liquidity in the secondary markets, GEMMS have the right to 'strip' coupon gilts. Stripping means that the titles to the coupon payments and the face value are traded separately. The technique originated in the US and is now commonly used in major government bond markets. Japanese government bonds are called JGBs. As well as straight coupon bonds the Japanese government also issues bonds whose payments are linked to inflation. A system of primary dealers has been created in the Japanese market. Most JGBs are held by domestic investors although the authorities have been marketing them actively to international investors in recent years. In the eurozone the major government bond issuers are Germany, France, and Italy. Longer-maturity coupon bonds are called bunds (Germany), OATs (France), and BTPs (Italy). These are all quoted in the secondary market on a clean price basis, though settlement is based on the dirty price. As at end-2007 the total central government debt in Italy stood at over 100 % of GDP, one reason why Italian government bonds were rated less highly than German and French bonds in terms of sovereign risk.

5

Bond Price Sensitivity

5.1 CHAPTER OVERVIEW

This chapter explores the sensitivity of bond prices to changes in market interest rates or yields. Key terms are defined such as Macaulay's duration, modified or adjusted duration, and the price value of a basis point (PVBP). The chapter looks at how to calculate these measures and at their interrelationships. Duration measures are approximations, and for large changes in market yields they can become increasingly inaccurate. This is because the relationship between bond price and yield is not entirely linear. In the case of a straight bond with no call features the graph of the price/yield relationship is convex. Various methods of estimating this convexity effect are illustrated, as well as how duration and convexity combined can be used to produce a more accurate estimation of the change in the price of a bond for a significant yield change. Finally, the chapter explores practical applications of duration in portfolio management. It looks at how duration can be used to create a portfolio of bonds matching future payment obligations, and how to construct a duration-based hedge against the effects of changes in interest rates on a bond portfolio.

5.2 BOND MARKET LAWS

The bond pricing model introduced in Chapter 4 shows that the price of a fixed coupon bond changes inversely with its yield. This arises from the fact that the bond's cash flows are discounted more or less heavily depending on current market interest rates. It does not follow, however, that all bonds change in value to the same extent for a given change in interest rates.

Consider the two bonds in Table 5.1. Both have a coupon rate of 10% p.a. (paid semi-annually) but the first bond has a maturity of five years and the second of 20 years. Both bonds are currently trading at par so they yield 10% p.a. The current prices and yields are shown in bold. The table also shows the present values of the bonds per $100 par value

Table 5.1 Comparing the interest rate sensitivity of two bonds

Yield (p.a.)	PV of 10% 5-year bond	PV 10% 20-year bond
9.96%	100.1546	100.3441
9.97%	100.1159	100.2579
9.98%	100.0773	100.1718
9.99%	100.0386	100.0859
10.00%	**100.0000**	**100.0000**
10.01%	99.9614	99.9143
10.02%	99.9228	99.8286
10.03%	99.8843	99.7431
10.04%	99.8457	99.6578

for a range of different yields between 9.96 % and 10.04 % p.a. Table 5.1 demonstrates some important results:

- the change in price for a given change in yield is not the same for the two bonds;
- the longer maturity bond is more sensitive to changes in yield than the shorter maturity bond.

The phenomenon can be explained intuitively, in terms of interest rate exposures. If interest rates rise the values of both bonds will drop because the coupon rates are now less attractive. However the longer maturity bond falls more sharply in value because cash is tied up in the investment for a much longer period of time. On the other hand, if rates fall the longer maturity bond will be paying a more attractive coupon for 20 years compared to only five years on the other bond, and its price will rise more sharply. The exposure to changes in interest rates is much greater in the case of the 20-year bond.

5.2.1 The Price/Yield Relationship

Table 5.1 also shows other key relationships:

- for small changes in yield (such as one basis point) the percentage change in a bond price is roughly the same whether the yield is increased or decreased;
- for a larger change in yield the percentage rise in the bond price if the yield is decreased is greater than the percentage fall in the bond price if the yield is increased.

For example, for a one basis point rise/fall in yield the price of the five-year bond falls/rises by 0.0386 %. For a four basis point change the fall is only 0.1543 % but the rise is 0.1546 %. For even larger changes in yield the difference is more exaggerated.

If the numbers for one of the bonds in Table 5.1 were plotted on a graph this would show that the relationship between the price of a bond and its yield is in fact nonlinear. The shape of the price/yield relationship for straight bonds without embedded options is **convex**. This is illustrated in Figure 5.1.

The fact that the price/yield graph is convex tells us that if yields rise by a large amount then the fall in the bond price is less pronounced than it would be if the relationship between yield and price were linear. On the other hand if yields fall the rise in the bond price is

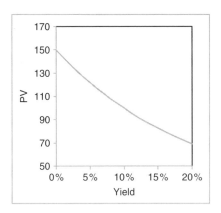

Figure 5.1   Price/yield relationship for a straight bond without call features.

more pronounced than it would be if the relationship between price and yield were linear. Convexity has the effect of accelerating the rise in the bond price as yields fall, but slowing down the fall in the bond price as yields rise.

5.3   OTHER FACTORS AFFECTING PRICE SENSITIVITY

Bond price sensitivity is also related to the coupon rate:

• the lower the coupon on a bond, the more sensitive it is to changes in market interest rates – the bigger its percentage price change for a given change in yield.

The effect is most exaggerated with a zero coupon bond: if yields rise the increase in the discount rate used to present value the single future cash flow due on the bond is magnified by the time to the receipt of that cash flow, and the bond price falls sharply. Put another way, with a zero there are no intervening coupons to reinvest to help offset the effect of rising yields. By contrast, the holders of coupon bonds have the compensation of being able to reinvest the coupons at higher interest rates, which will serve to cushion the fall in the price of the bonds. This reduces their effective exposure to interest rate rises.

On the other hand if market yields fall, zero coupon bonds will tend to do better than coupon bonds with the same maturity. Investors in the zeros are locked into a fixed return whereas holders of coupon bonds will suffer because the coupons will now be reinvested at lower interest rates.

5.3.1   The Interest Rate Environment

One further conclusion can be drawn by inspecting the price/yield graph in Figure 5.1:

• in a low interest rate environment a given change in yield produces a larger change in the price of a bond than in a high interest rate environment.

In fact this is a very straightforward effect. A 100 basis point increase in yield from 1 % to 2 % will have a much larger effect on the price of a bond than an increase from 10 % to 11 %. The absolute yield change in both cases is the same, but the proportional change is very different.

5.4   MACAULAY'S DURATION

Consider the following securities:

• a 5 % coupon bond maturing in 15 years;
• a 10 % coupon bond maturing in 30 years.

It is not easy to tell by simple inspection which of the two bonds is likely to be more sensitive to changes in yields. The first bond has a lower coupon, but the second bond has a longer term to maturity. We need a measurement that allows us to combine both factors. This measurement is known as **duration**.

The earliest measure of duration was formulated by Frederick Macaulay in 1938. **Macaulay's duration** is the weighted average life of a bond's cash flows, where each cash flow is weighted by its present value as a proportion of the bond's total present value. Macaulay's duration is a measure of a bond investor's effective exposure to interest rate changes. It blends the bond's term to maturity with the size of its coupon payments. The longer the term to maturity and the lower the coupon, the higher the duration of a bond – the more sensitive it is to changes in market yields.

> **Definition**
>
> Macaulay's duration is the weighted average time to maturity of a bond's cash flows. The weight assigned to a cash flow is its PV as a proportion of the total PV (dirty price) of the bond.

5.5 CALCULATING MACAULAY'S DURATION

To illustrate the method this section takes a three-year annual coupon bond trading at par. The coupon rate is 10 %, the yield is 10 % and there are exactly three years until maturity. There are three cash flows due on the bond:

1 year	$ 10 coupon
2 years	$ 10 coupon
3 years	$ 10 coupon + $ 100 par or nominal value

The full calculation of Macaulay's duration for this bond is set out in Table 5.2:

Column (1) is the year when a cash flow is received.

Column (2) is the size of the cash flow.

Column (3) is the present value of the cash flow discounted at 10 % (the bond's yield).

Column (4) is the present value in column (3) divided by the bond's total present value ($ 100).

Column (5) is column (1), the time when the cash flow is received, multiplied by column (4).

Macaulay's duration is the sum of the column (5) figures. In this example it is approximately 2.74 years.

5.5.1 Interpreting Macaulay's Duration

What does it mean? Although the bond in the example has three years to maturity, its sensitivity to interest rate changes is a little less than that might suggest, because of the

Table 5.2 Duration calculation for three-year 10 % coupon par bond

(1) Year	(2) Cash flow ($)	(3) PV at 10 % ($)	(4) PV/total PV	(5) (PV/total PV) × time
1	10	9.09	0.0909	0.0909
2	10	8.26	0.0826	0.1653
3	110	82.64	0.8264	2.4793
		Total PV = 100.00		Duration = 2.7355 years

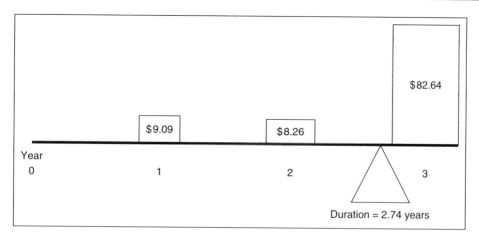

Figure 5.2   Duration as a balance.

interim coupon payments. The fact that coupons are paid and can be reinvested at current market interest rates reduces the effective life of the investment and the exposure to interest rate changes. The larger the coupons, all other things being equal, the lower the duration.

The duration calculation can be visualized as a balance, as shown in Figure 5.2. The bond's cash flows (actually their present values as a proportion of the total present value) are the weights placed on the balance. The duration – the effective life of the bond – is the balancing point measured in years.

5.6   DURATION OF A ZERO

To help understand the duration measure a little more clearly, this section calculates the Macaulay's duration of a three-year zero coupon bond also yielding 10 % p.a. The calculation is set out in Table 5.3.

The three-year zero coupon bond has a Macaulay's duration of exactly three years. If interest rates rise the price of the zero coupon bond will fall more sharply in percentage terms than the price of a three-year coupon bond. The one and only cash flow that is due on the zero bond will be received in three years, and the investor is missing out on higher interest rates in the meantime.

The three-year 10 % coupon bond has a Macaulay's duration of less than three years. The fact that coupons are paid and can be reinvested at current market interest rates reduces

Table 5.3   Duration calculation for three-year zero coupon bond

(1) Year	(2) Cash flow ($)	(3) PV at 10 % ($)	(4) PV/total PV	(5) (PV/total PV) × time
1	0	0	0	0
2	0	0	0	0
3	100	75.13	1	3
		Total PV = 75.13		Duration = 3 years

Figure 5.3 Balancing point for three-year zero coupon bond.

the effective life of the investment and the exposure to interest rate changes. In fact a three-year 10 % coupon bond yielding 10 % with a duration of 2.74 years will have the same sensitivity to (small) changes in interest rates as a 2.74-year zero coupon bond also yielding 10 %. Figure 5.3 shows the balancing point for the three-year zero coupon bond. It is exactly three years.

The Macaulay's duration of a zero coupon bond is always the same as its maturity. An investor receives only one cash flow on the bond and if interest rates rise in the meantime the investor has nothing to reinvest and is exposed for the full maturity of the bond. The price of the bond will fall sharply. The process works in reverse, though. If an investor buys a zero bond and rates fall the investor is locked in at a higher yield; the investor will not suffer from falling reinvestment rates because there are no intervening coupons to reinvest. The price of the bond will rise sharply, more than a coupon bond with the same maturity, which will suffer from falling reinvestment rates.

5.6.1 Duration of Money Market Investments

At the other extreme, the Macaulay's duration of cash is zero. If interest rates change an investor holding cash can invest immediately at the new market interest rates and is not locked in for any period of time. The exposure to changes in market interest rates is zero. The duration of a one-week money market term deposit placed today is exactly one week. The funds will be repaid in seven days and can be reinvested at whatever the prevailing LIBOR rate happens to be then. The duration of a newly issued floating rate note with a coupon that re-fixes in three months' time is three months.

5.7 MODIFIED DURATION

Another widely used measure of the sensitivity of the price of a bond to changes in interest rates is **modified duration**, also known as adjusted or Macaulay modified duration. It is simply Macaulay's duration discounted at the bond's yield-to-maturity. The three-year 10 % coupon par bond yielding 10 % explored above has a Macaulay's duration of 2.7355 years.

Therefore:

$$\text{Modified Duration (MOD)} = \frac{2.7355}{1 + 0.1} = 2.4869$$

In practical terms the MOD figure means that if the bond's yield shifts by 1 % or 100 basis points its PV (dirty price) will change in percentage terms by about 2.4869 %. Note that if the bond pays a semi-annual coupon and its Macaulay's duration is expressed in years the yield in the denominator must be divided by two to derive modified duration.

Modified duration assumes that the cash flows on a bond are not affected by changes in yields. This is a reasonable assumption for straight Treasury bonds paying regular coupons on regular dates with a fixed maturity date. It may not be so for callable and putable bonds. If yields fall it becomes more probable that callable bonds will be redeemed early by the issuers and less likely that putable bonds will be retired early by investors. There is also a problem with high-yield corporate bonds. Increases in interest rates may make it more difficult for the issuer to make payments on its debt, which increases the risk of default.

5.7.1 Estimating Modified Duration

Modified duration is sometimes estimated using a bond calculator or on a spreadsheet, using the following steps.

- **Step 1.** Work out the change in the dollar price of the bond for a one basis point rise in yield.
- **Step 2.** Work out the change in the dollar price of the bond for a one basis point fall in yield.
- **Step 3.** Average the results from Steps 1 and 2. An average is necessary because Steps 1 and 2 will not produce exactly the same result due to the convex price/yield relationship.
- **Step 4.** Calculate the answer to Step 3 as a percentage of the starting price of the bond.
- **Step 5.** Multiply the answer to Step 4 by 100 to approximate the percentage price change for a 100 basis point change in yield.

5.8 PRICE VALUE OF A BASIS POINT

From modified duration it is easy to estimate the profit or loss on a bond in cash terms for a given change in yield. The normal market convention is to measure the profit or loss on a bond if its yield shifts by 0.01 % or one basis point. This is known as the **price value of a basis point** (PVBP). It is also called basis point value and (for US bonds) the 'dollar value of an 01' or simply 'DV01', where '01' represents a one basis point shift in yield.

In the case of the three-year 10 % annual bond the starting bond price is $ 100. Modified duration is 2.4869 so the percentage change in the bond's PV for a 100 basis point shift in its yield is about 2.4869 %. Therefore:

$$\text{PVBP} = \frac{\$\,100 \times 2.4869\,\%}{100} = \$\,0.0249$$

This means that the change in the bond PV per $ 100 nominal for a one basis point shift in its yield is roughly two and a half cents. Dividing by 100 in the calculation simply adjusts from a 100 to a one basis point yield change. Note that if modified duration is used to calculate PVBP it should properly be applied to the *dirty price* of a bond, which is the PV. In practice the clean price may be used if there is little accrued interest.

5.9 CONVEXITY

Duration can estimate the change in the price of a bond regardless of whether yields rise or fall. However this can only be an approximation. This is because it assumes that the relationship between bond price and yield is linear. In fact the actual relationship, as shown in Figure 5.1, is nonlinear and (for a straight bond with no call features) convex.

PVBP is the slope or tangent on the bond price curve at a given yield, and Figure 5.1 shows that PVBP is not a constant. In practical terms this means that the actual change in the price of a straight bond for a 10 or a 50 basis point yield shift is not simply PVBP times 10 or 50. Because of the curvature in the bond price/yield relationship the greater the yield movement the less accurate PVBP tends to be in predicting the actual change in the bond price.

5.9.1 Testing Modified Duration

The modified duration of the three-year 10 % bond suggests that the change in its dirty price for a 100 basis point shift in yield is about 2.4869 %. In fact revaluing the bond at different yields using the bond pricing model shows that this is not completely accurate.

- The actual percentage rise in the price of the bond for a 100 point fall in yield is 2.5313 %, more than predicted by modified duration.
- The actual percentage fall in the price of the bond for the same level of increase in yield is 2.4437 %, less than predicted by modified duration.

Duration is a first approximation and is good only for small changes in interest rates. (Mathematically it is the first derivative of the bond pricing model.) It can be improved by taking into account the effects of the curvature in the price/yield relationship, which is known as convexity. A long position in a normal 'straight' bond with no call features is said to exhibit **positive convexity**. In fact for the purchaser of a bond positive convexity is a benefit – the bond falls by less in price and rises by more in price for a given yield change than predicted by duration on its own.

5.10 MEASURING CONVEXITY

Convexity can be measured in a similar way to Macaulay's duration. Table 5.4 shows the first stages of the calculation for the 10 % coupon three-year annual bond trading at par. In columns (4) and (5) 'TPV' stands for total present value, the sum of the present values in column (3). In this example TPV is $ 100. The bond is trading at par and the yield is the same as the 10 % coupon rate.

The final step is to discount at the yield squared:

$$\text{Convexity} = \frac{10.595}{(1 + \text{Yield})^2} = \frac{10.595}{1.1^2} = 8.756$$

Table 5.4 First stages of convexity calculation

(1) Year	(2) Cash flow ($)	(3) PV at 10 % ($)	(4) PV/TPV	(5) (PV/TPV) × time × (time + 1)
1	10	9.09	0.0909	0.1818
2	10	8.26	0.0826	0.4959
3	110	82.64	0.8264	9.9174
	Total =	100.00	Total =	10.5950

This convexity measure can easily be converted to work out the approximate percentage change in the bond's price for a given yield shift that is caused by the curvature in the price/yield relationship. The formula is:

$$0.5 \times \text{Yield Change}^2 \times \text{Convexity} \times 100$$

For a 100 basis point shift in yield the result for the example bond is:

$$0.5 \times 0.01^2 \times 8.756 \times 100 = 0.0438\,\%$$

In this calculation 0.01 is simply 100 basis points (1 %) expressed as a decimal. For a 1 % fall in yield the estimated rise in the price of the bond is:

Modified duration prediction	2.4869 %
+ Percentage convexity	0.0438 %
= Estimated change in price	2.5307 %

Given some rounding errors, this is much closer to the actual result – a change of 2.5313 % – than is suggested by modified duration alone. For a 1 % rise in yield the estimated fall in the price of the bond is:

Modified duration prediction	−2.4869 %
+ Percentage convexity	+0.0438 %
= Estimated change in price	−2.4431 %

The actual fall in price as calculated by the bond pricing model is −2.4437 %. Figure 5.4 illustrates the fact that modified duration becomes increasingly accurate as a predictor of changes in the bond price for larger yield movements. Note that convexity for a long position in a straight bond is *additive*: it boosts the rise in the bond price as yields fall, and reduces the decline in the price as yields rise.

5.10.1   Estimating Convexity from Yield Changes

Convexity is sometimes approximated from the discrepancy between the percentage change in the price of a bond for a given fall in yield and the percentage change in the bond price for an equal rise in yield. By discounting the cash flows at different yields the following data for the three-year 10 % bond can be calculated:

- PV of bond at 10 % yield = $ 100 ('starting bond price')

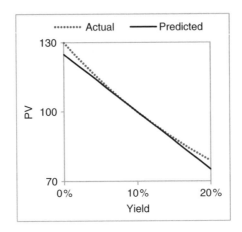

Figure 5.4 Change in PV predicted by duration against the actual change.

- PV of bond at 9 % yield = $ 102.5313. Change = 2.5313 %
- PV of bond at 11 % yield = $ 97.5563. Change = 2.4437 %
- Discrepancy for 2 % yield difference = 2.5313 % − 2.4437 % = 0.0876 %
- Percentage convexity for 100 basis point yield change ≈ 0.0876 %/2 = 0.0438 %

5.11   CONVEXITY BEHAVIOUR

Table 5.5 has a sample of annual bonds, all yielding 10 % p.a. In each case it shows modified duration (MOD) and then convexity (CNX) in percentage terms based on a 1 % change in yield.

Modified duration is higher the lower the coupon and the longer the term to maturity. Table 5.5 shows that convexity obeys the same rules. The graph in Figure 5.5 shows the price/yield relationships for two of the bonds in the Table: a five-year 15 % coupon bond and a 15-year zero coupon bond. The modified duration of a short maturity high coupon bond is relatively low. The exposure to interest rate changes is only a little greater than that of holding cash and a change in yield has relatively little effect on this position. Furthermore, the bond's present value changes in a fairly linear fashion in response to yield changes.

Table 5.5   Modified duration and convexity for nine different bonds

Coupon rate (%)	Maturity (years)	MOD	CNX
0	5	4.5455	0.1240
0	10	9.0909	0.4545
0	15	13.6364	0.9917
10	5	3.7908	0.0968
10	10	6.1446	0.2640
10	15	7.6061	0.4342
15	5	3.5938	0.0898
15	10	5.7101	0.2359
15	15	7.0832	0.3858

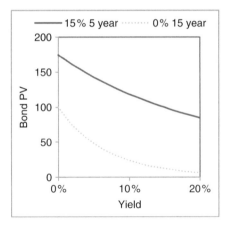

Figure 5.5 Price/yield relationship for a coupon bond and a zero bond.

At the other extreme, the modified duration of a long maturity zero coupon bond is high and the change in the bond price in response to a change in yield is far less linear – it is a more convex investment.

As noted before, positive convexity is in itself a 'good thing'. If yields fall the percentage rise in the bond price is greater than that predicted by modified duration. If yields rise the percentage fall in the bond's price is less than that predicted by duration. We would therefore expect that if two bonds have the same credit risk and time to maturity then the more convex bond would offer a slightly lower return than the less convex bond.

5.12 PORTFOLIO DURATION

The duration of a bond portfolio is the weighted average duration of the securities in the portfolio. The weights are established by the market value (PV or dirty price) of each bond divided by the total market value of the portfolio. For example, take a portfolio consisting of the three annual coupon bonds shown in Table 5.6. The total par value of the portfolio is $100 million, made up of:

- $30 million par value of the 10% three-year bond;
- $50 million par value of the 7% 10-year bond;
- $20 million par value of the 14% 13-year bond.

The total market value of the portfolio is calculated in Table 5.7 (there is some rounding in the values).

Table 5.6 Portfolio of three annual coupon bonds

Bond	PV (per $100 par)	Yield	MOD
10% 3 year	100.0000	10.00%	2.4869
7% 10 year	81.5663	10.00%	6.5624
14% 13 year	128.4134	10.00%	6.6779

Table 5.7 Market value of the bond portfolio

Bond	Par value × PV	=	Market value ($ million)
10% 3 year	$30 million × 100%		30.0000
7% 10 year	$50 million × 81.5663%		40.7831
14% 13 year	$20 million × 128.4143%		25.6827
		Total market value =	96.4658

The modified duration (MOD) of the portfolio is:

$$\left(\frac{30}{96.4658} \times 2.4869\right) + \left(\frac{40.7831}{96.4658} \times 6.5624\right) + \left(\frac{25.6827}{94.4658} \times 6.6779\right) = 5.3257$$

The modified duration measure means that for a 1% shift in the yield of all three bonds the market value of the portfolio will change by approximately 5.3257%. The PVBP of the portfolio is:

$$\$96.4658 \text{ million} \times \frac{0.053257}{100} = \$51,375$$

In fact the actual change in the portfolio value for a one basis point rise and fall in yield averages out at exactly $51,375. However the actual percentage rise in the portfolio value for a 1% fall in yield is 5.5593%. The discrepancy compared to the modified duration estimate of 5.3257% is caused by the convexity of the portfolio.

5.13 DEDICATION

The sum of money achieved at the maturity of an investment in a coupon bond will depend to some extent on the actual rate at which coupons are reinvested over the life of the bond. This contrasts with a zero coupon bond, where a sum of money can be invested and a known future cash flow achieved. If the zero is a 'strip' (see Chapter 4) issued by a major government such as the US government then the future value is effectively guaranteed. This explains why zeros are so highly regarded in fixed income portfolio management. The future cash inflows can be matched off against the projected future cash outflows from an insurance company or a pension fund. This strategy is known as **dedication**.

Dedication Example

A fund has a liability of $100 million that must be paid in exactly four years. Annually compounded interest rates are currently 10% p.a. The fund's portfolio manager buys a four-year zero coupon bond. If the yield is 10% with annual compounding then the purchase price is $100 million/$1.1^4$ = $68.3013 million. The maturity value is exactly $100 million. The portfolio manager has locked into a 10% per annum return over the desired investment horizon.

5.13.1 Dedication with a Coupon Bond

But what if no such zero bond exists or the fund's portfolio manager does not like the zeros that are on offer – perhaps because they are not sufficiently liquid? An alternative approach is to buy a four-year coupon bond. Suppose there is such a bond with 10 % annual coupons trading at par and yielding exactly 10 %. On the assumption that coupons can be reinvested at 10 % p.a. the portfolio manager needs to buy bonds costing $68.3013 million. Since it is a par bond the nominal value is also $68.3013 million so annual coupons will be:

$$\$68.3013 \text{ million} \times 10\% = \$6.8301 \text{ million}$$

The first coupon payment due in one year can be reinvested for a further three years at (on our assumption) 10 % p.a. This will grow to become:

$$\$6.8301 \text{ million} \times 1.1^3 = \$9.0909 \text{ million}$$

The total cash generated by the bond at maturity is shown in Table 5.8.

The problem with this strategy is that it assumes coupons can always be reinvested at 10 % p.a., which may or may not turn out to be true. Suppose that immediately after the portfolio manager invested in the bond yields fell to 8 % p.a. and stayed at that level for the remaining four years. The total cash generated by the bond at maturity in this case is recalculated in Table 5.9.

The annualized return actually achieved in this second scenario is:

$$\left[\sqrt[4]{\left(\frac{99.0787}{68.3013} \right)} \right] - 1 = 9.75\% \text{ p.a.}$$

Table 5.8 Value at maturity with coupons reinvested at 10 % p.a.

Year	Cash flow ($ million)	Maturity value with coupons reinvested at 10 % p.a. ($ million)
1	6.8301	9.0909
2	6.8301	8.2645
3	6.8301	7.5131
4	75.1315	75.1315
		Total = 100.0000

Table 5.9 Value at maturity with coupons reinvested at 8 % p.a.

Year	Cash flow ($ million)	Maturity value with coupons reinvested at 8 % p.a. ($ million)
1	6.8301	8.6040
2	6.8301	7.9667
3	6.8301	7.3765
4	75.1315	75.1315
		Total = 99.0787

This demonstrates that if reinvestment rates fall the portfolio manager will fail to achieve the expected rate of return and the target cash flow at maturity. On the other hand if rates rise the manager will exceed the target return and future value.

5.14 IMMUNIZATION

Another alternative for the portfolio manager is to buy a bond with a maturity *greater* than four years. When rates fall reinvestment income will also fall. However the portfolio manager has a shorter investment horizon than the maturity of the bond and will be able to sell the bond after four years at a favourable price that reflects falling interest rates.

If rates increase then interest on interest arising from the reinvestment of coupons will be higher, but the bond has to be sold before its maturity at a higher yield. These two factors – the reinvestment effect and the proceeds from the sale of the bond before maturity – offset each other when the Macaulay's duration of the assets matches the desired investment horizon. The process of constructing such a portfolio is known as **immunization**. The purpose is to lock into a required rate of return at the time of purchase of the bonds regardless of what happens subsequently to interest rates.

5.14.1 Immunization Example

The story as before is that the portfolio manager is trying to match a \$ 100 million liability due in four years. Suppose there exists in the market a suitable five-year annual bond with a coupon of 13.75 % yielding 10 %. The present value of the bond is \$ 114.2155 per \$ 100 and its Macaulay's duration is approximately four years. To generate the required cash flow, bonds should be bought with a total purchase price (PV) of \$ 68.3013 million. The total par value will therefore be:

$$\frac{\$ 68.3013 \text{ million}}{1.142155} = \$ 59.8004 \text{ million}$$

The annual coupons received will be:

$$\$ 59.8004 \text{ million} \times 13.75 \% = \$ 8.2226 \text{ million}$$

Table 5.10 shows the value of the coupons generated and reinvested at the end of four years if the reinvestment rate over the period turns out to be 8 % p.a.

Table 5.10   Value of reinvested coupons from five-year bond in four years reinvested at 8 % p.a.

Year	Coupon (\$ million)	Future value (\$ million)
1	8.2226	10.3581
2	8.2226	9.5908
3	8.2226	8.8804
4	8.2226	8.2226
	Total =	37.0518

However, on the assumption that the yield on the bond is still 8 % with one year remaining to maturity we can also work out its sale price at the end of the four-year investment horizon. At maturity the bond will pay a final coupon of $ 8.2226 million plus the par value of $ 59.8004 million, a total of $ 68.023 million. Therefore the sale price with one year to maturity at an 8 % yield is:

$$\frac{\$\,68.023 \text{ million}}{1.08} = \$\,62.9843 \text{ million}$$

Add this to the cash flow from the reinvested coupons of $ 37.0518 and the total cash generated at the end of the four-year investment horizon is $ 100.036 million. The return achieved over the four-year investment horizon is calculated as follows:

$$\left[\sqrt[4]{\left(\frac{100.036}{68.3013}\right)}\right] - 1 = 10\%$$

5.14.2 Cash Flows if Interest Rates Rise

What happens if the portfolio manager buys the five-year bond and then rates rise, let us say to 12 %? As Table 5.11 shows, the total cash generated by reinvesting coupons after four years would increase to $ 39.2984 million.

However the sale value of the bond at a 12 % yield is less than at an 8 % yield:

$$\frac{\$\,68.023 \text{ million}}{1.12} = \$\,60.7348 \text{ million}$$

The total cash due in four years in this scenario is approximately $ 100 million and the return achieved over the investment period is again 10 % p.a.

It seems that whether interest rates rise or fall the portfolio manager will achieve the required return and the required future cash flow. The reason this works is because the five-year bond in the example has a Macaulay's duration of four years and behaves rather like a four-year zero. The problem with the strategy in practice is that the composition of the portfolio may have to be adjusted periodically to match the duration of the liabilities.

Table 5.11   Value of reinvested coupons from five-year bond in four years reinvested at 12 % p.a.

Year	Coupon ($ million)	Future value ($ million)
1	8.2226	11.5521
2	8.2226	10.3144
3	8.2226	9.2093
4	8.2226	8.2226
	Total =	39.2983

5.15 DURATION-BASED HEDGES

When constructing a hedge against the fall in the price of a bond portfolio due to changes in yield the appropriate measure to use is PVBP rather than Macaulay's or modified duration. The strategy is to select a hedging vehicle whose change in dollar value for a given yield change offsets that of the bond portfolio to be hedged.

Hedge Example

A trader holds $ 10 million nominal value of an annual 8 % coupon 10-year bond trading at par and yielding 8 % p.a. The PVBP of the bond is $ 0.0671 per $ 100 nominal. The trader wants to hedge against the risk that interest rates will rise.

The total profit/loss on the portfolio of 8 % bonds for a one basis point yield change is $ 6710:

$$\frac{\$ 0.0671}{100} \times \$ 10 \text{ million} = \$ 6710$$

Since the trader owns the bonds, in market jargon this is a 'long position'. The trader will make money if the bond price rises (yields fall) and will lose money if the bond price falls (yields rise). The trader decides to hedge against the risk of rising interest rates by shorting a 14 % coupon annual bond with a 10-year maturity also yielding 8 %. Then if yields rise the trader can buy the short bond back more cheaply at a profit, reducing or cancelling out the loss on the long position. The present value of the 14 % bond to be shorted is $ 140.2605 per $ 100 par. The PVBP of this second bond is $ 0.08526 per $ 100 nominal. Clearly the trader does not need to short $ 10 million par value of the higher coupon bond to implement the hedge.

The profit/loss on the 14 % coupon bond for a one basis point yield change on a $ 10 million nominal position would be:

$$\frac{\$ 0.08526}{100} \times \$ 10 \text{ million} = \$ 8256$$

This is greater than the profit and loss (P&L) on the long bond to be hedged and the position is over-hedged. The problem is clearly that the short bond will generate a greater P&L for a one basis point yield change than the long bond. The amount sold has to be reduced in proportion. The hedge ratio calculation is:

$$\frac{\text{PVBP of Bond to be Hedged}}{\text{PVBP of Hedging Vehicle}} = \frac{0.0671}{0.08526} = 0.787 \text{ or } 78.7\%$$

The amount of the hedging bond to be shorted is approximately:

$$\$ 10 \text{ million} \times 0.787 = \$ 7.87 \text{ million par value}$$

Then for a one basis point yield change the profit/loss on these bonds would be:

$$\frac{0.08526}{100} \times \$7.87 \text{ million} = \$6710$$

This matches the expected P&L on the 8% coupon bond owned by the trader.

5.16   CONVEXITY EFFECTS ON DURATION HEDGES

In practice the hedge just assembled would rarely work exactly, especially for large movements in yields. This is not simply because of rounding in the calculation of PVBP and the hedge ratio.

Consider Table 5.12. This shows the P&L on the 8% coupon bond for a 1% and a 2% rise and fall in yields starting from 8%. It then shows the P&L on the 14% coupon bond shorted by the trader as a hedge, using the same yield change assumptions. Note that the trader has a $10 million par value long position in the first bond but shorted only $7.87 million par value of the second bond.

For small movements in yields starting from 8% the P&Ls will more or less cancel out. The trader has successfully hedged against losses on the long bond position, at the expense of not being able to make a profit if the bond rises in price – any profits will be offset by losses on the bonds that are shorted. However for larger movements in yields it appears that the trader always makes a (small) profit. This is shown in Figure 5.6.

Table 5.12   P&Ls on the long and on the short bond starting from an 8% yield

Yield (p.a.)	P&L on long bond ($)	P&L on short bond ($)	Net P&L ($)
6%	1,472,017	−1,465,410	6607
7%	702,358	−700,791	1568
8%	0	0	0
9%	−641,766	643,152	1386
10%	−1,228,913	1,234,191	5277

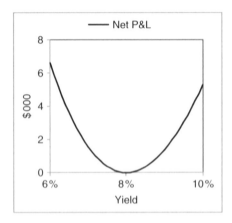

Figure 5.6   Net P&L on the long and on the short bond in the duration hedge.

The reason is *convexity*. The long 8% coupon bond has greater convexity (0.3%) compared to the short 14% coupon bond (0.26%) because it has a lower coupon rate. This has implications:

- for large falls in yield the trader will make more money on the long bond compared to losses on the short bond, because positive convexity gives the rise in value of the long bond a greater 'boost';
- for large rises in yield the trader will lose less money on the long bond compared to profits on the short bond, because positive convexity holds up the fall in value of the long bond.

In this example both the bonds have 10 years to maturity. However suppose the trader had hedged the exposure on the 10-year bond by shorting the appropriate amount of (say) a five-year bond, calculated using the hedge ratio method we employed before. Then there is an additional risk. As long as yields shift by the same amount and in the same direction at the five and at the 10-year points then the profits and losses on the two bonds would more or less cancel out. In practice this may well not happen.

Chapter 6 discusses the concept of a **yield curve**, a graph showing the yields on a given class of bonds (such as government bonds) against their time to maturity. Duration measures are based on the simplifying assumption that the yield curve shifts in parallel. In reality the yield curve is subject to non-parallel shifts. It is possible, for example, for yields to rise at the 10-year point but at the same time fall at the five-year maturity, so that the trader in the example could actually lose on both the long and the short position. This is sometimes known as **curve risk**.

5.17   CHAPTER SUMMARY

The price of low coupon, long maturity bonds is highly sensitive to changes in market yields. This is because most of the cash flows occur far out into the future and cannot be reinvested at new levels of interest rates for a long time. The weighted average life of a bond's cash flows is measured by Macaulay's duration. A zero coupon bond has a Macaulay's duration equal to its maturity. The duration of a coupon bond and its effective exposure to interest rate changes are less than its maturity because the coupons can be reinvested at the prevailing market rate. Modified duration is a related measure which can be used to estimate the change in the money value of the bond for a 0.01% yield change. This is known as the price value of a basis point or basis point value. Duration can be used to put together a portfolio of bonds which matches expected future cash flows. This technique is called immunization. Duration can also be used to construct a hedge against the fall in the value of a bond portfolio. Duration is an approximate measure because the relationship between the price of a bond and its yield is nonlinear. Convexity is a measure of this curvature. It can be used to provide a better estimate of the actual change in the price of a bond for a substantial yield change.

6
The Yield Curve

6.1 CHAPTER OVERVIEW

Chapter 4 explored the bond markets and the traditional measure of return on bonds: yield-to-maturity, or internal rate of return. This chapter extends the discussion and considers the relationship between bond yield and time to maturity. It reviews the components of a quoted or nominal interest rate, and the concept of annual equivalent rate. It then moves on to the yield curve itself and prevalent theories about the shape of the curve. Most investors and traders agree that the curve builds in expectations of future interest rates, although others believe that there may be other factors at work, such as the preference investors have to 'keep their options open' by favouring short-dated securities. The chapter looks at how to extract forward interest rates from the yield curve. To do this it uses a methodology called 'bootstrapping' to derive zero coupon or spot rates from the yields on coupon bonds trading at par. Forward interest rates are derived from the spot rate curve and the results are related back to the expectations theory of yield curves. Finally, the chapter shows how to derive discount factors which can be applied directly to future cash flows to calculate present values, without making reinvestment assumptions, and how discount factors and forward interest rates are related.

6.2 REAL AND NOMINAL INTEREST RATES

The cost of borrowing money for a period of time (its time value) is measured by the interest rate for the period. Interest rates and bond yields are usually quoted on a **nominal** basis. A nominal rate has two components:

- **Inflation Rate.** This compensates the lender for the assumed erosion in the value of the money over the time period.
- **Real Rate.** This compensates the lender for the economic use of the funds over the time period.

The relationship can be expressed in a formula (with the rates inserted as decimals):

$$1 + \text{Nominal Rate} = (1 + \text{Inflation Rate}) \times (1 + \text{Real Rate})$$

It follows that:

$$\text{Real Rate} = \left(\frac{1 + \text{Nominal Rate}}{1 + \text{Inflation Rate}} \right) - 1$$

If the nominal interest rate for one-year money is 10% p.a. with annual compounding and the assumed rate of inflation over the period is 5% p.a. then the real interest rate is calculated as follows.

$$\text{Real Rate} = \left(\frac{1+0.10}{1+0.05}\right) - 1 = 0.0476 = 4.76\%$$

6.2.1 Volatility of Interest Rates

Inflation rates and market expectations about inflation rates are usually more volatile than real interest rates, which are determined by fundamental factors such as the supply and demand for credit in the economy. Short-term interest rates in major economies are strongly influenced by the activities of the central bank, which drives the rate up and down depending on whether it wishes to rein in inflation or stimulate the economy. To a large extent long-term interest rates are determined by bond prices and bond yields, which build in a market consensus expectation about inflation and the future direction of interest rates.

6.3 COMPOUNDING PERIODS

Chapter 4 explained that some bonds pay coupons annually and others semi-annually. The traditional method of calculating the yield on a bond is to find the single discount rate that equates the market dirty price of the bond with the present value of the bond at that discount rate. This is an **internal rate of return** calculation. If the bond is semi-annual then the annualized return is calculated by simply doubling the figure. One problem with this convention is that the yield on a semi-annual bond is not directly comparable with that on a bond that pays annual coupons. This is why an annual equivalent rate (AER) is often calculated, also known as the effective annual rate. It is the rate expressed with annual compounding that is equivalent to a rate expressed with more frequent compounding, such as semi-annual, or quarterly, or monthly. The formula for calculating the effective annual interest rate or yield when interest is compounded m times per annum is as follows.

$$\text{AER} = \left(1 + \frac{\text{Nominal Rate}}{m}\right)^m - 1$$

For example, a nominal rate of 10% p.a. with semi-annual compounding is equivalent to 10.25% p.a. with annual compounding.

$$\text{AER} = \left(1 + \frac{0.1}{2}\right)^2 - 1 = 0.1025 = 10.25\%$$

A par bond that yields 10% p.a. on a semi-annual basis has the same effective return as a bond that yields 10.25% p.a. with annual compounding. Table 6.1 shows what happens to the annual equivalent rate as interest is compounded more frequently.

Note that capital markets professionals may refer to a bond as yielding 10% semi-annual. Conventionally this does *not* mean that the bond pays a return of 10% every six months. It means that it pays a return of 10% p.a. expressed with semi-annual compounding. This is equivalent to a yield of 10.25% p.a. expressed with annual compounding i.e. the AER is 10.25% p.a.

Table 6.1   Annual equivalent rates

Quoted rate p.a.	Compounding frequency	AER
10%	Annually	10.0000%
10%	Semi-annually	10.2500%
10%	Quarterly	10.3813%
10%	Daily	10.5156%

As interest is compounded more and more frequently the annual equivalent rate approaches a limit. This is defined by what is known as **continuous compounding**, a method of calculating interest commonly used with derivatives. The effective annual rate where interest is compounded continuously is calculated as in the following example. The value e is the base of natural logarithms and is approximately 2.71828.

Example

A quoted rate of 10% p.a. expressed with continuous compounding is equivalent to 10.5171% p.a. with annual compounding.

$$AER = e^{0.1} - 1 = 0.105171 = 10.5171\%$$

6.4   THE YIELD CURVE DEFINED

A yield curve is a graph plotting the yields on a set of debt securities against time to maturity. The securities are selected to be comparable in all respects apart from their time to maturity. There are separate yield curves for US Treasury bonds, government agencies, municipal authorities, top-rated corporate bonds and so on. The US Treasury curve shows the yields on dollar investments for a range of maturities that carry minimal credit or default risk. The curve is normally constructed from the yields on the most recently-issued and liquid bonds trading around par.

Note that the following discussion on the shape of the yield curve is based on government bonds that are highly unlikely to default, such as US Treasuries. For any given maturity an investor will demand extra yield over and above that available on US Treasuries (a risk premium) for holding bonds denominated in US dollars that carry additional credit risk. This includes dollar bonds issued by corporations and foreign governments. The size of the risk premium will depend on the likelihood of default and the money that can be recovered in the event of default. Credit risk on bonds is covered in more detail in Chapter 7.

6.4.1   Shape of the Yield Curve

The shape of the yield curve varies over time. There are four main types (see Figure 6.1).

- A **positive** or upward sloping or 'normal' curve occurs when yields on longer maturity securities are higher than those on shorter maturities. It tends to occur when short-term interest rates have been cut to relatively low levels.

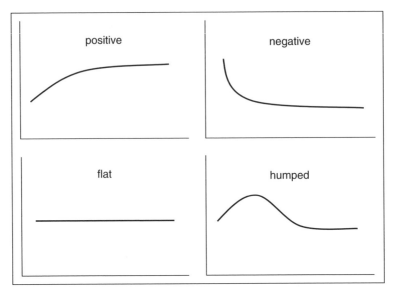

Figure 6.1 Basic yield curve shapes.

- A **negative** or downward sloping or inverted curve occurs when yields on shorter maturity securities are higher than those on longer maturities. It tends to occur when short-term interest rates have been raised to high levels by the central bank.
- A **flat curve** occurs when yields on short and long maturity securities are roughly equal.
- A **humped** curve occurs when yields rise gradually from short to medium term but then fall off at the longer maturities.

The slope of the Treasury yield curve tends to level off after 15 or so years. The market tends to lump the longer maturities together and sees little distinction between (for example) 20 and 30-year bonds. There are many variations on the four basic types. For example, the curve may develop a 'kink' within a certain maturity range rather than describing a smooth curve.

6.5   THEORIES OF YIELD CURVES

Many theories have been promoted to explain why yield curves take the shapes they do. The most popular are:

- market expectations theory;
- liquidity preference theory;
- preferred habitat or institutional theory.

The following discussion is based on the curve for government securities such as US Treasuries. This ignores for the moment issues concerning default risk, which are considered later. The main risk on an investment in US government bonds is **market** or price risk – the risk of making a loss because of changes in the market price/yield of the securities as a result of changes in general market conditions, such as a rise in interest rates.

6.5.1   Market Expectations Theory

This is the most widely held view. It says that a positive yield curve is a sign that the market expects rises in interest rates. Intuitively, if interest rates are rising then investors in short-term securities will be paid back soon and will be able to reinvest the proceeds at the new higher interest rates. On the other hand investors buying longer-term securities are locking their money away for longer and will not be able to take advantage of reinvesting at the new higher interest rates to the same extent. They will demand a higher return on their investment in compensation.

Conversely, a negative yield curve is held to be a sign of falling interest rates. In a declining interest rate environment holders of longer-term paper are content to lock in at relatively low yields, because they think that yields on short-term paper are currently high and are due to fall. In this situation investors who buy short-term debt securities would suffer from falling reinvestment rates when their paper matures.

6.5.2   Empirical Evidence

Negative yield curves often occur in circumstances in which short-term interest rates have been raised to relatively high levels by the central bank in order to control inflation. Market expectations theory holds that the yield curve is negative in this environment because investors believe that the medicine will work and rates will eventually fall.

Empirical evidence suggests that the yield curve is not in fact a particularly good predictor of future interest rates. Proponents of the expectations theory will argue that this is not particularly relevant. The market's view on future interest rates is an unbiased consensus based on all the currently available information. This information will change over time and is always incomplete. If the yield curve shows the current market consensus on the direction of interest rates then at least it allows market participants to decide whether or not they agree with the consensus – and act accordingly.

In the early 2000s the yield curves for US Treasuries and UK gilts were negative for prolonged periods of time. Most market practitioners accepted that this had little to do with expectations on interest rates and was mainly caused by a lack of supply of longer-dated Treasuries. This caused prices to rise and yields to fall. It was exacerbated by the authorities buying back longer maturity bonds.

6.5.3   Liquidity Preference Theory

This argues that since the price or market risk of a bond increases with the term to maturity investors will demand a risk premium for holding longer maturities. Longer-duration bonds are more sensitive to changes in interest rates than shorter-duration bonds. All other things being equal, investors prefer to have their money in short-term securities so that they can quickly respond to changes in market interest rates.

If this theory was interpreted simplistically it would imply that yield curves should always be positive, which is clearly not the case. In fact adherents tend to argue that the yield curve should incorporate *both* interest rate expectations and a risk premium for holding longer-term bonds. This means that a positive yield curve may predict rises in interest rates. Alternatively, there may be no such expectation and the upward slope is entirely explained by the liquidity risk premium effect.

Liquidity Premium

Pure expectations theory suggests that an investor who agrees with the market consensus on the future direction of interest rates should not demand a liquidity premium. Such an investor would be indifferent between investing in a one-year Treasury bill and investing in a 30-year Treasury bond with the intention of selling it after one year. This is because future interest rates expectations and hence bond prices can be predicted from the current shape of the yield curve. The method is explained later in the present chapter.

6.5.4 Preferred Habitat Theory

This theory accepts the view that the term structure reflects the expectations of future interest rates and also includes a risk premium. However proponents deny that the risk premium is due to a preference for shorter maturity securities. They argue that investors and borrowers have preferences for particular maturities. If there is an excess of demand for funds at a given maturity additional investors can only be attracted out of their 'preferred habitat' by offering a risk premium. If there is an over-supply of funds then further borrowers can only be attracted by lowering interest rates at that maturity.

6.6 ZERO COUPON OR SPOT RATES

All the theories discussed in the last section agree that the yield curve incorporates market expectations about future or 'forward' interest rates. In fact using a simple arbitrage argument it is possible to derive interest rates for future time periods from the yield curve for government bonds. These are called **implied forward rates**. The curve for government bonds such as US Treasuries is used to set aside issues relating to credit risk.

Unfortunately the yields-to-maturity on coupon bonds cannot be used directly to establish forward rates, since they actually assume that coupon payments can be reinvested for all future periods at a constant rate. To help explore the difficulties this causes this section considers a yield curve based on one, two, and three-year annual coupon bonds trading at par. This is known as a **par yield curve**. The rates are set out in Table 6.2. The bonds in this example are presumed to be free of default risk.

6.6.1 Coupon Stripping

Suppose a trader carries out the following strategy today.

- **Step 1.** Buy $ 100 of the two-year 9 % coupon bond trading at par.

Table 6.2 Par yield curve for annual coupon bonds

Maturity	Coupon rate p.a.	Yield-to-maturity p.a.
1 year	8 %	8 %
2 years	9 %	9 %
3 years	10 %	10 %

- **Step 2.** Sell off the title to the first $9 coupon on this bond due in one year's time to another investor.

Effectively, the trader has 'stripped' out the first coupon and created a one-year zero coupon bond with a future value of $9. Since the yield on one-year maturity annual bonds is 8% it seems reasonable that the trader should sell off this $9 future cash flow at a yield of 8%. The present value received from selling the bond is:

$$\frac{\$9}{1.08} = \$8.3333$$

- **Step 3.** Next, the trader sells off the title to the final coupon and the par value of the 9% coupon bond both due in two years' time.

Now the trader has 'stripped' out the final cash flow on the 9% coupon bond and created a two-year zero coupon bond with a future value of $109. The yield-to-maturity on two-year coupon bonds is currently 9% (from Table 6.2). Assuming that the $109 cash flow is sold at a 9% yield the present value received is:

$$\frac{\$109}{1.09^2} = \$91.7431$$

To summarize the position, the trader has:

- bought the two-year 9% coupon bond for $100;
- sold the title to the first $9 cash flow from the bond for $8.3333;
- sold the title to the second and final $109 cash flow from the bond for $91.7431.

The outgoing today is $100 and the total receipts are $100.076. If the trader carries this 'coupon stripping' exercise out on billions of dollars' worth of bonds he or she is going to make a great deal of free money!

6.6.2 Calculating the Two-Year Spot Rate

Since there is a risk-free or arbitrage profit here something must be wrong. The first $9 cash flow was discounted at 8% and this is correct because 8% is the yield on one-year annual bonds with no intervening coupons. The problem arose over discounting the second cash flow of $109 using the 9% yield on two-year *coupon bonds*. This yield measure assumes that the interim $9 coupon is received and reinvested for a further year at 9%, and that on top of this a further $109 is received at maturity. It cannot be used to price the two-year $109 cash flow on the bond when this is sold off separately without receiving the intervening $9 coupon.

From the data provided it is possible to calculate the appropriate discount rate at which the year two $109 cash flow should be sold off today such that there are no arbitrage profits available. Recall that the trader:

- paid $100 for the two-year 9% coupon bond;
- sold the title to the first $9 coupon at the one-year yield of 8% for a present value of $8.3333.

There are no intervening coupons to reinvest on a one-year annual bond so this 8 % yield can be applied directly to present value any one-off risk-free dollar cash flow due in one year. It is the one-year zero coupon rate, also known as the **spot rate** for the period. We will call it z_1. In this case $z_1 = 8\%$.

The question to be resolved is how much the trader has to receive today for the title to the year two cash flow of $109 to exactly break even on stripping the bond.

- Cost of two-year 9 % coupon bond today = $100.
- Received for title to the year one cash flow at z_1 (8 %) = $8.3333.
- Required for title to year two cash flow to break even = $100 − $8.3333 = $91.6667.

To just break even on the coupon stripping exercise the trader has to be paid $91.6667 today for the title to the two-year cash flow of $109. The yield on this investment is the two-year zero coupon or spot rate z_2. How is this calculated? The present value (PV) formula used in the bond markets is as follows:

$$PV = \frac{FV}{(1+r)^n}$$

where FV is the future value, r is the discount rate per compounding as a decimal period, and n is the number of compounding periods in the investment. Rearranging this gives:

$$r = \left[\sqrt[n]{\left(\frac{FV}{PV} \right)} \right] - 1$$

In the example the future value is $109. The present value is $91.6667. The investment period is two years with annual compounding, so that there are two compounding periods to the receipt of the FV. The two-year zero coupon rate is therefore:

$$z_2 = \left[\sqrt[2]{\left(\frac{109}{91.6667} \right)} \right] - 1 = 0.090454 = 9.0454\%$$

6.7   BOOTSTRAPPING

The lesson from the previous section's exercise is that the 9 % yield on two-year coupon bonds cannot be used directly to present value a one-off cash flow due in two years' time with no intervening coupons to reinvest. For this we need z_2, the two-year zero coupon or spot rate. If liquid zero coupon bonds exist in the market then the yield on such bonds can be observed directly and used as spot rates. Otherwise, spot rates can be extracted from the cash flow on par coupon bonds using the methodology employed above to calculate z_2.

The methodology is often called **bootstrapping** in the capital markets. To see why, recall that we started by assuming that the one-year yield on annual coupon bonds establishes z_1, the one-year spot rate. This was used to calculate z_2, the two-year spot rate. The methodology can be taken a step further by using z_1 and z_2 to calculate z_3, the three-year spot rate. We 'pull ourselves up by our bootstraps'.

6.7.1 Calculating the Three-Year Spot Rate

The methodology is the same used before to calculate the two-year spot rate.

- Assume a three-year 10% annual coupon bond is purchased for $100.
- Sell off the one-year $10 coupon at the one-year spot rate $z_1 = 8\%$:

$$\text{Present Value} = \frac{\$10}{1.08} = \$9.2593$$

- Sell off the two-year $10 coupon at the two-year spot rate $z_2 = 9.0454\%$:

$$\text{Present Value} = \frac{\$10}{1.0904542} = \$8.4098$$

- Calculate how much has to be received for the title to the three-year cash flow of $110 to exactly break even on the exercise:

$$\text{Breakeven Price} = \$100 - \$9.2593 - \$8.4098 = \$82.3309$$

- Calculate z_3 the yield that an investor would make on this year three cash flow if purchased at the breakeven price of $82.3309:

$$z_2 = \left[\sqrt[3]{\left(\frac{110}{82.3309} \right)} \right] - 1 = 10.1395\%$$

The complete set of par yields and spot rates is shown in Table 6.3 and in Figure 6.2.

Table 6.3 Par yields and spot rates

Maturity	Par yield	Spot rate
1 year	8%	8%
2 years	9%	9.0454%
3 years	10%	10.1395%

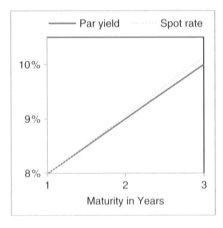

Figure 6.2 Par and spot rates in a positive yield curve environment.

6.8   SPOT RATES AND THE PAR CURVE

There is a clear relationship in the example between the par yield curve and the spot rates.

- The two-year spot rate is higher than the yield on two-year coupon bonds trading at par.
- The three-year spot rate is higher than the yield on three-year coupon bonds trading at par.

This result can be explained intuitively in terms of the expectations theory of yield curves. The par curve in the example is positive or upward sloping – three-year yields are higher than two-year yields, which are higher than one-year yields. This builds in an expectation of future increases in interest rates. An investor who buys a two-year or three-year zero coupon bond will miss out on the ability to reinvest interim cash flows at rising interest rates. The investor has to be compensated through a higher yield than is available on coupon bonds with the same maturity.

Negative Curve

If the yield curve is inverted or downward sloping then zero coupon yields will be below the yields on par coupon bonds. A negative curve builds in expectations of falling reinvestment rates. Intuitively, investors in zero coupon bonds will not suffer from this since they have no interim coupons to reinvest, unlike investors in coupon bonds. To compensate they earn lower returns.

6.9   PRICING MODELS USING SPOT RATES

Traditionally, as shown in Chapter 4, bonds are valued by discounting each cash flow at exactly the same discount rate. This is equivalent to assuming a constant reinvestment rate for future cash flows. However, this is a simplifying assumption and applying the yields-to-maturity on coupon bonds to present value one-off future cash flows such as those from zero coupon bonds produces inaccuracies. More sophisticated pricing models in the capital markets employ spot rates. A financial instrument is broken down into its individual cash flows and each is discounted at the specific spot rate for the period of time to the receipt of that cash flow. No assumption need be made about reinvestment rates. If there is a risk that a cash flow may not be received it can be discounted at the spot rate for Treasuries plus a spread representing credit risk.

6.9.1   Outright Risk and Curve Risk

Duration measures use the traditional bond pricing model, which is based on constant reinvestment rates. They assume implicitly that the yield curve moves in parallel shifts. Modified duration can be used to measure what is sometimes known as **outright risk** – the profits and losses that result from parallel movements in the yield curve. However bond traders also have to take into account the profits and losses that might result from 'twists' in the shape of the curve. This is sometimes called **curve risk**. For example, a positive curve might shift upwards but also flatten, such that short-term interest rates rise more steeply than long-term interest rates. (This is a common phenomenon.)

One advantage of breaking a security down into its component cash flows and discounting each cash flow at the appropriate spot rate is that potential profits and losses can be calculated for non-parallel movements in the curve. For example, it might be assumed that one-year spot rates increase by 50 basis points but 10-year rates by only 25 basis points, flattening the curve.

6.10   FORWARD RATES

Previous sections started with a par yield curve and used this to calculate the spot rates for each time period using the bootstrapping methodology. It is also possible to calculate the forward interest rates implied in the par yield curve between two time periods using an arbitrage argument. The example is based on the spot rates in Table 6.3. (This example ignores spreads on borrowing and lending rates which would apply in practice.)

Suppose a trader is able to borrow $\$1$ for two years at the two-year spot rate z_2 which is 9.0454 %. The future value to be repaid on the loan at maturity is as follows.

$$\text{Future Value} = \$1 \times 1.090454^2 = \$1.1891$$

Next, the trader invests the $\$1$ today for one year at z_1, the one-year spot rate, which is 8 %. The future value in one year will be $\$1.08$. Finally, the trader arranges to reinvest the $\$1.08$ proceeds due to be received in one year for a further year at a fixed rate of interest. We will call this rate f_{1v2}, because it is a forward rate of interest for investing money in one year for one year. The investment will mature two years from today.

If the trader can earn more on the two investments combined than the $\$1.1891$ to be repaid in two years on the loan then there is an arbitrage opportunity available. Assume that no such opportunity exists (if it did the market would quickly exploit it and it would soon disappear). In that case the cash flow received in two years from the two investments will exactly match the repayment amount due on the loan. In an equation:

$$(1 + z_2)^2 = (1 + z_1) \times (1 + f_{1v2})$$

To put this equation into words, the repayment due on the $\$1$ borrowing for two years at z_2 must equal the proceeds from investing the money for one year at z_1 and reinvesting for a further year at the forward rate f_{1v2}.

By turning this equation round and inserting the values for z_1 and z_2 a value can be found for f_{1v2}:

$$f_{1v2} = \left[\frac{(1 + z_2)^2}{(1 + z_1)} \right] - 1 = \left[\frac{1.090454^2}{1.08} \right] - 1 = 10.1009\,\%$$

The cash flows involved in this example are set out in Figure 6.3. The first line shows the cash flows from the two-year borrowing. The second line shows the $\$1$ invested for one year at z_1 and then reinvested for a further year at f_{1v2}.

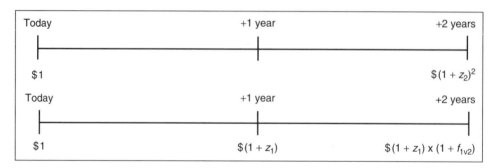

Figure 6.3   Cash flows for the forward rate calculation.

6.10.1   Explaining the Result

Again, the result can be explained in terms of expectations theory. The par yield curve is positive or upward sloping so the one-year forward rate is higher than the rate for investing today for one year, the cash market rate of 8 %. The curve builds in expectations of future rises in interest rates.

6.10.2   Extending the Argument

The forward rate f_{2v3} for a one-year period starting in two years can be calculated from the spot rates using the same methodology.

- Borrow $ 1 for three years at the spot rate z_3 which is 10.1395 %. The repayment amount in three years is $ 1.3361.
- Invest the $ 1 for two years at the spot rate z_2 which is 9.0454 %. The future value in two years is $ 1.1891.
- Calculate f_{2v3} as the rate for reinvesting money in two years for a further year such that all the transactions break even. In this example f_{2v3} equals 12.3607 %.

6.11   DISCOUNT FACTORS

Market professionals often prefer to work with discount factors rather than spot rates. This is really a matter of convenience since a discount factor is simply the present value of $ 1 discounted at the spot rate for a given future date. For example, if the one-year spot rate z_1 is 8 % then the one-year discount factor DF_1 is calculated as follows:

$$DF_1 = \frac{1}{1.08} = 0.9259$$

If the two-year spot rate z_2 is 9.0454 % then the two-year discount factor DF_2 is given by:

$$DF_2 = \frac{1}{1.090454^2} = 0.8410$$

Table 6.4 Spot and forward rates and discount factors

Maturity	Par yield	Spot rate	Forward rate	Discount factor
1 year	8 %	8 %		0.9259
2 years	9 %	9.0454 %	10.1009 %	0.8410
3 years	10 %	10.1395 %	12.3607 %	0.7485

A discount factor can be applied directly to a future cash flow to establish its present value. For example, if an investor is due to receive $5 million in two years' time and the spot rate for that time period is 9.0454 % p.a. then the present value of the cash flow is given by:

$$\text{Future Value} \times DF_2 = \$5 \text{ million} \times 0.8410 = \$4.205 \text{ million}$$

6.11.1 Discount Factors and Forward Rates

Table 6.4 summarizes the par, spot, and forward rates and discount factors used in the examples in this chapter.

There is an important relationship between discount factors and forward interest rates:

$$\text{Period Discount Factor} = \frac{\text{Discount Factor for the Previous Period}}{1 + \text{Forward Rate between the Two Periods}}$$

For example:

$$DF_2 = \frac{DF_1}{1 + f_{1v2}} = \frac{0.9259}{1.101009} = 0.8410$$

This relationship can be very useful in practice. For example, if DF_2 is 0.8410 and the forward rate between years two and three, f_{2v3}, is 12.3607 %, then the year three discount factor DF_3 can be calculated as follows:

$$DF_3 = \frac{DF_2}{1 + f_{2v3}} = \frac{0.8410}{1.123607} = 0.7485$$

This produces the same result as that produced by deriving DF_3 from the three-year spot rate:

$$DF_3 = \frac{1}{(1 + z_3)^3} = \frac{1}{1.101395^3} = 0.7485$$

This relationship is useful since in major currencies forward interest rates can be observed directly because of the existence of derivative products such as forward rate agreements and interest rate futures (see Chapter 11). The relationship is used when pricing interest rate swaps in Chapter 14. Note that when using discount factors in practice it is usually necessary to use around six to eight decimal places to obtain accurate results.

6.12   CHAPTER SUMMARY

Interest rates and bond yields are normally quoted on a nominal basis which includes inflation expectations. The real rate of interest is the nominal rate adjusted for the inflation assumption. Bond yields quoted with annual and with semi-annual compounding cannot be directly compared. Instead the semi-annual yield has to be converted to an annual equivalent rate (or vice versa). In the derivatives market interest is often compounded on a continuous basis. The yield curve is a graph based on a certain class of bonds which plots bond yield against maturity. There is a yield curve for government bonds and also curves for bonds that carry additional credit or default risk. The expectations theory of yield curves holds that a positive or upward sloping curve builds in expectations of rising interest rates. The par yield curve is the curve for coupon bonds trading at par. Using arbitrage arguments it is possible to extract from the par curve zero coupon or spot rates and forward interest rates. Deriving spot rates is called bootstrapping. Spot rates can be applied directly to present value future cash flows since they make no reinvestment assumptions. The spot rate derived from government bonds has to be adjusted if the cash flow carries additional credit risk. A discount factor is the present value of $1 at the spot rate for the time period. Discount factors can also be derived from observed forward interest rates in the market.

7

Credit Spreads and Securitization

7.1 CHAPTER OVERVIEW

This chapter explores credit risk on debt securities issued by non-sovereign borrowers, as well as credit default swaps and securitization. In developed markets the credit spread on a bond issued by a corporation is traditionally measured as the additional return or yield on that bond over a Treasury security with a similar maturity. The spread depends on the probability that the bond will default, and on the cash amount that can be recovered in the event of default. However it is also affected by liquidity factors. The chapter explores the activities of the credit ratings agencies in assessing default risks. It also considers so-called 'risk-neutral' models which can estimate a bond's default probability from its credit spread or vice versa. Next the chapter explores credit derivatives, and in particular credit default swaps (CDS), which allow traders and investors to hedge or speculate on changes in the creditworthiness of entities such as corporations, financial institutions, and sovereign states. It considers the standard CDS structure and how CDS contracts are used to create credit-linked notes. Finally the chapter discusses securitization which is the process by which bonds are created and sold to investors backed by the cash flows generated by a pool of assets. It considers collateralized debt obligations (CDOs) which are bonds sold to investors via a special purpose vehicle (SPV) in different classes or tranches with different risk and return characteristics. The SPV is used to assemble a set of assets which generates the cash to repay the CDOs. The chapter considers cash deals in which the portfolio consists of actual debt assets, and synthetic structures in which the portfolio consists of single-name credit default swaps.

7.2 BASICS OF CREDIT SPREADS

As discussed in Chapter 6, a yield curve is a graph showing the relationship between the time to maturity of bonds of a certain class and the yields or investment returns on those bonds. The US Treasury yield curve establishes what is sometimes referred to as the 'risk-free' return for dollar investments for a range of different maturities. In practice the market does not believe that the level of credit risk on US government debt is zero, especially with longer-dated securities and in extreme market conditions (see Chapter 5). Nevertheless the risk is very low.

It makes sense to construct a yield curve using only US Treasuries because the different securities are all obligations of the US government denominated in the same currency. They differ only in their remaining time to maturity. Chapter 6 discussed the shapes that yield curves can take and the market view that these build in expectations about future interest rates.

If a corporation or a foreign government issues a bond denominated in US dollars then investors normally demand a higher yield on that security compared to the yield on US Treasuries with a similar maturity. This extra return is known as a **credit spread**.

It exists primarily because bond issuers such as corporations may default on their debt obligations. The extent of the credit spread is affected by the probability of default and by how much money is likely to be recovered in the event of default (see section 7.4 below).

A credit spread is often quoted in terms of a number of basis points over the return on a benchmark government bond. For example, if the 10-year US Treasury yields 6% and a corporate bond with the same maturity yields 8% then the credit spread is 200 basis points. In a bank or securities house bonds that pay credit spreads are typically analysed and traded by individuals who specialize in assessing default risk. Major government bonds such as US Treasuries and German Federal bonds are normally dealt with by colleagues who focus primarily on the effects of interest rate changes on bond prices (given the very low likelihood of default).

In developed markets such as the US and Europe the **asset swap spread** may be used as an alternative measure of default risk on debt securities. This is discussed in Chapter 13. In addition, section 7.5 of the current chapter discusses the **credit default swap** market which also provides a market-based assessment of the risk that a borrower will default on its debt.

Default Probability and Recovery Rate

The probability that a borrower will default on its debt is a key determinant of the credit spread. In the case of a corporation it is affected by the health and prospects of the business, its revenues and outgoings, its assets, and the total amount of debt the firm has outstanding. The likelihood of corporate default is influenced by business and economic cycles. In an economic downturn some firms are especially vulnerable. The credit spread is also affected by forecasts of the recovery rate. This measures the cash that debt holders are likely to recover from the borrower in the event of default, through asset sales and other means. It is often expressed as a percentage of the face value of the debt.

Debt securities of corporations and other entities carrying credit risk can be issued in **domestic markets**, in which case they are subject to the control of local regulatory bodies such as the Securities and Exchange Commission (SEC) in the US. They can also be issued in **international markets** in centres such as London. In the latter case they were traditionally called Eurobonds, although to avoid confusion with the new European single currency they are now often known as international bonds. These securities are typically issued via a syndicate of underwriting banks and sold on to international investors. Most still are denominated in US dollars.

International bonds are issued not only by corporations but also by governments and their agencies, by state and regional authorities, by international agencies, and by banks and financial institutions. They may have a **call feature**, such that the issuer can retire the bond early at a specified price and on specified dates. This is a disadvantage to the investor because the issuer will tend to call a bond back when interest rates fall and when it can refinance the debt at a lower rate. The investor should be compensated through a higher yield compared to similar bonds without the call feature. Some bonds have a **put feature** which allows the investor to retire the bond early.

7.3   THE ROLE OF THE RATINGS AGENCIES

Many investors do not have the resources to carry out a detailed credit risk analysis and rely on the work of the ratings agencies. Two of the most important agencies are Standard & Poor's (S&P) and Moody's Investor Services. Borrowers raising funds through the issuance of bonds normally require a credit rating to attract investors, and pay the major ratings agencies to carry out an analysis. In some cases the agencies carry out credit analysis as a service to investors and without a request from the borrower. Their ratings scales are set out in Table 7.1.

The agencies offer **issuer ratings** which are general assessments of the creditworthiness of particular entities. They also rate specific obligations issued by those entities. The same organization can have debt securities on issue with different credit risks because some bonds have a **higher ranking** in the capital structure. This means that they have to be paid before the lower-ranking debt is paid. Some bonds are also secured on specific assets. In a company's capital structure **subordination** refers to the order in which its debt is paid. The order is as follows.

- senior secured debt;
- senior unsecured debt;
- senior subordinated debt;
- subordinated debt.

As discussed further in Chapter 8, debt has to be paid before any payments are made to the equity holders. In legal terms, the equity holders have a **residual claim** on the assets of the firm.

Table 7.1   Credit ratings

Standard & Poor's	Moody's	Quality
AAA	Aaa	Highest quality, extremely strong
AA+	Aa1	
AA	Aa2	High quality, very strong
AA−	Aa3	
A+	A1	
A	A2	Upper medium quality
A−	A3	
BBB+	Baa1	
BBB	Baa2	Medium quality, adequate protection
BBB−	Baa3	
BB+	Ba1	
BB	Ba2	Very moderate protection
BB−	Ba3	
B+	B1	
B	B2	Speculative and vulnerable
B−	B3	
C	C	Highly speculative, major risk of non-payment
D	D	Default

Source: Ratings agencies.

The agency credit ratings range from top quality AAA or Aaa paper to speculative bonds where there is a much higher risk of default. Issues rated BBB− and above are commonly referred to as **investment grade**. Issues below that level are called 'below investment grade' or sometimes 'junk bonds'. In many markets institutional investors such as pension funds are restricted to investment grade paper. Generally, asset management companies use the ratings to help in their allocation decisions and to place restrictions on the structure of a particular fund. For example, limits may be imposed on the percentage of bonds held below an AA rating. Non-rated bonds do exist but tend to be the province of specialist investors.

The credit ratings are not associated with a specific numerical default probability value extracted from a mathematical model. Nor are they associated with specific investment horizons. Essentially what they offer is a ranked assessment of how likely it is that a given entity or debt obligation will default. The ranking means that it is expected that on average the default rate will be greater on lower-rated compared to higher-rated paper. As the next section shows, it is possible to create mathematical models which extract specific implied default probability values from bond credit spreads. However such values change constantly as the market price of a bond changes.

Instead, what the ratings agencies aim to produce are relatively stable indicators of under-lying or 'intrinsic' credit risk. The ratings are intended to offer a practical guide for issuers and investors. If they were constantly changing based on the market price of debt it would be impractical for institutional investors to use them in asset allocation decisions. It would also be more difficult for borrowers and their advisors to assess the rate of interest they have to offer on new debt issues to attract investors. The agencies seek to cope with changes in the circumstances of issuers and in the general business and financial environment by their ratings review procedures and by making disclosures on when specific credit ratings are under review.

The agencies use a structured procedure based on a rating committee. They consider a range of both quantitative *and* qualitative factors in assigning a credit rating, which means that there is a significant element of judgement involved. In the case of corporate debt the key factors considered can include the following:

- **Business Fundamentals.** The nature of the company and the sector; the size, growth, and prof-itability of the business and its competitive position in the market; the business strategy; the quality of management; the extent to which revenues and profits vary across business cycles; vulnerability to technological change; the regulatory environment; and the nature of the countries within which the business operates.
- **Financial Characteristics.** The financial strength of the company; its assets and liabilities; its cash flow generation powers; the amount of debt outstanding; the nature and maturity of that debt; other financial obligations that might affect the business; and contingencies such as legal claims outstanding.

In general, credit analysts tend to place great reliance on the ability or otherwise of a corporation to generate sufficient cash to pay back debt across business cycles. In some circumstances it is possible for a commercial organization to have a higher credit rating than the sovereign state in which it is based, such as when the business owns valuable natural resources. In the case of a financial institution such as a commercial bank, credit analysts assess factors such as the quality of the loan book and the amount of capital set aside to protect against loss. They will also look at the regulatory environment and the countries in which the bank operates.

Bonds that default are labelled 'D' by the agencies. They start to trade in the markets at their assumed recovery rate, that is, the percentage of face value the market thinks can be recovered from the assets of the issuer. There is a market for so-called **distressed debt** which is either in default or close to that level. Buyers hope that the actual recovery rate will be greater than forecast at the time of default or that outright default is avoided.

7.4   CREDIT SPREADS AND DEFAULT PROBABILITIES

Bonds normally trade on a price basis. From the bond price it is possible to calculate the yield, and then the spread over a benchmark government security. Some highly speculative bonds are quoted by dealers directly in terms of the credit spread. As shown below, given an assumption about the recovery rate, it is possible to 'back out' from the credit spread the default probability implied in that spread.

Alternatively, assumptions about the recovery rate and default probability can be used to estimate the 'fair' or theoretical credit spread on a bond. This can then be compared with the actual value in the market. If a bond is trading in the market at a spread that is too high it is cheap. If the market spread is too low the bond is expensive. Its price does not adequately reflect the potential losses from default.

7.4.1   Implied Default Probability: A Simple Model

A corporate bond trading at par yields 6 % p.a. The return on safe Treasuries with the same maturity is 5 % p.a. so the credit spread on the corporate bond is 1 %. This means that investors expect to lose about 1 % each year in principal due to defaults. If the recovery rate was zero the implied default probability would also be about 1 % p.a. However suppose the forecast recovery rate is 40 %. This means that the implied probability of default is rather higher. The following approximation is useful here.

$$\text{Implied Default Probability} \approx \frac{\text{Spread}}{1 - \text{Recovery Rate}} = \frac{0.01}{1 - 0.4} = 1.67\,\% \text{ p.a.}$$

The model is based on the idea that an investor should be indifferent between investing in Treasuries and in risky bonds, on the assumption that the credit spread compensates for the expected losses arising from default. It is what is sometimes called a 'risk-neutral' model rather than one based on actual market data about historical default rates. (The '1' in the formula represents the principal amount that is at risk from default.)

7.4.2   Credit Spreads in Practice

When implied default probabilities on bonds are derived from risk-neutral models it is not unusual to find that they are higher than the actual historical default rates on bonds with similar characteristics, such as the same credit rating and maturity. To put it simply, the market spread can seem 'too high' given the actual levels of default in the past.

One explanation for this phenomenon is that the spread over Treasuries is not only concerned with credit risk. It also reflects liquidity risk. Investors demand a risk premium for holding a bond that is difficult to trade. It is also arguable that models such as the one used above fail to take fully into account the possibility of extreme movements in debt markets which can severely affect market values and increase volatility. In such markets bond prices fall steeply and contagion effects set in, so that default by one entity affects the credit standing of other organizations.

It can also be difficult in practice to find relevant historical data on defaults and recovery rates to compare with the implied default probability for a bond derived from a model. The sample may be small and the average values may be subject to a great deal of variation. Finally, it is not always clear what the risk-free rate used to calculate the credit spread on a bond should be. In practice traders often compare bond yields with the rates on interest rate swaps rather than Treasury yields. Interest rate swaps are discussed in Chapter 13 below.

A risk-neutral model can also be used to derive the 'fair' credit spread for a bond, given assumptions about the probability of default and the recovery rate. Rearranging the formula used above gives the following equation:

$$\text{Fair Credit Spread} \approx \text{Default Probability} \times (1 - \text{Recovery Rate})$$

The fair spread can then be compared with actual credit spreads in the market (making an adjustment for liquidity risk). If it looks like a bond's spread in the market is too high it is a potential 'buy' because the spread exaggerates the likely losses arising from default. Note that the above equation implies that the higher the default probability and the lower the recovery rate the higher the credit spread on a bond should be. These factors increase the expected losses arising from default.

Estimates of the fair credit spread or the implied default probability for a debt security can also be compared with the values used in relevant derivatives markets. Particularly important here are asset swap spreads (see Chapter 13) and the premiums on credit default swap transactions, which are discussed in the next section.

7.5 CREDIT DEFAULT SWAPS

In general terms, a **credit derivative** is a product whose value depends on the creditworthiness of an entity such as a corporation or a sovereign state. Sometimes it is based on a basket of such entities. The most popular product is the **credit default swap** (CDS). According to the International Swaps and Derivatives Association (ISDA) the total notional amount outstanding on CDS contracts reached $62 trillion by the end of 2007. This exceeded the amount of actual debt worldwide. ISDA publishes standard legal terms for CDS contracts.

Definition

A credit default swap is used to transfer credit risk between two parties. The buyer of protection pays a regular premium or spread to the seller of protection. In return, the protection seller makes a contingent payment if the reference entity specified in the contract defaults on its debt. A swap can also be based on a basket of different reference entities. The most common maturity for CDS deals is five years.

In a CDS contract the **reference entity** specifies the corporation or other organization on which protection is bought and sold. The **reference obligation** is a security used to

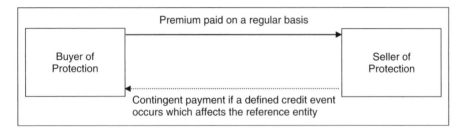

Figure 7.1 Credit default swap.

determine which assets of the reference entity can be delivered against the contract in the event of default; it is normally at the senior unsecured level of the capital structure. A **credit event** is an occurrence defined in the CDS contract that triggers the contingent payment from the protection seller to the protection buyer, such as if the reference entity is declared bankrupt or defaults on certain debt obligations. The protection seller is sometimes said to be 'long the credit risk' because the position is economically equivalent to buying a debt asset which carries credit risk.

Figure 7.1 illustrates the basic structure of a single name CDS. The swap premium (spread) is paid at an agreed rate on a regular basis. The market standard is for quarterly payments made on 20 March, 20 June, 20 September, and 20 December. For example, if the swap notional is $ 10 million and the CDS premium is 2 % p.a. then the quarterly payment is approximately $ 50,000. (More precisely, it is calculated using the actual/360 day-count convention described in Chapter 2.) In effect the premium is the cost of purchasing insurance against default by the reference entity.

At the time of writing (2008) most CDS contracts are **physically settled**. This means that if a credit event occurs the protection buyer has the right to deliver certain debt assets of the reference entity to the protection seller and to be paid their par value. These are called **deliverable obligations**. They can include bonds or loans or other forms of debt. However they must not be subordinated to the reference obligation that is specified in the contract. If the CDS settlement process is triggered the loss to the protection seller is the par value paid for the assets less their recovery value. The CDS premium is paid by the protection buyer up to the date of the credit event.

Some CDS contracts are **cash settled** i.e. if a credit event occurs the protection seller pays the buyer of protection a cash sum. For example, suppose the swap principal is $ 10 million and a credit event occurs. The cheapest available eligible deliverable asset of the reference entity has a recovery value of $ 40 per $ 100 par value. The protection seller compensates the buyer for the loss of face value on the asset, a total of $ 6 million. In some cases CDS contracts are based on a cash settlement amount pre-determined in the contract. This is sometimes called a **binary CDS**. Cash settlement may become more common in future.

A single name CDS is designed to provide protection against the generic default risk on a particular entity. Since CDS contracts are over-the-counter deals (i.e. made directly between two parties) a wide range of credit events could be specified. Certain types of events have become common, although practices differ in different locations.

- **Bankruptcy.** The reference entity becomes insolvent.
- **Failure to Pay.** It fails to pay principal and interest on its debt obligations.

- **Debt Restructuring.** The structure of its debt is changed in a way that affects its creditworthiness e.g. the maturity or coupon is changed.
- **Obligational Acceleration/Default.** It defaults and/or a debt obligation becomes due before the maturity date originally scheduled.
- **Repudiation/Moratorium.** It renounces its debt obligations and refuses to pay.

7.5.1 CDS Applications

Perhaps the most obvious use of a CDS occurs when an investor or a commercial bank buys protection against losses on debt assets such as bonds and loans. In effect, the CDS provides a form of insurance, though at a cost of paying the premium. It is important to be selective here. An investor that covers *all* the default risk on a portfolio of debt securities using CDS contracts will be left with a return close to that on Treasuries (in practice it will probably be rather less than this because of transaction costs).

Credit default swaps are also invaluable for traders and hedge funds. It allows them to take a view on credit spreads narrowing or widening without having to buy or short physical debt securities. A standard CDS is an **unfunded** structure which means that unlike buying a cash bond an investor does not have to make an initial payment.

For example, suppose that a trader thinks that the creditworthiness of a particular reference entity is likely to deteriorate. The trader buys protection on a CDS and pays a premium of (say) 1 % p.a. If the credit risk on the entity does increase the trader will be able to sell protection on the same reference entity and earn a higher level of premium. Alternatively, if a credit event occurs the trader can purchase the reference entity's bonds cheaply in the market, deliver them against the CDS contract, and receive their par value.

CDS contracts can have the additional advantage that they can be highly liquid at certain maturities. CDS contracts also allow traders to take views on default risk over maturities that are not available with the underlying cash bonds. Finally, financial institutions such as insurance companies can earn additional income and also diversify their current activities by selling protection on CDS contracts. The danger is that losses can snowball if the level of defaults rises. The US insurance giant AIG Inc. had to be bailed out by the US government in September 2008 because of losses on CDS and other types of insurance written to protect banks against losses on loans. The US authorities decided to rescue AIG because of the systemic risk to the financial system if it failed to meet its obligations.

7.5.2 CDS Premium and Spreads on Cash Bonds

As mentioned above, selling protection on a CDS is similar to buying a cash bond issued by the reference entity, or 'going long the credit'. The protection seller earns a premium or spread which depends on the default probability and the forecast recovery rate. These are key inputs to pricing a CDS contract.

CDS Premium: A Simple Example

A CDS trader sells protection on a one-year par bond which has a credit spread of 1 %. The forecast recovery rate is 40 %. According to the 'risk-neutral' formula used in the previous section the bond has a roughly 1.67 % chance of default (1 % divided by one minus the recovery rate). If it defaults the trader will have to pay $ 100 par value to the buyer of protection for bonds which will then be worth $ 40. This is a loss of $ 60. The bond has a 98.33 % chance of survival in which case the trader will pay nothing on the CDS. The *expected loss* to the trader is therefore approximately $ 60 × 1.67 % = $ 1 per $ 100 par value or 1 %. The trader should therefore charge a CDS premium of about 1 % to compensate for the expected loss.

In theory, then, the premium on a CDS should be close to the credit spread earned on a position in the underlying cash bond. In practice, however, the picture is complicated by differences between the way that CDS contracts operate compared to investments in cash bonds. For example, the seller of protection in a CDS may receive one of a number of deliverable obligations at the choice of the buyer of protection, who will tend to choose the cheapest. This creates a so-called 'cheapest-to-deliver option' which has value.

Furthermore CDS contracts can be more liquid than cash bonds, especially at standard maturities and with frequently traded names. This will affect the premium at which they trade. In developed markets now 'the tail wags the dog' since CDS spreads are used to determine the prices and yields of the underlying cash bonds.

Another difference is that (as traditionally constructed) CDS contracts carry an additional element of **counterparty risk**. This is because they are made directly between two parties, one of which may fail to perform its duties. For example, if a credit event occurs the seller of protection may be unwilling or unable to proceed with the settlement process.

The threat of this happening, and the potential collapse of the CDS market as a result, was one reason why the US government arranged the $ 85 billion bailout of AIG in September 2008 and the rescue of Bear Stearns. At the time of writing (late 2008) central clearing arrangements for CDS transactions in the US are being created. In the plan this would start with index CDS deals (described in the next section) and later be extended to single-name CDS. Such arrangements would greatly reduce counterparty risk because the central counterparty (CCP) would guarantee delivery and settlement.

7.6 INDEX CREDIT DEFAULT SWAPS

It is also possible to trade an **index** based on CDS premiums. In Europe the key product is the iTraxx Europe index maintained by Markit Group Limited which is based on the CDS premiums on 125 top European investment grade names or reference entities. The names are equally weighted and each comprises 0.8 % of the index. The composition of the index is reviewed or 'rolled' every six months in March and September based on the most actively traded CDS names established through dealer polls. A new series is created based on the particular names specified in that portfolio, which can then be traded in an over-the-counter market.

Suppose at the issue of a given series a trader takes EUR 25 million five-year iTraxx Europe credit exposure in unfunded form from a market maker (i.e. in the form of a CDS transaction). The premium (credit spread) is 100 basis points. This is based on the CDS premiums on the 125 names in the index. The market maker pays the trader 1 % p.a. on a quarterly basis on EUR 25 million for five years. If no credit events occur that affect the names in the index the market maker will pay the premium until maturity. However if a credit event does occur during the five years the trader will have to make a payment to the market maker. In this example it will be:

$$\text{EUR } 25 \text{ million} \times 0.8\% = \text{EUR } 200{,}000$$

In return for this payment the market maker delivers EUR 200,000 par value of deliverable bonds of the reference entity which defaulted. The notional on the CDS index transaction is then reset to EUR 24.8 million. The market maker continues to pay 1% on this value until maturity, unless further credit events occur affecting names in the index. Markit also owns the Markit CDX family of indices, including indices covering North America and emerging markets.

Banks and institutional investors can use an index CDS to hedge the risk on loans and bond portfolios. Traders can use it to speculate on a basket of names as represented by the index components. They can also construct various **spread** or relative value trades in which they buy one index and sell another. It is normally cheaper in terms of transaction costs to trade an index than to buy CDS contracts on the individual names in the index. It is also possible to trade options on CDS indices, otherwise known as **swaptions**. The holder has the right but not the obligation to enter into a CDS contract as the buyer or the seller of protection at a predetermined price.

7.7   BASKET DEFAULT SWAPS

In an nth to default basket swap the payment from the protection seller to the buyer is triggered by the default of the nth reference entity in the basket. The swap then terminates. The protection buyer pays a regular premium to the seller until maturity or until a credit event occurs affecting the nth asset. Contracts can be cash settled or physically settled.

In a **first-to-default** (FTD) deal $n = 1$. The settlement process is triggered by the first credit in the basket to default. For example, suppose a trader sells protection on an FTD basket of five corporations. The principal is $10 million and the maturity is five years. The protection buyer pays a premium of 200 bps or 2% p.a. If one of the names defaults the protection seller has to take delivery of $10 million par value of bonds issued by that name and pay the par value to the buyer of protection. The FTD deal then terminates. The premium is paid by the buyer of protection up to termination or maturity, whichever is the sooner. The deal is illustrated in Figure 7.2.

Establishing the premium on an FTD swap is a complex matter and requires the use of a mathematical model. Some aspects are more straightforward than others. For example,

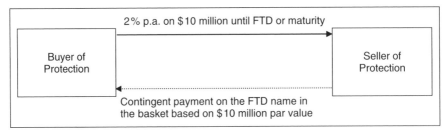

Figure 7.2   FTD credit default swap.

other things being equal the premium will tend to increase the greater the number of names in the basket and the lower their credit quality. The more names that are included, the more likely it is that one will default over the life of the FTD deal. However pricing an FTD also requires an assumption about the so-called **default correlation** between the various assets in the basket. This measures their tendency to default together and to survive together. The broad effects are as follows.

- **Default Correlation is High.** The protection seller in an FTD takes much the same risk as on a CDS on the riskiest name in the basket. This means that the premium on the FTD should be close to the premium on a CDS on that name. If it survives it is highly likely that the other names in the basket will also survive.
- **Default Correlation is Low.** The names in the FTD basket are largely independent of each other in terms of their tendency to default and each poses distinctive risks for the protection seller. This means that the premium on the FTD should be close to the sum of the premiums on CDS contracts on the individual names in the basket.

Intuitively, default (and survival) correlation can be thought of as reflecting the business and economic factors that affect a reference entity. Names with low default correlation pose distinctive credit risks because default is affected by different factors. Names with high default correlation pose similar risks. If the riskiest survives the others are also likely to survive. Note that the market convention is not to use the term 'negative correlation'. Instead the market refers to low, medium, and high correlation.

Because default correlation assumptions are so important in pricing basket CDS contracts (and subject to so much debate) these products are often considered as vehicles for taking a view on correlation. The **implied correlation** on a product such as an FTD can be 'backed out' from its current market premium using a pricing model. If a trader thinks that the market implied correlation is too high he or she can buy FTD protection at a relatively low premium. Then if correlation assumptions fall in the market (other things being equal) the FTD premium will increase.

In a **second-to-default** (STD) basket default swap $n = 2$. Nothing is paid for the first credit event. Then the deal becomes an FTD on the remaining names in the basket. In an STD high default correlation actually tends to *increase* the risk to the seller of protection, because if one entity defaults another is likely to follow suit. This increases the premium. By contrast, low default correlation tends to reduce the STD premium because the names in the basket are less likely to default together. Intuitively, they are affected by different market factors.

7.8   CREDIT-LINKED NOTES

A credit-linked note (CLN) is a debt security which contains an embedded credit derivative. They can be attractive to investors who cannot trade credit derivatives directly or who have restricted access to certain debt assets e.g. in emerging markets.

Figure 7.3 illustrates a credit default linked note issued by a bank on a specific reference asset. Unlike a credit default swap, this is a **funded structure**, which means that an investor who buys the CLN pays par at the outset to the issuer. The issuer uses this payment to buy the underlying asset. The investor earns an enhanced coupon on the CLN and this continues until maturity provided the asset does not default. However if it does default the CLN terminates early. The investor is paid the par value of the note less the loss on the

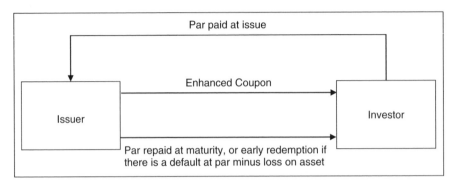

Figure 7.3   Credit default linked note.

underlying asset. In effect the investor is selling protection on a CDS to earn an enhanced return.

One variant on the CLN structure is a **first-to-default note** on a basket of names. The investor earns an enhanced coupon as before. However if any one of the reference entities defaults the note terminates and the investor is paid par minus the loss on the defaulting asset. The default correlation between the entities in the basket has an effect here. The lower the default correlation, the greater the risk to the investor that one of the entities will default. The investor should be compensated for this with a higher yield on the note.

7.9   SECURITIZATION AND CDOs

One of the most significant developments in the capital markets in recent years has been the growth of **securitization**. Essentially it is the process by which bonds are created from future cash flow streams.

Mortgage-backed securities (MBS) are based on a pool of mortgage loans. The bonds may be simply **pass-through** structures, which means that the cash flows from the loans are passed through on a pro-rata basis to make the principal and interest payments to the bondholders. Or different classes of bonds may be created with different characteristics. For example, IO (interest only) bonds are paid from the interest cash flows from the mortgage pool while PO (principal only) bonds are paid from the principal redemption cash flows.

A **collateralized debt obligation** (CDO) is a bond that is created and sold to investors by a Special Purpose Vehicle (SPV) set up by a financial institution such as an investment bank which acts as the deal structurer. The SPV is used to assemble a pool of loans or debt securities and to sell securities to investors backed by the cash flows generated by the asset pool. Three or more different classes or **tranches** or securities are sold which have different risk and return characteristics. The least secure class (known as the equity tranche) takes the first loss if any of the loans or debt securities in the asset pool suffer from default. The middle or mezzanine tranches suffer the next losses. The senior tranche is the most secure and is designed to be safe unless the pool of assets suffers severe losses. Depending on the nature of the underlying assets in the pool a CDO may be called a Collateralized Loan Obligation (CLO) or a Collateralized Bond Obligation (CBO).

The basic CDO structure is illustrated in Figure 7.4, although in practice there are many variations. The SPV is a tax-exempt trust or company which raises capital by selling CDOs

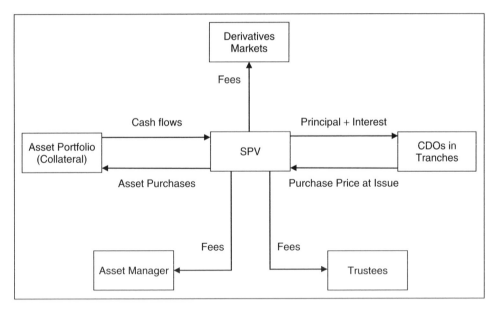

Figure 7.4   CDO Structure.

and which buys the collateral or asset portfolio. This may be a **static** asset pool, in which case the SPV effectively acts as a conduit to collect the cash flows and make the agreed payments to the CDO holders. In other cases the portfolio is **actively managed** within set guidelines, in which case an asset manager is appointed to make investment decisions. The interest rate and currency risks on the portfolio are managed using a range of derivative products. The **trustees** have a safekeeping duty to ensure that the assets are protected and maintained for the benefit of the CDO investors.

The process of creating different tranches is a **credit enhancement** feature. It means that the senior tranche can obtain the highest rating (AAA) because the more junior tranches suffer the first losses and are also paid after the senior tranche. The system of payments in a CDO structure is sometimes called the cash flow **waterfall**. The tranches are paid in sequence out of the cash flows from the collateral, from the highest to the lowest ranking, with the equity tranche paid last. Other credit enhancement techniques include over-collateralization (excess assets are added to the collateral pool) and obtaining guarantees from a third party organization such as an insurance company to make good any shortfalls on the cash flows from the collateral.

The senior tranche in a CDO structure is the largest. The bonds pay the lowest coupons, but they are also intended to have the lowest risk to investors. They are generally intended to be attractive to institutional investors such as insurance companies. The middle or mezzanine tranches are sold to investors who are prepared to take on more default risk for a higher yield. The equity tranche is the most subordinated and has the highest default risk. It may be attractive to more speculative investors such as hedge funds. One of the key features of a CDO is that its value depends entirely on the performance of the asset pool and not on that of the creditworthiness of the entity or entities that originally created the assets (such as a commercial bank).

7.10   RATIONALE FOR SECURITIZATION

Some CDO structures are what is known as **balance sheet CDOs**. If a bank originates a loan portfolio and retains the assets on its balance sheet it is required by the regulators to set aside capital against potential losses. However the bank can sell the assets to an SPV which funds the purchase by issuing CDOs. The bank reduces its credit risk and the amount of capital it has to hold against this risk. It also frees up cash which it can use to create further loans. In some cases it may be able to sell off non-performing loans. The investors in the CDOs gain an exposure to loan portfolios which they could not access directly. At the time of writing (late 2008) regulators are debating whether the ability of banks to move loan assets off their balance sheets should be curtailed.

Most CDO structures are in fact what is known as **arbitrage CDOs**. These are assembled by a sponsor which arranges the purchase, restructuring, and management of a portfolio of bonds or loans. Normally certain rules are set specifying the overall composition of the portfolio. The sponsor may be a fund management business or a bank. It can seek to profit by making more money on the asset portfolio than it pays out on the CDOs. Alternatively, the sponsor may just take a management fee. In some cases the individual assets in the portfolio may be illiquid or unattractive to investors by themselves (and hence cheap to purchase). However by pooling them together the sponsor may be able to create CDOs in different tranches that appeal to various classes of investors.

Bowie Bonds

Since the 1990s banks have created many new types of securitization deals. Bonds have been issued based on the cash flows from credit card and auto loans, trade receivables, commercial banking loans, even unpaid tax due to the Italian government. As long as a reasonably predictable stream of future cash flows could be isolated it seemed that bonds could be sold and funds raised from investors against the projected cash flows. In 1997 the so-called Bowie bonds took the market into a new sphere. $55 million was raised by selling 7.9% coupon bonds against the future royalties due to the rock singer David Bowie from 25 albums.

At the time of writing (in late 2008) it remains to be seen whether the regulators decide to tighten up on CDO issuance and on the market for securitized debt in general. In the 'credit crunch', which started in 2007 and which accelerated in 2008, financial institutions were left holding what became known as 'toxic assets', especially securities backed by failing US mortgage loans. The 'toxic assets' became illiquid, so that it was impossible to establish their fair value and the extent of the losses suffered by investors. Major financial institutions failed due to their exposure to the bad debt as well as their inability to secure funding in the money markets. In September 2008 the US government was forced to nationalize two giant government-sponsored firms Fannie Mae (FNMA) and Freddie Mac (FHLMC) which issue and guarantee mortgage-backed securities.

7.11   SYNTHETIC CDOs

In a synthetic CDO structure the collateral is a portfolio of single name credit default swaps rather than loans or bonds. The arranging or sponsoring organization (typically a bank) enters into a set of CDS contracts with the SPV which sells credit protection and receives

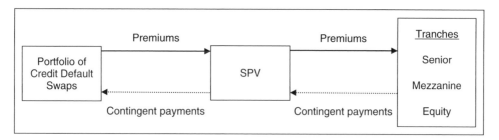

Figure 7.5   Synthetic CDO structure.

the CDS premiums. The premiums are passed over to the CDO investors, who assume credit risk on the names in the portfolio of CDS contracts. If different tranches of CDOs are issued, the lowest ranking classes suffer the first losses on the swap portfolio.

Individual tranches can be in unfunded form, which means that the investors are simply paid their share of the premiums from the CDS portfolio. Or they can be in funded form, like a credit-linked note: the investors pay par at the outset and earn an enhanced return, including their share of the premiums, but risk losing some or all of their capital if defaults occur on the names in the portfolio of CDS contracts. Many variants have been developed but Figure 7.5 illustrates a very simple example of a synthetic CDO structure.

For example, suppose the underlying portfolio consists of 100 credit default swaps each on $10 million notional. The total notional is therefore $1 billion. The (unrated) equity tranche assumes the first 3% or $30 million of losses. It is paid a high premium. The mezzanine tranche is rated BBB and suffers the next $70 million of losses. It is paid a lower premium. The AAA-rated senior tranche on the remaining $900 million takes the remaining losses and is paid the lowest premium. In theory this tranche is very safe because it would only be affected by a very high level of defaults. If the average recovery rate on the names in the portfolio is one third then the senior tranche is protected against 15 defaults in the CDS portfolio.

$$\text{Loss on Portfolio from 15 Defaults} = 15 \times \$10 \text{ million} \times \frac{2}{3} = \$100 \text{ million}$$

The portfolio of CDS may be static or it may be actively managed by an asset manager to maximize the returns.

There may be as many as seven tranches in a deal. If the senior tranche is rated AAA and if the portfolio could suffer several defaults before it is affected it may be called **super senior**. The next tranche down may then be called the senior tranche.

By contrast **single tranche CDOs** are customized deals arranged between a bank and a client. The two parties agree on the nature of the CDS portfolio and the level of subordination the investor will take e.g. at the mezzanine level. The advantage for the investor is that it can take exactly the type and level of credit risk exposure it wants. The advantage for the arranging bank is that it does not have to find investors willing to buy all the tranches.

As with cash securitization deals (based on portfolios of real bonds and loans) there has been much innovation in the synthetic securitization business. One example is the complex so-called **CDO-squared** structures which are based on a portfolio of other CDOs, and which can only be priced by using a set of assumptions which may break down in difficult market conditions. Some of the more exotic structures are likely to disappear as markets and regulators and political legislators learn more about the risks involved, not only to the investors but also to the financial markets as a whole.

7.12 CHAPTER SUMMARY

In developed markets such as the US the return on Treasury securities is traditionally used as the benchmark to measure the additional return paid on a debt security such as a corporate bond that carries an additional degree of credit risk. This is called a credit spread. It depends on the probability that the risky bond will default and on the rate at which money can be recovered in the event of default. However it is also influenced by other factors such as liquidity. The ratings agencies assess the default risk on borrowers and on individual debt securities issued by borrowers. The same organization can have different bonds on issue with different credit ratings because the higher-ranking debt has to be paid before the subordinated debt. The ratings agencies aim to produce a judgement about the underlying creditworthiness of an entity using a mix of qualitative and quantitative information. It is also possible to use a mathematical model to estimate the probability that a given bond will default based on its credit spread (or vice versa) given an assumption about the recovery rate.

A credit derivative is a product whose value depends on the creditworthiness of a particular entity or name such as a corporation or a financial institution or a sovereign state, or a basket of such entities. The most commonly traded structure is the credit default swap (CDS). In a standard single-name CDS the buyer of protection pays a regular premium to the seller of protection. In return, if a defined credit event affects the name referenced in the contract the protection seller has to make a payment to the protection buyer. The contract can be settled through the physical delivery of debt assets or in cash. CDS contracts can also be based on an index or basket of names. They can be used to construct credit-linked notes in which the investor earns an enhanced yield in return for assuming credit risk. In general terms, securitization is the process in which bonds are sold to investors who are repaid from the cash flows generated by a pool or portfolio of assets. The underlying portfolio (also known as the collateral) can be static or it can be actively managed. A collateralized debt obligation (CDO) is a bond issued via a special purpose vehicle (SPV) which is a company or trust set up by an arranging financial institution. The SPV buys a portfolio of assets such as bonds or loans and uses the cash flows these generate to pay interest and principal on the CDOs. Normally different classes or tranches of CDOs are issued with different risk and return characteristics. The high-risk equity tranche takes the first losses arising from any defaults in the underlying portfolio. The senior tranche is only affected if a number of defaults occur, but it pays the lowest return compared to the other tranches. In a synthetic securitization the asset pool consists of a portfolio of credit default swaps rather than actual bonds or loans. Huge losses on CDOs in the 'credit crunch' starting in 2007 prompted intense debate on the future regulation of the market.

8

Equity Markets and Equity Investment

8.1 CHAPTER OVERVIEW

Previous chapters have explored short and long-term debt securities. This chapter sets the scene for later material by reviewing the operations of equity markets. It considers the differences between debt and equity securities for corporate issuers and for investors. One of the most hotly debated subjects in finance is the extent to which markets are efficient. The practical implications of this debate for share traders and investors are assessed. Equity portfolio investment is discussed, as well as the theory and the practice of portfolio diversification. The chapter considers the key stages of an initial public offering (IPO) of new shares and looks at how further shares are issued through general cash offers or rights issues. Unlike bond markets, most share trading around the world is conducted on organized stock exchanges. The chapter looks at quote-driven markets based on dealers, and order-driven markets in which buy and sell orders are directly matched. Market operations are illustrated by considering a number of major organizations such as the New York Stock Exchange and the London Stock Exchange. The remaining sections of the chapter explore the markets for depository receipts, stock borrowing and lending, and portfolio trading.

8.2 COMPARING CORPORATE DEBT AND EQUITY

Most companies are funded through a mixture of debt capital and equity capital. Debt is provided by commercial banks in the form of loans, or by investors who buy commercial paper and bonds issued by the company, or by trade suppliers who offer terms of credit. Equity capital is provided by the company's common stockholders (known in the UK as ordinary shareholders) who are part-owners of the business. As discussed in section 8.4 below, preferred stock is sometimes also classified as a form of equity, although it is actually a hybrid form of investment. In this chapter the focus is on common stock, also referred to simply as 'shares'.

8.2.1 Features of Standard or 'Straight' Corporate Debt

- The lenders normally demand lower returns than the common stockholders.
- This is because the debt is a lower risk – the company has a legal obligation to repay interest and the loan principal. It does not have to pay dividends on common stock.
- Debt may be secured on assets such as land and property, further reducing risk to the lenders.
- A company with a substantial proportion of debt is said to have **high leverage** (US) or gearing (UK). Leverage is a double-edged sword. If a company borrows money and uses it effectively it will have more than enough funds to pay the interest, and the profits accrue to the shareholders. If the company performs badly it still has to pay the interest. Increased leverage increases the risk of **financial distress** – action by creditors to recover money owed, or outright bankruptcy.
- In most countries companies can offset interest payments against their tax liabilities thereby reducing their effective cost of debt; this is not the case with the dividends paid on shares.

- There are limits to how much debt a company can raise – either imposed by the existing creditors through legal covenants or by the capital markets which will stop lending beyond a certain level as the risk of financial distress increases.

8.2.2   Features of Common Stock (Ordinary Shares)

- The holders – known as common stockholders in the US and ordinary shareholders in the UK – are part-owners of the business and (usually) have voting rights.
- Common stock is **risk capital**. The owners have the lowest ranking in the capital structure of the company, which means that other investors must be paid out first. Common stockholders have a residual claim on the assets of a firm – if a company is put into liquidation they are paid last.
- A company is not obliged to pay dividends on its common stock. It must pay interest (though in extreme circumstances it may try to obtain the agreement of creditors to suspend payments for a period of time).
- Common stockholders benefit from the growth in the value of the company through an increasing share price and/or a rising dividend stream.
- Common stock is normally more expensive for a company to service than debt, because investors demand higher returns to compensate for higher risk (and also because dividend payments are not tax deductible). On the other hand if it gets into difficulties, a company can cut or miss a dividend payment.
- New start-up companies are often funded largely through common stock since shareholders are prepared to wait for their return on capital, perhaps by selling their stake later on in a public offering.
- Some companies have a class of non-voting shares. This means that control over business direction is maintained by the voting shares, which in turn often trade at a premium to the non-voting shares. The purpose of a dual-class share structure may be to ensure stability over strategy and to make the company more difficult to acquire in a takeover. Critics who believe in shareholder democracy argue that it creates 'second class' investors lacking a voice.

8.2.3   Limited Liability

A limited company is defined in law as a 'legal person' separate from the shareholders who own the company. The company can enter contracts and litigate in its own right. The shareholders have the advantage of limited liability. If the company fails, the most they can lose is their equity stakes. Shareholders are not liable to further compensate the company's creditors out of their own personal resources (although the directors may be subject to personal action for wrongdoing or negligence).

8.3   ADDITIONAL FEATURES OF COMMON STOCK

When shares are first issued they may be given a nominal or par value. However, the market value of most common stock bears no relationship to the nominal value. The **market capitalization** of a company is the total value of its shares on the market:

$$\text{Market Capitalization} = \text{Common Stock Outstanding} \times \text{Current Share Price}$$

In practice, stock market analysts often calculate market capitalization on a **fully diluted** basis. This means that they take into account the shares that have actually been issued but also those that would be created through, for example, the exercise of stock options and convertible bonds.

8.3.1 Share Capital

A share may be partly paid. When it was issued a proportion of the price was paid to the company, which has the right to call in the remainder from the shareholder on a set date or dates. In the UK, publicly-owned firms have often been privatized through share issues in which the price was payable in a number of instalments. In its memorandum of association (UK) or articles of incorporation (US) a firm sets out its authorized share capital, the amount of common stock it may issue (though it can seek approval from shareholders to increase the amount).

8.3.2 Dividends on Common Stock

Cash dividends may be paid annually, or in two six-monthly instalments, or quarterly. When a share is trading **ex-dividend** (xd) the buyer is not entitled to receive the next dividend payment – it will go to the seller. A share 'goes xd' a week or so before the dividend payment. During this period it would be difficult for the company to change the share register in time to reflect the new ownership. On the xd date the market price of the stock will drop by approximately the amount of the forthcoming dividend. A share bought cum-dividend carries entitlement to the next dividend payment. Most dividends are paid in cash. In a **stock dividend** the payment is made in the form of additional shares.

8.4 HYBRID SECURITIES

Some securities are 'hybrids', sharing some of the characteristics of debt and of equity. They are designed to appeal to different categories of investors.

- **Preferred Stock (Preference Shares in the UK).** The dividend (normally fixed) is paid before dividends are paid to the common stockholders. 'Prefs' have no maturity date and rank above common stock in the event of liquidation, but do not carry voting rights.
- **Cumulative Preferred Stock.** If the dividend is not paid one year, it must be paid in the following year or whenever the company generates sufficient profits. The arrears must be paid off before any dividend is paid on the common stock or on other preferred stock with a lower ranking.
- **Convertible Preferred Stock.** Preferred stock that can be converted into common stock. Before conversion it is lower risk than the common stock because it has higher ranking and (normally) pays a fixed dividend.
- **Convertible Bond (CB).** A bond that can be converted into (normally) a fixed amount of common stock at the option of the holder on or before a fixed date. CBs are considered in Chapter 20.

Technically, preferred stock can be classified as a form of equity because it is a residual claim – the holders are paid after the debt (though before the common stockholders). However for valuation purposes it is better to treat preferred stock that pays a fixed dividend as a type of fixed-income debt security. The following sections focus solely on investments in common stock.

8.5 EQUITY INVESTMENT STYLES

Shares are bought by individual investors, corporations, and governments and by large investing institutions such as pension funds, insurance companies, and mutual funds. Mutual funds are collective investment vehicles which may invest in shares, bonds, and other assets. The portfolios of assets are run by professional managers for a fee. Chapter 1 has further information on institutional investors and the services provided to them by investment banks.

Fund managers are sometimes called the 'buy side' of the market. Securities trading and broking operations are the 'sell side'. Traditional fund managers such as those managing the assets of pension funds are said to run **long-only** funds. This means that unlike hedge funds (see Chapter 1) they do not run short positions. There are two principal approaches to running a 'long-only' fund: passive style and active style management.

- **Passive Management.** The fund manager seeks to track a benchmark index. These are also known as index tracker funds. Because it can be expensive in terms of transaction costs to buy all the shares in the index the manager may use a 'sampling' methodology and buy a subset of the shares. If so, the manager runs the risk of making a tracking error.
- **Active Management.** The fund manager seeks to outperform a benchmark index. This could be a country-specific index such as the S&P 500 in the US; or a global benchmark such as the MSCI World Index. The index normally represents a highly diversified portfolio of securities.

Outperforming a benchmark index, adjusted for risk, is sometimes known as 'generating positive alpha'. (The concept of alpha is discussed in Chapter 10.) Active managers use a wide variety of investment styles to try to achieve this task. Two widely used approaches are growth investment and value investment.

- **Growth Investment.** Buying shares in high-growth businesses such as TMTs (technology, media, and telecommunications companies) and companies whose growth prospects are reckoned to be under-estimated by the market. Profits are realized primarily through capital gains on the stock.
- **Value Investment.** Buying shares in companies that are reckoned to be undervalued by the market, perhaps because they have recently suffered from a downturn in business or operate in an un-fashionable sector of the economy. Profits are realized through capital gains and/or high dividends.

On top of this, many fund managers place a great deal of emphasis on their **asset allocation** process. In this system the fund is typically apportioned between different asset classes (e.g. bonds, shares, cash), different geographical locations (e.g. the US, Europe, the Far East), and different business sectors (e.g. pharmaceuticals, manufacturing, retail). After the allocation process is completed, decisions are taken on which securities in each category to buy. In a **tactical asset allocation** approach the weightings are adjusted from time to time in line with economic and market forecasts.

Tactical Asset Allocation Example

The asset allocation committee of a global equity fund decides to 'go overweight' the US equity market for the next quarter. The benchmark weighting is currently 40% i.e. the US equity market is currently 40% by market capitalization of the global index. The committee increases the proportion of the fund's assets to be invested in US shares to 50%. The actual decisions on which stocks to buy are taken by the team of fund managers that specializes in US equities.

A fund management firm that operates an asset allocation process is sometimes said to use a **top-down** methodology. By contrast, a **bottom-up** fund manager starts with individual stock selections and builds the fund up from there. The essence of successful asset allocation is timing. Top-down funds that use tactical asset allocation seek to add value by being in the right market at the right time as well as picking the right stocks. They often tend to take a **contrarian** approach. That is to say, they tend to buy after a market has declined and may be undervalued. They tend to sell when a market is felt to have reached a peak and may be overvalued.

In recent years asset allocators have favoured a range of alternative investment assets in addition to the traditional mix of shares, bonds, and cash. This includes investments in commodities, property, hedge funds and also in private equity funds which buy stakes in unlisted companies and seek to achieve high levels of capital growth. Private equity funds typically look to sell on their stakes within a three to five-year time horizon, through an initial public offering, or by selling their shares on to another investor, or through a trade sale of the whole company to a large corporation.

Chinese Walls

Fund management businesses that form part of a larger banking group must be separated from the rest of the bank by a so-called Chinese Wall. This is a set of arrangements to ensure that the fund managers act on behalf of their investing clients and that their decisions are not influenced by any of the other activities of the parent bank (in particular, the broking, trading, and new issuance operations).

8.6 EFFICIENT MARKETS

In part the movement towards passive or index-tracking funds in the US and Europe has been fuelled by an increasing recognition that it is very difficult to outperform the market benchmark on a consistent basis. Even when it seems that an active fund has outperformed for a number of years this may be no more than a random result. In fact, there is a tendency for funds that have outperformed in recent times to underperform over the next few years – which may simply be because their long-term performance is reverting to the market average, or because a style of investment that works well in one set of market conditions works less well when circumstances change.

The argument about the merits or otherwise of active portfolio management turns on whether or not capital markets are **efficient**, and if so how efficient. Broadly speaking, an efficient stockmarket is one in which information is already fully reflected in share prices. E.F. Fama and others have categorized three levels of market efficiency.

- **Weak Form.** The past history of the shares is fully reflected in current prices.
- **Semi-strong Form.** All publicly available information is already reflected in share prices.
- **Strong Form.** All information including information that is not publicly available is already reflected in share prices.

This is one of the most controversial topics in finance, and one where the opinions of market practitioners and academics have tended to diverge sharply in the past. If a share price reflects all available information then the only thing that will move the price is some new piece of information. By definition this is unknowable; it could equally well be 'good news' or 'bad news' for the share. Therefore the next movement in the share price is random and there is nothing we can do with the existing information we have available to predict that movement with any accuracy. Share prices will follow a so-called **random walk**.

8.6.1   Practical Consequences

There are real-world implications of the efficient markets debate.

- **Technical Analysis.** If share prices follow a random path then it is not possible to predict future price movements efficiently by analysing historical data. Many traders believe that there are clearly discernable patterns in historical share price charts that will recur in the future. Exploring such patterns is known as technical analysis or 'chartism' in the finance markets.
- **Fundamental Analysis.** If a market is semi-strong efficient then it should not be possible to identify on a consistent, non-random basis stocks that are under- or overpriced through the analysis of financial statements or any publicly available information. All of this information should already be built into the current share price. In practice stock analysts and active investment managers do believe that they can find shares that are trading on prices that do not accurately reflect 'the fundamentals' – perhaps because of panic selling, or over-exuberant buying.
- **Insider Dealing.** If the strong form theory were true then even inside traders could not profit from their activities. The information they have is already reflected in the share price.

8.6.2   Research on Market Efficiency

Few if any people believe in strong form efficiency. But even if the semi-strong form is true it should be impossible to develop a technique that would consistently outperform a market index such as the Dow-Jones Industrial Average in the US or the FT-SE 100 in the UK. A strategy that involves picking potential 'winners' and 'losers' from amongst the constituent shares could succeed for a time through sheer good luck.

Research is focusing these days on exactly *how efficient* different types of market are. It may be that the prices of major blue-chips more-or-less accurately reflect all available information, but it is far less certain that this is the case with smaller capitalization companies. If this is true then there are implications for how funds are operated. The proportion of the fund earmarked to buy large blue-chips should perhaps be put into a tracker fund with transaction costs kept to a minimum. The proportion allocated to 'small cap' companies should be given to an active fund manager who can exploit market efficiencies and 'beat the index'. There has been a trend in this direction, especially in the US, although some commentators argue that active managers of blue-chip funds will come back into their own in a falling market when tracker funds are by definition losing money.

Market Bubbles

One reason why financial markets may not be entirely efficient is the possibility that 'bubbles' may appear, in which the share prices of certain companies reach extravagant levels unsupported by fundamentals. The 'dot-com' bubble, which burst in 2000, saw shares in some web-based retailers rise to levels that could not be sustained by credible sales and profitability forecasts. Some people argue that it may not be entirely irrational to knowingly participate in a bubble market. The so-called 'bigger fool' investment strategy involves buying shares not because they are believed to be worth the price but because it is thought that they can be sold on at a profit to someone else before the inevitable collapse occurs. This is obviously very risky, however, and is based on a conviction that the investor has some special insight into market timing and on when bubbles are likely to deflate. In practice, the collapse may be triggered by some entirely random and unpredictable piece of bad news, which is then followed by panic selling.

8.7   MODERN PORTFOLIO THEORY (MPT)

Portfolio management is based on the basic insight that risks can be reduced by investing in a diversified pool of assets. In an article in the *Journal of Finance* in 1952 Harry Markowitz found a way to quantify this concept. The basic proposition is that a rational investor will only take on additional risk if he or she is compensated by additional return. Markowitz suggested that the riskiness of an asset can be measured as the standard deviation of the expected returns on the asset. (Standard deviation is a statistical measure of the extent to which a set of values deviates from the average or mean value.) Furthermore, it is possible to reduce the risk (standard deviation) of a portfolio by choosing stocks that do not exactly move in line with each other. This is the diversification effect. As a result, it is necessary to analyse investments according to their contribution to the risk and return on a portfolio of assets rather than in isolation.

To see how Markowitz diversification works, consider two shares A and B. Based on historical experience we believe that the expected return on stock A over a given time horizon is 20%. The expected return on stock B over the same horizon is 25%. However, also based on historical experience, it is believed that the returns on stock A have a standard deviation of 30% while those on B have a standard deviation of 35%. These values are shown in Table 8.1 below. The symbol σ is conventionally used to mean standard deviation. Variance is an alternative measure of dispersion and is calculated as standard deviation squared (σ^2).

Suppose a portfolio consists of 70% of stock A and 30% of stock B. The return on the portfolio is just a weighted average.

$$\text{Portfolio Return} = (20 \times 0.7) + (25 \times 0.3) = 21.5\%$$

The weighted average risk is also easy to calculate.

$$\text{Weighted Average Risk} = (30 \times 0.7) + (35 \times 0.3) = 31.5\%$$

Table 8.1   Expected return and risk values for two shares A and B

Stock	A	B
Return (%)	20	25
Risk σ (%)	30	35
Variance σ^2	900	1225

However this ignores the diversification effect, assuming that the two shares do not exactly move in line with each other. For example, there will be cases where stock A falls in value but stock B rises. This reduces the portfolio diversified risk. Suppose that based on historical experience we believe that the correlation between the returns on the two stocks is +0.4. This means that there is some positive correlation between movements in the two stock prices, but it is not perfect, so that there will still be occasions when one stock falls in value and the other rises, or falls by less. (Perfect positive correlation would be +1 and would mean that the prices of the two stocks always rose and fell in complete alignment with each other.) Using the Markowitz approach, taking into account the diversification effect, variance and risk are calculated as follows.

$$\text{Portfolio Variance } \sigma^2 = (30 \times 0.7)^2 + (35 \times 0.3)^2 + (2 \times 30 \times 0.7 \times 35 \times 0.3$$

$$\times \, 0.4) = 727.65$$

$$\text{Portfolio Diversified Risk } \sigma = \sqrt[2]{727.65} = 26.97\,\%$$

This means that the 70:30 portfolio has a higher return than stock A on its own (21.5 % as against 20 %). In addition, it also has a lower risk compared to stock A on its own (26.97 % as against 30 %).

Figure 8.1 graphs the relationship between risk and return for a range of portfolios consisting of different proportions of stock A and stock B, assuming that the correlation factor is kept constant at +0.4. A portfolio consisting of 100 % of stock A has a risk of 30 % and a return of 20 %. A portfolio of 100 % of stock B has a risk of 35 % and a return of 25 %. In between, different mixes of stocks A and B produce different risk and return values.

Figure 8.1 shows that, up to a point, by progressively adding stock B to a portfolio consisting solely of stock A returns can be enhanced whilst also reducing overall risk. However beyond a certain level, in order to keep enhancing return, it is necessary to take on more risk, in this case by adding more and more of stock B to the portfolio.

Next, Figure 8.2 shows the effects on portfolio risk of changing the correlation assumption. This is based on a portfolio consisting of 70 % of stock A and 30 % of stock B. It shows

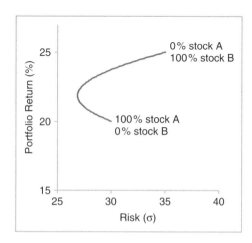

Figure 8.1   Risk-return relationship for different proportions of two shares.

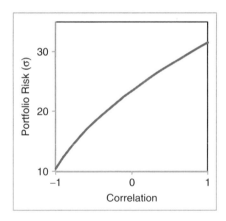

Figure 8.2   Diversification gains from lower levels of correlation.

that the less highly positively correlated the assets are, the lower the portfolio risk – in other words, the greater the diversification benefit.

8.7.1   Developments with Portfolio Theory

In practice, it is unlikely that an investor will have only two stocks in a portfolio. By choosing more and more stocks it is possible to further enhance risk and reduce return. Taking this approach, Markowitz described what he called **efficient portfolios**. These are diversified portfolios which produce the maximum return for any given level of risk that is selected. It would be irrational to construct a portfolio that is less than efficient because an alternative could produce higher returns for the risks assumed (or lower risks for the expected returns).

Further developments in MPT, building on Markowitz, depend on additional assumptions made in the Capital Asset Pricing Model (CAPM) which is discussed in Chapter 10. Based on such assumptions it can be shown that the best risk-return profiles can be generated by investing in a mix of a risk-free asset (such as a Treasury bill) and a holding in a highly diversified market portfolio. If an investor wishes to take zero risk he or she should invest 100 % in the risk-free asset. To assume the overall level of risk in the market the investor should put 100 % into a market portfolio. To take on additional risk still, the investors should borrow money and invest over 100 % in a market portfolio.

One of the problems with the Markowitz framework is the assumption that investors share the same expectations on the returns and risks on an asset. It is also assumed that the standard deviation measure can be used as a proxy for risk. In practice, it may fail to take into account extreme circumstances in which the losses on risky assets such as shares and loans are exaggerated, perhaps through market panics or liquidity crises. In statistical terms, the chances of large losses may be greater than those that can be captured using a model based on the standard 'bell curve' or normal distribution.

In addition, it cannot be assumed that portfolio diversification will work effectively in all market conditions. In extreme circumstances, such as market crashes, the correlation between the movements in asset prices often tends toward one – in other words they all move in the same direction (downwards) and at more or less at the same rate. Finally, MPT assumes that there is a risk-free asset with a standard deviation of zero. In practice, there is some dispute over what this asset should be taken to be. Some analysts use short-dated Treasury bills, whilst others use longer-dated Treasury bonds.

8.8   PRIMARY MARKETS FOR COMMON STOCK

A **primary market** is one in which securities are sold to investors for the first time. A **secondary market** is one in which existing securities are traded (such as a stock exchange).

An initial public offering (IPO) is a first offer to sell shares in a company to the investing public. The stock may be existing shares owned by the founders of the business who wish to realize profits from their investment, or new shares issued to raise additional capital for the company. Often it is both at the same time. The company is normally advised by an investment bank. The business unit that works on IPOs and other new share issues in an investment banking operation is normally known as the **Equity Capital Markets** (ECM) group.

8.8.1   Issuance Methods

Perhaps the simplest way for a company to issue shares would be to fix a price and offer them to potential investors at that price. If there is uncertainty about the pricing, the shares might be auctioned (in the UK this is called a **tender issue**). The danger with a fixed price offer is that the price may be set too high (there is insufficient demand) or too low (the company raises less money than it should). The risk with an auction is that the bids may come in too low, or investors may be unclear about what to bid and stay out of the bidding process altogether. This may be a particular problem with retail investors.

Nowadays many IPOs around the world are conducted using a modification to a straight-forward fixed price offering. In this system the financial institution advising the issuer values the business and puts out a price range. The actual issue price is set towards the end of the process, after having established the level of demand for the shares. In practice, it is very difficult to value many companies in the modern world, since their main assets are intangible – brands, patents, the skills of the workforce, client relationships and so on. It is wise to test a theoretical valuation against the opinions of investors and general market sentiment before finally fixing the issue price.

8.8.2   Elements of an IPO

There are many variants, but a modern IPO is likely to contain a number of inter-related elements.

- **Lead Manager(s).** The company appoints an investment bank or securities house (sometimes more than one) as lead manager or bookrunner of the issue. The lead has primary responsibility for the whole IPO process, working with other advisors such as auditors, lawyers, registrars, investor relations specialists and so on. The lead will also deal with the regulators and the exchange(s) on which the shares are to be listed.
- **Syndication.** In a larger issue the lead manager(s) will assemble a syndicate of financial institutions which help in the process of selling and distributing the shares. Typically the syndicate will also underwrite the issue, which guarantees the issuer that it will raise the capital it needs. The underwriters assume the risk that they may be left holding the stock. Their fee is the difference

between the issue price and the price paid to the company for the shares. If the issue is especially risky the lead manager may decline to underwrite it and agree only to use its best endeavours to sell the shares.

- **Valuation.** The company will be valued for the IPO using a range of techniques – assessing its assets, sales, and profits; looking at the valuations of similar businesses; forecasting future cash flows. A price range is set and this is used to assess demand for the shares.
- **Initial Prospectus.** A preliminary document is issued setting out details of the company, its management, and how it intends to invest the IPO proceeds. In the US the initial prospectus is sometimes known as a **red herring** because of the warning printed in red that the IPO registration has not yet been approved for accuracy by the Securities and Exchange Commission (SEC). The red herring does not carry an offer price and the shares cannot be sold until SEC approval is granted. It may be revised a number of times.
- **Bookbuilding.** Investor roadshows are run to publicize the issue and the underwriters assess demand for the shares at a range of different prices. Sometimes the feedback suggests that the whole price range has to be reviewed. A fixed issue price is set and an allocation procedure determined that will clear the available stock. The issue price is listed in a final prospectus which also contains full details about the company and the underwriting arrangements. The company and its underwriters control the allocation process, including the proportion of shares going to institutional and to individual investors.
- **Greenshoe Option.** In an IPO the syndicate often tries to sell more shares than are actually being offered in the 'basic' deal. A greenshoe is an over-allotment option which allows the underwriters to purchase additional shares (typically up to 15 % more) to satisfy unexpectedly high demand from investors. If the option is exercised the company creates the extra shares and/or they are sold by the existing shareholders. (The strange name comes from the Green Shoe Manufacturing Company, the issuer involved when the technique was originated.)
- **Aftermarket.** The underwriters usually provide support after the shares have been issued by acting as market makers. This helps reassure investors that there will be an active and liquid market.

A greenshoe option can help to smooth out excessive fluctuations in the share price after the IPO date. For example, suppose the underwriters negotiate a greenshoe option to obtain an extra 15 % of stock from the issuing company at a fixed price for a period of 30 days after the IPO issue price is announced. In the IPO they manage to sell 115 % of the announced shares. In effect they are short 15 % of the shares. If the share price rises sharply after issue they will exercise the greenshoe option to obtain the extra shares. This will increase the supply of stock in the market. On the other hand, if the share price falls the underwriters will not exercise the greenshoe and will buy the additional 15 % of shares in the market, so increasing demand and helping to stabilize the price.

New issues may be traded in the **grey market** before the official launch on the secondary market. An investor who sells in the grey market is effectively selling short, since if he or she does not receive the expected allocation the shares will have to be purchased in the secondary market to complete the sale, potentially at a higher price.

Private Placements and Direct Auctions

A cheaper alternative to a full IPO is for a company's advisors to place the shares directly with major institutional investors. The procedure may be used with smaller issues. The costs are appreciably lower than with a full public offering. In its 2004 IPO Google chose a different method which was to auction its shares directly to investors without the use of underwriters.

Google eventually priced the shares at $85 each, the low end of the revised $85–$95 range and well below the original filing range of $108–$135. It also reduced the number of shares offered. It seems unlikely that this approach will supplant the traditional IPO method except in unusual cases.

8.8.3   Reversing the IPO Process: Taking a Company Private

One of the features of capital markets in recent times has been the number of occasions in which the IPO process has effectively been put into reverse, by **private equity** firms buying up the shares of a listed company and removing that firm from the stock market. It then becomes a private limited company whose shares are held by a small group of investors. There are a number of motivations for doing this. It may be felt that the shares are undervalued in the stock market, perhaps because investors there are taking a short-term view of the company's prospects. In private hands, also, the management team can be provided with strong personal incentives to boost performance, over a somewhat longer time horizon, unencumbered by the need to prepare the regular reports that are required by the stock market authorities. Typically, the management team will take an equity stake in the business, and this will form a major component of their compensation package.

After a period of time in private hands the company may be returned to the stock market through an IPO. This will allow the private equity investors and management to realize the gains from their investment in the business.

8.9   SUBSEQUENT COMMON STOCK ISSUES

A company that has already conducted an initial public offering can then sell additional shares to raise further equity capital. The principal method used in Europe is a **rights issue**. The full legal name is 'pre-emption rights'. In this method additional shares are offered to existing shareholders in proportion to their existing holding, usually at a discount to the current market price. Normally shareholders can either take up their rights or sell them on to another investor. By contrast, rights issues are uncommon in the US. A listed US company that wishes to sell new stock normally makes a **general cash offer** to existing and new shareholders alike via underwriters.

The fact that a rights issue is made at a discount to the current share price has a dilution effect on the value of the company's shares, as the following example illustrates. The example also uses a simple and widely followed method for valuing the rights if an existing investor decides to sell them rather than taking them up.

8.9.1   Rights Issue Example

Dilution Inc. has one million shares on issue currently worth $5 each. The company as a whole is therefore worth $5 million. It needs $1 million to invest in a new project. It raises the cash through a rights issue. It offers existing shareholders one new share for every four shares already owned, at a specially discounted price of $4 per new share. In effect, the shareholders are given options to buy new shares at a 20% discount.

Suppose a shareholder in Dilution Inc. decides to sell on his or her rights 'nil paid' to someone else. 'Nil paid' means that whoever acquires the rights will later have to pay $4 per share to Dilution Inc. to exercise the rights and purchase shares. What is a fair price to charge for the rights? It is not zero, because the rights confer an option to purchase shares at a special discount. It might be thought that it is $1 per new share, since the rights provide an option to acquire a share for $4 that was worth $5 before the rights issue was announced. However this does not take into account the fact that the discounted issue price dilutes the previous value of the shares.

- The total number of shares after the rights issue is 1.25 million.
- If we assume that after the rights issue, which raises $1 million in cash, the total value of the company increases from the original $5 million to $6 million, then the value of each share will now be only $4.80.

$$\frac{\$6 \text{ million}}{1.25 \text{ million shares}} = \$4.80 \text{ per share}$$

- Someone who acquires the right to buy a new share 'nil paid' will later have to pay Dilution Inc. $4 per share to exercise that right. By doing so they will acquire a share that (taking the dilution effect into account) will be worth $4.80. Therefore (in theory) the fair price to pay the original owner for the 'nil paid' rights is the difference between $4.80 and $4 which is $0.80 per share.

8.9.2 Shareholder Choices

Take the case of a shareholder who, before the rights issue is announced, owns a portfolio consisting of 100 Dilution Inc. shares worth $500 plus $100 in cash, a total value of $600. The shareholder has the right to buy 25 new shares (one for four) at $4 each. In theory, the shareholder's position is not affected by the discounted rights price, and it does not even matter if the investor takes up the rights or sells them to someone else 'nil paid'.

- **Takes up the Rights.** The shareholder will now own 125 shares worth $4.80 each, a total of $600.
- **Sells the Rights.** The shareholder will now own 100 shares worth $4.80 each, plus 25 × $0.80 in cash raised from the sale of the rights at the theoretical value, plus the initial $100 in cash. This is a total of $600.

However matters are not at all that simple. The actual value of the company after the rights depends on how well the market believes the cash raised will be used, and on the future prospects for the business. In the above example it was assumed that the $1 million raised in cash simply adds to the previous market capitalization of the business. In practice, a rights issue may be used as a means of raising cash in difficult circumstances where other alternatives are unattractive or unavailable. It may be taken by investors as a signal of hard times ahead. For example, in mid-2008 a series of UK banks launched rights issues to raise additional funds from their shareholders following losses on credit markets and severe problems with raising cash in the interbank lending market. These were generally taken as adverse signals over future business prospects, and raised major fears amongst investors that further announcements of losses in credit markets were imminent.

8.9.3 Stock Splits

A stock split (bonus or capitalization issue in the UK) occurs when a share price becomes too high and unwieldy. For example, a company whose stock is currently trading at $100 each might decide to issue 100 new shares for every one existing share. Unlike a rights issue the company is not raising any new equity capital and in theory at least the price of each new share after the split should settle at $1. The purpose is to increase the attractiveness of the stock to investors and the number of shares traded. An active or liquid market is an advantage for a shareholder. It is easier to buy and sell the stock without affecting the price. In practice, the liquidity improvement may actually improve the value of the new shares.

A stock split may also be taken as a signal by investors that management has confidence in the business. It is unlikely to go through the process if the shares are set to decline sharply in value and trade at very low levels. Less common is a **reverse stock split** in which a company combines numbers of existing shares together into new shares each with a higher value. It sometimes occurs because the value of the existing shares has fallen to such a low level that they do not meet the requirements of the stock exchange on which they are listed. It may be taken as a negative signal from management that the existing low share price level is unlikely to improve.

8.10   SECONDARY MARKETS: MAJOR STOCK MARKETS

A secondary market is one in which existing shares created through a primary market are traded. Stock markets use a variety of trading methods to achieve this purpose. Some are **order-driven** (or order-matching) markets, in which buy and sell orders from investors and dealers are directly matched on trading floors and/or using computer systems. Some are **quote-driven** markets in which market makers post bid and offer prices acting as principals, buying and selling stock from their own inventory; the other market users transact with the market makers rather than directly with each other. In practice, as described below, some markets such as the New York Stock Exchange and the London Stock Exchange combine both methods, though in somewhat different ways.

Figure 8.3 shows the ten biggest stock markets in the world by domestic market capitalization at end-2007. The figures are in US dollars and exclude investment funds.

The New York Stock Exchange (NYSE) originated with the 24 brokers who formed the first organized stock market in New York in 1792, meeting under a buttonwood tree in Wall Street. On 28 October 1997 for the first time over one billion shares were traded. Today the NYSE combines traditional auction-based open-outcry trading on its physical trading floor with the use of advanced electronic systems. Apart from exchange staff there are two main types of market participants on the NYSE trading floor: floor brokers and specialists.

- **Floor Brokers.** These act on behalf of clients, for a commission fee, transacting buy and sell orders and seek to obtain the best available price. The trades can be executed in person or using electronic systems.
- **Specialists.** These are the auctioneers in the system and act as the contact point bringing together brokers with buy orders and brokers with sell orders. They operate from trading posts on the NYSE floor and act to ensure that bids and asks are reported in a timely manner and that buyers and sellers achieve the best available price on the market. Each stock listed on the NYSE is allocated to a specialist and trading in that stock occurs at the relevant trading post. Nowadays most of the orders are delivered to the trading post through an electronic routing system and many of the activities of

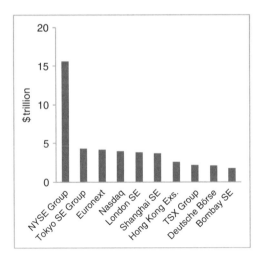

Figure 8.3 Largest stock exchanges by domestic market capitalization at end-2007.
Source: World Federation of Exchanges, reproduced with permission.

the specialist have been automated. Where there is an imbalance in supply or demand the specialist will also buy and sell stock from inventory, acting as a principal.

On the NYSE the floor brokers are agents, operating on behalf of clients. The main responsibility of the specialists is to ensure an orderly market in which shares are auctioned at the best available price and buy and sell orders are matched fairly and efficiently. However, specialists also act as a type of 'emergency' market maker in order to provide liquidity in the market. For example, if there are too many sellers in a stock then the specialist will buy shares into their own inventory. If there are too many buyers they will sell out of inventory. This is a comfort to investors who know that in turbulent market conditions there is always a buy and sell price available.

NASDAQ® is the largest electronic screen-based share trading market in the US. By contrast with the NYSE, NASDAQ is fully electronic, with no trading floor, and is an entirely quote-driven system, based on market makers which buy and sell shares from inventory in transactions with investors and with other dealers. Normally there is more than one market maker for each stock so that investors can 'shop around' and operate in a competitive market. The market makers are required to post firm two-way prices in their stocks.

Recent years have seen rapid consolidation of stock markets in the US. In 2007 NASDAQ agreed to buy the Philadelphia and the Boston stock exchanges. In early 2008 the group operating the NYSE announced that it was acquiring the American Stock Exchange (Amex).

8.10.1 Major European Exchanges

Euronext was created in 2000 by the three-way merger of the domestic stock exchanges in Amsterdam, Brussels, and Paris (formerly known as the Paris Bourse). Euronext later acquired LIFFE, the London-based derivatives market, and merged with the Portuguese exchange. Share trading on Euronext is based on electronic matching of buy and sell orders using sophisticated information technology. In April 2007 Euronext combined with the NYSE group to form a new group called NYSE Euronext. It is structured as a limited company and its stock is listed on the NYSE and on the Paris exchange.

Traditionally, the London Stock Exchange (LSE) was a quote-driven market, based on market makers (formerly known as 'jobbers'). The main advantage of a quote-driven market is that bid and offer prices are always available. This means that even in extreme market conditions such as the October 1987 crash an investor can find a price at which to sell their shares. In a pure order-matching system without market makers this may not be the case – there may not be enough buyers and the whole market may dry up. (The main practical difficulty in the 1987 crash, before the days of automated trading systems, lay in getting through to the market makers on the telephone.) The downside of a quote-driven system is that market making is a potentially dangerous business and the traders maintain bid-offer spreads as a means of making a profit and protecting themselves against losses. In turbulent markets they are inclined to widen those spreads.

In 1997 the LSE introduced a new order-matching electronic trading system called SETS. This was designed to cut dealing costs and spreads for the most actively traded shares, and to ensure that prices were established in an open and transparent market. Since 2007 SETS has operated as a single platform for trading the more liquid UK shares, including the constituents of the FT-SE All Share Index. SETS now combines an automatic order-driven trading service with market making services, ensuring two-way prices in all securities. Settlement in order book trades in UK stocks is guaranteed by a central counterparty operated by the London Clearing House. The LSE also operates a separate trading system for less actively traded stocks including a number listed in its Alternative Investment Market (AIM).

Deutsche Börse Group operates the Frankfurt Stock Exchange, by far the largest in Germany, as well as the derivatives market Eurex which is a joint venture with the Swiss Exchange (SWX). The Group has been a listed company since 2001. It also owns Clearstream International which is a leading organization in the clearing and settlement of securities trades. Share trading takes place on the trading floor of the Frankfurt Exchange or on the Xetra® electronic platform. On Xetra buy and sell orders are collected in a centralized order book and matching orders are executed. Share trades are settled through the central counterparty (CCP), which effectively eliminates counterparty risk for users of the Exchange. The central counterparty system also reduces transaction costs because the proceeds from buy and sell orders are netted out so that only the balance is settled.

8.10.2 The Tokyo Stock Exchange

The Tokyo Stock Exchange (TSE) was re-established under new legislation in 1949. The trading floor closed in 1999 and now all trading is based on an electronic order book which matches buy and sell orders. Settlement is also computerized. During a trading session bids and offers are continually matched using an algorithm called the *Zaraba* method. A somewhat different algorithm called the *Itayose* method is used to establish the opening and closing prices of shares for the morning and afternoon sessions. It arises because orders are accepted before trading begins, so that there is a range of buy and sell orders for a given stock outstanding at various prices. The *Itayose* method is designed to execute these different orders at a single price.

The TSE is a pure order-driven market, without specialists or market makers helping to form prices. It uses two techniques to prevent excessive volatility in share prices. Firstly, immediate order execution only takes place if the price is within a certain range of the previously executed price. Secondly, there is a system of price limits which stipulates a maximum and minimum share price move during a trading day.

8.10.3 Major Markets in China and India

The Hong Kong Stock Exchange (HKEx) dates back to the nineteenth century. In 2000 it merged with the Hong Kong Futures Exchange, the market for derivative products. Share trading on the Hong Kong Stock Exchange is based on an order-driven system. Trading is conducted through terminals in the Exchange and also on off-floor electronic systems based in the offices of market participants.

The Shanghai Stock Exchange (SSE) was founded in 1990 and is now the largest stock market in mainland China calculated by the number of shares listed and traded. It is currently (as at 2008) a non-profit-making membership institution governed by the China Securities Regulatory Commission (CSRC). Buy and sell orders on SSE are electronically matched. These can be submitted through terminals situated in the dealing floor or in the offices of member firms throughout the country. Trading is paperless and securities are held in the form of a book-entry system maintained by the central clearing organization.

Finally, the Bombay Stock Exchange (BSE) dates back to 1875. Its current growth mirrors that of the fast-developing Indian economy. In 1995 the BSE moved from an open outcry system to an online screen-based order-driven trading system. As at end-December 2007 the market capitalization stood at about $1.8 trillion. The BSE also had the largest number of listed companies of any exchange in the world, over 4700. It is now structured as a corporation with institutional and individual shareholders and has forged strategic partnerships with Deutsche Börse and the Singapore Exchange. As well as equity trading the BSE also supports transactions in debt securities and derivative products.

8.11 DEPOSITORY RECEIPTS

Depository receipts (DRs) are negotiable (tradable) certificates issued by a bank in local currency for a deposit of shares in a foreign company. They allow companies to tap a pool of international capital, and to increase liquidity in their shares. From a local investor's perspective, depository receipts provide a relatively simple means of investing in foreign securities. The certificates are quoted in the domestic currency and trades are settled using local procedures.

The biggest market is for American depository receipts (ADRs). These were first introduced in 1927 to bypass restrictions preventing UK companies from registering their shares abroad. US investors could invest in the UK market by lodging British shares with the London branch of a US bank which would then issue ADRs in the US. Since then exchange-listed ADRs have become popular in the US. The main advantage for investors these days is ease of use. ADRs:

- are quoted and pay dividends in US dollars;
- normally trade on US stock markets and can be bought and sold like US shares.

A global depository receipt (GDR) is a certificate representing ownership of a number of shares in a foreign company which is typically based in a developing country. GDRs are issued by a bank, normally in two or more markets, and can be traded separately from the underlying shares. They are denominated in major currencies such as the US dollar or the euro and are listed on markets such as the London Stock Exchange. The first GDR in London was issued in 1994 for shares in East India Hotels, then India's second-largest hotel chain. The company raised $ 40 million from the offering, which was led by Merrill Lynch. GDRs have proved an effective means of raising capital abroad for companies in developing countries. In some cases it has allowed international investors to take stakes in markets where there are restrictions on the direct foreign ownership of shares.

8.12 STOCK LENDING

The stock lending market allows holders of financial assets, such as portfolio managers or traders, to make extra returns by lending their shares to a borrower for a fee. An intermediary may bring the lender and borrower together. The borrower of the stock might be:

- a trader who has agreed to sell the shares but for some reason is unable to purchase them outright;
- a trader who is running a short position i.e. selling a share he or she does not own in the expectation of buying it back later at a cheaper price. The short seller has to borrow the shares and replace them later;
- an options trader who needs to hedge by taking short positions in the underlying shares.

The fees paid to the lender of shares will depend on the type and quantity of shares borrowed, supply and demand for the shares in the market, and the term of the loan. The term may be a fixed period, or the loan may be rolled over by mutual agreement on a daily basis.

8.12.1 Collateral

Lenders of shares normally demand collateral to guarantee that the borrower will return the shares or compensate them in cash. Collateral may be in the form of cash, or securities such as government bills or bonds. When securities are used as collateral they may be valued at some discount to their actual market value – this is sometimes known as a **haircut**. In addition, if the shares that are borrowed rise in value during the loan the lender may require additional collateral. If the collateral posted is cash the lender of shares will pay some rate of interest that reflects current money market rates, less the lender's fee. If the collateral takes the form of securities the lender's fee may be quoted as a percentage of the market value of the shares lent.

Figure 8.4 illustrates a stock lending agreement where the borrower is a short seller. The short acquires the shares through the arrangement and then sells them into the stockmarket at the current price. The intention is to buy them back from the market later and return the shares to the lender, the original owner. If the price has fallen then the short seller can profit from the deal. If it rises then he or she will make a loss.

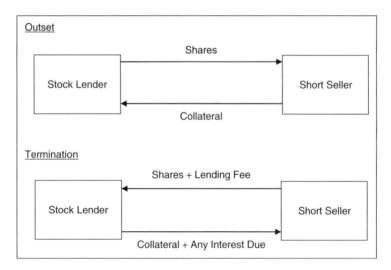

Figure 8.4   Basic structure of a stock lending arrangement with a short seller.

8.12.2   Termination

The borrower or lender of shares can normally terminate the arrangement early. The borrower might do this when the shares become available to purchase or when he or she decides to close out a short position. The lender might choose to terminate the deal in order to sell the shares. Once the stock is returned to the lender (the original owner) the borrower's collateral is returned and any outstanding lending fees are paid.

8.12.3   Ownership and Manufactured Dividends

When shares are loaned out the actual ownership is transferred, so that the borrower can sell them on to another party. The borrower agrees to compensate the lender for any dividends paid on the shares during the loan. This is sometimes called a **manufactured dividend**. Similarly, if the company whose shares have been loaned out launches a rights issue the stock borrower must take the rights up on behalf of the lender or reimburse the lender for the value of the rights.

8.12.4   Naked Short Selling

Naked short selling occurs when a trader sets up a short position without first having taken steps to locate and borrow the stock. Critics argue that it can allow speculators to launch aggressive attacks on ailing companies. The US Securities and Exchange Commission has banned what it calls 'abusive' practices in which a trader sells stock short without having it available for delivery and intentionally failing to deliver the stock in time for settlement.

The concern is that such activity can be used to manipulate share prices and to create a false market.

8.13   PORTFOLIO (BASKET) TRADING

Portfolio trading specialists help institutional clients to analyse and execute buy and sell orders on large portfolios of shares. Deals are implemented on a **risk** or an **agency** basis.

- **Principal/Risk Basis.** The broker/dealer quotes a price to acquire a portfolio from or for an institution, at a discount or premium to the current market value, and takes the risk that it may make a loss on dealing at that price.
- **Agency Basis.** The broker acts as an agent for a commission and seeks to execute the order to buy or sell the portfolio at the best available price on the market.

Principal trades can be advantageous to the broker/dealer firm since they create substantial deal flows for the trading book. In agency deals the broker is sometimes set a target to execute the portfolio trade at or around the **volume-weighted average price** (VWAP) for the day the trade was executed. VWAP is believed by some to be a better benchmark indication of where a share was actually trading on a given day than the closing price or the simple arithmetical average of the trade prices that day. If a portfolio trader executes a deal at or around VWAP this is a sign that he or she has handled the deal effectively and has minimized the market impact of dealing in volume.

8.13.1   Implementing Portfolio Trades

Portfolio traders use a number of strategies to help implement orders. For example, they may be able to arrange a 'cross' by looking for buyers and sellers amongst their client base rather than dealing on the open market. When they transact in the market, portfolio traders can analyse dealing patterns to assess when the shares are most actively traded and when most orders are likely to be brought to the market. They can also automate the execution of deals and 'parcel' them up into a larger number of smaller transactions to help minimize market impact (although software tools have also been developed to help other market participants detect such tactics).

8.14   CHAPTER SUMMARY

Common stock (ordinary shares) differs from debt securities in that the holder is a part-owner of the business and benefits from the growth of the company. However, there is no requirement for the company to pay dividends and common stock has the lowest ranking in the capital structure. Shareholders in public companies benefit from limited liability. In developed countries most shares are held by institutions such as pension funds and insurance companies. A passive fund seeks to track a benchmark index and an active fund to outperform an index. Many active portfolio managers operate an asset allocation process and some tactically switch resources between asset classes. If a market is perfectly efficient it should not be possible to consistently outperform the market index by picking stocks that appear to be mispriced. Modern portfolio theory (MPT) is based on ideas set out by Markowitz in 1952. It explains how the principle of diversification can be used to construct optimal portfolios of assets.

Common stock is firstly made available to the general public through initial public offerings. In many IPOs, a lead manager investment bank or securities house manages the whole process and underwrites the issue, often with a syndicate of sub-underwriters. Some issues are directly placed with investors. In the UK and Continental Europe companies raise additional share capital mainly through rights issues in which new shares are offered to existing shareholders at a discount. In the US new shares are usually made available to all investors. After they are issued shares are traded in exchanges such as the NYSE and the London Stock Exchange. In an order-driven market buy and sell orders are directly matched. In a quote-driven market deals are transacted with market makers who post bid and ask (offer) prices. Depository receipts are negotiable (tradable) titles to a deposit of shares in a foreign company held by a bank. They make it easier for investors to gain access to foreign equity markets. Shares are borrowed and lent through stock lending agreements. Borrowers include traders taking short positions (selling shares in the expectation of buying them back more cheaply later on) and option traders hedging their books. Portfolio or basket traders carry out trades in large portfolios of shares for institutional investors. They can act on a risk basis by quoting fixed prices for the shares; or as an agent using their market knowledge to buy or sell shares at the right time with minimum impact on the price.

9
Equity Fundamental Analysis

9.1 CHAPTER OVERVIEW

When assessing the current condition and future prospects of a company, investors, and analysts often tend to start by assessing the information contained in the financial statements. This is known as fundamental analysis. Although the analysis is typically based on current and historical data, this is normally used as a starting-off point to make forecasts about the future. This chapter looks at the key items in a company's balance sheet and income statement (profit and loss account). It sets out the balance sheet equation and explains the concept of accruals accounting. It explores what is meant by shareholders' equity as it appears in a balance sheet, and compares it with market capitalization. Equity analysts use a range of financial ratios to extract information about a company from its financial statements. The chapter defines the main ratios and illustrates how they are used. In attempting to value shares and make investment recommendations, equity analysts use a range of valuation multiples. This chapter looks at the most widely used, the price/earnings ratio, and explores the applications and limitations of this measure. Finally, it considers some alternative valuation tools including the price/book ratio and a measure that is now widely used by professional equity analysts, the firm value/EBITDA multiple. All of these multiples are based on accounting numbers, although EBITDA is the closest to cash flow. The following Chapter 10 explores equity valuation methodologies based on discounted cash flow techniques.

9.2 PRINCIPLES OF COMMON STOCK VALUATION

Common stock (ordinary shares) provides an investor with a share in the total net assets (total assets less total liabilities) of a company plus the right to receive dividends if they are distributed. Unlike a fixed income security such as a bond there is no pre-determined return on an investment in a share. Nor is there a fixed redemption date. This makes the valuation of common stock a complex and uncertain process. There are many factors to take into account:

- the value of the company's assets including intangible (non-physical) resources such as brands, patents, reputation, and client relationships;
- its liabilities including bank loans and money owed to trade creditors;
- forecasts of future sales, costs, profits, and dividends;
- the company's business strategy, its sources of competitive advantage, its order book, the quality of the management and workforce;
- the nature of the business sector in which it operates, the levels of competition and profitability, and the scope for future revenue growth.

The starting point for information about a company for many investors is its **financial statements**. The main items are the balance sheet and the income statement.

- **Balance Sheet.** This shows the financial position of the company at a particular moment in time, such as the end of the financial year. It lists the company's assets, then its liabilities and its equity capital. Total net assets – total assets less total liabilities – equals shareholders' equity.
- **Income Statement.** This shows the company's income and expenditures over a defined period of time. The latest annual report will have the figures for trading activity in the last financial year, although companies listed on stock exchanges also issue interim financial statements during the course of the year. In the UK the income statement is known as the profit and loss account.

The annual report of a listed company will also contain a **cash flow statement**. This is similar to the income statement in that it deals with trading activities over a period of time. The difference is that it shows how cash has been generated and spent by the company. Some items in the income statement, such as the depreciation of fixed assets, are internal book entries and do not represent actual cash flows. The company will explain in its accounts how the operating profit (the profit arising from normal trading activities) shown in the income statement is reconciled with the net cash flow generated from operating activities.

9.3   THE BALANCE SHEET EQUATION

At its simplest the basic balance sheet equation says that:

$$\text{Assets} = \text{Liabilities} + \text{Shareholders' Equity}$$

The assets of the company can be divided into **fixed assets** and **current assets**. Fixed assets are longer-term resources for use in the company's business operations rather than for resale. They can be further divided into tangible and intangible items.

- **Tangible Assets.** This will include items such as land and buildings, plant and machinery, vehicles. Such assets are normally shown at their original cost less depreciation to date. In some countries such as the UK land and property may be shown at a market value based on a revaluation rather than historic cost. Depreciation is a charge for the employment of an asset over its useful life.
- **Intangible Assets.** It is common accounting practice in the US and internationally now that only intangible assets that are acquired in the takeover of another business are valued and placed on a company's balance sheet. A value for internally generated intangible assets, such as brands built in-house by a company, is *not* put on the balance sheet. The matter is highly controversial, with some arguing that this treatment is anomalous.

The balance sheet may also list under fixed assets long-term investments in other businesses and in joint-ventures.

Current assets are short-term assets used in the operation of the business. They consist in cash plus other items which can be turned into cash in less than one year, including:

- inventory or stocks of finished or unfinished goods and raw materials;
- accounts receivables (called debtors in the UK);
- short-term investments such as Treasury bills.

9.3.1   Sources of Funds: Liabilities and Shareholders' Equity

A company has two main sources of funds to purchase assets: liabilities (debt) and shareholders' equity. In a balance sheet the liabilities are normally divided into two broad categories:

- current or short-term liabilities;
- creditors falling due after one year (long-term liabilities).

Current liabilities include short-term debt such as credit facilities with a bank and accounts payable or money owed to trade creditors. Creditors falling due after one year include longer-term bank loans and bond issues.

Shareholders' equity (also known as shareholders' funds or net worth) has two main components. The first is the cash paid by investors to buy shares in the company. The second is **retained earnings** which is accumulated profits due to the shareholders but not paid out in the form of dividends. Instead it is reinvested in the business. It helps to increase the value of the company and also the value of an equity stake in the company.

The balance sheet equation reminds us that shareholders' equity is **risk capital** in the sense that it is a residual claim on the assets of the business. If the company is put into liquidation and broken up then the assets are used in the first instance to pay off liabilities such as money owed to trade creditors and lenders. Anything that remains belongs to the shareholders. Note that in this chapter the word 'share' is used to refer to common stock (ordinary shares). If a company has issued preferred stock then the preferred dividends have to be deducted from net income (the 'bottom line' profit figure) to calculate the profit that belongs to the common stockholders.

9.3.2 The Balance Sheet Equation Illustrated

Figure 9.1 illustrates the basic balance sheet equation. Essentially, it says that current and long-term liabilities comprise the debt capital used to operate the business. Together with shareholders' equity they form the total capital base of the company, debt plus equity,

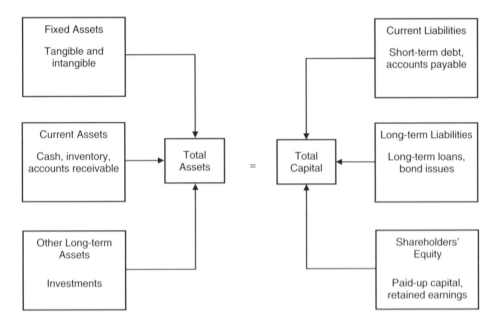

Figure 9.1 The basic balance sheet equation.

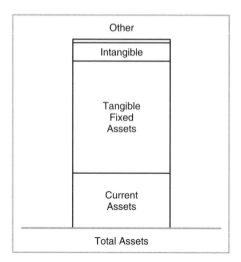

Figure 9.2 Breakdown of Wal-Mart balance sheet assets at 31 January 2008.
Source for data: Wal-Mart Inc. 2008 Annual Report.

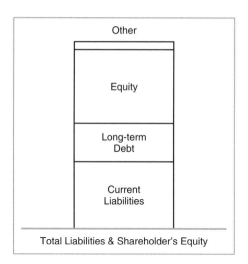

Figure 9.3 Breakdown of Wal-Mart liabilities and equity at 31 January 2008.
Source for data: Wal-Mart Inc. 2008 Annual Report.

which equals total assets. The debt holders have first claim on those assets. Figures 9.2
and 9.3 give a breakdown of the balance sheet for the retailer Wal-Mart Stores Inc. as at
31 January 2008. Total assets were about $ 163.5 billion, which equalled total liabilities and
shareholders' equity combined.

9.4   THE INCOME STATEMENT

The income statement (profit and loss account in the UK) shows how a company has
performed over a specific period of time. It lists the sales and the profit (or loss) generated

over that period. The key concept used in compiling the income statement is that of **accruals accounting**. This says that revenues and costs are accounted for in the period in which the revenue is earned and the cost incurred. For example, if a company delivers goods worth $ 1000 in a given financial year the sale is recorded in that year's income statement even if the cash payment is not received until the next financial year. In addition, any expense the company incurred in making that sale would be matched with the sale and recorded in the same income statement. This system is quite different from cash-based accounting in which sales and costs are only recorded when cash actually changes hands.

9.4.1   Example of Income Statement: Wal-Mart Stores Inc.

Table 9.1 shows a somewhat simplified income statement for Wal-Mart for the financial year ended 31 January 2008.

Gross profit equals sales revenues minus the direct cost of goods sold (COGS), such as wages paid to employees operating the retail stores and the cost of purchases from suppliers. The **operating profit** (or operating income) is then calculated by deducting SG&A expenses for support activities (such as marketing). Operating profit is a measure of a firm's earning capability from its ongoing business activities. The **net income** figure is the so-called 'bottom line'. It represents the profit from that year's trading activities that is attributable to the shareholders. Wal-Mart paid some of this out in the form of dividends and reinvested the rest in the business. In accounting terms, it was added to the shareholders' equity figure in the balance sheet as retained earnings.

Note that there is a separate entry for **exceptional items** in the Wal-Mart income statement. This represents non-recurring items. Equity analysts like to see these isolated because it allows them to explore the underlying trend in profits rather than having the figures distorted by one-off expenses (or gains). Typical exceptional items include charges for business restructurings or the costs associated with managing the acquisition of another firm. The **minority interest** item in the income statement represents the profits attributable to the outside shareholders who have a stake in a subsidiary business partly owned by Wal-Mart; this has to be deducted from operating profit to establish the net income that belongs to Wal-Mart's own shareholders.

Some analysts call the operating profit figure as calculated in Table 9.1 **Earnings before Interest and Tax** (EBIT). Strictly speaking, when calculated in this way EBIT is a

Table 9.1   Wal-Mart income statement for year ended 31 January 2008

Item	$ millions
Revenues	378,799
Cost of goods sold (COGS)	286,515
Gross profit	92,284
Selling, general and administration expenses (SG&A)	70,288
Operating profit	21,996
Net interest expense	1798
Income tax expense	6908
Exceptional items	153
Minority interests	406
Net income (including exceptional items)	12,731

Source: Wal-Mart Inc. 2008 Annual Report.

'normalized' value. That is to say, it excludes exceptional items such as restructuring costs. The idea is that normalized EBIT allows an analyst to compare the underlying profitability of a company across time. It also allows the analyst to build forecasts of its future profitability with greater certainty, because the distorting effects of exceptional items have been removed. By excluding interest, EBIT also focuses on the underlying profitability of the business and not on its capital structure (the proportions of debt and equity). By excluding tax, it strips out the distortions arising from different tax regimes.

EBIT is not a *cash flow* figure, however, because it is calculated after deducting non-cash items, such as depreciation and amortization. Depreciation involves writing off a tangible asset over its economic life through a series of charges to the income statement. Amortization is the same procedure but with an intangible asset. In recent years many analysts have preferred an alternative measure of profitability called **EBITDA**, which stands for Earnings before Interest, Tax, Depreciation and Amortization. EBITDA is closer to cash flow, although it is still not quite the same thing. (This is discussed further in Chapter 10.) One advantage of EBITDA is that it reduces the distortions produced by the fact that different firms use different procedures for depreciation and amortization. The EBITDA calculation for Wal-Mart for the year ended 31 January 2008 is as follows:

EBIT (normalized)	$ 21,996 million
Add back: depreciation and amortization charges	$ 6317 million
Equals: EBITDA (normalized)	$ 28,313 million

EBITDA is not a universally admired measure. Critics such as the investor Warren Buffett have argued that depreciation *should* in fact be taken into account in assessing profitability, even though it is a non-cash item, because it roughly approximates to the expenditure in a given year required to maintain the firm's base of fixed assets. In addition, EBITDA used on its own does not take into account how much capital is employed in the business and what it costs to service that capital. The next Chapter 10 explores how capital expenditures and the cost of capital can be incorporated into equity analysis.

9.5   EARNINGS PER SHARE (EPS)

In simple terms, earnings per share (EPS) is net income divided by the number of shares (common stock) outstanding. It measures the profit from a given period (such as a year) that is attributable to each share. However, in practice there are a number of complications in the calculation:

- some companies have issued preferred stock so the preferred dividends have to be deducted from total net income to establish the net income that is attributable to the common stockholders;
- there is the question of whether or not to include exceptional items in net income;
- most analysts think that it is more accurate to calculate EPS using the weighted average number of shares outstanding over the reporting period rather than the figure at a particular point in time.

In addition, analysts often favour a measure called **diluted earnings per share**. This takes into account not just the actual number of shares outstanding (the 'basic' weighted average figure) but also the potential new shares that would be created through the exercise of employee stock options and similar instruments. Table 9.2 shows a range of EPS figures for Wal-Mart for the financial year ended 31 January 2008.

Table 9.2 Wal-Mart EPS figures for year ended
31 January 2008

Basic EPS including exceptional items	$3.13
Basic EPS excluding exceptional items	$3.17
Diluted EPS including exceptional items	$3.13
Diluted EPS excluding exceptional items	$3.16

Source: Wal-Mart Inc. 2008 Annual Report.

The diluted weighted average number of shares outstanding in the financial year was roughly 4072 million. The total net income was $12,731 million. Adding back $153 million in exceptional expenses produces an adjusted net income figure of $12,884 million. The diluted EPS values are therefore calculated as follows.

$$\text{Diluted EPS Inc. Exceptionals} = \frac{\text{Total Net Income}}{\text{Diluted Weighted Average Shares}} = \frac{12,731}{4072} = \$3.13$$

$$\text{Diluted EPS Excl. Exceptionals} = \frac{\text{Adjusted Net Income}}{\text{Diluted Weighted Average Shares}} = \frac{12,884}{4072} = \$3.16$$

Typically, in the larger broking firms there is a 'rule book' which sets out the 'house' method for adjusting or 'normalizing' EPS figures to reflect the underlying health of the business and to capture the underlying trends. Clients of the firm studying its research notes will then know that earnings figures are calculated on a consistent basis. One of the other problems with EPS figures published by companies is that they reflect all the accounting conventions that the firm has used to calculate net income (such as its depreciation policy). In addition, EPS does not take into account how much capital was used to generate that level of profit. Some firms may be more efficient in the use of capital than others and able to generate earnings using fewer resources.

9.6 DIVIDEND PER SHARE (DPS)

During the financial year to end-January 2008 Wal-Mart paid dividends of $0.88 on its common stock. The diluted EPS was $3.13. The **dividend payout ratio** measures the proportion of earnings paid out in dividends. Its reciprocal, dividend cover measures the number of times a company could have paid the dividend out of that year's earnings. The numbers for Wal-Mart for the year ended 31 January 2008 were as follows:

$$\text{Dividend Payout} = \frac{0.88}{3.13} \times 100 = 28.1\,\%$$

$$\text{Dividend Cover} = \frac{3.13}{0.88} = 3.6 \times$$

Wal-Mart could have paid the dividend more than three times from the profits attributable to the common stockholders that year. This is a comfortable margin and is a reassurance to investors. It can be compared with other retailers, some of which will face a greater struggle to maintain dividends than Wal-Mart with its strong selling power and its effective controls over expenses.

9.6.1 Dividend Policy

In theory companies pay dividends that vary according to their profits. In practice this is not necessarily true. Shareholders generally like to see steadily rising dividend payments, smoothing out the effects of economic booms and downturns on the company's earnings. Many companies operate a **dividend policy** to meet this requirement. Even if a company fails to make a profit in a given year the directors are likely to maintain or even increase the dividend, paid out of earnings retained from previous years' trading activity. Of course this cannot be sustained indefinitely.

High-growth firms (such as Microsoft in earlier years) tend not to pay any dividends at all to their shareholders, and to reinvest all their profits in the business. The shareholders are willing accept this situation if they believe that the company is able to reinvest the funds in new projects at high rates of return, bearing in mind the level of risk that is assumed. However, when the growth rate starts to slow down it is common for companies of this kind to start paying out dividends so that investors can reinvest at least some of their profits in other assets.

Figure 9.4 shows the trends in earnings per share and dividend per share figures for Wal-Mart in the 10 financial years from 1999 to 2008. It illustrates the extent to which the firm has progressively reinvested in its global business operations, whilst paying a steadily rising dividend stream to its shareholders.

9.7 RATIO ANALYSIS

The balance sheet and income statement are valuable sources of information about the past performance of a company, and a starting point for forecasts of future performance. The base case for a forecast of next year's expected earnings per share is the historical EPS and the historical growth rate in EPS. This has, of course, to be balanced against what is known about changes in the company and the environment in which it operates, which could affect expectations of future growth rates.

Equity analysts use a number of financial ratios when assessing the information contained in company accounts:

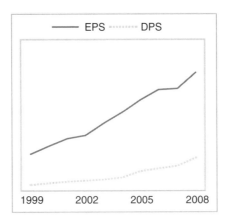

Figure 9.4   Trends in Wal-Mart EPS and DPS figures 1999–2008.
Source: Wal-Mart Annual Reports.

- **liquidity ratios** measure the ability of the company to raise cash when it has to make urgent payments;
- **profitability ratios** measure profit margins and returns on capital invested;
- **leverage (gearing) ratios** measure the proportion of debt and equity in the business and the ability of the company to pay its interest bill.

There are many variations in the way in which these numbers are calculated, some relatively minor. It is very important that an analyst uses consistent methods so that the results obtained for different companies can be directly compared. The following sections describe commonly-used ratio calculations and provide some illustrations using data drawn from Wal-Mart's financial statements.

9.8   LIQUIDITY RATIOS

The key measures are the **current ratio** and the **quick ratio**, also known as the acid ratio.

$$\text{Current Ratio} = \frac{\text{Current Assets}}{\text{Current Liabilities}}$$

$$\text{Quick Ratio} = \frac{\text{Current Assets} - \text{Inventory}}{\text{Current Liabilities}}$$

These numbers provide an idea of how easy it is for a company to clear its most immediate liabilities with the cash it holds and the assets it can most easily raise money on. A current ratio of one means that current liabilities are exactly matched by current assets. The quick ratio is a more rigorous measure since it excludes inventory, which in some industries may not be all that readily turned into cash to pay off creditors.

The current and quick ratios for Wal-Mart for the financial year 2008 were 0.8 and 0.2 respectively. This means that current liabilities exceeded current assets. In some industries such as heavy engineering this could be a major cause for concern. A company in that sector might struggle to sell off its inventory of work in progress and finished goods quickly enough to pay off its short-term creditors in a hurry. In a fast turnover retail business, however, a current ratio of less than one is not something that causes too many concerns; it may actually be a sign of efficiency. Goods for resale can be purchased on trade credit terms from suppliers. Provided they move off the shelves and are quickly turned into cash the suppliers can be paid. This minimizes the amount of capital the retailer has tied up in running the business, and boosts its profitability.

A firm's **working capital** is its current assets less current liabilities. Typically, the faster a business grows the more it will have to invest in working capital. For example, it will need to hold more cash and inventory.

9.9   PROFITABILITY RATIOS

The main numbers used to measure a company's profitability and efficiency are:

- profit margin;
- return on equity (ROE);
- return on total assets (ROTA).

There are a number of ways of calculating profit margin, depending on whether the focus is on gross profit, operating profit, or net income:

$$\text{Gross Profit Margin} = \frac{\text{Gross Profit}}{\text{Sales}} \times 100$$

$$\text{Operating Profit Margin} = \frac{\text{Operating Profit}}{\text{Sales}} \times 100$$

$$\text{Net Profit Margin} = \frac{\text{Net Income}}{\text{Sales}} \times 100$$

Net profit margin measures the 'bottom line' profit that is extracted from each dollar of sales. A high figure means that the company is able to charge prices that comfortably exceed the total costs of running the business. In some industries such as luxury goods and perfumes the profit margins can be extremely high. In other sectors such as food retailing intense competition keeps the margins down. The large retailers fight back through effective cost containment measures, including sourcing from a large number of suppliers, and using the scale advantages of their huge purchasing power. They also seek to boost profit margins by selling own-brand labels and selling higher-margin items such as prepared foodstuffs. Wal-Mart's net profit margin for the financial year 2008 was a healthy 3.4 %. The operating profit margin was 5.8 %.

9.9.1 Return on Equity

Return on equity (ROE) is a measure of the returns made by the common stockholders from a given year's trading activities in relation to the equity tied up in the business. It is normally calculated as follows.

$$\text{ROE} = \frac{\text{Net Income}}{\text{Shareholders' Equity}} \times 100$$

If the company has preferred stock the preferred dividends have to be first deducted from net income to establish the earnings that belong to the common stockholders. In the ROE calculation some analysts use an average figure for shareholders' equity over a period of time.

Note that ROE is an accounting measure and is not based on actual cash flows; as a result it cannot be compared directly with the returns on bonds or money market investments. The numerator is profit attributable to the common stockholders, which is calculated after the deduction of non-cash items such as depreciation and amortization. The denominator is the value of shareholders' equity as it appears on the balance sheet, and not the actual market capitalization of the company on the stockmarket. The next chapter explores how the returns on shares can be measured in cash flow rather than accounting terms.

9.9.2 Return on Total Assets (ROTA)

ROE measures the return achieved by the common stockholders in relation to the shareholders' equity tied up in the business. ROTA measures the return the common stockholders achieve in relation to *all* the assets used by the company (which by the balance sheet equation is equal to the total capital employed, debt plus equity).

$$\text{ROTA} = \frac{\text{Net Income}}{\text{Total Assets}} \times 100$$

Again, if the company pays preferred dividends these have to be deducted from net income to establish the element of net income that is attributable to the common stockholders. In the ROTA calculation some analysts take an average figure for total assets over a period of time. There is a useful relationship between ROTA, net profit margin, and a ratio called **asset turnover**.

$$\text{Asset Turnover} = \frac{\text{Sales}}{\text{Total Assets}}$$

Asset turnover measures the quantity of sales a company extracts from each dollar of total assets tied up in the business. It is a measure of how efficiently the assets are put to use. If one retailer can generate more sales per square metre of floor space than another then it will tend to have a higher asset turnover. Based on the definitions of ROTA and net profit margin used above it can be shown that:

$$\text{ROTA} = \text{Net Profit Margin} \times \text{Asset Turnover}$$

This equation tells us that a company can deliver a superior return on assets compared to other firms operating in its industry through two factors:

- an ability to achieve higher profit margins than its competitors;
- an ability to generate a higher level of sales for each dollar of assets tied up in the business.

9.10   LEVERAGE RATIOS

These ratios measure the proportion of debt used to fund the business and the ability of the company to service that debt. (In the UK leverage is known as gearing.) Most analysts base the calculation on long-term debt.

$$\text{Debt to Equity Ratio} = \frac{\text{Long-term Debt}}{\text{Shareholders' Equity}}$$

Leverage may also be calculated as the proportion of long-term debt to debt plus shareholders' equity combined. A further variant is to subtract cash held by the company from long-term debt. Note that all the above measures are accounting numbers, since they are based on the **book values** of the equity and the debt – the values that appear in the balance sheet. The market value of a company's shares (market capitalization) is normally appreciably higher than the book value, especially if it benefits from internally developed intangible assets which are not listed on the balance sheet.

9.10.1   Effects of Leverage

The effect of leverage (the use of debt by a company) on the common stockholders is on the risk profile of their investment. Typically it is cheaper for a company to raise money through debt because shareholders demand higher returns to compensate them for taking on additional risks. Furthermore, interest payments are normally tax deductible for a company whilst dividend payments are not.

A highly leveraged company is one with a large proportion of debt to equity. If such a company puts its borrowings to good use, it will generate sufficient cash not only to pay the interest on the debt but also to boost profits for the shareholders. However if the company gets into difficulties and profits fall it still has to make the interest payments. There may be little or no money left over for the common stockholders. Shares of highly leveraged companies are a riskier investment in the sense that the returns are more variable. In the extreme, there is a greater chance that the company may be forced into liquidation.

Private equity firms often invest in companies on a **highly leveraged basis** i.e. a large proportion of the cash that is required is borrowed from banks and only a small amount is injected as share capital. The company invested in is then saddled with a lot of debt which has to be serviced. If it meets or exceeds the private equity firm's expectations in terms of business performance then the debt can be redeemed and the private equity shareholders will own a thriving and valuable business. However the risk is that too much is paid for the business, based on over-optimistic forecasts, and it proves impossible to sustain the levels of debt taken on. The risk of this happening can increase if a number of private equity houses bid against each other to invest in a business.

9.10.2   Interest Cover

Analysts assess the ability of a company to pay its interest bill using a measure called interest cover.

$$\text{Interest Cover} = \frac{\text{Operating Profit}}{\text{Interest Expense}}$$

The figure for Wal-Mart for the financial year 2008 was over 10. This means that it could comfortably meet its interest expenses out of earnings before interest and tax. Obviously if a company's interest cover is approaching a value of one this is danger sign. It may be in imminent danger of failing to meet its obligations. Interest coverage is closely related to the willingness of lenders to supply additional funds and to corporate credit ratings.

9.11   INVESTOR RATIOS AND VALUATION

The information from the financial statements must be looked at in the context of the current market price of a share. An investor has to decide whether the stock is undervalued or whether it is the right time to sell. Two of the main ratios used by analysts and investors searching for value in shares are the price/earnings ratio (p/e) and the dividend yield.

$$\text{Price/Earnings Ratio} = \frac{\text{Market Price per Share}}{\text{Earnings per Share}}$$

$$\text{Divident Yield} = \frac{\text{Dividend per Share}}{\text{Market Price per Share}}$$

Both ratios can be calculated on a **historic** basis using EPS and dividend values from past financial statements, or on a **prospective** basis, based on estimates of future earnings and dividends.

9.11.1   The Price/Earnings Ratio

The p/e ratio is used to rate which shares in a given sector are 'cheap' and 'dear' relative to each other. Effectively, it is a payback measure. If a share has prospective p/e of 20 then the current share price is 20 times next year's forecast EPS – it would take 20 years of earnings at that level to recoup the purchase price. It is relatively more expensive than a share with a market price that is only 15 times forecast EPS.

It makes sense to compare the p/e ratios of similar companies. They are in the same line of business and their performance is affected by the same kinds of factors. If one is rated more highly than another in terms of the prospective p/e ratio this is typically because the market sees it as more likely to grow its earnings at a faster rate, or as a lower risk investment. Investors are prepared to pay a 'premium' for high growth expectations in the form of a high p/e ratio. P/e ratios are also affected by the general level of interest rates. For a given set of earnings assumptions, as interest rates fall p/e ratios will generally tend to rise. In practice, though, changes in interest rates will also tend to have an effect on corporate earnings. Chapter 10 has further details on the factors that affect p/e ratios.

9.11.2 Dividend Yield

The dividend yield measures the income return from a share, which can be compared to the general level of deposit rates in the money markets. It does not take into account returns arising from the growth in the share price. Often high growth stocks have high p/e ratios (building in expectations of strong future earnings growth) and low dividend yields (the dividend is low in comparison to the high share price). Many growth companies pay no dividends at all – shareholders expect to achieve their returns from the growth in the share price.

A high dividend yield can arise from a number of circumstances. In some cases investors are uncertain about the future of the business and so the share price has collapsed, even though the company seems able to sustain its dividend payment (at least for a time). In other cases high-yielding stocks are actually low risk but have limited growth prospects. The classic example is a utility stock which is purchased primarily for dividend income rather than capital gains.

9.12 APPLYING VALUATION MULTIPLES

The p/e ratio is still the most widely used valuation tool in the equity markets. It is commonly used by analysts and investment banks pricing new shares in an IPO. When valuing a company for sale using a p/e multiple two numbers are required:

- a figure for earnings;
- an earnings multiple, normally established by taking the average multiple for similar businesses that are already publicly traded.

Suppose that Flotation Inc. is expected to make $10 earnings per share net year, based on recent results. The average p/e multiple for similar businesses is 20 times. Therefore the theoretical ('fair') value of one Flotation share is calculated as follows:

$$\text{Fair Value} = \$10 \times 20 = \$200$$

9.12.1 Practical Difficulties with PE Valuation

Valuing a company for an IPO using an average p/e multiple is very simple in theory, but in practice there are often difficulties.

- **Comparability.** It is important to ensure that the earnings figures for the different companies are directly comparable. For example, different companies may use different methodologies for depreciation of fixed assets and amortization of goodwill.
- **Sample Group.** The sample group used to establish the average p/e multiple must be engaged in similar business activities and have similar growth prospects and risk characteristics. (This was a problem in the Google IPO in 2004.)
- **Fair Value.** The shares in the sample group must be trading at a fair value otherwise their p/e ratios are distorted.
- **Negative Earnings.** The p/e multiple is of little use when the company to be valued has negative earnings.

The p/e is also used as a measure of **relative value** when comparing listed companies. If a company has a lower p/e than a rival in the same area of business it may represent good value for a potential investor. However, it has to be remembered that prospective p/e ratios build in average expectations about future growth prospects. The rule is as follows. If an investor thinks that a stock has *more* growth potential than is already built into the share price then it is a 'buy'. However if the investor thinks the growth prospects have been overplayed by the market and the stock price is inflated then it is a 'sell'.

Websites such as http://moneycentral.msn.com publish comparative p/e ratios and consensus EPS forecasts for popular stocks based on estimates produced by analysts in broking firms. For example, as at mid-2008 the consensus estimate was that Wal-Mart would grow its earnings by over 10 % in the financial year 2009.

9.12.2 Companies with no Earnings

There are other multiples that can be used to value shares in a company which is not currently making a profit but is expected to do so in the future. (The dot.com bubble which burst in 2000 reminded investors that a company that will *never* make money is worth nothing.) Two of the most common measures are:

- the price/sales ratio;
- the price/book ratio.

Applying a price/sales ratio involves finding a sample group of similar firms, calculating the average multiple of total sales to market capitalization, then applying the multiple to the company to be valued. As with the p/e ratio, it is critically important that the sample group is comparable.

The price/book ratio compares the market capitalization of a company with its shareholders' equity – that is, with total assets minus total liabilities. The market capitalization is based on forecast sales and profits, whereas the book value of the common stock is based on the historic cost of the assets less depreciation and total liabilities. The price/book ratio has some advantages as a valuation tool:

- it is intuitive and easy to work with;
- it is reasonably stable over time;
- it can be used to price a company with negative earnings.

However the ratio is based on the accounting measurement of net assets. When it is used to compare the valuation of different companies care has to be taken to ensure that adjustments are made for factors such as different depreciation policies.

9.13   FIRM OR ENTERPRISE VALUE MULTIPLES

A different approach is to calculate and compare EBITDA multiples for different firms.

EBITDA

Earnings before interest, tax, depreciation and amortization. EBITDA permits a more transparent comparison between the profitability of different firms because it is not distorted by factors such as differing depreciation policies. It is more akin to actual cash flow.

However, EBITDA is a stream of earnings that is used to make interest and principal repayments on debt, as well as to reward the common stockholders. Therefore the appropriate valuation measure is not EBITDA as a multiple of equity, but EBITDA as a multiple of equity and debt combined – the total value of the firm (also known as enterprise value).

$$\text{Firm or Enterprise Value} = \text{Market Value of Debt} + \text{Market Value of Equity}$$

The market value of the equity is simply market capitalization. In theory the debt ought to be valued at current market interest rates, although if it pays interest at a rate close to current market levels the par value will be a reasonable approximation. The EBITDA multiple is calculated as:

$$\frac{\text{Firm Value}}{\text{Earnings before Interest, Tax, Depreciation and Amortization}}$$

In an IPO the 'fair' firm or enterprise value of a company can be established by multiplying the EBITDA forecast for the company by an EBITDA multiple derived from similar businesses. Subtracting the value of the debt then establishes a theoretical value for the equity.

9.13.1   Tobin's q Ratio

A further valuation tool is to estimate the *replacement* rather than the book value of the firm's total assets (reflecting what it would actually cost in current market conditions to establish its resource base) and to compare this with firm or enterprise value. This measure is named after the economist James Tobin.

$$\text{Tobin's q ratio} = \frac{\text{Firm Value}}{\text{Replacement Value of the Firm's Assets}}$$

The theory is that, in an efficient market, a firm should be valued at what it would cost to assemble the bundle of assets or resources it uses to compete in the marketplace (i.e. the Tobin's q should be around one). This leads to some simple decision rules (economists will recognize these as equilibrium arguments).

- **Overvalued Firm: Go Short.** If a company is actually valued on the market at *more* than the replacement value of its assets (the Tobin's q is more than one) then competitors could undercut it by setting up a rival business with a similar asset base but at a lower cost. The prospect of this happening should cause the company's firm value on the market to fall and its Tobin's q value to return to one.
- **Undervalued Firm: Go Long.** If a company is actually valued on the market at *less* than the replacement value of its assets (the Tobin's q is less than one) then it is a takeover target. Competitors could buy it as a cheap way to enter the industry or to expand their current operations. The prospect of this happening should cause the company's firm value to rise and its Tobin's q value to return to one.

In practice though when analysts calculate Tobin's q they tend to use the replacement value of the *tangible* assets in the denominator, and not to take into account the intangibles. This means that for many companies the q value will normally be greater than one, because firm value *does* take into account the cash flows generated by intangible assets such as brands and reputation. If Tobin's q is calculated in this way the above decision rules are not so clear-cut. Instead, q values can be interpreted as follows:

- **High q** companies are expensive but add value to their tangible assets with some unique competitive advantage e.g. brands, patents, know-how. They have an incentive to increase capital investment.
- **Low q** companies tend to operate in highly competitive and 'commoditized' industries. Or they are takeover targets for smarter investors and managers who could 'sweat' the physical assets harder.

9.14   CHAPTER SUMMARY

Forecasts of a company's future profits and cash flows normally start with the historical information contained in the financial statements. The main documents are the balance sheet, the income statement, and the cash flow statement. The balance sheet lists assets owned by the company then its liabilities and equity. Equity is total net assets, that is, total assets minus total liabilities. Assets can be divided into fixed assets such as property and plant, and current assets such as cash and inventory. Liabilities are divided into short-term liabilities such as accounts payable and long-term liabilities such as bond issues. The income statement shows income and expenditures over a period of time. Sales are recorded when they are made and expenses when they are incurred. The 'bottom line' profit after interest and tax is called net income. After any preferred dividends are paid, net income is attributable to the common stockholders (ordinary shareholders). This is paid out as dividends or added to shareholders' equity in the balance sheet as retained earnings. Earnings per share is a measure of the profits attributable to each common stock. It may be adjusted for non-recurring items.

The price/earnings ratio is a key valuation tool in the equity markets. On a historic basis it is the current share price divided by last year's earnings per share. It can also be based on forecast earnings. The p/e is used as a measure of value to compare different businesses in the same sector. A high p/e typically indicates that the market as a whole expects significant future earnings growth. If an investor believes that the growth prospects are overstated then the share can be judged as overpriced. Analysts apply a range of other ratios to assess the health and prospects of a company. Liquidity ratios measure the ability of the firm to pay its short-term liabilities. Profitability ratios measure profit margins, cost efficiency, capital efficiency, and return on capital. Leverage ratios give an indication of the amount of debt in the business and whether the company may have difficulties in meeting interest payments. EBITDA measures earnings before interest, tax, depreciation, and amortization. Firm value is the total value of a company, debt plus equity. Measures such as the p/e ratio and the firm value/EBITDA ratio are based on accounting measures of earnings (although EBITDA is closer to actual cash flow). The next chapter considers equity valuation methods based on discounting expected future cash flows.

10

Cash Flow Models in Equity Valuation

10.1   CHAPTER OVERVIEW

Multiples such as the price/earnings ratio are widely used to value shares. This is a relative valuation method. In an initial public offer the shares are often valued using the average p/e ratio for similar firms. This assumes that the sample is comparable and that the share prices in the sample are fairly valued. Discounted cash flow methods offer an alternative approach. This chapter explores models in which the expected dividend stream from a share is discounted to establish its fair value. It considers a version in which dividends continue to grow at a constant rate in perpetuity, and practical issues with applying such models. The links between dividend discount models and the p/e ratio and dividend yield are also explored. The chapter briefly considers the equity risk premium and the implications for stock market value. It then looks at how to estimate a fair or theoretical value for a firm by forecasting and discounting free cash flows. Firm or enterprise value is the total value of a company, debt plus equity. Cash flow models require a discount rate, which is the required return on the cash flows given the degree of risk. The chapter explores an industry standard model for establishing the discount rate and links between this model, portfolio theory, and the optimal levels of debt and equity in a firm.

10.2   THE BASIC DIVIDEND DISCOUNT MODEL

The return to a shareholder from owning a share consists in dividends plus capital gains. Suppose that an investor can buy a share in the spot market at a fair price of $ 100, hold it for a year, earn a $ 10 dividend and then sell the share for $ 110. The holding period return on the investment is calculated as follows.

$$\text{Holding Period Return} = \left(\frac{10 + 110}{100} \right) - 1 = 0.20 = 20\,\%$$

The investment return consists of 10 % income plus 10 % capital gains. Alternatively, the calculation can be rearranged to work out the fair value of the share today. Call this S_0. The above equation tells us that:

$$\left(\frac{10 + 110}{S_0} \right) - 1 = 0.2$$

Therefore:

$$S_0 = \frac{\$\,120}{1.2} = \$\,100$$

This is a present value calculation. $\$100$ is the present value of the $\$120$ cash flow due on the share in one year at a 20 % discount rate. It establishes a fair value for the share on the assumption that the one-year cash flow will be $\$120$ and the appropriate rate of return for an investment of that type is 20 %. The formula is as follows:

$$S_0 = \frac{d_1 + S_1}{1 + r_e}$$

where:

$S_0 =$ spot value of the share
$S_1 =$ value of the share in one year
$d_1 =$ expected dividend due in one year
$r_e =$ required return on the share p.a. as a decimal

10.2.1 Extending the Basic Model

The formula can easily be extended to cope with situations in which cash flows are due in more than one year. For example if the holding period is two years then the fair spot value S_0 can be calculated as follows:

$$S_0 = \frac{d_1}{1 + r_e} + \frac{d_2 + S_2}{(1 + r_e)^2}$$

where:

$S_2 =$ value of the share in two years
$d_2 =$ expected dividend due in two years

This approach can be extended indefinitely by taking longer and longer holding periods. If the holding period has no limit then the fair value of the share can be calculated as the present value of the expected dividend stream extending to infinity:

$$S_0 = \frac{d_1}{1 + r_e} + \frac{d_2}{(1 + r_e)^2} + \frac{d_3}{(1 + r_e)^3} + \cdots$$

This formula says, in effect, that a share price discounts all known information about future dividends. It is also consistent with the idea that valuing the equity in a company should employ the same method used to value all the individual projects making up the company. The individual projects are valued by discounting their anticipated future cash flows. The equity is valued by discounting expected future dividend payments that are generated by the sum of the company's investment projects. (Note that this version of the formula assumes that the next dividend payment is in one year's time, and the one after that in two years' time, and so on.)

10.3   CONSTANT DIVIDEND GROWTH MODELS

The first version of the dividend discount model developed in the last section requires an estimation of the resale value of the share at the end of the holding period. This seems unrealistic – if we know that why don't we know the value today? The second version of the model avoids this criticism, but at the expense of requiring a forecast of dividends in perpetuity (or for a long time to come). Most equity analysts are prepared to forecast earnings and dividends for a few years ahead but beyond that point the exercise becomes increasingly speculative.

10.3.1 Perpetuity Formula

Luckily there is a formula for valuing a perpetuity with constant cash flows. Assuming the next cash flow is due in exactly one year it is as follows:

$$PV_0 = \frac{CF_1}{r}$$

where:

PV_0 = present value of the perpetuity
CF_1 = cash flow due in one year (the same for all subsequent years)
r = required return on the investment p.a. as a decimal

The formula can be used to value a perpetual bond. For example, suppose a perpetual bond pays a 4% coupon. If the required return on the bond in current market circumstances is 5% p.a. then its value per $100 par is as follows:

$$PV_0 = \frac{\$4}{0.05} = \$80$$

If the bond is trading at $80 it has a current yield of 5%. Intuitively what is happening in the perpetuity formula that the far-dated cash flows are discounted more and more heavily and cease to have any meaningful impact on the present value calculation. In this way the calculation can be 'collapsed' into the simple formula.

10.3.2 Constant Dividend Growth

Assuming that the dividends on a share are not constant but grow at a constant rate g then the perpetuity formula can easily be modified. It becomes:

$$S_0 = \frac{d_1}{r_e - g}$$

where:

S_0 = spot value of the share
d_1 = next year's expected dividend
r_e = required return on the share p.a. as a decimal
g = constant annual growth rate in dividends p.a. as a decimal

Next year's expected dividend d_1 can be calculated from last year's dividend payment d_0 and the expected dividend growth rate. In symbols:

$$d_1 = d_0 \times (1 + g)$$

10.3.3 Constant Dividend Growth Model: Example

DDM Inc. paid a dividend last year of $5 on earnings per share of $10. This is a 50% dividend payout ratio. It is expected that earnings will grow at 8% p.a. and that the company will maintain the same payout ratio in future. The required return on equity is 12 % p.a. The fair value of the company's shares, S_0, is calculated as follows.

$$S_0 = \frac{\$5 \times 1.08}{0.12 - 0.08} = \$135$$

The decision rule is a simple one. If the share is trading below $135 on the market it is a 'buy', and if it is trading above $135 it is a 'sell' (though of course transaction costs have to be taken into account). Note that if earnings grow at a constant 8 % and the payout ratio is constant then dividends will also grow at 8 % in perpetuity.

10.4   THE IMPLIED RETURN ON A SHARE

All dividend discount models require a decision to be made on the required return on the share, also known as the **cost of equity**. One answer is to use the Capital Asset Pricing Model (CAPM) which is explored in section 10.9 below. An alternative is to turn the constant growth formula around. Rather than calculating the fair value of the share from a known discount rate, it is possible to work out the rate of return implied in buying the share at its actual market value and receiving the predicted dividend stream.

Suppose it was somehow possible to buy DDM Inc. shares at *less* than the estimate for fair value, say for $120 each. Last year's dividend was $5. Assuming the 8 % dividend growth rate is correct, next year's forecast dividend is $5.4. The constant growth model says that the implied return on the stock if purchased at $120 is as follows.

$$\text{Implied Return} = \frac{5.4}{120} + 0.08 = 0.125 = 12.5\%$$

This is greater than the 12 % estimate for the required return on the stock given the level of risk, and suggests a bargain. Some equity analysts rank companies in the same sector or country by their returns calculated in this fashion. Companies that return above the sector or market average are classified as potential buys. Those that return below the average are potential sells. This methodology cannot be applied in an indiscriminate fashion, however. There may be good reasons why investors demand a higher return on one share compared to another. Typically, it is because the future cash flows are more uncertain and the stock bears higher risks. However the analysis may reveal possible pricing anomalies in the market that bear further investigation.

Note that the implied return as calculated above is the sum of two terms. The first is the share's prospective dividend yield based on next year's forecast dividend ($5.4) and the purchase price of the share ($120). The second term is the constant dividend growth rate (8 % or 0.08 as a decimal).

10.5   DIVIDEND YIELD AND DIVIDEND GROWTH

Reshuffling the basic constant growth dividend discount model reveals the following expression:

$$\frac{d_1}{S_0} = r_e - g$$

This calculates the share's prospective dividend yield, which is next year's forecast dividend d_1 divided by the current value of the share S_0. The equation says that it equals the required rate of return on the stock less the expected constant growth rate in dividends. In practical terms it shows that a growth stock may have a high expected overall return but the prospective dividend yield is restrained by the fact that dividends are expected to grow at a fast rate. By contrast, a high dividend yield income stock such as a utility normally has a low required rate of return (reflecting low risk) but it also has a low dividend growth rate.

The constant growth model also reveals the expression:

$$g = r_e - \frac{d_1}{S_0}$$

This formula says that the market's expectations on dividend growth rates can be deduced from a share's required return less its prospective dividend yield. Take the case of DDM Inc. Assume that the share is trading at a $\$135$ fair value, the required return is 12% p.a. and next year's forecast dividend is $\$5.4$. In that case:

$$\text{Prospective Dividend Yield} = \frac{5.4}{135} \times 100 = 4\%$$

$$\text{Constant Dividend Growth Rate} = 12\% - 4\% = 8\%$$

A trader or investor using the constant growth model and considering an investment in the share would have to decide whether it is likely that the dividend growth rate could continue at 8% in perpetuity. If not (and assuming that the other inputs to the model are correct) then the share may be overpriced at $\$135$. Suppose a trader decides that the constant dividend growth rate is more likely to be 7.52%. Then the share should actually trade at $\$120$ on a fair value basis:

$$\text{Fair Value } S_0 = \frac{\$5 \times 1.0752}{0.12 - 0.0752} = \$120$$

10.6 PRICE/EARNINGS RATIO

The constant growth dividend discount model also offers valuable insights into the meaning and interpretation of p/e ratios. The model says that:

$$S_0 = \frac{d_1}{r_e - g}$$

Let b be the share's dividend payout ratio. Then next year's dividend d_1 must be the dividend payout ratio times next year's earnings per share e_1:

$$d_1 = b \times e_1$$

Substituting the right-hand part of this equation for d_1 in the constant growth model gives:

$$S_0 = \frac{b \times e_1}{r_e - g}$$

This can be rearranged as follows:

$$\frac{S_0}{e_1} = \frac{b}{r_e - g}$$

This equation calculates the share's prospective price/earnings ratio – the current share value divided by next year's forecast earnings per share. According to the constant growth model it is equal to the dividend payout ratio divided by the difference between the required return on the share and the constant dividend growth rate.

10.6.1 Price/Earnings Ratio Calculation

The results for DDM Inc. can be checked using the original values inserted into the constant growth model:

- Fair value of the share = $ 135
- Constant growth rate in earnings and in dividends = 8 %
- Last year's earnings per share = $ 10
- Forecast earnings per share = $ 10.8
- Dividend payout ratio = 50 % (constant)
- Required return on equity = 12 %

The prospective p/e ratio of 12.5 is the share value of $ 135 divided by next year's forecast earnings per share of $ 10.8. It is also the dividend payout ratio divided by the required return less the growth rate in dividends:

$$\frac{135}{10.8} = \frac{0.5}{0.12 - 0.08} = 12.5$$

10.6.2 Reinvestment Rates

The formula for the p/e ratio just derived may seem odd at first sight, since it appears that a company can boost its p/e ratio simply by increasing the dividend payout ratio. However this would also reduce the proportion of earnings reinvested and would in all probability impact on the future growth in earnings and dividends.

The critical issue here is the rate at which a company can reinvest retained earnings. All other things being equal, the higher the reinvestment rate on earnings the higher the price/earnings ratio. High internal rates of return, over and above the required return on equity, lead to rapid earnings growth and a high price/earnings ratio. If the reinvestment rate is above the required return on equity then cutting the dividend payout ratio can boost the share's p/e ratio. Since investors are benefiting from internal rates of return above that which can be achieved on similar stocks in the market they should be content to have a large proportion of earnings reinvested in the firm rather than having the money paid out in dividends.

In real-world terms, a company is liable to benefit from high reinvestment rates if it has some source of competitive advantage not readily available to its rivals. This could include the ownership of intellectual property such as brands or patents, or a favourable position in a network of customers and suppliers, or a set of unique competencies in new technologies.

The price/earnings formula also suggests that, other things being equal, the lower the required rate of return on a share the higher its p/e ratio. Intuitively, future cash flows will be discounted less heavily and the stock's fair value and hence its p/e ratio will increase. If market interest rates fall the required returns on shares will also fall and price/earnings ratios generally will rise.

10.7 STAGE DIVIDEND DISCOUNT MODELS

The constant growth model works fairly well for utilities which tend to pay a steadily rising dividend stream (assuming they are not under threat from government regulators). In other cases it is simply not realistic to assume that a share's earnings and dividends can increase at a constant rate indefinitely.

A new company can achieve phenomenal growth rates for a number of years. However, the growth often tends to slow down over a period of time and revert to a rate that is nearer to the sector or economy average. In fact if a firm continued to grow at a rate that is much faster than the economy average in perpetuity then sooner or later it would become the entire economy! To cope with this problem some analysts use **two-stage** dividend discount models. The stages are as follows.

- **Stage One.** The company's earnings per share and dividend per share are forecast for a set number of years ahead. This can be done by assuming a constant growth rate over the period or by making an explicit forecast for each year, in which case the growth rate does not have to be regular. Forecast dividends are then discounted to a present value at the required return on equity.
- **Stage Two.** The terminal or continuing value of the share at the end of the forecast period is calculated and discounted back to a present value. This is added to the present value of the forecast dividends calculated in stage one, to establish the fair value of the share today. Terminal value can be calculated by assuming a constant growth rate in dividends from that point on and valuing this cash flow stream as a perpetuity.

10.8 TWO-STAGE MODEL: EXAMPLE

Recall the case of DDM Inc. which paid a dividend last year of $ 5. It was initially expected that dividends would grow at 8 % in perpetuity. The required return on equity is 12 %. On this basis the fair value of the share is $ 135.

Suppose, however, that the average earnings growth rate in the sector is only 6 %. A more conservative approach is to assume that DDM's growth rate will converge towards the sector average after a time. Existing competitors may start to fight back, perhaps cutting prices and reducing profit margins in the industry, or new players may enter the sector attracted by the high earnings and erode DDM's market share. Assume that DDM can sustain its 8 % growth rate for five years but growth will reduce to 6 % after that point and stay at that level in perpetuity. The present value of the first five years' dividend stream is shown in Table 10.1.

Assuming that the company will continue to trade after five years it will have a continuing or **residual value** at that point. If dividends grow at 6 % p.a. in perpetuity the value of the share at year five can be calculated using the constant growth perpetuity formula.

$$\text{Residual Value at Year } 5 = \frac{\$\,7.35 \times 1.06}{0.12 - 0.06} = \$\,129.85$$

Table 10.1   Present value of five years' forecast dividends

Year	Forecast dividend ($)	PV at 12 % ($)
1	5.40	4.82
2	5.83	4.65
3	6.30	4.48
4	6.80	4.32
5	7.35	4.17
		Total = 22.44

The value of this *today* is $129.85 discounted at the 12 % required return on equity:

$$\text{PV of Residual Value} = \frac{\$129.85}{1.12^5} = \$73.68$$

The total value of the share today is therefore $22.44 plus $73.68 which is $96.12.

10.8.1   Multi-stage Models

Some equity analysts use three and even four-stage dividend discount models. In practice this involves making a series of different assumptions about dividend growth rates over time. For example, it might be assumed that DDM Inc. can sustain an 8 % growth rate for five years, a 7 % growth rate for a further five years, and only then will the growth rate revert to the 6 % sector average. For the record, this analysis would produce a fair value for DDM of $99.27. A more complex alternative is to assume that the company's growth rate will steadily revert to the sector average and then subsequently to the total economy growth rate over some period of time, rather than in a sudden movement. It could also be assumed that the required return on the share reduces during the 'steady state' perpetuity phase, when the company is more established and therefore a lower risk investment.

10.9   THE CAPITAL ASSET PRICING MODEL (CAPM)

Models such as the dividend discount model require a discount rate to present value future cash flows. Intuitively, the discount rate should be appropriate to the riskiness of the future cash flows. If a company operates in a relatively safe sector then the required return on equity and the discount rate should be substantially less than that for a company operating in a highly cyclical industry with considerable variance in earnings. An example of the first type of company is a utility; the second might be a high-technology firm.

Many capital markets practitioners establish a discount rate (required return) by using the CAPM developed by William Sharpe and others in the 1960s. CAPM starts with the intuition that the returns on shares (dividends plus capital gains) are normally higher, but subject to more variation, than those achieved on government securities such as Treasury bills. The minimum return that investors will demand in a major currency such as the US dollar is established through the yield or return on government securities. This is the **risk-free** rate of return. Investors will demand an additional **risk premium** to invest in other securities.

The **market risk premium** is the excess return over the risk-free rate demanded by investors to hold a highly diversified portfolio of assets. If an individual share has the same risk profile as the market as a whole then the required return on that share is exactly the same as the market portfolio return. If a share is more or less risky than the market its return is adjusted by a factor known as **beta** (Greek letter β).

10.9.1 The CAPM Formula

CAPM says that the required return r_a on a risky capital asset (i.e. a security such as a share) is the risk-free rate plus a risk premium which is the market risk premium times the beta of the security. In symbols:

$$r_a = r_f + [\beta \times (r_m - r_f)]$$

where:
r_a = required return on the security
r_f = risk-free rate for the expected holding period of the security
β = the security's beta, a measure of how sensitive it is to movements in the market portfolio
r_m = the return on a diversified market portfolio
$r_m - r_f$ = the difference between the market portfolio return and the risk-free rate, i.e. the market risk premium

10.10 BETA

Statistically, beta measures the sensitivity of the expected excess return on a security relative to that on the overall market. (Excess return is the difference between a return and the risk-free interest rate.) If a share has a beta of one, it tends to move in line with the market. For example, if the market as a whole beats the risk-free rate by 1 % over a given time period then we could expect the stock also to achieve an excess return of 1 %.
 Consider the following market data:

$$r_f = 6\%$$

$$r_m = 10\%$$

In this case the market risk premium $r_m - r_f = 4\%$. According to CAPM the required return on a security with a beta of one is calculated as follows:

$$6\% + [1 \times (10\% - 6\%)] = 10\%$$

This is exactly the same as the market return. Blue-chip shares that are very representative of the economy as a whole tend to have betas around one. The events that move the stock market as a whole – changes in interest rates, oil prices, foreign exchange rates and so on – tend on average to affect the returns on such assets to more or less the same extent. Since it has the same risk profile as the market, CAPM says that the required return on a share with a beta of one is the market return.

10.10.1   High and Low Beta Shares

On the other hand a share with a beta of two is twice as risky as the market portfolio. If the market as a whole returns an excess 1 % we could expect the stock to beat the risk-free rate by 2 %. In other words, it amplifies movements in the overall market. Using a 6 % risk-free rate and a 4 % market risk premium the required rate of return on a share with a beta of two would be:

$$6\% + [2 \times (10\% - 6\%)] = 14\%$$

This is higher than the expected return from the market portfolio. Adding such a share to a market portfolio adds risk. By comparison, the required return on a share with a beta of less than one would be less than the market return. Adding such a share to a diversified portfolio actually reduces the overall level of risk. In practice, high beta shares tend to be those of companies operating in volatile or cyclical sectors such as technology and construction which are very sensitive to changes in the overall economy. Low beta securities include utility shares and investment grade corporate bonds, which are relatively stable. (Note that the beta of a **portfolio** of securities can be calculated as the weighted average of the betas of the constituent assets.)

10.11   ESTIMATING THE MARKET RISK PREMIUM

How can we establish the market return and therefore the market risk premium that is required by the CAPM? One approach is to compare the *actual returns* achieved on a diversified portfolio of securities with the returns achieved on Treasury bills or bonds over a historical time period and measure the average excess returns on the former. The assumption is then that this value can be used to forecast the expected future risk premium.

In theory the market portfolio used in this calculation should include investments in all available securities including equities and bonds. In practice it is common to use an equity index and compare the average returns achieved on the stock market over a long time period with those on Treasury bills or bonds. This will calculate an **equity risk premium** based on historical evidence – the additional returns achieved on a diversified portfolio of shares compared to risk-free returns. On the assumption that it is a good forecast for the future, this risk premium can then be added to the current nominal yield on Treasuries to establish the required return on the stock market (the nominal Treasury yield builds in current inflation expectations). To establish the required return on an individual share the equity risk premium is then adjusted by the beta of the share.

10.12   THE EQUITY RISK PREMIUM CONTROVERSY

The historical equity risk premium calculation is extremely tricky and the subject of great controversy. The US risk premium calculated by researchers based on data available from 1926 to the mid-1990s tended to come out at around 7 %−8 % (excess arithmetical returns over Treasury bills), although adding pre-1926 data and data from the early 2000s suggests a smaller figure.

Some analysts argue that the market risk premium derived from such calculations is excessive. It is based on a period of unparalleled growth in the US economy in a country which did not suffer the interruptions to financial markets suffered by countries such as France, Germany, and Japan. In short, the figure may represent a (fortunate) historical aberration and we have no reason to expect similar returns on equities in the future. The practical problem is that if shares are valued today using an excessive risk premium derived from the past then the actual level of risk involved in making equity investments today will be exaggerated and the true value of the stock market will be understated.

In an influential study published in the *Journal of Applied Corporate Finance* in September 2002, Dimson, Marsh, and Staunton developed *forward-looking* or expected risk premia. This study suggests a forward-looking risk premium figure for the US market of only 5.3 %, much lower than the values normally cited based on the analysis of historical data. The corresponding (arithmetical) risk premia figures for the UK and for the world index calculated in the study are 3.6 % and 3.9 % respectively. If correct, these values suggest that investors cannot expect the same (very high) level of excess returns on stock markets in the future that were achieved over most of the twentieth century. The authors also argue in favour of taking a global approach to estimating the equity risk premium, given the international nature of modern capital markets.

10.12.1   Changes in the Equity Risk Premium

One possible reason for the high values for the equity risk premium derived from historical data is that (as it turned out) stock markets performed much better in the twentieth century than expected. As a result using this data produces a risk premium value that exaggerates the actual level of risk involved in making equity investments. It may be that *looking forward* twentieth century investors expected a much lower level of returns on shares than was actually achieved, based on a more modest assessment of the level of risk involved.

It is also possible that the risk premium demanded by investors to invest in shares has declined over the years. There are a number of possible reasons why this might be so:

- investors have more opportunities these days to diversify their portfolios both domestically and internationally, which reduces the risks on share portfolios;
- the transaction costs associated with domestic and international diversification have fallen sharply;
- increased participation in the equity markets means that shares are more liquid and more fairly priced than they were historically.

10.12.2   Deriving a Risk Premium Using the Dividend Discount Model

It is also possible to derive an equity risk premium using the dividend discount model, based on the current level of an index. This often tends to produce a lower risk premium than the historical method. For simplicity in the following example the constant growth version is used, although it is probably better to use a stage model which can capture expected changes in future growth rates.

Suppose that an index is trading at 1000. The forecast average dividend yield on the stocks in the index is 3 %. The risk-free rate is 4 %. Earnings and dividends are also forecast to grow at 4 % p.a. in perpetuity, based on the expected nominal long-run growth rate in the economy (inflation plus real growth). Based on historical evidence the market risk premium is estimated at 4.5 %. Using the constant growth dividend discount model:

$$\text{Index Fair Value} = \frac{\text{Next Year's Forecast Dividends}}{\text{Required Return on the Index} - \text{Constant Dividend Growth Rate}}$$

Next year's dividends (in index points) can be calculated using the current index level of 1000 and the 3 % forecast dividend yield:

$$\text{Next Year's forecast Dividends} = 1000 \times 0.03 = 30$$

The required return on the index can be calculated using CAPM given a 4 % risk-free rate and a 4.5 % market risk premium (the index beta is assumed to be one):

$$\text{Required Return on the Index} = 4\% + 4.5\% = 8.5\%$$

Then:

$$\text{Index Fair Value} = \frac{30}{0.085 - 0.04} = 667$$

This is a great deal less than the current market level of 1000. However it may be that the market risk premium used in the calculation is excessive. The market risk premium that is *implied* in an index level of 1000 (assuming that the other inputs to the model are correct) is in fact 3 %. This produces a required return on the market of 7 % (the 4 % risk-free rate plus 3 %) and a market value of 1000:

$$\text{Market Value} = \frac{30}{0.07 - 0.04} = 1000$$

In a two-stage dividend discount model it could be assumed (for example) that dividends will increase at an above average rate for the next five years and then revert to the long-term growth rate for the economy. Examples such as these also show how sensitive equity valuations are to assumptions made about the equity risk premium.

10.13   CAPM AND PORTFOLIO THEORY

The CAPM analysis is closely related to modern portfolio theory, which is discussed in more detail in Chapter 8. This says that the risk on a portfolio as measured by the variation in its returns is less than the weighted average risk of the constituent shares. Intuitively, this is because market events that are bad for some stocks are beneficial for others, so the overall volatility of the returns on the portfolio is reduced. The principle holds true provided the stocks in the portfolio do not exactly move in line with each other. In the real world there are likely to be 'offsetting' effects in a portfolio of securities, and hence its risk is reduced through diversification.

10.13.1 Diversifiable Risk

The risk that can be reduced and potentially eliminated through diversification is called diversifiable, specific, or **unsystematic risk**. In practice it is possible to greatly reduce the variation of returns in a portfolio by choosing between 10 and 20 securities at random. Thereafter the effect tends to level off. The risk that remains in a fully-diversified portfolio is known as undiversifiable, market, or **systematic risk**. CAPM makes the assumption that a rational investor holds a fully diversified portfolio and is not rewarded for unsystematic risk. Therefore it is not the *total variation* in the returns on a security that explains its required return, only the systematic element which cannot be diversified away, and that is measured by beta. Beta measures how much risk a stock contributes when added to the market portfolio.

10.13.2 Estimating Beta Using Historical Data

Beta is commonly estimated by comparing the percentage returns on a share against the returns on a suitable market index on a monthly, weekly, or daily basis over a period of time (some analysts use five years, others two years or less). If the stock pays a dividend then the yield is added to the return for that period. To illustrate the general method, Table 10.2 shows the returns on a share and on the market index for 10 time periods. These are expressed here as excess returns i.e. returns over and above those achieved on Treasury securities. (Market practitioners often simplify the calculation by using total rather than excess returns.)

The graph in Figure 10.1 plots the data in Table 10.2. It shows the stock excess return for each time period on the vertical axis against the market excess return on the horizontal axis. A 'best fit' straight line has been drawn as closely as possible to the plotted points using the statistical technique of regression analysis.

10.13.3 Beta and Alpha

The slope or tangent of the straight line in Figure 10.1 is one. This is the beta of the share. It means that, if the future follows the past, then on average we would expect the stock to move fully in line with the market as a whole. If the overall market excess return is

Table 10.2   Market return and stock return

Time period	Market excess return (%)	Stock excess return (%)
1	3	6
2	2	3
3	−2	−4
4	3	5
5	−5	−4
6	1	2
7	−3	1
8	2	3
9	5	4
10	−1	−3
Average	0.5	1.3

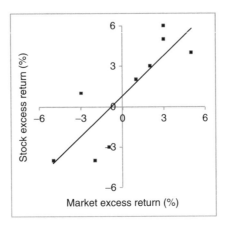

Figure 10.1 'Best fit' straight line.

1 % in a given future time period then the best guess is that the stock will also achieve a 1 % excess return. Note that the line does not exactly pass through the origin (zero). The 'intercept' where it passes through the vertical axis in this example is 0.8 %. This is known as the security's **alpha**. It measures the 'abnormal' or excess return on the stock, above that which is explained by its beta.

Active fund managers are sometimes evaluated according to whether they are able to generate **positive alpha** on a portfolio. This is calculated by working out the extra return achieved beyond that predicted by its beta. The objective is to assess whether or not the fund manager has actually 'added value' through tactical asset allocation and/or stock-picking. If this adjustment is not made a fund manager can produce what looks at first glance like a superior level of return simply by investing in very risky (high beta) stocks or sectors. However when beta is taken into account it may be that the portfolio has actually failed to exceed its expected return.

10.13.4 Arbitrage Pricing Theory (APT)

CAPM is a simple model, which partly explains its enduring popularity. It says that the relevant measure of risk on a stock is not its total risk (variability in returns) considered in isolation. Instead, it is its systematic risk as measured by one single factor: beta. This is because investors are assumed to hold highly diversified portfolios. As a result, CAPM says that the required return on a stock is in direct proportion to its beta. However the model makes a number of problematical assumptions. It supposes that:

- investors always hold well-diversified portfolios;
- beta captures all the risks on an asset or a portfolio that are relevant to making investment decisions;
- investors share the same expectations on return and risk;
- there is a risk-free asset with a known return;
- markets are efficient, with many buyers and sellers, and prices are not distorted by transaction costs or liquidity problems or irrationality.

An alternative approach known as **arbitrage pricing theory** (APT) tackles one potential problem in CAPM, by taking a multi-factor approach to risk. It argues that the risk premium on a share is the sum of the risk premia associated with various economic factors, adjusted by the stock's sensitivity to each factor. In effect it breaks market risk down into a series of component factors. The basic argument is that if two securities have the same level of sensitivity to the key risk factors then in an efficient market they will have the same expected return. In APT, as in CAPM, the required return on a stock is based solely on systematic risk, because it is assumed that investors can eliminate the risks that are unique to that stock through portfolio diversification.

APT does not itself specify what the economic factors are. They could include items such as the level of interest rates, the consumer price index, gross domestic product, credit spreads on corporate bonds, commodity prices etc. For example, we might expect the stock of a large-scale manufacturing company to be especially sensitive to changes in commodity and energy prices. Some fund managers and consulting firms have adapted the APT framework to try to assess the extent to which a given portfolio is exposed to changes in key macroeconomic variables (such as the oil price), rather than as a means of assessing the required return on the portfolio.

10.14   FREE CASH FLOW VALUATION

Many analysts value companies by discounting free cash flows rather than dividends. Partly this is because dividends are less important as a proportion of the total returns on shares than they were historically. Companies that do not pay dividends often have positive free cash flows, or at least will start to generate positive free cash flows over a forecast period.

Free Cash Flow

Also known as Free Cash Flow to the Firm (FCFF). The cash flow generated by a firm from its operating activities, after making the investments required to support it as a going concern and after tax expenses. It is available to make payments to debt providers and other non-equity claimants and then (residually) to the common stockholders.

A company's fair value can be established by discounting the projected free cash flows generated by its operating activities back to a present value. To this is added the present value of any non-operating assets, which could include:

• investments in marketable securities such as Treasury bills or shares in listed companies;
• excess cash and bank deposits, beyond the operational needs of the business.

Note that if operating free cash flow is negative for a given year it means that the providers of capital are putting money into the company that year. If it is positive it means that free cash is available to be paid out to the investors from that year's trading (even though some may actually be retained in the business).

10.14.1   Debt and Equity Streams

If a company is entirely funded by share capital then free cash flows are available to the common stockholders (ordinary shareholders). If it is funded through a mixture of debt and equity then it splits its free cash flows into two streams. One is a relatively safe stream of interest and principal payments due to the debt holders. The other is a more risky cash flow stream available to the common stockholders. The net present value of the free cash flows plus the present value of non-operating assets therefore measures the total value of the firm. It is **firm value**, also known as enterprise value. (The present value of any overfunded pension plans should also be added in the calculation of firm value, and the present value of any underfunded pension schemes subtracted.)

Equity Value

The value of the equity is firm value less the value of the debt. The value of the debt can be measured by present valuing the future interest and principal payments at current market interest rates. For ease of calculation the value of the debt is sometimes taken simply as its book value or its face value.

10.15   FORECASTING FREE CASH FLOWS

Forecasting free cash flows is of course the key to the whole exercise. It is a lengthy process, if the company to be valued is of any size. Typically the analyst builds a spreadsheet with forecasts of sales, direct and overhead costs, capital expenditures, and working capital requirements for a number of years ahead. Normally the faster a business grows the more it will have to invest in fixed assets and working capital. The forecast free cash flows for each year are then discounted at the required return on capital and summed to establish enterprise value. In practice it is an iterative process. The result from the model is checked against valuations using other methods such the enterprise value/EBITDA multiple and the sensitivity of the model to changes in input values is investigated.

10.15.1   Deriving Free Cash Flows: A Simple Example

The 'base case' for estimating a company's future cash flows is normally the data contained in previous historical financial statements. This is then used to forecast future cash flows based on assumptions about the rate at which the company can grow its sales and the level of costs and capital investments that will be required to sustain this growth. Suppose that a company's earnings before interest and tax (EBIT) last year is as set out in Table 10.3.

As discussed in Chapter 9, EBITDA is close to cash flow but not quite the same thing. This is because the company has still to meet its tax expenses out of EBITDA, plus the

Table 10.3   EBIT calculation: figures in $ millions

Sales	4000
Cost of Goods Sold (COGS)	2200
Selling, General, Administration (SGA)	1000
EBITDA	800
Depreciation and Amortization	100
EBIT	700

Table 10.4   Free cash flow calculation: figures in $ millions

EBITDA	800
Tax Expense (at 30% of EBIT)	210
Capital Expenditure	200
Increase in Working Capital	40
Free Cash Flow to the Firm (FCFF)	350

cost of the investments in fixed assets and additional working capital required to sustain its growth level. All of this reduces the amount of cash that is available to pay out to the firm's debt and equity holders i.e. its free cash flow. Suppose that the company pays tax on its EBIT at a rate of 30%, and so its tax expense last year was $210 million. It made capital expenditures of $200 million and increased its working capital by $40 million. With these values, Table 10.4 calculates last year's free cash flow.

The next step in FCFF valuation is to use last year's base level free cash flow of $350 million to forecast future cash flows. These can then be discounted back to today to calculate the present value of the free cash flows. Adding the value of any non-operating assets calculates firm or enterprise value. Finally, equity value is calculated as firm value less the value of the debt.

10.16   WEIGHTED AVERAGE COST OF CAPITAL (WACC)

Calculating the present value of free cash flows requires a discount rate. Suppose that the company in the previous section is funded through a mixture of debt and equity. The following information is available about the firm.

- Required return on equity (cost of equity) = 10%
- Required return on debt (cost of debt) = 6%
- Proportion of equity to total capital = 65%
- Proportion of debt to total capital = 35%
- Tax rate = 30%

The cost of equity can be established using the CAPM. This requires a beta for the company's shares. If the shares have little or no trading history to establish a beta then a **proxy** can be used – in other words, the beta for a listed company which operates in a similar business sector and which has similar risk characteristics. The cost of debt can be established by taking the yield on Treasuries and adding a credit spread that depends on the credit rating of the company's debt. Or alternatively it can be derived from CAPM using a beta value for the debt.

However the problem here is that the company is funded through a mixture of debt and equity. Discounting the company's free cash flows at the cost of debt to establish the present value would not fully take into account the risks faced by the equity investors, and would overstate the company's value. On the other hand using a 10% discount rate (the cost of equity) would understate the company's true value since it is not entirely funded by equity. The debt holders are taking lower risks and require lower returns.

10.16.1 Calculating WACC

A common solution to this problem is to discount the free cash flows at the company's **weighted average cost of capital** (WACC). This is an average of the cost of equity and of debt weighted by the proportions of each. A slight complication is that interest payments are tax deductible. As a result the effective cost of debt to the firm is somewhat less than the gross 6% actually paid to debt holders (assuming that it is paying tax). On the assumption that interest payments can be fully offset against tax at 30% then the effective cost of debt is calculated as follows:

$$\text{Effective Cost of Debt} = 6\% \times (1 - 0.3) = 4.2\%$$

To put it another way, if the firm pays $6 interest on a $100 loan then its tax bill is reduced by $1.80. This tax saving means that the effective cost of the debt is only $4.2 or 4.2%. Since the cost of equity is 10%, the effective cost of debt is 4.2%, and the proportions of equity and debt are 65% and 35% respectively the WACC is as follows:

$$\text{WACC} = (10\% \times 0.65) + (4.2\% \times 0.35) = 8\%$$

The weights (in this case 65% and 35%) should be established by the market value of the equity and of the debt. The former can be taken as the company's market capitalization, total shares outstanding times the current market price per share. The market value of the debt can be established by present valuing the future stream of interest and principal repayments at the appropriate rate for debt carrying that level of risk. This is a common method, but it does assume that the current capital structure of the firm is optimal – in other words, that it has the correct mix of debt and equity. It also assumes that the market capitalization is fair.

10.17 RESIDUAL VALUE

In practice it is not possible to forecast free cash flows for more than perhaps six or eight years ahead, 10 at the outside. In calculating firm value, then, it is necessary to estimate a **residual** or terminal value at the end of the forecast period. This is the value of the company's operational activities as a going concern at that point in the future. Firm value then is:

- the present value of the forecast free cash flows for n years (where n is the number of years free cash flows are forecast);
- plus the present value of the residual value of the firm at year n;
- plus the present value of any non-operating assets such as portfolios of listed shares.

There are a number of techniques used in the securities industry to estimate residual value. One common method is to apply an EBITDA multiple to the year n forecast EBITDA. The multiple can be derived from the average EBITDA multiple at which similar businesses are trading. It builds in an assumption about the company's future growth in earnings and cash flows. Alternatives include estimating terminal value as:

- a multiple of the forecast book value of the firm's operating assets at year n;
- the replacement value of the operating assets at year n;
- the resale value of the firm's operating assets at year n.

This last approach (resale value) simply ignores any value the firm might have as a continuing entity. It assumes that it is worth no more than the physical break-up value of its operating resources.

Finally, residual value can be estimated by forecasting the growth in free cash flow from year n onwards and then using the constant growth perpetuity formula. For example, if the forecast free cash flow for year n is $\$500$ million and it is assumed that this will grow at 4% in perpetuity then the free cash flow for year $n+1$ will be $\$520$ million. Assume that the WACC is 8%. Then the terminal value at year n is calculated as follows:

$$\text{Residual Value} = \frac{\$520 \text{ million}}{0.08 - 0.04} = \$13,000 \text{ million}$$

This residual value has to be discounted back n years and then added to the present value of the free cash flows that were forecast for n years plus the present value of non-operating assets. The constant free cash flow growth rate (here presumed to be 4%) can be based on the forecast long-term growth rate for the economy.

Note that it may be necessary to recalculate the WACC used in the residual value calculation compared to that used in present valuing the n years of forecast cash flows. There are two main reasons for this. Firstly, during the n years the company may be in a high-growth phase, with an equity beta above one. However after that, during the 'steady growth' phase, the company's stock will tend to move in line with the market as a whole, so it can be assumed that the equity beta will be one. Secondly, calculating the WACC is based on an assumption about the optimal mix of debt and equity for the firm. This may be different in its long-run steady-growth phase than during the next n years. A firm with a low degree of leverage may be able to sustain higher levels of debt if it becomes a more established business.

10.18   WACC AND LEVERAGE

There is an obvious objection to the use of WACC in discounting free cash flows. Clearly the fact that interest payments are tax deductible is an advantage. However even if this effect is taken away it seems that if a firm increases its leverage (the proportion of debt used to fund the business) it can reduce its WACC at a stroke. In that case why do companies not simply replace expensive equity with cheaper debt? It appears that this would increase the present value of free cash flows by lowering the discount rate.

There does seem to be something wrong with this result. Intuitively it seems that the value of a firm should depend on 'real world' factors such as profitability and return on capital, not on how it happens to be funded. After all, a single investor could in theory buy up a company's equity and debt. It seems strange that the value of the investment could be affected by the way in which the investor chooses to take returns out of free cash flows – via interest or via dividend payments.

10.18.1   Return on Assets

One response to this problem is to argue that the assets or resources of a firm generate a stream of free cash flows. What WACC is trying to measure is the required return on that bundle of assets, a rate that in the absence of tax distortions is unaffected by the proportions of equity and debt capital funding the business. The rate can be applied to the free cash flows to calculate firm value. In the absence of tax effects, the argument runs, firm value is *not* affected by leverage. What leverage affects is how firm value is *apportioned* between the equity and debt stakeholders. In the following sub-section a case study is set out based on this argument.

10.18.2 Constant Return on Assets: Case Study

To eliminate tax distortions the case assumes that interest payments cannot be offset against tax. Suppose that we have the following data to establish a company's cost of capital.

- Risk-free rate = 5 %
- Market risk premium = 4 %
- Equity beta = 1.2
- Debt beta = 0.2
- Proportion of equity to total capital = 70 %
- Proportion of debt to total capital = 30 %

The cost of equity and of debt for the company (the required returns) are calculated using CAPM:

$$\text{Cost of Equity} = 5\% + (1.2 \times 4\%) = 9.8\%$$

$$\text{Cost of Debt} = 5\% + (0.2 \times 4\%) = 5.8\%$$

Therefore:

$$\text{WACC} = (9.8\% \times 0.7) + (5.8\% \times 0.3) = 8.6\%$$

Assume that the WACC calculation establishes the required return on the company's assets and that the 8.6 % figure is not affected by leverage. What happens if the company increases the proportion of debt to (say) 40 % without any changes to the nature of the underlying business? The riskiness of the debt will increase, essentially because a higher level of debt means that the likelihood of default will increase. Suppose that the debt beta rises to (say) 0.3. Then the cost of debt has to be recalculated:

$$\text{Cost of Debt} = 5\% + (0.3 \times 4\%) = 6.2\%$$

It is assumed that the return on assets will stay constant at 8.6 %. So the cost of equity will no longer be 9.8 %. In fact it must be 10.2 %:

$$\text{Return on Assets} = 8.6\% = (10.2\% \times 0.6) + (6.2\% \times 0.4)$$

The required return on equity has increased because of the increased level of leverage – it has become a riskier investment. Note that in this example the cost of debt *and* the cost of equity have increased. However debt now accounts for a larger proportion of firm value and so the return on assets (the weighted average of the cost of equity and the cost of debt) is unchanged at 8.6 %.

10.19   ASSETS BETA METHOD

An alternative to using WACC is to establish the required return on assets directly by calculating an **assets beta** for the firm and inserting the result into the CAPM formula. This measures the systematic risk of the returns generated by the firm as a whole. However in theory a single investor could buy all of the firm, debt and equity, and own all the assets and their returns. So the assets beta is simply the weighted average of the betas of the firm's equity and of its debt.

The original example in the previous section used the following data.

- Risk-free rate $= 5\%$
- Market risk premium $= 4\%$
- Equity beta $= 1.2$
- Debt beta $= 0.2$
- Proportion of equity to total capital $= 70\%$
- Proportion of debt to total capital $= 30\%$

Therefore:

$$\text{Assets Beta} = (1.2 \times 0.7) + (0.2 \times 0.3) = 0.9$$

CAPM tells us that:

$$\text{Return on Assets} = \text{Risk-free Rate} + (\text{Asset Beta} \times \text{Market Risk Premium})$$

Therefore:

$$\text{Return on Assets} = 5\% + (0.9 \times 4\%) = 8.6\%$$

10.19.1   Increasing the Proportion of Debt

What happens if the proportion of debt rises to 40%? Assuming it is correct to say that (in the absence of tax distortions) the return on a company's assets is unaffected by leverage then it follows that the assets beta is also unaffected by leverage. However increased leverage will increase the riskiness of the debt. Assume as before that the debt beta rises to 0.3 when the level of debt is increased to 40% of total capital. If the assets beta stays unchanged at 0.9 it must be the case that the equity beta also increases. In fact it must rise to 1.3:

$$\text{Assets Beta} = 0.9 = (1.3 \times 0.6) + (0.3 \times 0.4)$$

Given the higher beta value, CAPM tells us that the cost of equity has also risen:

$$\text{Cost of Equity} = 5\% + (1.3 \times 4\%) = 10.2\%$$

This is the same value calculated in the previous section using the WACC method, when it was assumed that in the absence of tax effects return on assets is unaffected by leverage. The assets beta has remained the same even though the betas of the equity and debt have

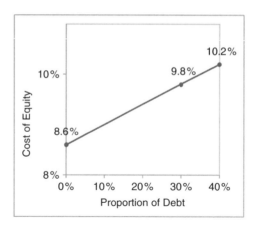

Figure 10.2   Relationship between leverage and cost of equity in the case study.

both risen, because the proportion of debt used to fund the business has increased. Note that if the company has *no debt* the cost of equity is the 8.6% expected return on assets. Figure 10.2 shows the relationship between the level of debt and the cost of equity in this example.

10.20   COMPANY VALUE AND LEVERAGE

This is a complex subject, but there may be reasons why a company's value and its required return on assets are not independent of the level of debt in the business. For one thing, the case study in the previous two sections ignored the effects of corporate taxation and of tax paid by investors. Companies do seem to replace equity with debt when the relative tax advantage for investors shifts in favour of holding debt securities. In these circumstances it seems that firms can increase leverage and also reduce their overall cost of capital.

What factors influence the assets beta for a whole company? High beta firms tend to operate in cyclical sectors such as information technology. They may also have high levels of fixed costs. In favourable circumstances demand for their products rises sharply and they outperform the market. In difficult trading conditions they are hit hard by falling sales and by having to support their fixed cost base out of shrinking revenues.

10.20.1   Levered and Unlevered Betas

The equity betas quoted in the capital markets are normally based on the degree of leverage the company has at the time they were calculated (sometimes average debt over a period of time is used). The previous section showed that equity beta is affected by leverage. Market practitioners therefore calculate what is known as the 'unlevered beta', which is what the equity beta would be if the company was 100% funded by equity and had no debt. The unlevered beta can then be 'relevered' to calculate the equity beta for any given level of debt.

The standard industry approach to unlevering equity beta is to take into account the benefits of tax relief on interest payments, whilst assuming that the debt is risk-free and has a beta of zero. This simplification produces the following equation:

$$\text{Unlevered Beta} = \frac{\text{Levered Beta}}{1 + (1 - \text{Tax Rate}) \times \dfrac{\text{Debt}}{\text{Equity}}}$$

For example, suppose that a firm is 80 % funded by equity and 20 % by debt. Its tax rate is 30 %. The levered equity beta at that level of debt is 1.2. Then:

$$\text{Unlevered Beta} = \frac{1.2}{1 + (1 - 0.3) \times \dfrac{0.2}{0.8}} = 1.02$$

This formula can be rearranged to calculate a 'relevered' beta from the unlevered value. Suppose the company increases its proportion of debt to 30 % of total capital. Then the 'relevered' beta of the equity at that level of debt is calculated as follows:

$$\text{Relevered Beta} = 1.02 \times \left[1 + (1 - 0.3) \times \frac{0.3}{0.7} \right] = 1.33$$

10.21   CHAPTER SUMMARY

A share (common stock) can be valued as the present value of the expected dividend stream. In practice, it is difficult to forecast dividends for more than a few years ahead. Therefore the dividend discount method requires an assumption that dividends will continue to grow at a given rate or rates after a certain point in time, or an assumption about the future resale value of the share. The constant growth dividend discount model shows that the prospective price/earnings ratio can be calculated from the dividend payout ratio, the required return on equity, and an assumed constant dividend growth rate. Many equity analysts use an alternative to the dividend discount model, which involves establishing firm or enterprise value by discounting free cash flows to the firm (FCFF). Free cash flows are derived from EBIT forecasts. The models require a discount rate. The Capital Asset Pricing Model developed in the 1960s remains a standard model used in the securities industry to establish the required return on a security given its risk. Risk in this context is measured not by the total variation in the returns on the security but by the risk that the security would add to a diversified market portfolio. This is established by the beta value. Free cash flows are conventionally discounted at a rate that blends the required return on a company's shares with the required return on its debt, taking into account the ability of the firm to offset interest payments against its tax liabilities. In practice tax effects mean that companies are sometimes able to reduce their overall cost of capital and boost firm value by changing the mixture of debt and equity used to fund the business. Equity betas are affected by leverage. The betas published in the capital markets industry are normally based on the current level of debt. An 'unlevered' beta is one calculated on the assumption that the firm has 100 % equity and no debt. It is used to estimate what the equity beta would be for any given level of debt.

11
Interest Rate Forwards and Futures

11.1 CHAPTER OVERVIEW

Interest rate forwards and futures are derivative contracts based on underlying money market interest rates. This chapter begins by discussing a key product known as a **forward rate agreement** (FRA). An FRA is a bilateral over-the-counter derivative contract directly negotiated between two parties fixing the rate of interest on a notional loan or deposit for a period of time in the future. The chapter sets out the FRA settlement procedure and how the forward interest rate can be established by cash market interest rates. It considers a typical hedging application for a corporate, using an FRA to lock into a future funding rate. **Interest rate futures** are the exchange-traded equivalents of FRAs. Because they are freely tradable they have the advantage of liquidity. The chapter explores the structure of key interest rate contracts such as the three-month Eurodollar futures traded on the Chicago Mercantile Exchange and the three-month EURIBOR futures contract traded on Eurex. It considers trading and margining procedures and the role of the clearing house. Finally, the chapter assesses the trading and hedging applications of interest rate futures and how they can be used to lock into a known investment or borrowing rate for a future period of time.

11.2 FORWARD RATE AGREEMENTS (FRAs)

An FRA is a bilateral contract agreed between two parties fixing the rate of interest that will apply to a notional principal sum of money for an agreed term in the future, the contract period. The principal amount never changes hands. It is used to calculate the settlement amount due on the transaction. One party to the agreement is the 'buyer' and the other is the 'seller', although in fact nothing is ever literally bought or sold.

- **Buyer.** The buyer of the FRA is compensated in cash by the seller if the benchmark interest rate for the contract period turns out to be above the rate agreed in the contract.
- **Seller.** The seller of the FRA is compensated by the buyer if the benchmark interest rate for the contract period turns out to be below the rate agreed in the contract.

Corporate borrowers wishing to hedge against rising interest rates are natural buyers of FRAs. Money market investors wishing to protect themselves against declining interest rates are natural sellers. An FRA is a derivative instrument in that its value is derived from underlying cash market interest rates.

FRAs are very similar to the interest rate futures contracts traded on exchanges, except that they are over-the-counter (OTC) transactions. An OTC derivative is a legal and binding agreement made directly between two parties. As such it cannot be freely traded and carries counterparty risk – the risk that the other party to the contract might fail to fulfil its obligations. Chapter 7 discussed the moves in the credit derivatives market to introduce central counterparty arrangements to ensure that trades are properly settled and due payments are made. In time similar arrangements may apply to a wide range of OTC derivatives.

11.2.1 Dealing Limits and Terms

FRAs are dealt by banks in a wide range of currencies. In the absence of a central counterparty guarantee, banks will only allow their dealers to enter into FRA contracts with known counterparties whose credentials have been checked by the bank's internal credit function. In addition, the bank will impose a limit on the value of contracts that can be entered into with a given counterparty at any one moment in time. This is in order to avoid **concentration risk** – the risk that if the bank has too many deals on its books with one counterparty it will incur serious losses if that organization suffers financial distress. In the London market FRAs are normally dealt on the terms and conditions laid out by the British Bankers' Association (FRABBA terms).

11.3 FRA APPLICATION: CASE STUDY

BIGCO is a corporate borrower with a loan from a bank. The company pays a rate of interest linked to current money market interest rates. The principal of the loan is $ 100 million and interest is paid every six months in arrears. The rate of interest is fixed twice a year at six-month dollar LIBOR plus a fixed spread of 100 basis points (1 %). The firm's borrowing rate for the next six-month period (183 days starting from spot) has just been set at 6 %. (Following market convention, all interest rates in this case are expressed on a per annum basis.)

BIGCO's chief finance officer (CFO) is concerned that rates for the following period may be appreciably higher. This would have a detrimental effect on the company's cash flows and profitability. The CFO buys an FRA from a bank. The terms are set out in Table 11.1. The trade date when the contract is agreed is today i.e. two business days before the value date which is spot. The contract period of 6v12 ('six against 12 months') means that the FRA covers a six-month contract period starting six months after spot. The actual number of days in this six-month period will be used to calculate the payments due under the FRA. In this example it is 182 days.

The FRA deal works as follows:

- If the six-month dollar LIBOR rate for the contract period turns out to be above the fixed contract rate of 5.25 % p.a. then the bank will compensate BIGCO.
- If the six-month dollar LIBOR rate for the contract period turns out to be below the fixed contract rate of 5.25 % then BIGCO will compensate the bank.

Table 11.1 FRA contract details

Contract amount	$ 100 million
Contract currency	US dollars
Contract rate	5.25 % p.a.
Trade date	Today
Value date	Spot
Contract period	6v12 months (a 182-day period)
Settlement date	6 months (183 days after spot)
Maturity date	12 months (365 days after spot)
Reference rate	Six-month US dollar LIBOR
Day-count method	Actual/360

11.3.1 Settlement Payment on the FRA

The settlement date on the sample contract is six months after spot. By that point the actual market interest rate for the period covered by the contract will be known to both parties. In this example it will be established by reference to the LIBOR rate for the period, which will be broadcast on the electronic news services.

Suppose that the LIBOR rate for the contract period is actually fixed at 6 % p.a. Then the bank that sold the FRA has to pay BIGCO a cash sum in compensation for the unexpected increase in interest rates, covering a period of 182 days. The payment will be calculated using the appropriate actual/360 day-count method for dollar LIBOR. If it was paid on the maturity date the payment would be as follows:

$$\text{Notional} \times (\text{LIBOR Fix} - \text{Contract Rate}) \times \frac{\text{Days in Contract Period}}{360}$$

$$\$\,100 \text{ million} \times (0.06 - 0.0525) \times \frac{182}{360} = \$\,379,166.67$$

11.3.2 Payment on Settlement Date

If the FRA was settled at maturity the compensation payment would indeed be $\$\,379,166.67$. However the payment is usually made on the settlement date, at the beginning of the contract period. The settlement date in this case is six months after spot. The relevant dates for the contract are shown in Figure 11.1.

The $\$\,379,166.67$ due at the maturity of the FRA would therefore be discounted back for 182 days at the LIBOR rate fixed for the contract period, which in this case was assumed to be 6 %:

$$\text{Settlement Sum} = \frac{\$\,379,166.67}{1 + \left(0.06 \times \dfrac{182}{360}\right)} = \$\,368,003.88$$

One advantage of making the settlement payment at the start of the forward period covered by the FRA is that it reduces the risk that the other party to the contract might default on its obligations.

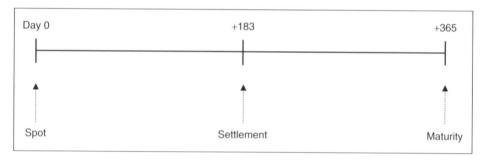

Figure 11.1 Relevant dates for the FRA.

11.3.3 Compensation Formula

The full compensation or settlement formula is as follows:

$$\text{Settlement Sum} = \frac{\text{Notional} \times (\text{LIBOR Fix} - \text{Contract Rate}) \times \dfrac{\text{Days in Contract Period}}{\text{Year Base}}}{1 + \left(\text{LIBOR} \times \dfrac{\text{Contract Days}}{\text{Year Base}}\right)}$$

The interest rates in the formula are per annum and in decimal format. The contract days are the actual number of calendar days in the FRA contract period. For dollars (and euros) the year base is 360. For sterling it is 365. Note that in accordance with its standard procedures the dollar LIBOR rate for the contract period will actually be fixed by the British Bankers' Association two business days before the FRA settlement date. For sterling FRAs the LIBOR rate is fixed on the settlement day.

11.4 BORROWING COSTS WITH AN FRA HEDGE

In the above case BIGCO is paying LIBOR + 1 % on its underlying borrowing. It buys an FRA at a rate of 5.25 %. If LIBOR turns out to be 6 % then it is paid an annualized 0.75 % on the FRA contract by the bank. This means that its effective cost of borrowing is:

$$6\% + 1\% - 0.75\% = 6.25\% \text{ p. a.}$$

This is simply the contract rate of 5.25 % plus the 1 % fixed spread over LIBOR paid on the underlying loan. In fact, whatever LIBOR turns out to be for the contract period BIGCO's net cost of borrowing will be fixed at 6.15 %. For example, if LIBOR is fixed at 5 % then BIGCO will have to pay 6 % on its loan *and* it will have to pay annualized compensation of 0.25 % on the FRA. The net funding cost for the period is:

$$5\% + 1\% + 0.25\% = 6.25\% \text{ p a.}$$

For BIGCO the FRA is simply a hedge against rising interest rates. The firm can lock into a known interest rate for the contract period. The hedge shares a common feature with other hedges assembled using forward or futures contracts. It establishes a fixed borrowing cost for the contract period, which is helpful in terms of managing the finances of the business. The disadvantage is that the firm cannot benefit from a fall in interest rates. It is locked in at a fixed rate.

11.4.1 FRA Payment Legs

Figure 11.2 illustrates the position of BIGCO after the FRA is dealt. It shows the payment due on the contract as two different legs, which in practice are netted out. In the FRA BIGCO pays the bank 5.25 % fixed. In return the bank pays LIBOR. If (for example) LIBOR turns out to be 6 % for the contract period then the bank owes a net 0.75 % to BIGCO. This is an annualized figure. In cash terms the bank pays $0.75\% \times 182/360 \times \$100$ million discounted back six months to the start of the contract period.

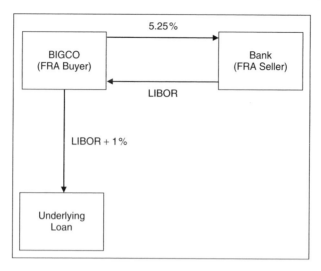

Figure 11.2   FRA plus underlying loan.

Figure 11.2 illustrates the fact that BIGCO's net cost of borrowing for the period covered by the FRA is 6.25 % p.a. The LIBOR leg received on the FRA simply cancels out the LIBOR element due on the underlying loan.

11.5   FRA MARKET QUOTATIONS

Dealers quote FRA prices on screens in much the same way as deposit rates. The screens show offer and bid rates for regular contract periods such as 3v6 and 6v12. The former (three against six) is for a three-month contract period starting in three months. The latter (six against twelve) is for a six-month period starting in six months. However dealers will also quote for irregular periods (sometimes called 'broken dates') on request.

Suppose that a dealer quotes the following rates for 6v12 month dollar FRAs:

Offer 5.25 % − Bid 5.21 %

- The dealer is selling FRAs at a rate of 5.25 %.
- The dealer is buying FRAs at a rate of 5.21 %.

Settlement is six months after spot. The maturity date is 12 months after spot. The contract period is a six-month period starting in six months. Imagine that as a result of making these quotes, the dealer sells a 6v12 month FRA at 5.25 %. The dealer is then lucky enough to find a second counterparty who wishes to deal on exactly the same dates and notional principal. However this time the dealer buys the FRA from the counterparty, at a rate of 5.21 %. The impact of making the two matched trades is shown in Figure 11.3.

11.5.1   Market Risk and Counterparty Risk

In Figure 11.3 the dealer makes a four basis point spread on the two deals combined. Furthermore, the market risk (the interest rate exposure) is fully hedged. If rates rise the

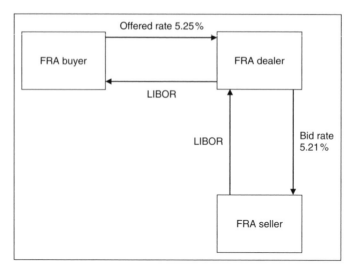

Figure 11.3   Matched FRA deals.

dealer will have to pay the FRA buyer, but will receive a compensating payment from the FRA seller. However the deals are made separately with the two counterparties so there is still an exposure to counterparty risk. This risk is not on the notional principal on the trades, because the notional is never exchanged. The risk is that a payment is made on one FRA, but nothing is received on the other deal. In practice counterparty risk can be managed by setting position limits and also by taking collateral from counterparties. It can also be managed if a third party such as a clearing house agrees to guarantee payments.

11.5.2   Shading FRA Rates

In reality the average FRA dealer will have many deals on the book and it is unlikely that all the interest rate exposures will exactly match out. If so, the dealer may decide to 'shade' or adjust the quoted bid and offer rates. For example, if the dealer has a net exposure to rising interest rates and wishes to reduce the market risk then he or she is a potential buyer of FRAs. The dealer may decide to quote rates into the market that will encourage sellers of FRAs to trade with the dealer rather than with other banks.

11.5.3   Shading Rates: Example

Suppose that the current market rates for 6v12 month dollar FRAs are as follows:

$$\text{Offer } 5.25\,\% - \text{Bid } 5.21\,\%$$

A dealer who is exposed to rising interest rates for this contract period may decide to increase his or her offer and bid rates for 6v12 FRA contracts as follows.

• **Offer Rate 5.26 %.** This is a less attractive rate than the market rate. It will tend to discourage buyers.

- **Bid Rate 5.22 %.** This is a more attractive rate than the market rate. It will tend to encourage sellers.

The dealer could also manage any residual interest rate risk on the trading book by using exchange-traded interest rate futures, which are discussed later in this chapter. Interest rate futures in major currencies such as the US dollar are quick and easy to transact and are highly liquid. In fact the prices on interest rate futures are commonly used by dealers to establish FRA rates.

Increasingly, the position limits imposed on traders to contain market risk are determined by complex risk calculations rather than by simple rules of thumb. For example, a dealer may be told to reduce the interest rate risk on a trading book when the potential losses (based on statistical analysis) look as though they could exceed a predefined level. This is the essence of the **value-at-risk** method for determining the risk on a trading book.

11.6   THE FORWARD INTEREST RATE

The contract rate on an FRA is not a cash market rate, starting now, but a rate for a future time period. The theoretical or 'fair' rate can be calculated from cash market rates using the same approach followed in Chapter 6 when deriving forward rates from the yield curve for par bonds. The difference is that most FRAs cover contract periods inside one year and the calculations are normally based on simple rather than compound interest.

11.6.1   Arbitrage Relationships

The task is to calculate the theoretical 6v12-month US dollar forward interest rate. Call this rate f_{6v12}. The following information is available on cash market interest rates.

- 6 months (183 days) rate $= 5\%$ p.a. actual/360
- 12 months (365 days) rate $= 5.18\%$ p.a. actual/360

To keep things simple here bid/offer spreads and other transaction costs are ignored. These interest rates and the time periods they apply to are illustrated in Figure 11.4. This also shows the 6v12-month rate f_{6v12}.

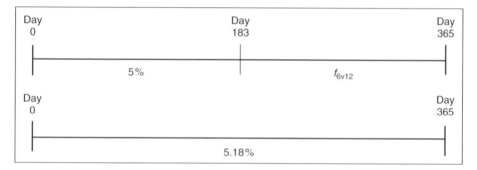

Figure 11.4   Cash market rates and the forward rate.

The cash market rates and the forward rate f_{6v12} cannot move too far out of alignment, otherwise profitable arbitrage opportunities will open up. Suppose, for example, it is possible to sell a 6v12-month FRA at a rate of (say) 5.50 %. This provides a simple arbitrage opportunity, taking the following three steps.

1. Borrow $ 1 for 12 months (365 days) at 5.18 % p.a.
2. Invest $ 1 for six months (183 days) at 5 % p.a.
3. Lock into a reinvestment rate of 5.5 % p.a. for the six-month (182-day) period starting in six months, by selling a 6v12-month FRA.

The repayment amount due on the borrowing is:

$$1 + \left(0.0518 \times \frac{365}{360} \right) = \$ 1.0525$$

The proceeds from the first six-month deposit are:

$$1 + \left(0.05 \times \frac{183}{360} \right) = \$ 1.0254$$

The proceeds from reinvesting this money for another six months (182 days) at a guaranteed rate of 5.5 % are:

$$1.0254 \times \left[1 + \left(0.055 \times \frac{182}{360} \right) \right] = \$ 1.0539$$

The arbitrage profit per dollar invested is:

$$1.0539 - 1.0525 = \$ 0.0014$$

11.6.2 The Fair Forward Rate

Clearly, the 'fair' 6v12 month forward interest rate cannot be 5.5 %. It must be less than that, for the arbitrage opportunity to disappear. Suppose the cash market and FRA rates are all in alignment and there is no arbitrage available. Then it must be the case that:

$$1 + \left(0.0518 \times \frac{365}{360} \right) = \left[1 + \left(0.05 \times \frac{183}{360} \right) \right] \times \left[1 + \left(f_{6v12} \times \frac{182}{360} \right) \right]$$

The left-hand side of this equation calculates the principal plus interest on a $ 1 one year loan at 5.18 % p.a. For there to be no arbitrage this must equal the proceeds from investing $ 1 for 183 days at 5 % p.a. reinvested at the fair 6v12 month forward rate for a further 182 days. Turning this equation round, the fair forward rate f_{6v12} is calculated as follows:

$$f_{6v12} = \left\{ \left[\frac{1 + \left(0.0518 \times \frac{365}{360} \right)}{1 + \left(0.05 \times \frac{183}{360} \right)} \right] - 1 \right\} \times \frac{360}{182} = 0.0523 = 5.23 \%$$

If the 6v12-month FRA can be sold at 5.23 % p.a. then the arbitrage profit disappears. The proceeds from investing a dollar for six months and locking into a reinvestment rate by selling a 6v12-month FRA will exactly equal the cost of borrowing for 12 months. The forward rate formula is as follows. This version is to be used with money market rates expressed with simple interest (the interest rates should be inserted as decimals):

$$\text{Forward Rate} = \left\{ \left[\frac{1 + \left(\text{Long Period Rate} \times \dfrac{\text{Days in Long Period}}{\text{Year Basis}} \right)}{1 + \left(\text{Short Period Rate} \times \dfrac{\text{Days in Short Period}}{\text{Year Basis}} \right)} \right] - 1 \right\}$$

$$\times \frac{\text{Year Basis}}{\text{Days in Forward Period}}$$

where:

Long period rate	= cash market rate to the second date in the forward period
Days in long period	= actual days to the second date in the forward period
Short period rate	= cash market rate to the first date in the forward period
Days in short period	= actual days to the first date in the forward period
Year basis	= 360 or 365 depending on the currency
Days in forward period	= actual days between the first and second date in the forward period

11.6.3 Forward Rates in Practice

The example in the previous sub-section ignores the effects of bid/offer spreads. To take this into account and to calculate the forward offer and the forward bid rate insert the following into the forward rate formula:

- **Forward offer.** Use the cash market offer rate for the 'long period' and the cash market bid rate for the 'short period'.
- **Forward bid.** Use the cash market bid rate for the 'long period' and the cash market offer rate for the 'short period'.

In practice FRA rates in major currencies such as the US dollar tend to be derived from the interest rate futures market (covered in the following sections). This is highly liquid and provides a relatively straightforward way for FRA dealers to manage the market risks on their trading books. As a result the bid/offer spreads on dollar FRAs may be narrower than the theoretical rates derived from cash market interest rates using the method shown in the previous section. On the other hand cash market rates, FRA rates, and the rates implied in interest rate futures prices cannot move too far out of alignment, otherwise profitable arbitrage trades will open up.

11.7 FINANCIAL FUTURES

Commodity futures contracts have been traded on exchanges such as the Chicago Board of Trade (CBOT) and the Chicago Mercantile Exchange (CME) for many years. (These two giant exchanges merged in 2007.) They are a natural extension of trading in physical commodities such as wheat, coffee, and orange juice. Farmers can sell futures as a means of locking into a price for selling their crops on future dates at an agreed price. Users of commodities can buy futures contracts as a means of fixing a purchase price on future delivery dates. By contrast, financial futures are relatively recent, first successfully introduced on the CME (known as the 'Merc') in 1972.

11.7.1 Definition

A common textbook definition of a financial futures contract is that it is an agreement made on an organized exchange:

- to buy or to sell;
- a standard amount of a specified financial instrument;
- on a specified date or range of dates in the future;
- at a price agreed up-front.

Some contracts such as the US Treasury bond futures traded on the CBOT follow this definition reasonably well, since there is indeed a physical delivery process (see Chapter 12 for more details). A buyer of US Treasury bond futures who has not closed out before the delivery month will take delivery of bonds and will be invoiced against delivery as if it were a cash market transaction. In practice, though, the great majority of contracts are closed out before delivery. However in the case of contracts such as interest rate futures the traditional definition can be a little misleading because there is no actual delivery process. The contracts are always **cash-settled**. In this respect interest rate futures are like their over-the-counter relatives, forward rate agreements.

11.7.2 Trading Futures Contracts

The traditional trading method is by open outcry in trading pits, in which traders call out the prices at which they are willing to buy and sell contracts. Increasingly, however, futures and options trading takes place through electronic screen-based systems which match buy and sell orders. The CME currently operates both methods in tandem. Its Globex® platform allows deals to be made by market participants operating from outside the physical trading floor and after the regular trading hours. The London International Financial Futures and Options Exchange (LIFFE) and Eurex, the combined Swiss-German exchange, are wholly electronic markets. Trades on LIFFE are made through its LIFFE-CONNECT® system which is operated in sites around the world; the physical trading floor finally closed for business in 2000.

Standardization and Performance

Unlike over-the-counter derivatives, financial futures are standardized products. This is to encourage active and liquid trading. They are also guaranteed by the clearing house associated with the exchange which virtually eliminates counterparty risk. The clearing house guarantees delivery and payment.

Table 11.2   CME Eurodollar futures contract

Unit of trading	Eurodollar time deposit with a principal value of $1 million and a three-month maturity
Contract listing	March, June, September, December in a quarterly cycle plus the four nearest serial contract months
Quotation	100.00 minus the implied rate of interest for the future time period covered by the contract
Full tick size	0.01 (representing in interest rate terms one basis point p.a.)
Full tick value	$25
Settlement method	Cash settled

Source: Chicago Mercantile Exchange.

11.8   CME EURODOLLAR FUTURES

The three-month Eurodollar futures contract traded on the CME is one of the most liquid financial futures contracts in the world. It is widely used by financial institutions to hedge short-term interest rate exposures or to take a leveraged position in anticipation of a rise or fall in interest rates. As discussed in Chapter 2, Eurodollars are US dollars held on deposit in international accounts. The CME contract is based on the LIBOR rate on a notional $1 million Eurodollar deposit starting at a specific date in the future. The contract specification is set out in Table 11.2.

The contract is based on the rate of interest for a notional $1 million three-month Eurodollar deposit commencing on the third Wednesday of the contract month (such as March 2009). The contract amount is purely notional – buyers and sellers simply receive the difference between the price at which they enter into contracts and the price at which they close the position. Open contracts are automatically closed on the last trading day, when cash settlement is made against the LIBOR rate for three-month dollar deposits established that day. The LIBOR is deducted from 100.00 to establish the final close-out price of the futures contracts.

11.9   EURODOLLAR FUTURES QUOTATIONS

The price of the Eurodollar futures contract is not quoted as an interest rate but as 100.00 minus the interest rate for the contract period. For example, a March futures price of 96.00 implies an interest rate of 4 % p.a. for the three-month period starting on the third Wednesday in March. In effect, this is the market's expectation of what the three-month LIBOR rate will be for that future time period. The quotation convention was adopted to make life simpler for traders because it makes the Eurodollar futures prices behave rather like the prices of fixed-income securities. Traders know that if expected interest rates are rising (falling) they should be thinking about selling (buying) interest rate futures.

Tick Size and Value

A one tick movement in the price of a Eurodollar futures contract is 0.01. In interest rate terms this represents one basis point or 0.01 % p.a. The contract is based on a $1 million three-month (90 day) LIBOR deposit. Each one tick move in the price of a contract represents a profit or loss of $25. This is the tick value.

$$\text{Tick Value} = \$1 \text{ million} \times 0.01\% \times \frac{90}{360} = \$25$$

The minimum price fluctuation on this contract is a half tick (worth $12.50), except for the nearest expiring month where it is a quarter tick (worth $6.25).

11.9.1 Overall Profits and Losses on Eurodollar Futures Trades

Suppose that the forthcoming March contract is currently trading at 96.00. This implies a future rate of interest for the three-month period starting in mid-March of 4 % p.a. A trader believes that interest rates are set to fall more steeply than anticipated by the market, as the Federal Reserve seeks to stimulate the flagging US economy. The trader buys 100 March Eurodollar futures contracts at 96.00.

The contracts cease trading on the Monday before the third Wednesday in March. On that day the BBA LIBOR rate for the three-month period covered by the contract is fixed. Suppose it is fixed at 3.90 %. The futures will therefore finally close at a price of $100.00 - 3.90 = 96.10$. Since the trader bought at 96.00 the profit is 10 ticks per contract, at $25 per tick. Ignoring funding and transaction costs, the net profit is as follows:

$$\text{Profit} = 10 \text{ ticks} \times 100 \text{ contracts} \times \$25 = \$25,000$$

In interest rate terms, the trader locked into a deposit rate of 4 % p.a. for the three-month (90 days) contract period. The total notional (based on 100 contracts) is $100 million. The actual LIBOR rate for the period was fixed at only 3.90 % p.a. The profit can also be calculated as follows:

$$\text{Profit} = \$100 \text{ million} \times (4\% - 3.90\%) \times \frac{90}{360} = \$25,000$$

11.10 FUTURES MARGINING

Only members are allowed to trade directly on a futures exchange. They may do so on their own account, or on behalf of clients or other brokers acting for clients. Once a deal is struck the clearing house associated with the exchange steps in and becomes the effective counterparty to both sides, virtually eliminating counterparty risk. This system also means that a trader who buys and sells the same number of contracts for the same contract month has a directly offsetting position and the trades simply cancel out.

The clearing house settles trades, regulates delivery, and also generates data about trading activities. In cases such as the CME and Eurex the clearing house is a division or subsidiary of the exchange. With LIFFE in London trades are cleared by LCH.Clearnet which is a separate organization. It also operates as the central counterparty for cash equities trades made on the London Stock Exchange's electronic order-matching system.

11.10.1 Initial Margin

As a safety measure the clearing house requires traders opening a position to put up collateral, commonly known as **initial margin**. (In US exchanges such as the CME and the CBOT it is now referred to as an **initial performance bond**.) This is a 'good faith' deposit designed to protect the clearing house, the members of the exchange, and their clients, against default. A client who is not a member of the exchange and who wishes to open a futures position must post initial margin with a broker which will handle all the payments with the clearing house. Smaller brokers do this via a clearing member of the exchange, a large investment bank, or securities house which settles directly with the clearing house.

The minimum initial margin is set by the clearing house according to the volatility of the contract that is traded, and can therefore change over time. However a broker may request a higher amount than the minimum from a client. It may be possible, depending on the terms and conditions offered by a particular broker, for a client to put up tradable securities such as Treasury bills against the initial margin requirement rather than cash.

11.10.2 Mark-to-Market

As a further safety measure futures position are also **marked-to-market** on a regular basis, normally at the end of the trading day. This means that the closing or settlement value of the contract is used to calculate a profit and loss figure which is credited to or debited from the client's account with their broker. The client may be called upon to deposit additional margin as a result of losses, or can withdraw cash from the account as a result of profits. The advantage of this system is that it prevents losses and profits from accumulating over time.

11.11 MARGINING EXAMPLE: EURIBOR FUTURES ON EUREX

To illustrate the operation of futures margining this section looks at the three-month EURIBOR futures contract traded on Eurex. (There is a very similar contract traded on LIFFE, which is part of the NYSE Euronext group.) EURIBOR® is the key reference rate for lending in the euro and is set by the European Banking Federation (FBE) and the Financial Markets Association (ACI). The Eurex contract specification is set out in Table 11.3. The daily settlement price is used for the daily mark-to-market calculation. The final settlement price is used for the final close out calculation on the last trading day. The tick value on the contract is calculated as follows:

$$\text{EUR 1 million} \times 0.005\,\% \times \frac{90}{360} = \text{EUR 12.50}$$

11.11.1 Trading Strategy: An Example

A trader believes that short-term interest rates in the euro are set to fall more sharply than are already factored into the price of EURIBOR futures. The March contract is currently

Table 11.3 Three-month EURIBOR futures contract traded on Eurex

Unit of trading	EUR 1 million three-month time deposit based on the Euro Interbank Offered Rate (EURIBOR).
Contract listing	March, June, September, December.
Quotation	100 minus the rate for interest for the contract period to three decimal places.
Tick size	0.005 (representing in interest rate terms a half a basis point)
Tick value	EUR 12.50.
Last Trading Day	Two exchange days before the third Wednesday in the contract month.
Daily settlement price	For the current contract month, based on an average of the prices of all transactions made during the minute before 17:15 CET.
Final settlement price	Based on the EURIBOR rate for three-month euro time deposits set at 11:00 CET on the last trading day.

Source: Eurex.

trading at 95.250. This implies a rate of interest in the euro for the three-month period starting on the third Wednesday of March of 4.75 % p.a.

The trader contacts a broker and arranges to buy 100 contracts at 95.250. The trader will have to lodge initial margin with the broker, who will handle all the margin payments to and from the clearing house. The settlement price at the end of the first trading day is 95.200. The fall in the contract price is 0.050, which represents five basis points in interest rate terms, or a 10 tick fall in the value of the contract. The trader has a long position in the futures so this is a loss. The trader is required to make good the loss by making a **variation margin** payment to the clearing house via the broker. The variation margin is calculated as follows:

$$100 \text{ contracts} \times 10 \text{ ticks} \times EUR\ 12.50 = EUR\ 12{,}500$$

This can also be calculated from the notional value of the position created. It is 100 contracts times EUR 1 million which is EUR 100 million. The implied interest rate for the period covered by the contract has changed by 0.05 % p.a. Therefore the loss on the trader's position must be:

$$EUR\ 100 \text{ million} \times 0.05\ \% \times \frac{90}{360} = EUR\ 12{,}500$$

11.11.2 Outcome of the Strategy

Table 11.4 summarizes variation margin payments and receipts on the assumption that the trader runs the position for three trading days. The assumed settlement price for the mark-to-market at the end of day one is 95.200. At the end of day two it is 95.280. On day three the trader closes the position by selling 100 March EURIBOR futures at a price of 91.310.

The final variation margin payment is due to the trader because the contracts were sold at 95.310, which is three basis points or six ticks above the settlement price used in the

Table 11.4   Margin payments and receipts from trading campaign

Day 1
Trader buys 100 March contracts at 95.250 and lodges initial margin
Settlement price = 95.200
Variation margin payable by the trader = 100 contracts × −10 ticks × EUR 12.50 = −EUR 12,500
Day 2
Settlement price = 95.280
Variation margin receivable by the trader = 100 contracts × 16 ticks × EUR 12.50 = EUR 20,000
Day 3
Trader sells 100 March contracts at 95.310
Variation margin receivable by trader = 100 contracts × 6 ticks × EUR 12.50 = EUR 7500
Trader also receives back the initial margin lodged on day one

mark-to-market calculation at the end of day two. When the 100 March contracts are sold the trader also receives back the initial margin. The position is closed and so it is no longer necessary to post any collateral.

11.11.3   Net Profit and Loss from Trading

The net profit and loss from the trading campaign (ignoring funding and transaction costs) can be calculated by totalling the variation margin payments and receipts:

$$\text{Net Profit} = -12,500 + 20,000 + 7500 = \text{EUR } 15,000$$

This can also be calculated directly from the prices at which the 100 futures contracts were bought and sold. They were bought at 95.250 and sold at 95.310, which is a difference of 12 ticks. The tick value is EUR 12.50. Therefore the net profit must be:

$$\text{Net Profit} = 100 \text{ contracts} \times 12 \text{ ticks} \times \text{EUR } 12.50 = \text{EUR } 15,000$$

11.11.4   Last Trading Day and Spread Trades

If the trader kept the position open until the last trading day of the contract the final settlement price would be based on the actual three-month EURIBOR rate fixed for the period covered by the contract. There would be a final variation margin calculation and the contracts would simply expire. If the trader wished to maintain the position he or she would have to 'roll' into another month by asking the broker to buy contracts in that month.

Many traders set up **spread trades** rather than simple long and short futures positions. At its simplest this involves buying one contract month (for example March) and selling another contract month (for example June). Since the risks offset each other to an extent, this has the effect of reducing the initial margin that has to be deposited at the outset of the trade. The daily variation margins will also net out against each other to some degree. The objective of a simple spread trade is to profit when the prices of the futures contracts converge or diverge (reflecting changes in the shape of the yield curve) and/or to profit from misalignments in the pricing of the contracts.

11.11.5 CME Performance Bonds

The CME operates a system in which a trader has to put up an initial performance bond to cover potential losses on futures positions. Then if the account falls below a specified maintenance level the trader will receive what is known as a **performance bond call** to bring the account back up to the initial performance bond level.

11.12 HEDGING WITH INTEREST RATE FUTURES: CASE STUDY

Like FRAs, interest rate futures can be used to hedge interest rate exposures. Consider the case of a money market investor. It is now mid-March. In mid-June the investor will have $ 10 million to reinvest in the money market for a further three-month (90-day) period. The risk is that short-term dollar interest rates will fall sharply in the meantime. Suppose the investor reckons that he or she will be able to deposit money with a bank for that future period at three-month LIBOR minus 0.0625 %. The problem is that the investor does not know in advance what the LIBOR component is going to be.

11.12.1 The Hedge Ratio

To hedge this risk the investor decides to buy June three-month Eurodollar futures on the CME. If interest rates fall the contracts will gain in value because they are priced in terms of 100 minus the rate of interest for the contract period. This will compensate for a loss of interest when the $ 10 million is reinvested in the money market. The notional size of the CME contract is $ 1 million so the investor has to buy 10 contracts to hedge the exposure. The tick size is 0.01 and the tick value is $ 25.

$$\text{Hedge Ratio} = \frac{\text{Position to Hedge}}{\text{Notional Contract Size}} = \frac{\$\,10 \text{ million}}{\$\,1 \text{ million}} = 10 \text{ contracts}$$

Suppose the investor buys 10 June futures at a price of 95.00. This implies an annualized rate of interest for the three-month period starting on the third Wednesday of June of 5 %.

11.12.2 The Hedge Performance

Next suppose that when the futures expire in mid-June the three-month dollar LIBOR rate is fixed at 4.90 %.

- The investor can therefore reinvest the $ 10 million at 4.8375 % p.a. (the LIBOR rate of 4.90 % minus 0.0625 %). At the end of the three-month reinvestment period this will generate interest of:

$$\$\,10 \text{ million} \times 4.8375\,\% \times \frac{90}{360} = \$\,120{,}937.50$$

- The Eurodollar futures will close at $100 - 4.90 = 95.10$ so the profit from the 10 futures contracts is:

$$10 \text{ contracts} \times (9510 - 9500) \times \$\,25 = \$\,2500$$

- Adding the interest plus the profit on the futures position generates a total of $123,437.50. The annualized return on $10 million is:

$$\frac{123,437.50}{10,000,000} \times \frac{360}{90} \times 100 = 4.9375\,\%$$

There is a simpler way to derive this value. It is the 5% figure the investor locks into through buying the futures contracts at 95.00, less the 0.0625% spread below LIBOR achieved on reinvesting the funds in the cash market:

$$5\% - 0.0625\% = 4.9375\,\%$$

11.13 FUTURES STRIPS

Chapter 14 looks at using a **strip** of interest rate futures with different expiry months to hedge interest rate swaps. This current section explores a similar kind of strip hedge, but this time for a bank that has to manage the risk on a fixed rate loan.

11.13.1 Strip Hedge: Example

A bank has to quote a rate of interest in mid-March for a one-year fixed rate Eurodollar loan to a corporate borrower. The loan principal is $10 million and interest payments will be made quarterly in arrears. The bank can fund itself at LIBOR flat. The LIBOR rate for the first period of the loan is 4.88% p.a. This can be locked in through borrowing in the money markets. The problem for the bank is that it does not know the rate of interest it will have to pay to refinance the loan on future dates. The situation is illustrated in Figure 11.5.

  For simplicity assume that the annual period covers 360 days and each three-month period has 90 days. The bank can lock into funding rates for the periods from June to September, September to December, and December to next March by selling an appropriate number of interest rate futures contracts. Since the exposure to be covered on each refunding date is always $10 million, the bank will have to trade 10 June, 10 September, and 10 December contracts. It has to *sell* contracts because if interest rates rise its funding costs will rise but it will profit from the short futures position. Interest rate futures prices move inversely with interest rates.

11.13.2 Futures Prices

Table 11.5 shows Eurodollar futures prices for the contracts that cover these periods and the rates of interest implied in these prices.

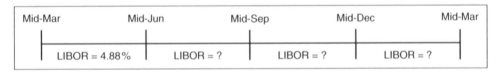

Figure 11.5 Bank's funding costs to finance a one-year loan.

Table 11.5 Interest rate futures prices

Future period	Contract month	Contract price	Implied interest rate (% p.a.)
Mid-Jun to mid-Sep	June	95.00	5.00
Mid-Sep to mid-Dec	September	94.83	5.17
Mid-Dec to mid-Mar	December	94.73	5.27

In a simple case like this it is often possible to approximate quite closely the funding rate the bank can achieve through the futures strip by calculating the arithmetical average of the first cash rate and the rates implied in the futures prices. In this example:

$$\frac{4.88\,\% + 5.00\,\% + 5.17\,\% + 5.27\,\%}{4} = 5.08\,\% \text{ p. a.}$$

The bank can lock into a rate of about 5.08 % by borrowing for the first three months at LIBOR and dealing a strip of interest rate futures to guarantee the rate for the subsequent periods. The next section shows how to calculate the result with more precision. This will be important when calculating a fixed interest rate from a longer strip of futures.

11.13.3 More Precise Calculation

The cost of funds to the bank is calculated as follows. Firstly work out the cost of funding $1 over the year at the cash market rate and the forward rates guaranteed by the strip of futures:

$$\left[1 + \left(\frac{0.0488}{4}\right)\right] \times \left[1 + \left(\frac{0.0500}{4}\right)\right] \times \left[1 + \left(\frac{0.0517}{4}\right)\right] \times \left[1 + \left(\frac{0.0527}{4}\right)\right] = 1.0518$$

Then subtract the $1 principal to derive the interest rate, which is 5.18 % p.a. This is an **annual equivalent rate**. It was calculated based on the actual amount of interest that would be due at the end of the one-year time period. Chapter 6 showed that a quoted rate of interest with quarterly compounding is always less than the annual equivalent rate (the rate expressed with interest compounded once a year). The quarterly compounded equivalent of 5.18 % p.a. with annual compounding is approximately 5.08 % p.a. It is calculated as follows:

$$(\sqrt[4]{1.0518} - 1) \times 4 = 0.0508 = 5.08\,\%$$

11.13.4 The Bank's Spread

Having calculated a break-even rate of 5.08 % (with quarterly compounding) the bank will then add on a spread to establish its lending rate. Note that in practice this calculation will only establish the approximate cost of funding for the bank. It was assumed that interest payments on the loan coincided with the expiry dates on the Eurodollar futures contracts, which in practice is unlikely to be the case. Transaction costs were also ignored.

11.14 CHAPTER SUMMARY

A forward rate agreement (FRA) is a cash-settled derivative contract based on the rate of interest for a period of time starting in the future. The buyer is compensated by the seller if the reference interest rate for the period (normally LIBOR) is fixed above the agreed contract rate. Otherwise the seller is compensated by the buyer. FRA dealers quote bid and offer FRA rates for regular dates on screens, although contracts can be tailored to meet the needs of individual customers. The theoretical rate for the forward period covered by an FRA can be calculated from cash market interest rates. In practice, FRA rates for major currencies such as the dollar are closely related to the prices of interest rate futures. Key contracts include the three-month Eurodollar futures traded on the Chicago Mercantile Exchange and the three-month EURIBOR futures contracts traded on Eurex and on LIFFE. Settlement is guaranteed by the clearing house associated with the exchange. A trader or hedger who wishes to buy or sell futures has to post initial margin as collateral and positions are marked-to-market on a daily basis. Interest rate futures are used to take speculative positions on changes in short-term interest rates. They are also used by corporations, investors, banks, and derivatives traders to hedge against interest rate risks. The prices of interest rate futures are taken to establish the market's overall expectations on the future direction of short-term interest rates.

APPENDIX: STATISTICS ON DERIVATIVES MARKETS

Table 11.6 shows the notional amounts outstanding on the global over-the-counter derivatives markets at the end of 2006 and 2007. Table 11.7 shows the notional amounts outstanding globally on organized exchanges.

Table 11.6 Notional amount outstanding on OTC derivatives in $ billions

Notional amounts outstanding	At December 2006	At December 2007
Grand total	414,845	596,004
Total FX contracts	40,271	56,238
Outright forwards and FX swaps	19,882	29,144
Currency swaps	10,792	14,347
Currency options	9597	12,748
Total interest rate contracts	291,582	393,138
FRAs	18,668	26,599
Interest rate swaps	229,693	309,588
Interest rate options	43,221	56,951
Total equity-linked contracts	7488	8509
Equity forwards and swaps	1767	2233
Equity options	5720	6276
Total commodity contracts	7115	9000
Total credit default swaps	28,650	57,894

Source: Bank for International Settlements.

Table 11.7   Notional amounts outstanding on exchange-traded derivatives markets in $ billions

Futures	At December 2006	At December 2007
Total	25,683.1	28,059.7
Interest rate	24,476.2	26,769.6
Currency	161.4	158.5
Equity index	1045.4	1131.6
Options	At December 2006	At December 2007
Total	44,760.6	52,516.2
Interest rate	38,116.5	44,281.7
Currency	78.6	132.7
Equity index	6565.5	8101.8

Source: Band for International Settlements.

12

Bond Futures

12.1 CHAPTER OVERVIEW

The previous chapter looked at futures contracts on short-term interest rates. Exchange-traded futures are also available on a range of major government bonds. The present chapter explores the structure and application of bond futures taking contracts on US Treasuries, UK gilts, and German bunds as examples. It explains contract specifications and basic trading strategies. These contracts have a physical delivery mechanism although they are based on notional bonds. The chapter explains how the delivery and settlement procedures operate and how the exchanges calculate the conversion factors that are designed to adjust for the relative values of the actual bonds that can be delivered. It looks at how bond forward and futures contracts are priced and explains concepts such as basis, basis risk, the implied repo rate, and the cheapest to deliver bond. It considers the limitations of the conversion factors and the behaviour of the cheapest to deliver bond. Finally, the chapter explores some practical applications of bond futures in hedging positions in underlying bonds and in implementing asset allocation decisions.

12.2 DEFINITIONS

A financial futures contract is an agreement to buy or to sell on an organized exchange:

- a standard amount of a specified financial instrument;
- at a specified date in the future (or within a range of dates);
- at an agreed price.

As illustrated in Chapter 11, a buyer or seller of futures contracts has to pledge collateral as a token of good faith. This is known as **initial margin** or performance deposit. If a trader keeps a position open it is regularly marked-to-market to stop losses and profits from accumulating. The current chapter focuses on bond futures contracts, their applications and how they are priced. The examples are based on: the US Treasury bond futures traded on the Chicago Board of Trade (CBOT); the bund futures traded on Eurex; and the UK gilt futures contracts traded on the London International Financial Futures and Options Exchange (LIFFE).

12.3 THE CBOT 30-YEAR US TREASURY BONDS FUTURES

The contract specification of the 30-year US Treasury bonds futures is described in Table 12.1. Each contract is on a $100,000 par value position in a notional US Treasury bond with a 6% coupon rate. The underlying bond is purely notional: there is no such instrument. The exchange publishes a list of **conversion factors** designed to adjust for the different values of the actual bonds that are deliverable against the contract.

Table 12.1   CBOT 30-year US Treasury bonds futures

Unit of trading	$ 100,000 par value of a notional US Treasury bond with a 6 % coupon rate
Contract months	March, June, September, December
Price quotation	The futures price is quoted as a percentage of par with a tick size (minimum price movement) of one-half of 1/32 %
Tick value	$ 15.625
Delivery	The contract is written on a purely notional bond. A range of actual bonds can be delivered against the contract provided they have a maturity of at least 15 years from the first day of the delivery month.
Delivery date	Any business day in the delivery month
Last trading day	Seven business days before the last business day of the delivery month

Source: Chicago Board of Trade.

The contract price is quoted as a percentage of par with a tick size of one-half of 1/32 %. For example:

- a quotation of 105-16 means that the contract is trading at $ 105 and 16/32 per $ 100 nominal, which is $ 105.50 in decimal format;
- a quotation of 105-165 means that the contract is trading at $ 105 and 16.5/32 per $ 100 nominal, which is $ 105.515625 in decimal format.

One half of 1/32 is 1/64, so the value of a one tick move in the price is calculated as follows:

$$\$ 100,000 \times \frac{1}{64} \% = \$ 100,000 \times 0.00015625 = \$ 15.625$$

This means that for every contract traded, every one tick movement in the value of the contract represents a $ 15.625 profit or loss on the position. Like the quoted prices of the underlying Treasury bonds, the bond futures price is a clean price (see Chapter 4). When a bond is delivered against a short futures position the seller will add the accrued interest on to the invoice.

12.4   INVOICE AMOUNT AND CONVERSION FACTORS

Most buyers and sellers of bond futures close out their positions before the delivery month is reached. However during the delivery month a trader who is short US Treasury bond futures is entitled to go through the delivery process and deliver bonds to an assigned trader who is long bond futures. The seller has the option of which business day in the delivery month to deliver bonds and receive the invoiced amount from the buyer.

The invoiced amount is based on the futures price adjusted by the **conversion factor** for the bonds that are actually delivered. The conversion factor is necessary because some bonds are more valuable than others, due (primarily) to differences in coupon rates. The clean price for delivering the bond is calculated as follows.

$$\text{Clean Price} = \text{Conversion Factor} \times \frac{\text{Futures Price}}{100} \times \$ 100,000$$

Table 12.2 Deliverable bonds and conversion factors

Coupon rate	Issue date	Maturity date	Conversion factor
5 %	15 Aug 2007	15 May 2037	0.8646
6 %	16 Feb 1996	15 Feb 2026	1.0000
7.5 %	15 Aug 1994	15 Nov 2024	1.1513

Source: Chicago Board of Trade, reproduced with permission.

To this is added the accrued interest on the bond that is delivered up to the delivery date. The conversion factors are calculated by working out the clean price of all the deliverable bonds at a 6 % yield – the coupon rate on the notional bond specified in the contract – on the first day of the delivery month. (The CBOT rounds the maturity date of the bond back to the nearest quarter year from the first day of the delivery month.)

Table 12.2 shows three bonds that (as at February 2008) were deliverable against the December 2008 CBOT US Treasury bond futures contract. Note that the middle bond listed has a conversion factor of exactly one. This is because the price of the bond at a 6 % yield is par. The 5 % coupon bond has a conversion factor lower than one because its clean price at a yield of 6 % is below par. The 7.5 % coupon bond has a factor above one because its clean price at a yield of 6 % is above par.

12.4.1 Delivery and Settlement

Notice of delivery has to be given by the seller to the CBOT before delivery actually takes place and the seller has to state which bond will be delivered. On the actual delivery date the bonds are transferred to the buyer and the invoice amount to the seller.

Suppose that a futures seller decides to deliver bonds on 12 December 2008 against a December 2008 contract. The futures settlement price is set by the clearing house at exactly 114-00. The seller notifies the exchange that the 7.5 % coupon Treasury bond maturing on 15 November 2024 is to be delivered. The conversion factor is 1.1513. The last coupon on the bond was paid on 15 November 2008 and therefore 27 days has elapsed since the last coupon up to delivery on 12 December. There are 181 days in the bond's current coupon period. The accrued interest on the bond on the delivery date is calculated as follows.

$$\text{Accrued Interest} = \frac{\$7.5}{2} \times \frac{27}{181} = \$0.5594 \text{ per } \$100 \text{ par}$$

On a contract size of $ 100,000 the total accrued will be approximately $ 559. The invoice amount is calculated as follows.

$$\text{Invoice Amount} = \left(\text{Conversion Factor} \times \frac{\text{Futures Price}}{100} \times \$100,000 \right) + \text{Accrued}$$

In this example the invoice amount (rounded) is as follows:

$$\text{Invoice Amount} = \left(1.1513 \times \frac{114}{100} \times \$100,000 \right) + \$559 = \$131,807$$

12.4.2 Problems with Conversion Factors

The conversion factor is a simple means of adjusting the Treasury bond futures price to a price that is appropriate for the particular bond that is delivered:

- bonds with coupons lower than 6% have factors below one, which reduces the invoice amount;
- bonds with coupons higher than 6% have factors above one, which increases the invoice amount.

Unfortunately, as shown later in this chapter, the conversion factor does not fully adjust for the real market value of the bonds that are deliverable against the futures contract. At any one time there tends to be one of the deliverable bonds that is the most attractive for a seller to hold and deliver against a short futures position.

12.5 LONG GILT AND EURO-BUND FUTURES

The long gilt futures contract on LIFFE has the following features:

- the contract is based on GBP 100,000 nominal notional gilts with a 6% coupon;
- delivery can take place any business day in the delivery month at the seller's option;
- bonds eligible for delivery have maturities of between 8.75 and 13 years;
- the contract months are March, June, September, and December;
- the price quotation is per GBP 100 par or nominal value;
- the tick size is 0.01 and the tick value is GBP $100,000 \times 0.01\% =$ GBP 10.

LIFFE publishes a list of conversion factors (which it calls price factors) designed to adjust for the relative values of the gilts that are deliverable against a given contract month. The price factor is calculated by working out the clean price of a bond per GBP 1 par value at a yield of 6% on the first day of the delivery month. The invoice amount on delivery is based on the futures settlement price adjusted by the price factor, plus accrued interest.

12.5.1 Euro-Bund Futures (FGBL)

The German government bond futures traded on Eurex is different in that there is only one delivery date in the delivery month, the 10th calendar day, or the next day if it is not a business day. The contract specification is set out in Table 12.3. The exchange publishes a

Table 12.3 Eurex bund futures contract

Unit of trading	EUR 100,000 par value of a notional German government bond with a 6% coupon rate
Contract months	March, June, September, December
Price quotation	The futures price is quoted as a percentage of par to two decimal places
Tick value	EUR 10
Delivery	The contract is written on a notional bond. Eurex lists a number of bonds that can be delivered.
Delivery date	10th calendar day of the delivery month or the next trading day if this is a non-business day.
Last trading day	Two exchange days before the delivery day

Source: Eurex.

list of deliverable bonds and conversion factors which adjust the invoiced amount based on which bonds are actually delivered. The seller has the option to choose one of the bonds on the list.

The settlement price for the daily mark-to-market in bund futures is determined using a closing auction. The final settlement price is fixed by Eurex at 12:30 CET on the last trading day, normally based on the average price during the last minute of trading.

The conversion factor of a deliverable bond is based on its clean price at a 6% yield on the delivery date. For example, one of the bonds deliverable against the December 2008 bund futures was the 4% coupon German government bond maturing on 4 January 2018. Its conversion factor was 0.860004. The factor is less than one because the bond's coupon rate is less than the 6% on the notional bund stipulated in the contract. If the bond was delivered on 10 December 2008 against a short futures position the seller would invoice (per contract) the final settlement price adjusted by the conversion factor applied to a notional contract size of EUR 100,000. To this would be added accrued interest on the delivered bonds up to 10 December 2008. In practice, though, few contracts ever go to delivery. Most are closed out before delivery or rolled over into the next contract month.

12.6 FORWARD BOND PRICE

Calculating the fair value for delivering a bond on a forward date is based on an arbitrage argument sometimes called the **cash-and-carry** method. Suppose that for settlement tomorrow the 8.875% US Treasury is trading at a clean price of $134.50 (in decimal format). Accrued interest is $2.0594 so the dirty price is $136.5594. A bank wishes to calculate a break-even price to deliver the bond to a client 30 days after tomorrow. This is a forward rather than a futures contract because it is agreed on an over-the-counter basis between the bank and the client.

The bank's strategy is to buy the bond in the cash market for a total settlement amount of $136.5594 so that it is available to deliver to the client after 30 days. It funds the position via repo. The repo rate is 4.5% p.a. After 30 days the bank will have to repay principal plus interest on the repo transaction:

$$\text{Interest Due} = \$136.5594 \times 0.045 \times \frac{30}{360} = \$0.5121$$

$$\text{Principal} + \text{Interest} = \$136.5594 \times \left[1 + \left(0.045 \times \frac{30}{360}\right)\right] = \$137.0715$$

To break even the bank has to charge the client a *dirty price* of $137.0715 on the forward delivery date to cover the principal and interest repayment on the loan. On that date the accrued interest on the bond will be $2.7949. Therefore the *clean price* the bank has to charge to break even on the forward contract is $137.0715 less accrued of $2.7949, which is $134.2766. It can be calculated directly as follows:

Forward Clean Price = Cash Dirty Price + Funding Cost − Accrued on the Forward Date

Forward Clean Price = $136.5594 + $0.5121 − $2.7949 = $134.2766

12.7   CARRY COST

The relationship between the forward clean price and the cash price of the bond can be expressed in terms of the net cost of carrying a position in the underlying bond for forward delivery:

$$\text{Net Carry} = \text{Coupon Income Earned} - \text{Funding Cost}$$

$$\text{Forward Clean Price} = \text{Cash Clean Price} - \text{Net Carry}$$

In the above example the coupon income earned over the 30-day period consists of net accrued interest of $\$2.7949 - \$2.0594 = \$0.7355$. The **net carry** is the coupon income earned over the holding period minus the interest cost of funding the bond position via repo. In the example it is $\$0.7355 - \$0.5121 = \$0.2234$. Subtracting this from the cash clean price of $\$134.50$ gives a break-even forward clean price of $\$134.2766$.

12.7.1   Positive and Negative Carry

The forward clean bond price in the example is actually *lower* than the cash clean price. This is because the accrued earned on the bond over the 30-day holding period is greater than the cost of funding the position via repo. The position is said to have **positive carry**. If the coupon income was *less* than the funding cost then holding the bond and funding the position via repo would result in **negative carry**. The break-even forward price would be above the cash bond price. Note that if a coupon is paid out on a bond during the 'carry' period this has to be factored into the calculation of net carry. It adds to the income earned on the bond over the period.

12.8   THE IMPLIED REPO RATE

A repo is a transaction in which a trader sells a bond at an agreed price and agrees to buy it back at a later date. In effect, the trader is borrowing money for the period of the repo using the bond as collateral. In a classic repo the title to the bond is transferred but any coupon payments are handed over to the original owner. The repo rate is the rate of interest charged by the lender of funds against the collateral. The interest on a dollar or a euro repo is based on the actual term of the deal divided into a 360-day year. (See Chapter 2 for more details.)

The previous section calculated the break-even or 'fair' forward price to deliver an 8.875% coupon US Treasury in 30 days' time. The clean price, based on a repo rate of 4.5%, was $\$134.2766$. It is also possible to work backwards from the actual forward price of a bond that is available in the market to calculate the repo rate that is implied in this price. This is known as the **implied repo rate**. We have the following equation:

Forward Clean Price $=$ Cash Dirty Price $+$ Funding Cost $-$ Accrued on the Forward Date

Suppose that it is actually possible to sell the bond forward at a clean price of $\$134.3125$ plus accrued interest. The cash dirty price as before is $\$136.5594$, the bond will be delivered in 30 days and the accrued interest on that date is $2.7949. Let IRP be the implied repo rate as a decimal. Inserting these values in the above equation produces:

$$\$\,134.3125 = \$\,136.5594 + \left(\$\,136.5594 \times IRP \times \frac{30}{360}\right) - \$\,2.7949$$

Rearranging this equation calculates that IRP = 4.8155%. This is a money market rate, quoted on a simple interest basis and using the actual/360 day-count convention.

12.8.1   Interpreting the Implied Repo Rate

The rules for interpreting the implied repo rate are simple.

- If the IRP is higher than the actual rate at which a cash bond position can be funded or 'carried' this is a sign that the forward contract is trading *above* its theoretical fair value. It may be possible to create a profitable cash-and-carry arbitrage by buying the cash bond and simultaneously selling the (overpriced) forward contract. The cost of funding the position at the actual repo rate will be more than offset by the settlement price received for delivering the bond on the forward date.
- If the IRP is below the actual funding rate via repo this means that the forward price is *below* the theoretical fair value. It may be possible to create an arbitrage by buying the underpriced forward contract and establishing a short position in the bond.

In practice, what looks like a profitable arbitrage opportunity can sometimes disappear when transaction costs and spreads are factored into the equation.

12.9   THE CHEAPEST TO DELIVER (CTD) BOND

The conversion factors published by the exchanges are easy to work with but do not provide an exact method for making deliverable bonds comparable to each other. They make certain simplifying assumptions. The CBOT conversion factors are based on a settlement date which is taken to be the first day in the delivery month, although in fact delivery can take place on any business day during the month. In addition, the maturity date of a bond is rounded down to the nearest quarter year.

These problems do not apply to the bund futures traded on Eurex, but one serious problem remains in the case of all bond futures contracts: the fact the conversion factors are based on pricing *all* bonds at the yield of the notional bond specified in the contract, regardless of maturity. In reality the yield curve tells us that the yields on bonds with different maturities are rarely identical. In addition, the shape of the yield curve changes over time. The advantage of the conversion factor system is that it is simple. It allows the exchange to calculate and publish conversion factors for deliverable bonds when the contract begins to trade, and they can remain constant throughout the life of the contract. This makes it easy to use bond futures for hedging purposes.

The disadvantage of the system is that at any one time one of the deliverable bonds tends to provide the greatest profit (or smallest loss) if it is delivered against a short position in the futures contract, compared to the other deliverable bonds. This is known as the **cheapest to deliver** or CTD bond. In practice a bond futures contract tends to behave as if it is a contract on the CTD bond since that is the issue most likely to be delivered against it.

12.9.1 Determining the CTD

The CTD can be established by calculating the **net basis** for each of the deliverable bonds. This measures the net cost of buying a cash bond (funded via repo) and delivering it into the futures contract. The key terms are defined as follows.

$$\text{Gross Basis} = \text{Cash Clean Price} - (\text{Futures Price} \times \text{Bond's Conversion Factor})$$

$$\text{Net Basis} = \text{Gross Basis} - \text{Net Carry}$$

Suppose the forthcoming US Treasury bond futures is trading on the exchange at 103-26, which is $\$103.8125$ in decimal format. The 8.875 % Treasury bond explored in sections 12.6 and 12.7 above is trading at $\$134.5$ in the cash market. The repo rate is 4.5 % and the bond's conversion factor is 1.2931. The net carry cost for this security was calculated in section 12.7 as $\$0.2234$, assuming that delivery takes place in 30 days' time. The cost of delivering this bond against a short position in the futures – its net basis – is therefore calculated as follows.

$$\text{Gross Basis} = \$134.5 - (\$103.8125 \times 1.2931) = \$0.2601$$

$$\text{Net Basis} = \$0.2601 - \$0.2234 = \$0.0367$$

This bond will be the CTD if it has the *lowest net basis* amongst the list of deliverable bonds. As mentioned above, it will also have the highest implied repo rate. Note that in this case $\$0.0367$ actually represents a *loss* resulting from carrying the bond to deliver against the futures. In section 12.7 it was calculated that at a 4.5 % repo rate the break-even clean price for delivering the bond in 30 days is $\$134.2766$. The clean price obtained by delivering the bond against the futures – sometimes called the Adjusted Futures Price – would be as follows.

$$\text{Adjusted Futures Price} = \text{Futures Price} \times \text{Bond's Conversion Factor}$$

$$\text{Adjusted Futures Price} = \$103.8125 \times 1.2931 = \$134.2399$$

This is $\$0.0367$ less than the break-even price. In other words, a trader would lose $\$0.0367$ per $\$100$ by carrying this particular bond to deliver against a short position in the futures contract in 30 days' time.

12.9.2 Sellers' Options

In fact it is a fairly common result, to lose money through carrying and delivering cash bonds against bond futures. It can apply even to the CTD bond. This may seem strange, since the fair value of a bond futures is often derived from the break-even cost of carrying a position in the CTD, as follows:

$$\text{Theoretical Futures Price} = \frac{\text{CTD Cash Dirty Price} + \text{Funding Cost} - \text{Accrued on Delivery}}{\text{CTD Conversion Factor}}$$

From this equation it seems as if the futures should trade at a price that produces zero profit and loss if a trader funds a position in the CTD and arranges to sell the bond by shorting the futures. What the equation ignores is the fact that the seller of bond futures is granted a number of options, which always includes the choice of which eligible bonds to deliver. In the case of US Treasury bond futures and UK gilt futures it also includes the option of which day in the delivery month to deliver bonds. These 'sellers' options' explain why the bond futures contract can trade below the theoretical fair value simply calculated from the cost of carrying the CTD. The seller of bond futures has valuable options, and in compensation the buyer demands a slightly lower futures price.

12.10   CTD BEHAVIOUR

As a futures contract approaches expiry, net carry diminishes to zero and the futures price adjusted by the CTD conversion factor should (in theory) converge on the price of the CTD. One problem, however, is that the CTD is not always the same bond. When the CTD changes the bond futures will suddenly start to track the new CTD, which makes its behaviour rather unpredictable. It is beyond the scope of this book to explore the CTD behaviour in detail, but one relationship is relatively straightforward, that between the CTD and market yields:

- when current market yields are above the coupon of the notional bond in a bond futures contract the CTD will tend to be a long-duration bond with a low coupon and a long maturity;
- when interest rates are low the CTD tends to be a high coupon, shorter-dated bond with lower duration.

To illustrate this effect, Figure 12.1 shows the price of two semi-annual 6% coupon bonds for a range of yields from 1% up to 11%. The bonds are identical except that one has 16 years and the other 28 years to maturity. At a yield of 6% both bonds trade at par. At yields below 6% the shorter-duration 16-year bond is the cheaper of the two, and at yields above 6% the longer-duration 28-year bond is the cheaper of the two.

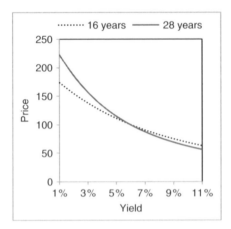

Figure 12.1   Price/yield curve for two bonds with different maturities.

12.11 HEDGING WITH BOND FUTURES

Bond futures are used by traders in bonds and interest rate derivatives, commercial banks, corporations, pension funds, mutual funds, insurance companies, and money managers. Each user has specific trading and risk management goals. These might include:

- protecting the value of portfolio assets;
- limiting opportunity losses;
- enhancing the returns on portfolios.

The first two objectives can be achieved through a variety of hedging strategies. For example, a pension fund manager holding a portfolio of US Treasury bonds may be anticipating a temporary rise in interest rates. If rates do rise the value of the portfolio will decline on a mark-to-market basis. To protect the value of the assets the manager sells US Treasury bond futures. If interest rates rise the bond futures position can be closed out at a profit which will help to offset any losses on the cash bonds. (Failing to close out would mean having to deliver up bonds.)

12.11.1 Hedging CTD Bonds: Example

Suppose that a portfolio manager holds $ 10 million nominal value of the current cheapest to deliver Treasury bond. It is a core holding in the fund and the manager does not wish to sell, but is concerned about the effect of a possible rise in interest rates. The bond is the 8.875 % US Treasury described in the previous sections. It is trading at $ 134.50 clean. Its conversion factor is 1.2931.

As a temporary hedge, the portfolio manager decides to short the near-dated Treasury bond future, which is trading at $ 103-26 or $ 103.8125 per $ 100 nominal. The manager might consider shorting 100 CBOT Treasury bond futures contracts with a total nominal value of $ 10 million. In fact this is not quite correct since in theory every one tick move in the futures price will be associated with a 1.2931 tick move in the CTD bond price. This is because the CTD bond's conversion factor is used in the calculation of the theoretical fair value of the futures contract:

$$\text{Theoretical Futures Price} = \frac{\text{CTD Cash Dirty Price} + \text{Funding Cost} - \text{Accrued on Delivery}}{\text{CTD Conversion Factor}}$$

Therefore the change (Δ) in the futures price should match changes in the CTD price divided by the conversion factor of the CTD:

$$\Delta \text{ Futures Price} = \frac{\Delta \text{ CTD Price}}{\text{CTD Conversion Factor}}$$

In the example it requires a change of 1.2931 ticks in the CTD bond to produce a change in the theoretical fair value of the futures contract of one tick. The manager therefore has to sell a slightly increased number of contracts:

$$\frac{\$ 10 \text{ million}}{\$ 100,000} \times 1.2931 = 129 \text{ Contracts (rounded)}$$

The total notional value of this position (given that each contract is based on $100,000) is $12.9 million.

12.11.2 Performance of the Futures Hedge

Suppose that soon after the hedge is put in place the bond price falls from $134.50 to $133.50 in decimal terms in response to rising interest rates. This is a loss of $1 per $100 nominal, or 1%. It represents a total loss of:

$$\$10 \text{ million} \times -1\% = -\$100,000$$

Expressed in terms of the tick size used in the futures contract (one half of 1/32) the loss on the CTD is 64 ticks. In theory the futures price should change by only 50 ticks because of the conversion factor:

$$\frac{64}{1.2931} = 50 \text{ ticks}$$

The tick value on the bond futures contract is $15.625. On a short position in 129 futures a 50-tick price change would generate a profit of:

$$50 \text{ ticks} \times 129 \times \$15.625 = \$100.781$$

The slight difference between this figure and the loss on the cash bonds is due to rounding, including the calculation of 129 futures contracts. Without rounding the hedge would (in theory) look perfect.

12.12 BASIS RISK

In practice the hedge will normally tend to work fairly well in the type of case just considered, because the futures contract will closely track the CTD bond. Any inaccuracy will primarily be due to the fact that the number of futures traded has to be rounded, and the fact that traded prices are rounded to the nearest tick. What dealers call **the basis risk** – the risk that the cash and the futures price may not move together as anticipated – is relatively small. There remains of course the risk that the CTD may change over the period and the manager's cash and futures positions will cease to track each other closely. In addition, the efficiency of the hedge will be affected by timing decisions on when to sell the futures and when to close out the position.

The hedge ratio used in the last section to determine the number of futures contracts to hedge the CTD bond was as follows:

$$\text{Hedge Ratio} = \frac{\text{Nominal Value of Portfolio}}{\text{Contract Nominal Value}} \times \text{CTD Conversion Factor}$$

Conversion factors approximate the relative price sensitivities of cash bonds in relation to the futures contract. For example, a conversion factor of 1.2931 means that the price sensitivity of the CTD cash bond is roughly 129% of that of the futures contract:

$$\Delta \text{ CTD Bond Price} \approx \Delta \text{ Futures Price} \times \text{CTD Conversion Factor}$$

Because this relationship holds it is possible to use the conversion factor to determine the hedge ratio – how many futures contracts must be sold to offset the losses on a CTD cash bond position. If the conversion factor were two the cash bond would be twice as volatile as the futures contract in terms of its price sensitivity. Therefore two futures contracts would have to be sold for every $100,000 nominal of the cash bond.

The hedging methodology used above has its limitations when the portfolio of bonds to be hedged consists of non-CTD bonds. Futures contracts track most closely the price changes in the CTD. The hedge ratio used was based on the assumption that the portfolio manager was hedging the CTD. As a result the calculation will fail to make the correct adjustment for the different price sensitivity on a non-CTD bond.

12.13 HEDGING NON-CTD BONDS

A way to describe the relationship between price changes in the CTD and non-CTD bonds is to use the concept of the price value of a basis point (PVBP). PVBP measures the change in the dollar value of a bond for a one basis point change in yield. The following relationship should hold:

$$\text{PVBP Futures} = \frac{\text{PVBP of CTD}}{\text{CTD Conversion Factor}}$$

A commonly used calculation for hedging a portfolio of non-CTD bonds is based on this relationship:

$$\text{Hedge Ratio} = \frac{\text{Portfolio Nominal Value}}{\text{Contract Nominal Value}} \times \frac{\text{PVBP of Portfolio}}{\text{PVBP of CTD}} \times \text{CTD Conversion Factor}$$

Suppose that the portfolio to be hedged consists of $10 million nominal of the 6.125 % US Treasury maturing on 15 August 2029. The CTD is the 8.875 % Treasury with a conversion factor of 1.2931. Chapter 5 shows how to calculate PVBP. Suppose the following values are calculated for the bonds in this example:

- **PVBP of Portfolio = $0.1429.** This means that for a one basis point change in yield the bonds in the portfolio to be hedged will change in value by approximately 14.29 cents per $100 nominal.
- **PVBP of CTD = $0.1299.** This means that for a one basis point change in yield the CTD bond will change in value by approximately 12.99 cents per $100 nominal.

The number of US Treasury bond futures that should be sold to hedge the portfolio is therefore:

$$\frac{\$10 \text{ million}}{\$100,000} \times \frac{0.1429}{0.1299} \times 1.2931 = 142$$

If the hedge was on the CTD bonds a total of 129 futures would have to be shorted, as shown in the previous section. However, in this case the bonds being hedged are more sensitive to changes in yield than the CTD (and hence the bond futures) so the number of futures contracts in the hedge has to be increased to 142.

12.14   USING FUTURES IN PORTFOLIO MANAGEMENT

A trader or portfolio manager can also buy futures to lock into a purchase price for a bond in anticipation of receiving cash in the future.

Suppose that a fund manager plans to invest $10 million in the current CTD in one month's time. This is the 8.875 % Treasury with a conversion factor of 1.2931. The manager is concerned that falling yields will drive up the bond price over the next few weeks and wishes to lock in a purchase price today by buying CBOT Treasury bond futures. The hedge ratio used above for hedging CTD bonds will calculate the number of futures to buy:

$$\text{Hedge Ratio} = \frac{\text{Nominal Value of Portfolio}}{\text{Contract Nominal Value}} \times \text{CTD Conversion Factor}$$

The manager should buy 129 contracts. If the bonds to be purchased are non-CTD bonds then the manager has to adjust for the PVBP of those bonds relative to that of the CTD.

12.14.1   Implementing Asset Allocation Decisions

Financial futures provide a quick and efficient means of adjusting the proportion of assets held in shares, bonds, and cash. Compared to cash market transactions the brokerage fees on futures are low, transaction times are short, and relatively large trades can be executed without major impact.

Suppose that a UK fund manager runs a portfolio worth GBP 100 million split 70 % in UK shares and 30 % in UK government bonds (gilts). The UK stock market index, the FT-SE 100, is currently trading at 5500. The manager anticipates a sharp fall in the index and wishes to increase the proportion of the fund held in gilts to around 40 %. One alternative is to sell shares and use the proceeds to buy bonds. However this is expensive in terms of brokerage. The fund manager may also wish to be able to move quickly back into the equity market if a recovery starts.

The current CTD on the nearest expiry gilt futures contract is the 8.75 % UK government bond maturing on 25 August 2017. It has a price (conversion) factor of 1.1887843. The gilts futures contract is based on GBP 100,000 nominal notional gilts with a 6 % coupon. Assuming that the manager wishes to establish a long position on GBP 10 million notional of the CTD then he or she should buy approximately 119 gilt futures contracts.

$$\frac{\text{GBP 10 million}}{\text{GBP 100,000}} \times 1.1887843 = 119 \text{ gilt futures (rounded)}$$

The next step is to establish a short position to the value of GBP 10 million on shares that track the FT-SE 100 index. This can be achieved by selling FT-SE 100 index futures (see Chapter 15 for more details). Each full index point on the FT-SE 100 futures contract traded on LIFFE is worth GBP 10. The notional value of each FT-SE 100 futures contract when the cash index is trading at 5500 is therefore 5500 × GBP 10 = GBP 55,000. Therefore in this particular example the portfolio manager must sell approximately 182 FT-SE 100 futures contracts.

$$\frac{\text{GBP 10 million}}{\text{GBP 55,000}} = 182 \text{ FT-SE 100 index futures (rounded)}$$

In the case of traditional 'buy side' portfolio managers the futures trades may be used as a temporary asset allocation mechanism, allowing the manager time to physically sell the shares and buy the bonds in the cash market. Alternatively, the manager might use the futures to make the switch quickly and then decide later whether to make it permanent or to restore the original asset allocation.

On the other hand 'long-short' hedge funds are prepared to take long or short positions in futures simply to implement their market view or their judgement on the relative values of two financial assets. A hedge fund manager, for example, could buy gilt futures and short US Treasury bond futures if he or she thought that UK interest rates had not yet reached their low point, whereas yields in the US were set to rise again from recent lows.

12.15   CHAPTER SUMMARY

A bond futures contract is an agreement made through an organized exchange to deliver or take delivery of a fixed nominal amount of a notional bond on a fixed date in the future, or between a range of dates. The 30-year US Treasury bond future traded on the CBOT is one of the most actively traded contracts in the world. Each contract is based on $ 100,000 par value of a notional US Treasury bond with a 6 % coupon. The seller decides which day in the delivery month to deliver bonds and receive the invoiced amount. The seller also decides which bonds to deliver. The exchange publishes a list of conversion factors designed to adjust for the different values of the deliverable bonds. The invoiced amount is the futures price adjusted by the bond's conversion factor, plus accrued interest up to the delivery date. Long gilt futures traded on LIFFE are similar to the 30-year US Treasury bond futures. Bund futures traded on Eurex differ in that there is only one delivery day. In all cases settlement on bond futures is guaranteed by the clearing house and contracts are subject to margin procedures.

The theoretical or 'fair' price for delivering a bond on a future date can be established through a 'cash-and-carry' argument. This establishes a break-even price based on the cost of buying the bond in the cash market and 'carrying' it for future delivery, funded via repo. The cheapest to deliver (CTD) bond is the bond that maximizes the profit or minimizes the loss resulting from carrying a bond to deliver against a short futures position. It has the highest implied repo rate. The CTD is not always the same bond, and it changes in response to factors such as market yields. Bond futures can be used to hedge bond portfolios. If the bonds to be hedged are not the CTD bonds then the hedge ratio has to be adjusted using a price risk measure such as PVBP. Bond futures can also be used to anticipate future purchases and to change a fund's asset allocations by overlaying positions in bonds with positions in futures contracts.

13

Interest Rate Swaps

13.1 CHAPTER OVERVIEW

This chapter explores one of the fundamental tools of the modern capital markets, the interest rate swap (IRS). A standard or 'plain' vanilla IRS is an agreement between two parties to exchange cash flows on regular payment dates. One leg is based on a fixed rate of interest and the return leg on a variable or floating rate of interest. The chapter considers how payments on the swap are calculated. It looks at the trading and hedging applications for corporate borrowers and institutional investors. Nowadays the market for swaps is extremely competitive and dealers working for major banks stand ready to quote two-way prices in a wide variety of currencies for a range of maturities (up to 30 years and beyond) and for a range of payment frequencies. The chapter discusses swap spreads which measure the relationship between the fixed rates on swaps and the returns on benchmark government securities. Spreads are affected by credit risk considerations, by liquidity, and also by supply and demand factors. Many issuers of fixed coupon bonds use swaps to switch their liabilities to a floating rate basis. The chapter considers why this is so and where the benefits lie. The final topic is cross-currency swaps, in which payments are made in two different currencies. The Appendix lists non-standard swap varieties.

13.2 SWAP DEFINITIONS

In the most general terms a swap is a contract between two parties:

- agreeing to exchange cash flows;
- on regular dates;
- where the two payment legs are calculated on a different basis.

A swap is a bilateral over-the-counter agreement directly negotiated between two parties, at least one of which is normally a bank or other financial institution. Once made, the contract cannot be freely traded. On the other hand, it can be tailored to meet the needs of a particular counterparty. As with other OTC derivatives there is a potential credit risk – the risk that the other party might default on its obligations. To counter this, collateral is normally exchanged.

A payment leg on a swap can be based on a rate of interest, an equity index, or the price of a commodity such as oil. However the most common type of transaction is the **interest rate swap** or IRS. In this deal both payment legs are based on a rate of interest applied to a notional principal sum of money. Normally one rate is fixed and the other is a floating or variable rate linked to a key money market reference rate, usually LIBOR. If payments are made on the same date they can be netted out so that one party pays the difference to the other. A range of different day-count conventions can be used to calculate the interest

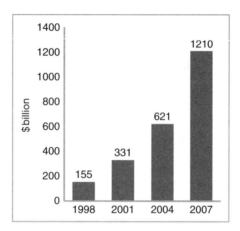

Figure 13.1   Global daily average turnover in interest rate swaps in April each year.
Source: Bank for International Settlements.

payments. The modern IRS market is huge and has grown at a rapid rate in recent years, as illustrated in Figure 13.1.

A **cross-currency** IRS is a deal in which the payments are made in different currencies. The payments can either be fixed or linked to a floating rate of interest. Note that this is a different type of deal to the FX swap described in Chapter 3. A cross-currency IRS is an agreement to exchange regular cash flows in two different currencies on regular dates. An FX or forward swap is an agreement to exchange two currencies for one value date (usually spot) and to re-exchange them on a later date.

13.3   THE BASIC INTEREST RATE SWAP ILLUSTRATED

The most common IRS is a fixed/floating deal in which the notional principal is not exchanged but is used to calculate the interest rate payments. This section introduces the basic structure, using a very simple example which ignores the practical complexities of different day-count conventions and payment frequencies. The example is one in which two parties A and B enter into a three-year IRS starting spot, with the following details.

- **Fixed Leg.** A agrees to pay B a fixed rate of 5 % p.a. on a notional $ 100 million i.e. $ 5 million.
- **Floating Leg.** In return B agrees to pay A 12-month dollar LIBOR on a notional $ 100 million.

The notional principal will not be exchanged. The interest payments will be made annually in arrears and will be netted out. There will be three payments in all. The first will be one year after spot; the second two years after spot; and the final payment three years after spot. The payment legs are illustrated in Figure 13.2.

The first net payment will occur one year after the contract starts. In fact the LIBOR rate used to calculate this payment will be set at the outset, when the swap is agreed. Suppose it is set at 4.5 %. Then:

- A will owe $ 5 million on the fixed rate leg.
- B will owe A $ 4.5 million on the floating rate leg (4.5 % of $ 100 million).
- The amounts will be netted out and A will pay a net $ 500,000 over to B.

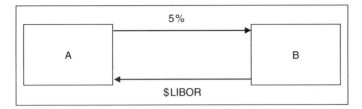

Figure 13.2 Payment diagram for interest rate swap.

However that is not the end of the story. At the point at which the first net payment is made the LIBOR rate will be reset for the second payment date, which will be due two years after the start of the deal. Suppose the LIBOR rate is reset at that point at 5.25 % p.a. Then on the second payment date:

- A will owe $ 5 million on the fixed rate leg.
- B will owe A $ 5.25 million on the floating rate leg (5.25 % of $ 100 million).
- The amounts will be netted out and B will pay a net $ 250,000 over to A.

At this point the LIBOR rate will be reset to establish the third (and final) net payment due on the swap.

13.3.1 Swap Structure and Terminology

Another way to look at the swap just described is as a package of spot and forward interest rate transactions. There are three components.

1. An agreement to make a payment in one year based on the difference between 5 % and the cash market one-year LIBOR rate.
2. An agreement to make a payment in two years based on the difference between 5 % and the forward LIBOR rate for the one-year period starting in one year.
3. An agreement to make a payment in three years based on the difference between 5 % and the forward LIBOR rate for the one-year period starting in two years.

The fact that a swap can be built from these basic components allows it to be priced. The methodology is illustrated in Chapter 14.

Why would A or B enter into the deal? Banks and corporates often use swaps to manage interest rate exposures. For example, suppose that A is a corporation which has a three-year loan outstanding on which it pays a variable rate of interest based on 12-month dollar LIBOR plus 1 %. Figure 13.3 shows that by overlaying the loan with the swap the company can effectively change from a floating to a fixed rate obligation. Its net cost of borrowing is fixed at 6 %. This is the 5 % swap rate plus the 1 % spread over LIBOR on the loan.

13.3.2 Terminology and Documentation

Some market participants refer to the **fixed rate payer** and the **fixed rate receiver**. In the above example A is the payer of the fixed leg and B is the receiver. Others would describe A as the **buyer** of the swap and B as the **seller**. Deals are normally agreed using the standard

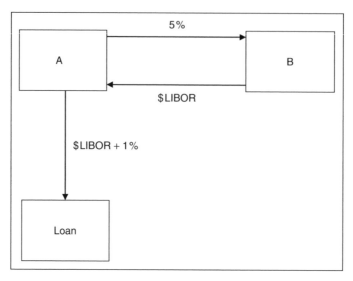

Figure 13.3   Using a swap to fix borrowing costs.

legal documentation developed by the International Swaps and Derivatives Association (ISDA). The two parties negotiate a master legal agreement using the ISDA terms and then any subsequent swaps are covered by this contract. This means that deals (at least standardized ones) can be transacted quickly by specifying the terms (fixed rate, maturity, payment frequency etc.) and stipulating that they are covered by the master agreement.

13.4   TYPICAL SWAP APPLICATIONS

Swaps can be used to take directional views on interest rates. For example, a speculator who believes that interest rates will rise beyond market forecasts could pay fixed and receive floating on an IRS. If rates do rise as predicted the floating receipts will exceed the fixed payments over the life of the deal. However, many uses of swaps are concerned with hedging exposures to changes in interest rates. Since an IRS is a contract directly negotiated between two parties the terms can be flexible. A dealer can adjust the payment dates and the notional principal amount to match the needs of a hedger. The following are four typical hedging applications.

1. **Fixing a Borrowing Rate.** A company has borrowed funds on a floating rate basis but is concerned that interest rates will rise. Solution: the company enters into an IRS with a bank paying fixed and receiving LIBOR. If rates do rise and LIBOR is higher than the fixed rate on the swap the corporate will receive net payments from the bank. This will offset its rising borrowing costs. Alternatively, the company can go back to the bank and terminate the swap. If rates have risen sharply it will receive a substantial close-out payment.
2. **Asset Swap.** An investor would like a return linked to money market rates. However money dealers will only pay LIBOR minus 1/16 %. Solution: the investor enters into an asset swap transaction with a bank. This consists, in effect, of buying a fixed-coupon bond and entering into an IRS paying a fixed rate to the bank and receiving a floating rate of interest linked to LIBOR. Depending on the yield on the bond (which will largely depend on its credit risk) the investor

can achieve a net return above LIBOR on this package deal, known as the **asset swap spread**. In exchange for this spread, the investor takes the risk that the bond will be downgraded or will default.

3. **Asset-Liability Management (ALM).** A bank is offering fixed rate mortgages to borrowers but funds itself primarily through short-term deposits. If interest rates rise it will pay more in funding than it receives on the mortgage loans. This is a classic ALM problem: the bank's assets (its loan book) are misaligned with its liabilities (its funding). Solution: the bank contracts an IRS paying away (some of) the fixed receipts from the mortgages and receiving in return a floating rate of interest which it can use to service its borrowing.

4. **Switching to a Fixed Return.** A money market depositor is concerned that interest rates look set to remain at low levels for a number of years ahead and may decline even further in a low inflation environment. Solution: the investor enters into an IRS to receive fixed and pay floating. The investor has locked into a fixed rate of interest and will not lose out as a result of declining money market rates.

13.5 INTEREST RATE SWAP: DETAILED CASE STUDY

The case is that of a company with debt of $ 300 million with five years remaining to maturity. The interest rate is set every six months on 6 June and 6 December at six-month US dollar LIBOR plus a 0.85 % credit margin. The Chief Finance Officer (CFO) is concerned that interest rates may be set to rise from their recent historical lows. Any increase in borrowing costs would have to be passed on to customers, making the company's products less competitive. Alternatively, it would have to absorb the cost itself, which would erode profit margins and affect the stock price.

13.5.1 IRS Agreement

The CFO enters into a 'vanilla' interest rate swap with a dealer. The terms are set out in Table 13.1. The company pays 5.5 % p.a. on $ 300 million for five years. This is payable in arrears in two semi-annual instalments. The accrued interest is calculated using the actual/actual day-count convention (see Chapter 4). In exchange, the swap dealer pays six-month dollar LIBOR on $ 300 million in arrears every six months for five years, whatever the LIBOR setting for a given period turns out to be. The accrued interest is calculated using the dollar LIBOR actual/360 day-count convention (see Chapter 2). To reduce credit risk on the deal, only the difference between the fixed and floating rate payments will be made, from one party to the other.

The trade date when the deal is agreed is Monday 4 June 2001. The swap actually starts on the spot date 6 June 2001; that is the day on which interest begins to accrue on each payment leg. The LIBOR rate for the first six-month payment period is already known on

Table 13.1 Swap agreement

Notional amount:	$ 300 million
Trade date:	4 June 2001
Start or effective date:	6 June 2001
Maturity date:	6 June 2006
Company pays fixed:	5.5 % semi-annual actual/actual
Dealer pays floating:	Six-month USD LIBOR actual/360
First floating fix:	5.32 %

the trade date since it is announced two business days before spot. In this case it has been fixed at 5.32 % p.a.

13.5.2   First Payment Date: 6 December 2001

The first payment is for the period 6 June–6 December 2001. The company's payment is:

$$\$\,300 \text{ million} \times \frac{0.055}{2} = \$\,8.25 \text{ million}$$

There are 183 actual days in the period. So the swap dealer's payment is:

$$\$\,300 \text{ million} \times 0.0532 \times \frac{183}{360} = \$\,8.113 \text{ million}$$

The company pays the difference between the two, which is $\$\,137,000$.

13.5.3   Second Payment Date: 6 June 2002

The second payment is for the period 6 December 2001–6 June 2002. The company's payment is still $\$\,8.25$ million. The LIBOR rate for the dealer's payment is set on 4 December 2001. Suppose it is set on that date at 5.7 % p.a. There are 182 actual days in the payment period. So the swap dealer's payment for the period is:

$$\$\,300 \text{ million} \times 0.057 \times \frac{182}{360} = \$\,8.645 \text{ million}$$

The dealer pays the difference $\$\,395,000$ on 6 June 2002. On 4 June 2002 the floating rate for the next period 6 June–6 December 2002 is reset according to the six-month dollar LIBOR announced that day.

13.5.4   Swap Payments and the Yield Curve

Since the swap has semi-annual payments and a maturity of five years there will be 10 payment dates. The final payment is due on 6 June 2006. A company using an IRS to change the nature of its underlying liabilities will normally arrange the swap payment dates to coincide with the dates on which it pays interest on its borrowings.

In this example the first net payment is from the company to the swap dealer. This is typical in a positive yield curve environment which builds in expectations of future increases in interest rates. The positive first cash flow gives the swap dealer a small cushion against its exposure to rising interest rates. The overall 'winner' over the five years will depend on whether interest rates are greater or less than the expectations built into the curve. In practice, though, the swap dealer will tend to hedge out most if not all of the interest rate risk on the deal.

13.5.5   Net Result of the Swap

The company's net position is illustrated in Figure 13.4. Its all-in cost of borrowing is fixed at approximately 5.5 % + 0.85 % = 6.35 % p.a. This is not quite correct because the 5.5 %

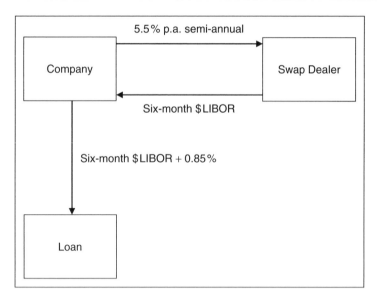

Figure 13.4 Loan plus swap.

element uses an actual/actual day-count whereas the 0.85 % element uses the actual/360 convention. As Chapter 2 shows, this latter convention understates the amount of interest payable. A simple way to correct for this is to multiply 0.85 % by 365/360 and then add it to 5.5 %, producing an all-in borrowing cost of 6.36 % p.a. This is payable on a semi-annual basis.

13.6 INTEREST RATE SWAP TERMS

The swap just described is a standard or 'vanilla' IRS contract. It has the following characteristics:

- one party pays a fixed and the other pays a floating interest rate;
- the notional principal is not exchanged;
- the notional principal remains constant over the life of the swap;
- the fixed rate is constant over the life of the swap;
- the floating rate is LIBOR flat (i.e. exactly LIBOR) and is set at the start of each payment period.

Payment periods can be annual, semi-annual, or quarterly. For example, the fixed leg may be paid semi-annually and the floating leg quarterly. Other day-count conventions may be used. For example, the fixed leg interest calculation may be based on the 30/360 convention in which each month has 30 days and each year 360 days. Sterling swaps will typically use the actual/365 day-count method, which is described in Chapter 2.

  In swaps the **modified following** rule is normally used. This says that if a payment is due on a non-business day it is moved forward to the next business day, unless that takes it into the next month, in which case it is moved back to the previous business day. This rule is widely used in the modern capital markets with a range of deals.

13.6.1 Overnight Index Swaps

An overnight index swap (OIS) is a fixed/floating IRS in which the floating leg is linked to an index based on overnight interbank interest rates. At maturity one party pays the other the difference between the fixed rate and the geometrical average of the overnight rates over the life of the swap, applied to the notional principal. The standard index for US dollar deals is the effective rate for overnight loans of Federal Funds as calculated by the New York Federal Reserve Bank. In euro deals it is the Euro Overnight Index Average (EONIA). In sterling deals the index is SONIA, which tracks overnight funding rates as experienced by money market participants.

The **LIBOR OIS Spread** measures the difference between three-month LIBOR and the OIS rate. It is used in the market as an indication of how much cash is available for interbank lending. On 10 October 2008, during the height of the 'credit crisis', the dollar LIBOR OIS spread rose to a record 365 basis points. Historically the typical spread was closer to 10–12 basis points. This indicated a strong reluctance of banks to lend to each other on a three-month horizon because of concerns over default risk. It is a 'fear gauge' reflecting worries over the health of the banking system.

13.7 COMPARATIVE ADVANTAGE

If there is a difference between the relative costs of funding in the fixed bond market and the floating rate bank loan market this can be exploited through an interest rate swap. This section explores why this is so, taking the case of two companies, Megacorp and Midicorp. Megacorp is a major multinational corporation with an AAA credit rating. It needs to borrow $ 500 million over a five-year maturity. Midicorp is a lower-rated but still well-regarded business. It too needs to borrow $ 500 million over five years. The costs of borrowing for the two companies in the fixed bond market and in the floating rate loan market for five years are set out in Table 13.2.

Megacorp would prefer a floating rate commitment, to obtain a balance between the amount of fixed and variable debt on its balance sheet. Meantime, Midicorp would prefer a fixed rate commitment, given concerns that increases in interest rates would affect the profitability of the business.

13.7.1 Fund Decisions and Swap Agreement

Despite their funding preferences the two companies start by raising money in precisely the way they would prefer not to. Megacorp issues fixed coupon bonds and Midicorp borrows on a floating rate basis linked to LIBOR. The amount raised in both cases is $ 500 million.

Table 13.2 Relative borrowing costs

Borrower	Fixed rate bond issue	Floating rate loan
Megacorp	5.5 % semi-annual	Six-month LIBOR
Midicorp	7.0 % semi-annual	Six-month LIBOR + 1 %
Spread	150 basis points	100 basis points

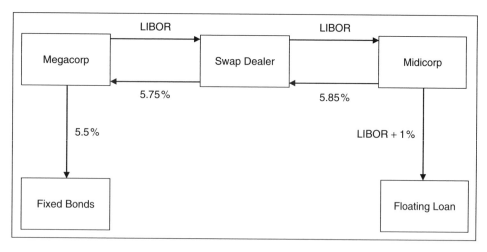

Figure 13.5 Swapping liabilities.

The two companies then contact a swap dealer who acts as an intermediary. The agreed terms for the swap deals are as follows:

- the swap dealer pays Megacorp 5.75 % semi-annually on a $ 500 million notional for five years in return for six-month LIBOR flat;
- the swap dealer receives 5.85 % from Midicorp semi-annually on a $ 500 million notional for five years and pays in return six-month LIBOR flat.

The net positions of all parties after the swap deals is shown in Figure 13.5. Comparing this result with the numbers in Table 13.2, it seems that 'everyone is a winner'.

- The net cost of borrowing to Megacorp is now LIBOR + 5.5 % − 5.75 % which is LIBOR minus 25 basis points. This is a saving of 25 basis points compared to its cost of borrowing in the floating rate loan market.
- The net cost of borrowing to Midicorp is now LIBOR + 1 % − LIBOR + 5.85 % which is 6.85 %. This is a saving of 15 basis points compared to its cost of borrowing in the fixed coupon bond market.
- The net benefit to the dealer is 10 basis points p.a. over the life of the swap transactions.

How can it be that everyone gains? The standard explanation is posed in terms of **comparative advantage**. In Table 13.2 Megacorp has an absolute advantage over Midicorp in its cost of funding in both the fixed and floating rate markets. It has a higher credit rating. However its relative advantage is greater in the fixed rate bond market. The market for corporate bonds tends to be 'name driven' – buyers like issuers they are familiar with – and some institutional investors can only invest in paper with a top credit rating. To tempt the bond investors Midicorp would have to pay a 7 % coupon rate, a full 150 basis points more than Megacorp. On the other hand the floating rate market is prepared to lend to Midicorp at only 100 basis points more than the rate for Megacorp.

13.7.2 Exploiting the Different Credit Spreads

In Table 13.2 the discrepancy between the different credit spreads in the fixed bond and floating rate loan markets is $150 - 100 = 50$ basis points. This is exploited through the swap market. Megacorp ends up saving 25 basis points by first borrowing through fixed coupon bonds (where its relative advantage is strong) and swapping into a floating rate liability. Midicorp ends up saving 15 basis points by borrowing floating and then swapping to a fixed rate basis. The dealer captures 10 basis points. These various 'gains' add up to 50 basis points.

13.7.3 Does Everyone Really Gain?

This is a complex and controversial point. One objection is that while the two companies have reduced their cost of funding they have also acquired credit risk on the swap transactions. In addition, there are costs associated with the swap deals. This includes transaction costs such as legal fees, but there may be other hidden costs. For example, Megacorp may insert a feature in its fixed coupon bond issue which allows it to 'call' the bond back early and replace it with cheaper debt. But if it does this it will also have to unwind the swap transaction.

13.8 SWAP QUOTATIONS AND SPREADS

In the early days of the market large corporations contracted swap agreements directly with each other. This exposed them to credit risk on the counterparty. It was also difficult to find a counterparty with matching needs.

Nowadays, most corporates, institutional investors, and commercial banks contract swap agreements with dealers working for banks and securities houses. Swap dealers quote two-way rates on electronic information systems and over the telephone in a range of currencies and for standard maturities. These may be **indication rates**, in which case the actual rate for a deal will be a matter for negotiation with the counterparty. Dealers will also quote rates on demand for non-standard maturity dates and for structures that are non-standard in some way – for example, deals in which the notional principal changes over the life of the contract.

13.8.1 Outright Swap Rates

Table 13.3 shows typical two-way swap quotations for two, five, and 10-year maturity euro interest rate swaps. These are fixed rates quoted on an annual bond basis i.e. with annual payments. They are against six-month EURIBOR. For example, the dealer will pay 4.4 % on a 10-year deal and ask in return six-month EURIBOR.

When a client asks a bank for a quotation the swap rates can be converted to a range of different bases. For example, the client may wish to receive floating payments every three

Table 13.3 Two-way rates for euro interest rate swaps

Maturity	Bid (%)	Offer (%)
2 years	4.13	4.18
5 years	4.25	4.30
10 years	4.40	4.45

months rather than every six months. Obviously in that case the fixed rate paid by the client will have to be adjusted upwards.

13.8.2 Swap Spreads

Dealers can also quote swap rates in terms of a spread over the yield on the appropriate government bond with the nearest maturity. This is known as the **swap spread**. For example, on the day the data in Table 13.3 was taken the yield on 10-year German government bonds was 3.85 %. This means that the spread on 10-year swaps (on the offer side) was 4.45 % − 3.85 % = 0.6 % or 60 basis points.

Swap spreads are widely taken as an indicator of the additional credit risk the market perceives on swap deals compared to the relatively safe returns that are available on government securities. Since most swaps are conducted between banks, swap spreads are sensitive to concerns about the banking system. At times of stress in financial markets they tend to rise. A spread of 60 basis points is high by historical standards, around double the long-run average going back to the early 1990s. The quotes in Figure 13.3 were taken in September 2008 in the midst of the interbank credit crisis, when rumours about possible bank losses and failures were rife.

13.9 DETERMINANTS OF SWAP SPREADS

Swap spreads are widely taken by dealers to reflect the market's current perceptions about credit risk, especially that on financial institutions, which are the main users of the swap market. Since in normal times the average credit rating on banks is typically somewhere around the AA level, swap spreads are influenced by the spreads currently available on bonds of this credit quality. As shown in Chapter 7, these are affected in turn by estimates of default probabilities and recovery rates. Nevertheless there are important differences between bonds and swaps from a credit risk perspective:

- if a financial institution buys a straight bond both the coupons and the redemption amount may not be paid, whereas if it enters into a single currency IRS the notional is never exchanged and is not at risk;
- in the swaps market banks use a range of techniques to mitigate the credit risk on deals e.g. collateral is taken; payments may be netted out; the deals may be regularly marked-to-market.

There are other factors that help to explain the existence of swap spreads, beyond credit risk. In major developed markets such as the US and Germany the government bonds used to measure the spreads are highly liquid investments, easily traded in volume, and held by investors around the world. They can also be used as collateral in repo transactions to secure cheap funding. These factors have a positive effect on their price and tend to lower their yield.

Swap spreads may also be affected by supply and demand. For example, if fears that interest rates are set to rise sharply start to affect corporate borrowers there will be an excess of demand from those who wish to pay fixed and receive floating on IRS transactions. Swap dealers will be able to demand higher fixed rates and higher spreads over Treasuries. Furthermore, the supply of Treasury bonds can have an impact. If the amount of Treasury bonds outstanding is reduced this tends to increase their prices and lower their yields, potentially increasing the swap spread.

Finally, as shown in the next section, one way to hedge a swap is to use Treasury bonds. For example, a dealer who is a net payer of fixed can buy Treasury bonds to hedge the interest rate risks, and fund the position via a repo deal. This suggests that the lower the repo rate, other things being equal, the greater the swap spread the dealer can afford to pay. Generally, the repo rate is likely to be lower than LIBOR because repo is a collateralized form of borrowing.

Hammersmith & Fulham

The London local authority of Hammersmith & Fulham transacted almost GBP 3 billion notional in swap transactions in the late 1980s. When UK interest rates rose sharply the contracts moved into loss. Unfortunately for the banks who were owed the money, the UK courts decided that the swaps were *ultra vires*, that is, that the local authority had no legal power to make the deals. The case entered the folklore of the market and led to greater caution (for a time at least) over the legal and credit implications of swaps.

As discussed previously, it remains to be seen at the time of writing whether in future more over-the-counter derivatives will be covered by central clearing arrangements. In a system of this kind market participants post collateral which is managed by a central counterparty, reducing the risks of settlement failures and of default.

13.10 HEDGING SWAPS WITH TREASURIES

The swap spread is linked to the fact that dealers can use Treasury bonds to hedge their swap positions. For example, a dealer who pays fixed on a 10-year dollar IRS can buy a 10-year US Treasury bond via repo to hedge the interest rate risk. This is illustrated in Figure 13.6. In the diagram 'T' is the Treasury yield. Assuming the repo rate is less than LIBOR then the dealer can afford to pay a spread over the Treasury rate on the IRS.

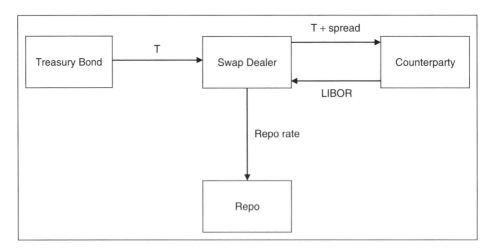

Figure 13.6 Hedging a swap with a Treasury bond.

13.10.1 Hedging in Practice

A swap dealer will have many deals on the book and much of the interest rate risk will cancel out. Sometimes the dealer will be paying fixed and sometimes receiving fixed. The dealer has to decide whether to hedge out any residual exposures to interest rate changes or whether this is a position he or she wishes to take.

Using Treasury bonds is not necessarily the best way to hedge interest rate risks on swaps. In times when the government is shrinking the supply of government debt there may be constraints on buying a sufficient quantity of bonds at a reasonable price. Government buy-backs of debt tends to push up the prices of Treasury bonds and to lower the yield.

This was a major factor in the widening of US dollar swap spreads in the early 2000s, particularly at longer maturities. In fact as the yield on longer-dated US Treasuries became distorted in this way they became less useful as benchmark rates to price corporate bonds. Swap rates were sometimes used instead, a reflection of the deep liquidity in the US dollar swap market. Chapter 14 explores another way to hedge shorter-dated swaps using interest rate futures.

13.11 CROSS-CURRENCY SWAPS: CASE STUDY

In a cross-currency IRS cash flows in one currency are exchanged on regular dates for cash flows in another currency. The principal is normally exchanged at the spot FX rate at the outset and re-exchanged at the same rate on the final payment date. The regular interest payments can be calculated on a fixed or a floating basis.

In the following case Americo Inc. is a highly-rated US company while Britco plc is a less highly-rated UK firm. Both wish to borrow on a fixed rate basis. Americo wishes to borrow GBP 100 million and pay interest in sterling to finance its UK operations. Britco wishes to borrow $180 million and pay interest in dollars to fund its US activities. The spot rate GBP/USD is 1.8000. Borrowing rates for each company are set out in Table 13.4.

Americo can borrow more cheaply in either currency, reflecting its higher credit rating. However its *comparative advantage* is greater in dollars than in sterling due to its higher 'name recognition' in the US market. So Americo borrows $180 million at 6% p.a. for five years. Its annual interest bill is $10.8 million. Britco borrows GBP 100 million at 7.75% p.a. for five years. Its annual interest bill is GBP 7.75 million. The two firms then approach a swap dealer who agrees the following transactions:

- **Swap with Americo.** The dealer takes the $180 million principal which Americo raised on its loan and gives the firm in return the GBP 100 million it needs for its business operations. The principals will be exchanged at the same FX rate in five years on the final swap payment date. The dealer also agrees to pay Americo 6% p.a. on $180 million each year for the next five years i.e. $10.8 million. In return Americo will pay the dealer 6.75% p.a. on GBP 100 million i.e. GBP 6.75 million.

Table 13.4 Borrowing costs for the two companies issuing fixed coupon straight bonds

Borrower	USD fixed rate funding (%)	GBP fixed rate funding (%)
Americo Inc.	6.00	7.00
Britco plc	7.50	7.75

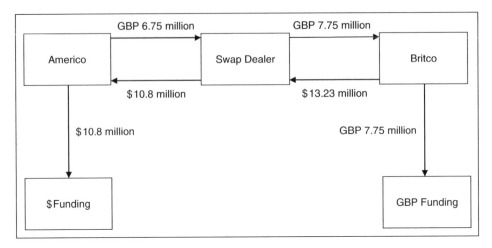

Figure 13.7 Annual interest payments on swaps and loans.

- **Swap with Britco.** The dealer takes the GBP 100 million principal which Britco raised on its loan and gives the firm in return $ 180 million. The principals will be re-exchanged at the same FX rate in five years on the final swap payment date. The dealer also agrees to pay Britco 7.75 % p.a. on GBP 100 million for five years i.e. GBP 7.75 million. In return Britco will pay 7.35 % p.a. on $ 180 million for five years i.e. $ 13.23 million.

13.11.1   Net Borrowing Costs to the Companies

Figure 13.7 shows the annual interest payments on the swaps and loans. The net cost to Americo is GBP 6.75 million or 6.75 % p.a. on GBP 100 million, which is a saving of 25 basis points compared to its funding cost if it borrowed sterling directly (see Table 13.4). The net cost to Britco is $ 13.23 million or 7.35 % on $ 180 million, which is a saving of 15 basis points compared to its funding cost if it borrowed dollars directly (see Table 13.4).

13.11.2   The Swap Dealer's Position

For the dealer the principal payments to Americo and Britco at the start and at the end of the swaps simply cancel out. The swap dealer is left with net cash flows from the annual swap payments as follows:

$$\text{\$ 13.23 million} - \text{\$ 10.8 million} = \text{\$ 2.43 million}$$

$$\text{GBP 6.75 million} - \text{GBP 7.75 million} = -\text{GBP 1 million}$$

There is a residual currency risk on this position since on a net basis the dealer is paying sterling and receiving dollars each year. However this can be hedged using forward FX contracts, as explained in Chapter 3. The deal could also be structured such that Americo or Britco take some or all of the foreign exchange risk.

13.11.3 Principal Exchange

It might seem odd that the dollar and sterling principal amounts are re-exchanged at the maturity of the swap at the same spot rate at which they were exchanged at the outset. Why is it not at the five-year forward FX rate? Chapter 3 showed that the fair forward FX rate is calculated from the spot rate and the interest rate differential between the two currencies. In a cross-currency swap the interest rate differential is already taken care of through the regular exchange of interest payments. So the initial spot rate of GBP/USD 1.8000 can be used for the re-exchange of the two currencies. This is helpful to Americo and Britco since they will need $ 180 million and GBP 100 million respectively to redeem their debt when it matures in five years. Note, though, that the principal re-exchange feature increases the credit risk on cross-currency swaps.

13.12 CROSS-CURRENCY SWAP REVALUATION

This next case illustrates how a cross-currency swap is revalued or marked-to-market. It concerns a dealer who entered into a cross-currency swap involving the dollar and the Swiss franc some time ago. At the outset the dealer paid over a principal sum of CHF 15.067 million and received in return $ 10 million. Exactly the same amounts will be re-exchanged at maturity. The interest payments due on the deal (paid annually in arrears) are as follows:

- Dealer pays: 5.45 % on $ 10 million.
- Dealer receives: 4.32 % p.a. on CHF 15.067 million.

Now there are exactly three years remaining until the maturity of the swap. The spot rate USD/CHF is now 1.5023. The fixed rate on dollar swaps is currently 5.22 %. The fixed rate on Swiss franc swaps is currently 3.58 %. (For simplicity it is assumed here that the yield curves are flat i.e. interest rates are the same at all maturities.) Given this data, what is the current market value of the swap transaction the dealer has entered into?

One way to calculate the mark-to-market value is to set out the swap cash flows in a spreadsheet and discount them at the current market swap rates. This is shown in Table 13.5.

Table 13.5 Cross-currency swap revaluation

Year	Payments ($)	PV @ 5.22 % ($)
1	−545,000	−517,962
2	−545,000	−492,266
3	−10,545,000	−9,052,149
	Total	−10,062,377

Year	Receipts (CHF)	PV @ 3.58 % (CHF)
1	650,894	628,398
2	650,894	606,679
3	15,717,894	14,143,818
	Total	15,378,894

Spot rate USD/CHF	1.5023	
USD Value of CHF receipts	10,236,899	
Swap NPV	$ 174,522	

The regular interest payment on the dollar leg of the swap is 5.45 % of $ 10 million which is $ 545,000. In year three there is also a principal repayment due of $ 10 million. These cash flows are discounted at the current swap rate of 5.22 % to establish a present value for the dollar payments. The present value of the Swiss franc receipts are also discounted, and converted to dollars at the current spot rate of 1.5023. The **net present value** (NPV) of the swap is $ 174,522. It is profitable.

13.13 CHAPTER SUMMARY

A standard or 'plain vanilla' interest rate swap (IRS) is a bilateral legal agreement made directly between two parties to exchange cash flows on regular dates based on a fixed and a floating rate of interest. Normally payments are made in arrears and the floating reference rate is LIBOR. The first floating payment is known when the contract is agreed. Thereafter it will depend on future LIBOR settings. There is a potential credit risk on swaps. However this is reduced by the use of credit management techniques such as collateralization. IRS rates are quoted by dealers working for major banks and securities houses. The rates are typically quoted in terms of the fixed rates versus LIBOR. A range of payment frequencies and day-count conventions may be used. The swap spread is the difference between the fixed rate on a swap and the yield on a reference government bond with a similar maturity. Swap spreads have been commonly taken in the market to reflect the general level of credit risk on financial institutions, although spreads can also be affected by liquidity issues and by supply and demand factors. Interest rate swaps can be hedged by buying or shorting Treasury bonds and using repo transactions. A cross-currency interest rate swap is one in which the payment legs are in two different currencies. Normally the principal is exchanged at the start and re-exchanged at the same FX rate at maturity. A company that has an advantage in borrowing in a particular market can raise funds in that market and use swaps to change the nature of its liabilities, with the possibility of reducing its overall borrowing costs.

APPENDIX: SWAP VARIANTS

There are many variants on the basic 'plain vanilla' interest rate swap. The following are some of the most common.

- **Accreting.** The notional principal increases during the life of the swap.
- **Amortizing.** The notional principal reduces during the life of the swap. This feature is useful for a corporate hedging an amortizing loan or bond in which the principal is paid off in instalments and decreases over time.
- **Basis Swap.** A floating-for-floating swap in which the two legs use a different reference rate. For example, one leg pays LIBOR and the other a cash flow linked to the commercial paper rate.
- **Callable.** The fixed payer can terminate the contract early.
- **Extendable.** One party has the option to extend the life of the swap.
- **Forward Start or Deferred.** The fixed rate is set when the swap is transacted but the swap starts on a date later than spot.
- **LIBOR-in-Arrears.** The LIBOR rate for the floating leg is fixed at the end of a payment period rather than at the beginning.
- **Margin swap.** The floating rate is LIBOR plus a spread, rather than LIBOR flat. The fixed rate is adjusted accordingly.

- **Off-market swap.** The fixed rate is different to the current market rate. One party makes a compensating payment to the other.
- **Putable.** The fixed receiver can terminate the contract early.
- **Rate-Capped.** The floating rate payment is capped at a maximum level.
- **Rollercoaster.** The notional principal increases then reduces over time.
- **Spread-Lock.** A forward start swap in which the swap spread is set at the outset. When the swap starts the spread is added to the yield on a reference government bond to establish the fixed rate.
- **Swaption.** An option to enter into an interest rate swap either as the payer or receiver of the fixed rate (see Chapter 20).
- **Zero Coupon.** A fixed against floating swap in which the fixed cash flow is calculated using a zero coupon rate. There are no interim payments on the fixed leg, only a lump sum payment at maturity. This potentially exposes the fixed rate receiver to a higher level of credit risk.

Interest Rate Swap Valuation

14.1 CHAPTER OVERVIEW

This chapter explores the value of an IRS when the deal is first agreed, and methods for revaluing a swap given subsequent changes in market interest rates. It shows how a standard single currency fixed-floating swap can be priced as a combination of a straight bond and a floating rate note. It illustrates an alternative valuation methodology using forward interest rates, which can be used with standard swaps but also with a range of 'non vanilla' deals. A par IRS is one in which the present values of the fixed and floating legs are equal. The chapter shows how spot and forward rates can be extracted from the fixed rates on par swaps, using the bootstrapping method. The final sections explore how swaps can be priced and also hedged using interest rate futures.

14.2 VALUING A SWAP AT INCEPTION

The example is based on the case of a swap dealer who has just entered into an IRS on a notional $ 100 million with exactly three years from the start date to maturity. The payment legs are as follows:

- the dealer pays a fixed rate of 8 % p.a. annually in arrears;
- The dealer receives 12-month dollar LIBOR annually in arrears.

For simplicity it is assumed that interest payments on both the fixed and floating legs are calculated using the actual/actual day-count method. The cash flows are illustrated in Table 14.1. At the end of each year the dealer pays $ 8 million and receives the LIBOR rate for that year applied to a notional principal of $ 100 million.
  The dealer's cash flows can be looked at in another way. They look as if:

- the dealer is short a three-year annual bond with a par value of $ 100 million and an 8 % coupon;
- the dealer is long a three-year floating rate note (FRN) with a par value of $ 100 million and an annual coupon based on the LIBOR rate set at the beginning of each year.

There does seem to be one important difference between the swap and the 'short bond long FRN' combination. In the swap the notional is never exchanged. However if the dealer was

Table 14.1 Swap cash flows

Year	Fixed Cash Flow ($ million)	Floating Cash Flow ($ million)
1	−8.0	100 × LIBOR%
2	−8.0	100 × LIBOR%
3	−8.0	100 × LIBOR%

actually long the FRN he or she would receive a $100 million redemption payment at the end of year three. But in fact this turns out not to matter at all. The $100 million due on the imaginary FRN at maturity would be matched by a $100 million redemption amount the dealer would have to pay on the hypothetical 8% coupon bond. These cash flows cancel out, so that the net cash flows on the short bond plus long FRN combination would be exactly the same as those shown in Table 14.1.

This tells us that the cash flows on the swap can be replicated by a combination of a straight bond and an FRN. If the 'bond plus FRN' package can be priced, it follows that the swap must have the same value. If two structures, however differently assembled, generate identical cash flows then they should have the same present value. Otherwise arbitrage deals can be constructed.

14.3   VALUING THE SWAP COMPONENTS

From the dealer's perspective then it must be the case that:

$$\text{Value of Swap} = \text{Value of FRN} - \text{Value of Fixed Bond}$$

To value the two components of the swap accurately it is necessary to use one, two, and three-year zero coupon or spot rates. These can be generated from the fixed rates on one, two and three-year annual swaps using the bootstrapping methods employed in Chapter 6. Suppose that current swap rates are as set out in Table 14.2.

Assuming that 6% is the spot rate for one year, then the two-year spot rate z_2 can be established through a bootstrapping argument. Suppose it is possible to buy $1 nominal value of a hypothetical two-year bond paying an annual 7% coupon and trading at par. Then the $1 cost of the bond must equal the receipts from selling the title to the first $0.07 coupon at the one-year spot rate 6%, plus the receipts from selling the title to the final $0.07 coupon plus the $1 redemption amount at the two-year spot rate z_2. In an equation:

$$1 = \frac{0.07}{1.06} + \frac{1.07}{(1 + z_2)^2}$$

Rearranging this equation calculates that $z_2 = 7.0353\%$. Chapter 6 showed that a discount factor is simply the present value of $1 at the spot rate for the period. So the two-year discount factor DF_2 is calculated as follows:

$$DF_2 = \frac{1}{(1 + z_2)^2} = 0.87286193$$

Using the same logic it is possible to establish from the swap rates in Table 14.2 the three-year spot rate z_3 and the three-year discount factor DF_3. These are shown in Table 14.3.

Table 14.2   Swap rates

Year	Swap rate (%)
1	6.0
2	7.0
3	8.0

Table 14.3 Swap rates, spot rates, and discount factors

Year	Swap rate (%)	Spot rate (%)	Discount factor (DF)
1	6.0	6.0000	0.94339623
2	7.0	7.0353	0.87286193
3	8.0	8.1111	0.79138828

14.3.1 Valuing the Fixed and Floating Legs of the Swap

The fixed leg of the dealer's swap is valued by calculating the present value of the cash flows on the equivalent short bond position using the discount factors from Table 14.3. The PV per $100 nominal is as follows:

$$PV\ Fixed\ Bond = (-8 \times 0.94339623) + (-8 \times 0.87286193) + (-108 \times 0.79138828)$$
$$= -\$100$$

The floating leg of the swap is valued by calculating the PV of the equivalent FRN. This requires a moment's thought. Assume that the first LIBOR rate used to establish the floating payment at the end of year one is set at 6% (the one-year swap rate from Table 14.2). Then the floating leg is equivalent to a long position in an FRN with a 6% coupon due in one year. At that point, however, the value of the hypothetical FRN would revert to its face value. Intuitively, this is because subsequent interest payments would be set according to future LIBOR rates, but these would be present valued at exactly the same rates. Therefore the FRN's total future value in one year will be its face value plus the 6% coupon payment. The one-year spot rate is 6% so the PV of the FRN per $100 nominal is as follows:

$$PV\ FRN = \frac{106}{1.06} = \$100$$

14.3.2 Swap Value

The net present value of the swap is therefore zero. This is called a **par swap** because the present values of the fixed and floating legs add to zero. In practice because of spreads and commissions a swap dealer will normally enter into an IRS at a positive net present value. This is sometimes called the **initial net present value** (INPV).

14.4 SWAP REVALUATION

Since the swap is equivalent to a fixed coupon bond and an FRN this fact can be used to revalue the swap if market interest rates change. Suppose, for example, that later on the same day the par swap explored in the previous sections was entered into, the three-year swap rate on the market rises to 8.1%. Rates for one and two-year swaps remain the same. This will affect the current market value of the swap, which will no longer be zero. To see why, Table 14.4 recalculates spot rates and discount factors based on the new market swap rates.

Table 14.4 Recalculated spot rates and discount factors

Year	Swap rate (%)	Spot rate (%)	Discount factor (DF)
1	6.0	6.0000	0.94339623
2	7.0	7.0353	0.87286193
3	8.1	8.2211	0.78897603

If the recalculated discount factors are applied to the fixed cash flows on the original swap agreed at 8 %, the PV is changed. The hypothetical fixed bond position is now worth less. Its value per $ 100 nominal is as follows:

$$\text{PV Fixed Bond} = (-8 \times 0.94339623) + (-8 \times 0.87286193) + (-108 \times 0.78897603)$$

$$= -\$99.7395$$

The value of the floating leg is unchanged at $ 100. So the net present value of the swap is now $ 100 − $ 99.7395 = $ 0.2605 per $ 100. On the notional of $ 100 million this is a profit of approximately $ 260,500. This is a **revaluation** or mark-to-market profit for the dealer who is paying fixed on the swap. If the dealer entered into an offsetting swap with the same payment dates and notional principal he or she would receive a fixed rate of 8.1 % on this second transaction, as opposed to the 8 % paid on the original deal. The gain of 10 basis points p.a. for three years would be worth about $ 260,500 in present value terms.

14.4.1 Approximate Swap Valuation

It is possible to produce an approximate revaluation for a single swap using a bond calculator. As before this involves revaluing the fixed leg of the swap as if it were a fixed coupon bond, but this time using a *single discount rate* rather than the spot rates or discount factors. The discount rate used is the current fixed rate on swaps with the same maturity. In the above example this would be 8.1 %, the new market rate on three-year swaps. In which case the fixed leg value per $ 100 nominal is estimated as follows:

$$\text{PV Fixed Bond} \approx \frac{-8}{1.081} + \frac{-8}{1.081^2} + \frac{-108}{1.081^3} = -\$99.7428$$

Given a value of $ 100 for the floating leg, this method estimates the swap NPV at $ 0.2572 per $ 100 nominal, or about $ 257,200 in total. This compares to about $ 260,500 using the more accurate zero coupon method.

14.5 REVALUATION BETWEEN PAYMENT DATES

If the swap is revalued after inception and between payment dates it is unlikely that the floating leg will still be worth par. Interest will have accrued, and current market interest rates may be above or below the LIBOR rate that was set at the start of the period. This parallels the situation with an FRN valued between coupon dates.

For example, suppose that the (annually paid) floating coupon on an FRN has been set at 6 % for a given year, but there are now only six months left in the coupon period. At the end of the year the FRN will have a total future value of $ 106. Suppose however that the six-month interest rate now is 7 % p.a. The present value of the FRN is as follows:

$$PV = \frac{106}{1 + \dfrac{0.07}{2}} = \$ 102.4155$$

This is a dirty price. The FRN has accrued $ 3 in interest during the current coupon period, so that its clean value is $102.4155 - 3 = \$ 99.4155$. This is below the par value of $ 100 because the 6 % coupon rate set for the period is lower than the discount rate used to price the FRN. Note that in practice interest payments on dollar FRNs will normally be calculated using the actual/360 day-count convention.

14.6 THE FORWARD RATE METHOD

Using spot rates to present value cash flows is an extremely powerful tool that can also be applied to less standard swaps, and indeed to entire portfolios of swaps. It derives its rigour from the fact that each future cash flow is discounted at the unique and correct rate for the period. However the approach used above to value the floating leg can seem a little strange at first – particularly the idea that the hypothetical FRN will reset to par at the start of each payment period. This section explores an alternative method to value the floating leg of an IRS, known as the **forward rate** method. The steps are as follows:

- calculate the forward rates implied in the swap yield curve;
- assume that the floating rates for forward periods on the swap will equal the implied forward rates;
- use the forward rates to calculate the floating rate cash flows;
- discount these cash flows at the appropriate spot rates.

Alternatively, forward rates can be directly observed from the prices quoted on FRAs and interest rate futures. These products are described in Chapter 11. Pricing a swap from interest rate futures is illustrated in section 14.9 below.

14.6.1 Forward Rate Method: Case Study

The example is the same swap agreement used in previous sections. The notional is $ 100 million and the term is three years with annual payments. The dealer has agreed to pay 8 % p.a. in arrears and will receive LIBOR. The dealer's position is the equivalent to being short a fixed coupon bond and long an FRN with a first floating coupon set at 6 % and annual resets based on LIBOR. The current fixed rates on par swaps in the market are shown again in Table 14.5. The table also shows the spot rates derived from these values using the bootstrapping method. In addition, it shows discount factors and the implied forward rates.

The implied forward rate f_{1v2} for reinvesting cash between year one and year two is 8.0808 %. This is calculated using the method explained in Chapter 6. For no arbitrage to occur, the return on a one-year investment at the one-year spot rate 6 % reinvested at f_{1v2} should equal the return on a two-year investment at the two-year spot rate 7.0353 %:

$$1.06 \times (1 + f_{1v2}) = 1.070353^2$$

Table 14.5 Spot and forward rates derived from swap rates

Year	Swap rate (%)	Spot rate (%)	Discount factor (DF)	Forward rates (%)
1	6.0	6.0000	0.94339623	
2	7.0	7.0353	0.87286193	$f_{1v2} = 8.0808$
3	8.0	8.1111	0.79138828	$f_{2v3} = 10.2950$

Therefore $f_{1v2} = 8.0808\,\%$. The implied forward rate f_{2v3} calculated in the same way is 10.295 %.

The fixed side of the swap is valued by present valuing the fixed cash flows on an 8 % coupon bond. The answer as before is $-\$100$ per \$100 nominal. The floating leg is valued like an FRN except this time it is assumed that the implied forward rates indicate what the cash flows will be in years two and three. The hypothetical FRN would therefore have cash flows (per \$100 nominal) of \$6 in year one, \$8.0808 in year two, and \$110.295 in year three. The next step is to discount these cash flows at the appropriate discount factors:

$$\text{PV FRN} = (6 \times 0.94339623) + (8.0808 \times 0.87286193) + (110.2950 \times 0.79138828)$$

$$= \$100$$

The fixed and floating legs are worth $-\$100$ and \$100 per \$100 nominal to the dealer, a net present value of zero. This has to be the case in this example, because the implied forward rates are derived from the par and spot rates.

14.6.2 Swap Revaluation Using Forward Rates

Section 14.4 showed that if the swap rate changed later on the start date to 8.1 % the value of the fixed leg changes to $-\$99.7395$ per \$100 nominal. The floating leg is unchanged at \$100. To recreate these results using the forward rate method the forward rates must be recalculated. As Table 14.6 shows, the change in the three-year swap rate to 8.1 % increases the implied forward rate between years two and three.

How does this affect the value of the floating leg of the swap? Per \$100 nominal it is equivalent to the PV of the following FRN:

$$\text{PV FRN} = (6 \times 0.94339623) + (8.0808 \times 0.87286193) + (110.6322 \times 0.78897603)$$

$$= \$100$$

Table 14.6 Recalculated forward rates

Year	Swap rate (%)	Spot rate (%)	Discount factor (DF)	Forward rates (%)
1	6.0	6.0000	0.94339623	
2	7.0	7.0353	0.87286193	$f_{1v2} = 8.0808$
3	8.1	8.2211	0.78897603	$f_{2v3} = 10.6322$

The forward rate method produces a net present value for the swap of $\$100 - \$99.7395 =$ $\$0.2605$ per $\$100$ nominal. On $\$100$ million this is about $\$260\,500$. This is the same revaluation profit calculated in section 14.4.

14.7 FORWARD RATE METHOD ON A SPREADSHEET

This section shows a variant on the forward rate method which is easy to set up on a spreadsheet. It can be used to value a wide range of standard and non-vanilla swaps. The aim here as before is to revalue the three-year annual swap on $\$100$ million. The fixed leg rate is 8% and the new three-year swap rate used to revalue the deal is 8.1%. This is taken from the swap curve i.e. the current market fixed rates on dollar swaps of various maturities. The swap is being revalued on the start date. The LIBOR rate for the first period has been set at 6%.

- **Step 1.** Calculate spot and forward rates from the fixed rates on par swaps in the market. The rates are shown in Table 14.6.
- **Step 2.** Calculate the fixed and floating cash flows on the swap, using the implied forward rates to establish the LIBOR rates for years two and three.
- **Step 3.** Net out the fixed and floating cash flows and discount the result at the appropriate discount rate for each period.
- **Step 4.** Sum the answers to step 3 to calculate the swap's net present value (NPV).

The results of steps 2 to 4 are shown in Table 14.7. The NPV is approximately $\$260,500$.

The fixed rate on a par IRS (with zero net present value) is simply the single rate which, when the fixed cash flows are calculated at that rate, produces a PV equal to the PV of the floating cash flows, where the forward LIBOR rates are established by forward interest rates. In the above example the dealer entered into a three-year swap paying 8% fixed. At inception the NPV was zero. However if the three-year swap rate changes to 8.1% on the same day (other things remaining equal) the swap NPV changes to approximately $\$260,500$.

Table 14.7 Swap net present value calculation with amounts in US dollars

Year	Dealer pays	Dealer receives	Net cash flow	Discount Factor	PV
1	−8,000,000	6,000,000	−2,000,000	0.94339623	−1,886,792
2	−8,000,000	8,080,808	80,808	0.87286193	70,534
3	−8,000,000	10,632,249	2,632,249	0.78897603	2,076,782
				NPV	260,523

14.8 SWAP RATES AND LIBOR RATES

The following relationship holds for a par swap: the fixed rate is the weighted average of the cash LIBOR rate for the first payment period and the forward rates for the subsequent periods, where each rate is weighted by the appropriate discount factor.

For example in the swap considered above the cash market one-year rate is 6%. This should be weighted by the one-year discount factor. The forward rate for one year starting in one year, f_{1v2}, should be weighted by the two-year discount factor. And so on. When the swap was entered into the weighted average was exactly 8 %:

$$\frac{(0.06 \times 0.94339623) + (0.080808 \times 0.87286193) + (0.102950 \times 0.79138828)}{0.94339623 + 0.87286193 + 0.79138828}$$

$$= 0.08 \text{ or } 8\%$$

14.8.1 Directly Observing Forward Rates

In the above example the forward interest rates were derived from the spot rates, and ultimately from the fixed rates on par swaps. In fact in developed markets such as the US and the eurozone, forward interest rates can also be *observed directly* because of the existence of products such as FRAs and interest rate futures.

As a result, the swap rate for a given maturity can be calculated from the observed FRA and interest rate futures prices. The method is valid because these products can be used to hedge the risks on a swap. A dealer will be prepared to pay fixed at a certain rate and receive LIBOR not only because he or she is able to forecast future LIBOR rates from FRA and interest rate futures prices, but also because the dealer can use these products to lock into future LIBOR rates. The case study in the next section shows how to price an IRS from the prices of interest rate futures contracts.

14.9 PRICING A SWAP FROM FUTURES

The case is that of a swap dealer paying fixed and receiving floating on a $ 100 million notional swap. Payments are made quarterly in arrears, two business days after the last trading date of the relevant Eurodollar futures contract. The swap contract details are shown in Table 14.8. The goal in this section is to establish a fair fixed rate for the deal so that it is a par swap: i.e. the present values of the fixed and floating legs add to zero.

The first payment is due on Wednesday 21 March 2001, two days after the last trading date of the March Eurodollar futures contract. The first period is a so-called 'stub' period because there are only 37 days from the swap start date rather than a full quarter of a year. The 4.175 % floating rate set for the stub period is the 37-day cash market rate.

Two business days before that first payment, on Monday 19 March 2001, the LIBOR rate for the next payment on the swap due on Wednesday 20 June 2001 will be fixed. Monday 19 March is also the last trading day of the March 2001 Eurodollar futures contract. Two business days before the second payment on the swap, on Monday 18 June 2001, the LIBOR

Table 14.8 Swap pricing case study contract details

Trade date:	8 Feb 2001
Start date:	12 Feb 2001
First payment:	21 Mar 2001
Final payment:	19 Mar 2003
Notional amount:	$ 100 million
Fixed rate day-count:	Actual/360
Floating rate day-count:	Actual/360
First floating fix:	4.175 %

Table 14.9 Eurodollar futures and implied rates

Swap payment	Days in period	Futures contract	Futures price	Implied rate (%)
20 Jun 01	91	Mar 01	95.82	4.18
19 Sep 01	91	Jun 01	95.66	4.34
19 Dec 01	91	Sep 01	95.35	4.65
20 Mar 02	91	Dec 01	95.17	4.83
19 Jun 02	91	Mar 02	95.08	4.92
18 Sep 02	91	Jun 02	94.98	5.02
18 Dec 02	91	Sep 02	94.88	5.12
19 Mar 03	91	Dec 02	94.79	5.21

rate for the September payment will be fixed. And so on. The following steps establish the fair fixed rate of the swap, assuming it is agreed at par.

14.9.1 Step 1: Establish Future Interest Rates

The Eurodollar futures prices covering the relevant swap payment periods are set out in Table 14.9. The 20 June payment on the swap (made in arrears) is based on the three-month LIBOR rate from 21 March 2001 to 20 June 2001. This is the period covered by the March 2001 three-month Eurodollar futures contract, which is trading at 95.82, implying a rate of 4.18 % p.a. for the period. The 19 September payment on the swap is based on the LIBOR rate from 20 June to 19 September 2001. This payment is covered by the June 2001 futures, which is trading at 95.66, implying a rate of interest for the period of 4.34 % p.a. And so on.

14.9.2 Step 2: Calculate Discount Factors

The spot rate for the stub period to 21 March 2001 is 4.175 %. The spot rate for the next period to 20 June 2001 can be calculated as follows. For no arbitrage to occur the return on $ 1 invested at the spot rate for the period to 20 June must be the same as that achieved by:

- investing $ 1 at 4.175 % on a cash deposit maturing 21 March;
- locking into a future interest rate of 4.18 % for the following three-month period to 20 June by buying March 2001 futures at 95.82.

If z is the spot rate to 20 June 2001 it must be true that:

$$\left[1 + \left(0.04175 \times \frac{37}{360}\right)\right] \times \left[1 + \left(0.0418 \times \frac{91}{360}\right)\right] = \left[1 + \left(z \times \frac{128}{360}\right)\right]$$

Solving this equation shows that $z = 4.1913\%$. It is easier to work with discount factors than spot rates. As shown previously, a discount factor is simply the present value of $ 1 discounted at the spot rate for the period. The factor for the 37-day stub period is:

$$\frac{1}{1 + \left(0.04175 \times \frac{37}{360}\right)} = 0.9957274$$

Table 14.10 Period discount factors

Payment date	Days	Cash/futures rate (%)	Discount factor
21 Mar 01	37	4.175	0.9957274
20 Jun 01	91	4.18	0.9853164
19 Sep 01	91	4.34	0.9746242
19 Dec 01	91	4.65	0.9633014
20 Mar 02	91	4.83	0.9516822
19 Jun 02	91	4.92	0.9399918
18 Sep 02	91	5.02	0.9282133
18 Dec 02	91	5.12	0.9163536
19 Mar 03	91	5.21	0.9044424

The factor for the next period to 20 June 2001 is the present value of $1 due on that date:

$$\frac{1}{\left[1 + \left(0.04175 \times \frac{37}{360}\right)\right] \times \left[1 + \left(0.0418 \times \frac{91}{360}\right)\right]} = 0.9853164$$

The following formula is a more direct way to work out discount factors:

$$\text{Discount Factor for a Period} = \frac{\text{Discount Factor for the Previous Period}}{1 + \left(\text{Future Rate Between Periods} \times \dfrac{\text{Days in Period}}{360}\right)}$$

For example, the discount factor for the period to 20 June 2001 is given by:

$$\frac{0.9957274}{1 + \left(0.0418 \times \dfrac{91}{360}\right)} = 0.9853164$$

Table 14.10 sets out the period discount factors for the payment dates of the swap. These are derived from the stub rate and then from the future interest rates implied in the Eurodollar futures prices.

14.9.3   Step 3: Present Value the Floating Leg Cash Flows

The floating leg cash flow on a given date is found by multiplying the swap notional by the cash rate for the stub period and by the future rates for subsequent periods, adjusted for the number of days in each period. Then each cash flow is present valued using the appropriate discount factor. For example, the PV of the floating leg cash flow due on 21 March 2001 is calculated as follows:

$$\text{Cash Flow} = \$100 \text{ million} \times 0.04175 \times \frac{37}{360} = \$429.097$$

$$\text{PV} = \$429.097 \times 0.9957274 = \$427.264$$

Table 14.11 shows the whole sequence of floating leg cash flows, their present values, and the sum of the present values.

Table 14.11 Floating leg cash flows and present values in US dollars

Payment date	Floating leg cash flow ($)	Present value ($)
21 Mar 01	429,097	427,264
20 Jun 01	1,056,611	1,041,096
19 Sep 01	1,097,056	1,069,217
19 Dec 01	1,175,417	1,132,281
20 Mar 02	1,220,917	1,161,925
19 Jun 02	1,243,667	1,169,036
18 Sep 02	1,268,944	1,177,851
18 Dec 02	1,294,222	1,185,965
19 Mar 03	1,316,972	1,191,126
	Total	9,555,761

14.9.4 Step 4: Find the Swap Rate for a Par Swap

The swap rate is the single fixed rate such that the present value of the fixed leg cash flows when calculated at that rate is also $9,555,761. It can be found by trial and error, by first making a guess at the answer. Each fixed leg cash flow is calculated as:

$$\text{Notional Principal} \times \text{Assumed Swap Rate} \times \frac{\text{Days in Period}}{360}$$

For example, if the swap rate is 5% then the fixed cash flow due on 21 March is as follows:

$$\$100 \text{ million} \times 0.05 \times \frac{37}{360} = \$513,889$$

The fixed cash flows are then present valued using the appropriate discount factors. At a fixed rate of 5% the sum of the present values is in fact more than $9,555,761 so the correct swap rate must be lower than 5%. By trial and error the correct rate is found to be 4.7439%. The fixed cash flows at that rate are shown in Table 14.12.

Mathematically the 4.7439% swap rate just calculated is the weighted average of the stub period interest rate and the future interest rates, where the weights are the discount

Table 14.12 Fixed leg cash flows and present values

Payment date	Fixed cash flow @ 4.7439%	Present value
21 Mar 01	487,566	485,483
20 Jun 01	1,199,150	1,181,542
19 Sep 01	1,199,150	1,168,720
19 Dec 01	1,199,150	1,155,142
20 Mar 02	1,199,150	1,141,209
19 Jun 02	1,199,150	1,127,191
18 Sep 02	1,199,150	1,113,067
18 Dec 02	1,199,150	1,098,845
19 Mar 03	1,199,150	1,084,562
	Total	9,555,761

Table 14.13 Weighting the cash and future interest rates by the discount factors

(1)	(2)	(3)	(4)
Payment date	Cash/future rate (%)	Discount factor × period days/360	Column (2) × Column (3)
21 Mar 01	4.175	0.102338645	0.427263845
20 Jun 01	4.18	0.24906609	1.041096255
19 Sep 01	4.34	0.246363347	1.069216926
19 Dec 01	4.65	0.243501193	1.132280549
20 Mar 02	4.83	0.240564106	1.161924632
19 Jun 02	4.92	0.237609042	1.169036485
18 Sep 02	5.02	0.234631696	1.177851113
18 Dec 02	5.12	0.231633839	1.185965256
19 Mar 03	5.21	0.228622939	1.191125510
	Totals	2.014330897	9.555760571

factors. In the example an adjustment also has to be made for the fact that the periods are of unequal length. The stub period has 37 days and the subsequent periods each have 91 days. The calculation is shown in Table 14.13. The weights are in column (3).

The weighted average of the cash and futures rates calculates the fixed rate for a par swap:

$$\frac{9.555760571}{2.014330897} = 4.7439\,\%$$

14.10   HEDGING INTEREST RATE RISK ON SWAPS

In the example in the last section if a dealer enters into the IRS at par then he or she will pay 4.7439 % and receive LIBOR. The notional is $ 100 million and the day-count method for both legs is actual/360. If the dealer does not have an offsetting swap, the deal can be hedged using interest rate futures. A common procedure is to recalculate the value of the swap for a one basis point change in future interest rates.

Assume, for example, that the March 2001 futures price rises from 95.82 to 95.83, implying a one basis point fall in the future interest rate from March to June 2001. The fixed and floating legs of the swap entered into at 4.7439 % can then be revalued based on this change in future interest rates. The results are as follows:

$$\text{Revalued PV floating leg} = \$9,553,498$$

$$\text{Revalued PV fixed leg} = -\$9,555,988$$

$$\text{NPV} = -\$2490$$

The price value of a basis point (PVBP) on a Eurodollar futures contract is $ 25. That is, each one basis point change in the interest rate is worth $ 25 profit or loss per contract. So to hedge this risk the dealer should buy 100 March 2001 futures:

$$\frac{2490}{25} \approx 100$$

To complete the hedge the dealer repeats this procedure for each of the payment periods of the swap and buys a 'strip' of interest rate futures. In theory the dealer should also hedge against changes in the rate for the stub period, although in practice this is often ignored for lack of a suitable hedging vehicle.

14.10.1 Convexity Effects

In the above example the dealer pays fixed, receives floating, and can hedge the risk of falling interest rates by buying interest rate futures. The hedge will work well for small changes in interest rates. However for larger changes it will become increasingly inaccurate. The dealer is effectively short a fixed rate bond and will suffer from **negative convexity**. This means that the losses on the swap will increase in a more than linear fashion as interest rates fall, while the profits will increase less sharply as rates rise. On the other hand the profit or loss on the futures contracts used to hedge the swap is always $25 per basis point move in interest rates. The dealer should charge for the effects of negative convexity by paying a lower fixed rate than that implied in the futures prices.

Precisely the opposite situation occurs if a dealer receives fixed, pays floating, and hedges by selling Eurodollar futures. The dealer is effectively long a fixed coupon bond. The **positive convexity** on this position means that the profit on the fixed leg will rise in a more than linear fashion as interest rates fall, while losses will be less pronounced as rates rise. But profits and losses on the futures always change in a strictly linear fashion; the imbalance this time is in the dealer's favour. The dealer should therefore pay for the benefits of positive convexity by receiving a lower fixed rate on the swap than that implied in the futures prices.

Note that pricing and hedging swaps with interest rate futures requires an active market in the futures contracts so that the prices reflect fair value. Even with major currencies the liquidity on futures tends to be highest with the near month contracts and to reduce in the case of contracts covering more distant time periods.

14.11 CHAPTER SUMMARY

A standard 'plain vanilla' single-currency interest rate swap can be considered as a combination of a fixed coupon bond and a floating rate note. The swap can be valued by working out the present values of the hypothetical straight bond and the FRN. To do this accurately the cash flows should be discounted at the appropriate spot rates or discount factors. An alternative method is to calculate forward interest rates from spot rates (or to derive them from FRA or futures prices) and use these to establish the payments on the floating leg of the swap. The net cash flows from the fixed and floating legs can then be present valued using the appropriate discount factors. A par swap is one in which the present value of the fixed and floating legs add to zero. The fixed rate on a par swap is a weighted average of the cash market rate that establishes the first floating payment, plus the future interest rates that establish subsequent floating payments. As a result, the fixed rate can be calculated from the market prices of interest rate futures or FRAs. Where available, these products can also be used to hedge the interest rate risks on swaps. A futures hedge will be somewhat inaccurate for larger changes in interest rates because the price value of a basis point on futures is constant whereas the profits and losses on swaps are not linear.

Equity Index Futures and Swaps

15.1 CHAPTER OVERVIEW

Index futures contracts are widely used to take trading positions and to hedge the exposures on baskets of shares. This chapter explores how they are quoted, traded, and settled as well as the operation of the margin system. It presents a number of applications of index futures in hedging, trading, and asset allocation. It considers how index futures are priced and the effect of the cost of carrying positions in the underlying shares. This leads to a discussion of the cash-futures relationship, known in the market as 'the basis'. A classic index arbitrage trade is assembled. Index and stock futures contracts are traded through exchanges and are standardized. Their equivalent in the over-the-counter market is the equity swap. The chapter looks at a standard or 'vanilla' equity swap and how the payments on the deal are calculated. It shows how equity swap traders can manage their risks using portfolios of shares or futures contracts. It explores the applications of equity swaps and also some important variations on the basic structure, including the floating principal deal.

15.2 INDEX FUTURES

An equity index futures contract is an agreement:

- made between two parties;
- on an organized exchange;
- to exchange cash compensation payments;
- based on the movement in the value of an equity index.

There is no physical delivery of the underlying portfolio of shares that comprise the index. This contrasts with commodity or bond futures where there is a physical delivery process. One of the most actively traded contracts in the world is the S&P 500 stock index futures contract traded on the Chicago Mercantile Exchange (CME). The contract was first introduced in 1982 and accounts for most US equity index futures trading. Trades can be transacted on the traditional trading floor or on the exchange's Globex® electronic trading platform. The underlying index is calculated by Standard & Poor's and is based on the value of 500 leading US shares weighted by market capitalization. It would be too cumbersome to deliver all the 500 shares in the correct proportions against the futures contract. Instead, each full S&P index point is assigned an arbitrary $250 monetary value and profits and losses on the futures are settled in cash.

Cash Settlement

A trader who buys one S&P 500 index futures contract at a level of 1200 points and who later sells at 1250 points will make a profit of $50 \times \$250 = \$12,500$ less brokerage.

The CME has introduced an 'E-mini' S&P futures contract mainly aimed at the retail market and which can be traded electronically. In this contract each full index point is worth $ 50. The CME offers a range of other contracts on well-known indices such as the Japanese Nikkei 225 (with points denominated in US dollars or in yen). Other major contracts include the FT-SE 100 futures, based on the index of the top 100 blue-chip UK shares, which is traded on LIFFE. Futures on the leading German index, the DAX 30, are traded on Eurex, the joint Swiss-German exchange.

15.2.1 Role of the Clearing House

The role of the exchange and the associated clearing house is to facilitate trading in the contracts. The clearing house acts as central counterparty and guarantees the settlement of all contracts. Opening an index futures position (whether buying or selling) involves depositing collateral called **initial margin** with a broker, which handles payments made to and received from the clearing house. (On the CME the initial margin is called a **performance deposit**.) Open positions are marked-to-market on a daily basis and are subject to margin calls from the clearing house.

15.3 MARGINING PROCEDURES

To illustrate the margining system, this section considers a short trading campaign based on FT-SE 100 index futures contracts. Trading in this contract is conducted electronically through the LIFFE CONNECT® computer system (the London trading floor was finally closed in 2000). The contracts are cleared and settlement is guaranteed by the London Clearing House (LCH). The contract specification is set out in Table 15.1.

15.3.1 Trading Campaign: Day One

The June FT-SE futures is currently trading at 5500 index points. A trader decides to buy 10 contracts. To transact the order the trader contacts a broker. The broker asks for an initial margin, a performance deposit. The LCH sets a minimum initial margin based on the volatility of the futures contract. However, a broker will normally ask for more than the minimum, depending on the relationship with the client. Suppose the broker in this case asks for GBP 3500 initial margin per contract and therefore GBP 35,000 on the whole trade. The trader lodges the money with the broker, who in turn pays margin over to the clearing house (via a clearing member, if the broker is not itself a clearing member).

The broker transacts the order electronically. Assume that 10 June contracts are bought at exactly 5500 index points. The other side of the trade is taken by the seller of the June

Table 15.1 FT-SE 100 index futures contract

Underlying:	FT-SE 100 index
Quotation:	FT-SE 100 index points
Point value:	GBP 10 per full index point
Tick size (value):	0.5 index points (GBP 5)
Expiry Months:	March, June, September, December

Source: LIFFE.

futures. However trading is anonymous and the buyer and seller are not known to each other. As soon as the deal is transacted the LCH interposes itself as central counterparty. It becomes the seller to the buyer, and the buyer to the seller. The clearing house does not itself initiate trades. It simply clears and guarantees that due payments will be made, and protects itself against default by operating the margin system.

The trader could close the long futures position out later the same trading day by selling June futures. Instead, the trader decides to retain the position overnight. In this case it will be marked-to-market based on the closing or settlement price of the June futures contract. Suppose that the settlement price is 5470 index points, 30 points below the purchase price. The trader will receive a margin call to pay GBP 3000:

$$\text{Variation Margin Due} = -30 \text{ points} \times 10 \text{ contracts} \times \text{GBP } 10 = -\text{GBP } 3000$$

The cash goes via the trader's broker to the clearing house. The clearing house needs this cash because if the futures fall in value the money collected from the longs is credited to the accounts of the shorts – the market participants who are short FT-SE 100 index futures contracts. If the trader does not meet the margin call the broker will close out the position, sell the 10 contracts, and return the initial margin minus any losses and costs.

15.3.2 Trading Campaign: Day Two

The trader has had to pay GBP 3000 variation margin, but the position is still open. Suppose that at the close of the next trading day the June futures close at 5520. This is a rise of 50 points from the previous day's settlement price. This time the trader *receives* variation margin:

$$\text{Variation Margin Received} = 50 \text{ points} \times 10 \text{ contracts} \times \text{GBP } 10 = \text{GBP } 5000$$

The futures price has risen, driven upwards by the cash FT-SE 100 index, ultimately by the prices of the constituent shares. This time variation margin payments are paid into the clearing house by the shorts (via their brokers) and are credited to the dealing accounts of the longs (via their brokers).

15.3.3 Trading Campaign: Day Three

Finally, on the third day the trader decides to close the position by putting in an order to sell 10 June futures either 'at best' (at the best available market price) or on a limit order basis (at a price that is not less than a stipulated level). Suppose the broker transacts the sell order at 5530. The trader is entitled to a final variation margin payment because the contracts have been sold 10 points above the last settlement price:

$$\text{Variation Margin Received} = 10 \text{ points} \times 10 \text{ contracts} \times \text{GBP } 10 = \text{GBP } 1000$$

The position is now closed. This is the effect of having one central counterparty. Effectively, the trader has bought 10 June futures with the clearing house acting as central counterparty. The trader is also short 10 June futures with the clearing house as counterparty. As far as the clearing house is concerned these trades simply cancel out and the trader has zero net position. The trader can take back the GBP 35,000 initial margin (with interest, if this has been negotiated in the brokerage agreement).

15.3.4 Net Profit and Loss

The net profit on the trading campaign (ignoring funding and transaction costs) is the sum of the variation margin payments:

$$\text{Net Profit} = -\text{GBP } 3000 + \text{GBP } 5000 + \text{GBP } 1000 = \text{GBP } 3000$$

Alternatively, it is the price at which the futures were sold less the price at which they were bought times the number of contracts traded times the point value:

$$\text{Net Profit} = (5530 - 5500) \times 10 \text{ contracts} \times \text{GBP } 10 = \text{GBP } 3000$$

15.4 FINAL SETTLEMENT AND SPREAD TRADES

On LIFFE the mark-to-market procedure is repeated every day until the FT-SE 100 futures position is closed out. The futures contracts expire on the third Friday of the contract month and trading ceases as soon as possible after 10:15 a.m. London time on that date. At the expiry all remaining open positions are settled in cash against the **EDSP** (exchange delivery settlement price).

- The EDSP is based on the value of the underlying cash FT-SE 100 index established through an auction run at the London Stock Exchange on the last trading day.
- In the absence of a physical delivery mechanism this procedure ensures that the futures contract value will converge on the cash index level at expiry.

If a position is retained until the last day there is a final variation margin payment based on the EDSP and then the contracts simply expire – there is no physical delivery of shares.

15.4.1 Margin and Brokerage Arrangements

On LIFFE there is a daily variation margin payment due if the settlement price has changed from yesterday's settlement even by a small amount. Some exchanges run a system of **maintenance margins**. The difference is that the settlement price of the contract has to move beyond a threshold level before there is a margin call. Some brokers are prepared to accept securities such as government bonds as collateral against the initial margin requirement. The securities cannot then be lent out elsewhere. The collateral may be subject to a **haircut**. This means that securities with a market value greater than the margin requirement have to be pledged, to protect the broker against a fall in their market value.

15.4.2 Spread Trades

If a trader buys one contract month, say the June FT-SE 100 futures, and sells another month, say the September contracts, then this is a **spread trade**. There is an offset in the profits and losses on the two positions but the total position is still open and will be marked-to-market on a daily basis. The two contract months are based on the same underlying but have different expiry dates and will normally trade at different prices. The long position does not completely match out with the short position, although the risk on the combined trade is less than if a trader has a simple long or short position in one delivery month. The initial margin requirement is adjusted to reflect the offset. Trades of this kind are used to take advantage of anomalies between the pricing of different contract months, or to take a view on whether the difference between the prices is likely to narrow or widen.

By contrast, an **intermarket spread** trade involves buying contracts on one equity index (such as the CME S&P 500 futures) and selling contracts on a different index (such as the CME Russell 2000 futures, based on an index of smaller capitalization companies). The objective of such a strategy is to profit from changes in the relative values of each market.

15.5 HEDGING WITH INDEX FUTURES: CASE STUDY

Index futures can be used to hedge against potential losses in a cash portfolio of shares due to short-term falls in the market. In the following case a portfolio manager owns a diversified portfolio of major US shares and wishes to use CME S&P 500 index futures to fully hedge the equity risk. The details are as follows:

- Current market value of the portfolio = $ 100 million
- Portfolio beta = 1.2
- Cash S&P 500 index = 1200

If the market falls sharply the portfolio manager runs the risk of failing to meet the quarterly performance targets on the fund. Of course the manager could simply liquidate the portfolio, sell the shares, and put the money on deposit. However this would incur transaction costs, and if the market rallied the manager would either have to start buying back shares, or run the risk of underperforming competitors who have stayed invested in the market.

Instead the portfolio manager decides to sell CME S&P 500 index futures as a temporary hedge or protection device. If the market falls the fund will lose money on the cash portfolio, but will earn variation margin payments on the short futures contracts in compensation. One problem to bear in mind though is that the portfolio is not a market portfolio and does not exactly replicate the behaviour of the S&P 500. The beta of 1.2 tells us that it is slightly more risky than the S&P 500 index. (Chapter 10 has details on the calculation and the applications of beta.)

15.5.1 Calculating the Hedge Ratio

The first issue to resolve is how many futures contracts the manager should sell to hedge against the risk of losses on the portfolio. This is the **hedge ratio**. One way to tackle the question is to take some arbitrary fall in the S&P 500 and calculate the loss on the portfolio. Then it is possible to calculate how many futures contracts the portfolio manager would have to be short to recover that loss. For example, assume that the index drops 120 points from its current level of 1200, a fall of 10%. The beta value predicts that the portfolio will fall by a greater amount:

$$\text{Percentage Change in Portfolio} = -10\% \times 1.2 = -12\%$$

On a $100 million portfolio this translates into a loss of $12 million. The final question to answer is how many futures contracts the manager would have to be short to recover a loss of $12 million. Assume for simplicity that the futures contracts move exactly in line with the cash S&P 500 index, and fall by exactly 120 points. Each full index point on the major CME S&P 500 futures contract is worth $250. Then the fund manager would have to be short 400 futures to recover the loss on the share portfolio.

$$400 \text{ Futures Contracts} \times 120 \text{ points} \times \$250 = \$12 \text{ million}$$

15.5.2 Hedge Ratio Formula

A simpler way to calculate the **hedge ratio** (the number of futures to sell) is to work out the notional value of the futures contracts. If the S&P 500 is trading at 1200 and each index point is worth $250 then each futures contract represents a notional position in a portfolio of index-tracking shares worth $300,000. (Some fund managers call this the 'associated economic exposure'.)

Buying one index futures is therefore equivalent to buying a portfolio of shares tracking the S&P 500 index worth $300,000. Selling one index futures is equivalent to running a short position in the market portfolio to the value of $300,000. The portfolio manager has to cover a long position in shares worth $100 million, so clearly selling one index futures is not sufficient. A first step is to divide the value of the portfolio by the nominal value of a futures contract:

$$\frac{\$100 \text{ million}}{\$300,000} = 333 \text{ futures}$$

However, the beta measure says that the portfolio is more sensitive to market events than the S&P 500 index, so the portfolio manager has to increase the number of contracts in the futures hedge:

$$\text{Number of Futures to Sell} = 333 \times 1.2 = 400$$

The complete hedge ratio formula is as follows:

$$\text{Hedge Ratio} = \frac{\text{Portfolio Value} \times \text{Portfolio Beta}}{\text{Cash Index Level} \times \text{Point Value}}$$

In the example the portfolio value is $100 million, the beta is 1.2, the cash index level is 1200, and the value of each S&P 500 index point is $250. When using the formula with FT-SE 100 index futures on LIFFE each full index point is worth GBP 10. When using the formula with the DAX® futures (code name FDAX) on Eurex each full index point is worth EUR 25.

15.6 HEDGE EFFICIENCY

There are a number of reasons why an index futures hedge such as the one just considered is liable to be less than perfect in practice.

- **Basis Risk.** It was assumed above that the cash S&P 500 index and the futures simply move in line with each other. In practice, futures contracts do not exactly track the day-to-day changes in the underlying index. The relationship between the cash index level and the futures price is known as

the basis. The basis can change over time and so there is basis risk on the hedge – the underlying index and the futures may not move exactly in line with each other.

- **Tracking Error.** The hedge ratio calculation assumes that beta is a reliable indicator of the tracking relationship between the portfolio and the S&P 500 index (and also that beta remains constant). Beta is often based on historical evidence and the future relationship between the portfolio and the index may not reflect past behaviour.

- **Liquidity Risk.** The daily profits and losses on the portfolio are unrealized (paper) profits and losses until the shares are actually sold. The futures position is marked-to-market and margin is paid or received on a regular basis. This can be an inconvenience for the portfolio manager (money has to be set aside to meet potential margin calls); at worst it could present a serious cash flow problem.

- **Rollover Risk.** The portfolio manager has to decide which expiry month to trade. In practice most market participants tend to trade the 'near month' futures, the contracts with the nearest expiry month. These are normally the most liquid and so it is easier to trade in size without moving the price. However when the contracts expire the portfolio manager will no longer have a hedge in place. If the manager wishes to extend the hedge further this will involve 'rolling' the futures – that is, selling the next expiry month. This gives rise to **rollover risk** – the risk that the new contracts may not be trading at their fair valuation and the manager may have to sell them too cheaply.

Portfolio managers who sell index futures to protect against market losses can use the contracts as a temporary hedge and buy contracts back if the market shows signs of recovery. The danger is that if they are fully hedged in a rising market any gains on their portfolio will be wiped out by losses on the futures, and they will underperform the competition. They face the risk of making an opportunity loss. One alternative is to reduce the number of futures in the hedge and to retain some level of exposure to market changes (i.e. some beta risk).

15.7   OTHER USES OF INDEX FUTURES

Portfolio managers can also use index futures to assist with their investment timing. For example, a mutual fund may decide to buy futures contracts to establish a position in a market before the cash is actually received from investors. The fund manager may not wish to delay the investment, in case the market rises in the meantime. Later on the futures contracts can be closed out and replaced with physical shareholdings.

Portfolio traders working for banks can employ the same type of strategy. If they need to buy a portfolio of shares they can buy futures in the first instance to establish a position in the market at a given level, and then purchase the actual shares over a longer period of time. Chapter 8 has information on the portfolio trading business.

15.7.1   Asset Allocation

Fund managers also use index futures as a means of tactically adjusting their asset allocations by 'overlaying' a position in shares with futures contracts. This can be a lot quicker and cheaper in terms of transaction costs compared to physically buying one portfolio of shares and selling another.

As an example, suppose that a US portfolio manager wishes to shift funds from the US to the UK. The S&P 500 is trading at 1200 and the FT-SE 100 at 5500. The sum to be reallocated is $30 million and the GBP/USD exchange rate is 1.5000. The current US portfolio has a beta close to one and the fund manager wishes to establish an exposure to the UK market that tracks the FT-SE 100 index. The fund manager should trade index futures contracts as follows:

$$\frac{\$\,30\ \text{million}}{1200 \times \$\,250} = 100\ \text{S\&P futures (sell)}$$

$$\frac{\text{GBP}\ 20\ \text{million}}{5500 \times \text{GBP}\ 10} = 364\ \text{FT-SE 100 futures (buy)}$$

The numerator here is simply the sterling equivalent of $\$\,30$ million at the spot FX rate. This strategy 'overlays' a cash portfolio of US shares with futures contracts in order to switch to an exposure in the UK market.

15.8   PRICING AN EQUITY FORWARD CONTRACT

The theoretical or fair value of an index futures contract is established using an arbitrage argument, sometimes known as a **cash-and-carry calculation**. Fair value is also known as **equilibrium value**: the futures price should not stray far from that level, otherwise there are opportunities for profitable arbitrage. The cash-and-carry method derives from pricing forward contracts and is extended to exchange-traded futures. The theoretical forward price of a commodity or financial asset is derived from the cost of buying the commodity or asset in the cash or spot market, plus the cost of 'carrying' the position for forward delivery.

Suppose that a bank is asked to quote a price to a counterparty to deliver a share in one year at a fixed price. This is a **forward contract** rather than a futures contract because it is an over-the-counter deal. The share is trading at $\$\,100$ in the cash market. The bank could try to establish the forward price by taking a view on the direction of the share price. For example, if it believes that the price is set to fall sharply it may be prepared to agree to deliver the share in a year at $\$\,100$, in the confident expectation that the stock can be acquired for a cheaper price nearer the date.

Derivatives Pricing

This strategy is speculation, not valuation. The general rule when pricing a derivative product is to start with what it would cost to hedge the risks on the product and then to add on a reasonable profit margin. In normal market conditions most of the risks in the derivatives business are due to the fact that the hedging mechanisms used are not always as efficient as they might be.

15.8.1   The Cash-and-Carry Method

The bank's problem is that it has to quote a fixed delivery price to its counterparty, but does not know what it will cost to buy the share in the future to complete the delivery process. However it *does* know that one share costs $\$\,100$ today. Its strategy is to buy the share in the cash market, borrow $\$\,100$ to do this, 'carry' the share, and then deliver it to the counterparty through the forward contract. The following additional information is available:

- interest payment due on a $\$\,100$ loan in one year = $\$\,5$;
- expected dividend income on the share during the next year = $\$\,2$.

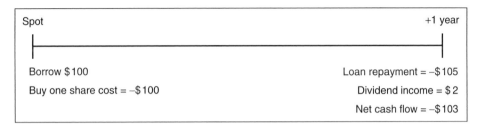

Figure 15.1 Cash flows resulting from carrying the share position.

The repayment on the loan in one year is $100 principal plus $5 interest, offset by $2 in dividends. Figure 15.1 illustrates the cash flows that result from carrying the position in the share to deliver against the forward contract. The bank's break-even price for delivering the share in one year (assuming it has covered all its costs) is $103.

15.8.2 Components of the Forward Price

The forward price has two components: the cost of buying the share in the cash market, and the net cost of carrying the position to deliver the share in the future. The carry cost in turn has two components: the funding charge (interest payable) minus the dividends received on the share:

$$\text{Break-even Forward Price} = \text{Cash} + \text{Net Cost of Carry}$$

$$\text{Net Cost of Carry} = \$5 - \$2 = \$3$$

$$\text{Break-even Forward Price} = \$100 + \$3 = \$103$$

Strictly speaking the net carry cost is likely to be slightly less than this because dividend payments received during the course of the year can be reinvested.

15.9 INDEX FUTURES FAIR VALUE

The fair value of a futures contract is established through a very similar calculation. It is the cost of buying a basket of shares in the cash market to have available to deliver on a future date, plus the cost of funding the position, less any dividends that will be received on the stock. Although there is no physical delivery on a futures contract, it is closed out at expiry against the index and therefore mirrors the behaviour of a market portfolio of shares that tracks the index.

The example this time is based on FT-SE 100 index futures. For simplicity transaction costs are ignored, although in practice this will have an effect on the fair value calculation. Short-term interest calculations are also rounded rather than using the actual/365 day-count convention that applies with sterling. The task is to establish the fair value of a three-month FT-SE 100 futures contract. The following data are available to complete the calculation:

- Cash FT-SE 100 index level = 5500.
- Three-month sterling interest rate = 4.5 % p.a.
- Dividend yield on the FT-SE 100 index = 2.5 % p.a.

The first step is to establish the carry cost. The quoted interest rate and dividend yield are divided by four because they are annual rates and the futures expires in three months:

$$\text{Net Cost of Carry} = 5500 \times \left(\frac{0.045 - 0.025}{4} \right) = 27.5$$

The fair futures is the cash index level of 5500 plus the net carry, a total of 5527.5. In one formula:

$$\text{Fair Futures} = 5500 \times \left[1 + \left(\frac{0.045 - 0.025}{4} \right) \right] = 5527.5$$

Positive and Negative Carry

The fair value in this example is above the cash index level because the funding rate is higher than the dividend yield on the index. There is a **negative** net cost of carrying the shares, which is passed on to the buyer of the futures by the seller. Not all trades have negative carry. For example, the coupon income on a bond is often higher than the cost of borrowing money to buy the bond. The seller of the futures can buy a bond to deliver against the futures and earn **positive** carry. This is passed over to the buyer of the futures in the form of a clean futures price at a discount to the cash clean price. See Chapter 12 for details on bond futures.

15.10   THE BASIS

The relationship between the cash and the futures price is known by traders as **the basis**. It can be calculated in different ways but the following definition commonly used by traders is used here:

$$\text{Basis} = \text{Cash} - \text{Futures}$$

The basis on the FT-SE 100 futures priced in the last section is therefore calculated as follows:

$$\text{Basis} = 5500 - 5527.5 = -27.5 \text{ index points}$$

The negative number means that there is negative carry involved. A buyer of the futures (if it is trading at fair value) will have to pay 27.5 index points in net carry cost to the seller. This is fair, because the buyer has the alternative of purchasing the underlying shares in the cash market rather than the futures. However in that case the buyer would also suffer from negative carry: the cost of funding a position in the shares (or the interest foregone from not being able to deposit the cash) would be greater than the dividend income earned.

15.10.1   Theoretical and Actual Basis

In fact −27.5 points is the **theoretical basis**. It is derived from the theoretical fair value of the futures. In reality futures contracts do not always trade exactly at fair value. This can be the result of sheer supply and demand factors in the equity market. For example:

- when the cash market starts to fall or look dangerous hedgers and speculators sell index futures aggressively;

- if the market starts to recover the shorts will look to close out their positions by quickly buying back contracts.

In practice, because of such factors, index futures can tend to exaggerate rather than simply track movements in the underlying index. However when futures contracts 'trade away' from their theoretical fair value then valuable arbitrage opportunities can open up. The next section shows how these can be exploited.

15.11   INDEX ARBITRAGE TRADE

Suppose there has been aggressive buying of the FT-SE 100 index futures contract that expires in three months' time. As before, the cash index level is 5500, three-month sterling LIBOR is 4.5 % p.a., and the forecast dividend yield on the index is 2.5 % p.a. The fair value of the futures is therefore 5527.5. However, a trader notices that the contracts are actually trading on the exchange at 5550. This provides an arbitrage opportunity. The strategy is as follows.

- **Long the Cash.** The trader borrows (say) GBP 110 million for three months at 4.5 % and buys a basket of shares in the cash market that tracks the index (beta = 1).
- **Short the Futures.** The trader sells an offsetting number of the overpriced futures contracts at 5550. The cash index is trading at 5500 and each point is worth GBP 10.

Therefore:

$$\text{Number of Contracts to Sell} = \frac{\text{GBP 110 million}}{5500 \times \text{GBP 10}} = 2000$$

By selling 2000 futures the trader neutralizes the market risk on a GBP 110 million portfolio of shares that tracks the index (i.e. the net beta is zero). The trader does not wish to take an outright position in the market but to exploit the mispricing of the futures contract.

Table 15.2 takes two possible scenarios for the level of the FT-SE 100 at the expiry of the futures. In both cases the profit is the same. For example, if the FT-SE is at 6000 at expiry this is a rise of about 9.91 % from a starting level of 5500, a profit of GBP 10 million on the GBP 110 million index-tracking share portfolio. The futures will also close at 6000, which is a loss of 450 points (they were initially sold at 5550). On 2000 contracts at GBP 10 per point this is a loss of GBP 9 million. The interest paid is 4.5 % p.a. on the GBP 110 million loan used to buy the shares. This is partially offset by the 2.5 % p.a. dividend yield on the stock.

15.11.1   Using the Basis Numbers

In fact the net profit on the strategy is always the same. A quicker way to establish this figure is to calculate and compare the **theoretical basis** and the **actual basis** (sometimes

Table 15.2   P&L on index arbitrage trade

FT-SE at expiry	P&L on shares	P&L on futures	Interest paid	Dividends earned	Net P&L
5000	−10,000,000	11,000,000	−1,237,500	687,500	450,000
6000	10,000,000	−9,000,000	−1,237,500	687,500	450,000

called the crude basis) of the futures. The former uses the fair value of the futures. The latter uses the actual price at which the futures are trading in the exchange.

$$\text{Theoretical Basis} = \text{Cash Index Level} - \text{Fair Futures Price} = 5500 - 5527.5 = -27.5$$

$$\text{Actual Basis} = \text{Cash Index Level} - \text{Actual Futures Price} = 5500 - 5550 = -50$$

There is a discrepancy here between the theoretical and the actual basis of -22.5 index points. This discrepancy (sometimes called by traders the **value basis**) is exploited through the index arbitrage trade.

$$\text{Value Basis} = \text{Fair Futures Price} - \text{Actual Futures Price} = 5527.5 - 5550 = -22.5$$

$$\text{Arbitrage Profit} = -22.5 \text{ points} \times -2000 \text{ futures} \times \text{GBP } 10 = \text{GBP } 450.000$$

The fact that the value basis is negative means that the carry cost built into the actual futures price is too high. It is also a signal that the appropriate strategy is to sell the futures and buy the cash index.

15.12   RUNNING AN ARBITRAGE DESK

In practice there are a number of constraints on index arbitrage trading that have to be factored into the equation.

- **Arbitrage Window.** Arbitrage opportunities of this kind do not persist for long in modern markets. The effect of traders selling the overpriced futures and buying the cash index will be to push down the futures price (and perhaps pull up the cash index). The arbitrage opportunity will quickly disappear.
- **Transaction Costs.** Even a large trading operation pays transaction costs when buying shares and selling futures. Against this, electronic trading is reducing such costs and making it easier to assemble baskets of shares to offset futures positions.
- **Tracking Error.** The arbitrage trader may decide to save on transaction costs by assembling a basket of shares that is *likely* to track the index, rather than buying all the shares in the index. This leaves open the risk that the basket may not accurately track the index (while the futures at expiry will close at the cash index level).
- **Dividend Assumptions.** The example was based on an assumption about the dividend yield the trader would receive on the basket of shares. It may be that this is inaccurate. In practice it is better to make an explicit forecast of the dividends likely to be earned on all the shares in the index over the life of the futures contract.
- **Borrowing Constraints.** The index arbitrage trade needs capital to generate a small (albeit a low risk) profit.
- **Funding Costs.** As with many transactions involving derivatives, the ability to fund the strategy at keen interest rates is very important. High funding costs will eliminate the arbitrage profit.
- **Stock Borrowing Fees.** If the futures is trading 'cheap' relative to its fair or theoretical value then the appropriate trade is to buy the futures and short the underlying stock. This incurs stock borrowing fees, and there is the risk that it may prove difficult (or expensive) to find the stock to borrow in the market.

Index arbitrage desks usually set a threshold level for the trade. If the futures deviates by more than this level from fair value the arbitrage trade is likely to be profitable, net of transaction costs. The threshold can differ between different financial institutions, because it depends on factors such as funding and trading costs.

15.13   FEATURES OF INDEX FUTURES

Equity index futures have a number of features that can offer advantages to investors and traders compared to buying and selling shares in the cash market:

- **Leverage.** A relatively small performance deposit (initial margin) provides access to a substantial equity exposure. For example, if the cash S&P 500 index is trading at 1200 then each of the major futures contracts is economically equivalent to a market portfolio of shares worth $1200 \times \$250 = \$300,000$. If an investor has $300,000 to invest, a percentage can be used to make the deposit on the futures and the rest can be kept in a safe money market deposit account.
- **Transaction Costs.** These are normally lower when compared to buying and selling underlying shares. Brokerage charges on futures are low, there is no need for custodians, and (in the UK) there is no stamp duty to pay to the government. It is relatively cheap and easy to switch exposures quickly using futures.
- **Diversification.** Index futures provide easy access to a diversified portfolio of shares.
- **Liquidity.** The major contracts such as the S&P 500 futures are very actively traded and there are many market participants. Market access is easy and prices are determined in an open and transparent manner. It is also just as easy to take a short position as it is to take a long position.
- **The Clearing House.** Settlement on futures contracts is guaranteed by the clearing house, which virtually eliminates counterparty risk.

There are some other features that can pose problems (although they can also provide trading opportunities):

- **Basis Risk.** The fact that futures prices do not exactly move in line with changes in the price of underlying cash market day-to-day (the basis is not constant) means that hedging with futures is not an exact science. It also poses problems for fund managers who are using futures to track an index.
- **Rollover Risk.** Index futures do not last for ever. When a contract expires a trader who wishes to retain the position will have to 'roll' into the next delivery month. This contract may be trading cheap or dear relative to fair value.
- **Margin Calls.** The margin system helps to protect the stability of the exchange and to ensure that the clearing house can always meet its obligations. However it does mean that a trader is subject to margin calls, and may be forced to sell securities quickly to make a payment.
- **Standardized Contracts.** In order to make index futures contracts as actively traded as possible they have to be standardized. This may not suit an investor who, for example, would like to take an exposure to a subset of shares in an index or to smaller companies.

The issue of standardization is now being addressed by the exchanges. Contracts have been introduced on a much wider range of indices, including the NASDAQ, the Russell 2000® index of smaller capitalization US companies, and the DJ STOXX® index based on 50 leading European shares.

In addition, futures contracts on **single stocks** can now be traded. As at end-2008 they were offered by LIFFE, Eurex, MEFF in Spain, on the Italian IDEM exchange, and on the US exchange OneChicago. The margin system means that only a percentage of the value of the underlying shares has to be deposited at the outset. In addition, some single stock futures contracts are settled in cash rather than through the physical delivery of shares, based on the difference between the price at which the futures were traded and the closing price of the underlying share at expiry. Cash settlement is a particular advantage in the UK because it avoids the government stamp duty tax on physical settlement.

15.14   EQUITY SWAPS

An equity swap is the over-the-counter answer to index and stock futures. In a standard contract:

- two parties agree to exchange cash flows at regular intervals over an agreed period of time;
- at least one payment leg is based on the change in the value of an equity index or a single stock.

If the deal is a **total return swap** then the equity leg payment includes a sum of money representing dividends on the underlying shares. The return leg can be based on a fixed or a floating interest rate or on another equity index. In some structures the notional is fixed over the life of the swap and in other cases it varies. Payments are normally made monthly, quarterly, semi-annually, or annually. The typical maturity (tenor) is one to three years.

Equity swaps can be more risky than interest rate swaps because the change in the value of the equity index can be negative as well as positive. If this happens the party *receiving* the equity return has to pay its counterparty for the fall in the value of the index. Figure 15.2 shows the global growth of equity forward and swap contracts.

15.14.1   Equity Swap Example

A portfolio manager wishes to make a tactical asset allocation switch over the next year and to increase the fund's exposure to the German stock market. The desired exposure is $100 million. Rather than selling off existing assets or liquidating holdings in cash and bonds, the manager decides to enter into an equity index swap on the DAX 30 index of the largest German companies with a dealer. The fixed notional is EUR 100 million. The manager:

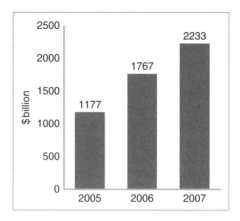

Figure 15.2   Notional amounts outstanding at end-year on equity-linked swaps and forwards. *Source*: Bank for International Settlements.

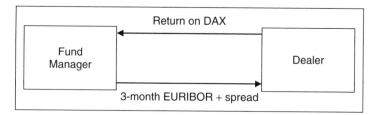

Figure 15.3 Payment diagram for equity index swap.

- pays three-month EURIBOR plus a spread on a quarterly basis for a year;
- receives the return on the DAX (positive or negative) on a quarterly basis for a year.

The payments on the swap are netted out. For example, suppose that in the first quarter of the deal the DAX rises by 5%. Then the manager is due a EUR 5 million cash payment on the equity leg of the swap. From this is deducted the interest payment due to the dealer. However if the index *fell* in the quarter by (say) −5% then the manager would owe the dealer EUR 5 million on the equity leg. This is in addition to the payment due to the dealer on the interest rate leg. The deal is illustrated in Figure 15.3. Note that the DAX is a **total return index** which means that it is assumed in the calculation that dividends are reinvested in additional shares.

The deal could also be structured such that the fund manager pays a fixed rather than a floating rate of interest. It is easy to convert between these alternatives using a fixed-floating interest rate swap. (See Chapter 13 for details of interest rate swaps.)

15.14.2 Floating Notional Equity Swap

In a floating notional total return equity index swap the notional is reset after a payment according to the change in the index over the period. It is designed to replicate the changing value of an underlying basket of shares, whilst also taking into account the cost of funding the position and the dividends received on the stock. By contrast, a fixed notional swap is designed to replicate the position of an investor who wishes to have a fixed amount of cash allocated to an investment, and who would sell off shares if the value increases, or add additional shares if the value falls.

15.15 MANAGING THE RISKS ON EQUITY SWAPS

The swap dealer in Figure 15.3 clearly has a significant exposure to changes in the DAX. Perhaps the ideal hedge would be to find another counterparty willing to pay over the return on the market over the same period and to accept EURIBOR less a spread. The counterparty might be a second fund manager holding a portfolio of blue-chip German shares who wishes to change from an equity exposure to a return based on EURIBOR for a period of time.

If an offsetting swap is not available, another way for the dealer to hedge the equity exposure is to buy a cash portfolio of shares tracking the DAX index, funded by a loan. The equity exposures will cancel out, since the dealer will earn the return on the DAX on the share portfolio and pay it away on the swap. If the dealer pays EURIBOR flat on the loan and receives EURIBOR plus a spread on the swap then he or she will capture the spread as a profit. However in practice there are still some risks outstanding.

- **Credit Risk.** The counterparty might default on the swap, and the hedge would have to be unwound or a replacement swap entered into (although the notional principal is not at risk since it is never exchanged). The dealer will typically ask for collateral to manage this risk.
- **Funding Risk.** The dealer may decide to fund the hedge on a weekly or even daily basis if rates are cheaper, and roll over the funding. This produces a mismatch since the rate received from the counterparty is based on three-month EURIBOR.
- **Tracking Error.** The dealer may decide to buy a basket of shares designed to track the DAX rather than all 30 shares, to save on transaction costs. Then there is a risk that the basket may not track the index accurately.

Alternatively, the dealer could hedge the swap by buying index futures to cover the next payment date and then 'rolling' the futures hedge into later month contracts to cover subsequent payment dates. Then if the DAX rises the payments the dealer has to make on the equity swap will be offset by profits on the futures contracts, which will increase in value. This strategy is likely to be cheaper in terms of transaction costs compared to buying a cash portfolio, but there is a **basis risk** – the risk that the futures position may not match the profits and losses on the swap. If the dealer has to buy index futures at a 'rich' price i.e. above their fair value this can produce a net loss.

15.16   STRUCTURING EQUITY SWAPS

Equity swaps are over-the-counter derivatives and can be tailored to meet specific client needs. They need not be based on a well-known index such as the DAX or the S&P 500. For example, a counterparty may wish to receive the return on a basket of shares drawn from a particular sector such as pharmaceuticals or oil. In a so-called **quanto** swap the returns on a basket of shares are paid in another currency. This allows investors to take positions in foreign equity markets without settlement and custodian complications and without having to make FX deals.

A swap may have two equity legs rather than just one. For example, a fund manager may decide to make a tactical asset allocation switch by paying a dealer the returns on a basket of US shares and receiving the returns on the DAX. Typically the fund manager will own an underlying portfolio of US stocks and will simply pass over the returns to the dealer. In effect, the manager switches the exposure to the DAX but without having to liquidate the US stock portfolio, which could be expensive in terms of transaction costs.

A further variant occurs when the equity leg of a swap is based on the higher of the returns on two market indices. Given the obvious attractions of such a structure the rate paid on the interest leg will be higher than on a standard or 'vanilla' equity index swap. A **blended swap** is one in which the equity payment is based on the weighted average of the returns on two or more indices.

Finally, an equity swap can be based on a **single stock**. For example, an investor who owns a share but who is unwilling or unable to sell the holding for a period of time can pay away the returns on the stock to a dealer in return for a floating or fixed rate of interest. Alternatively, the investor can be paid the return on a diversified portfolio of stocks.

15.17 BENEFITS AND APPLICATIONS OF EQUITY SWAPS

Equity swaps have a number of advantages for an investor or trader compared with holding actual share portfolios.

- **Leverage.** Normally the notional principal is not exchanged, so that it is possible to establish a position that replicates the profits and losses on a large number of shares without having to physically purchase the shares.
- **Transaction Costs.** There may be an upfront commission fee on an equity swap, or the dealer may simply make a return on the bid-offer spread. However, transaction costs can be appreciably lower than the cost of buying and holding the underlying shares (although there will be legal costs involved in setting up a master swap agreement).
- **Accurate Tracking.** Equity swaps are highly convenient for index funds. As well as lower transaction costs, they can track an index more accurately than strategies that involve buying a sub-set of the shares in the index. Index-tracking share portfolios also have to be restructured when there is a change in the composition of the index.
- **Tax Benefits.** Some countries impose a special withholding tax on dividends paid to foreign investors. A foreign investor can enter into a swap with a bank that has an operation in such a country that is not subject to the withholding tax. The bank purchases the shares and passes over the returns to the investor including gross (or nearly gross) dividends.
- **Market Access.** In some countries shares can be highly illiquid, or there may be restrictions on ownership. Equity swaps allow foreign investors to gain exposure to such markets. If the swap is structured as a 'quanto' the returns can be paid in the investor's home currency. In addition, there is no need for the investor to become involved with the different settlement, accounting, or regulatory systems of the foreign country.

Equity swaps also have some advantages compared to trading futures contracts.

- **No Basis Risk.** The return on a futures position depends not only on changes in the underlying market portfolio but also on unpredictable changes in the cash-futures relationship (the basis). The equity leg payments in a swap are based purely on the returns on the underlying index or basket of shares.
- **Customized.** Equity swaps are highly flexible and a dealer will be able to tailor a contract to meet the precise needs of the client.

One potential disadvantage of swaps is that they are over-the-counter contracts and therefore inherently illiquid. The more customized contracts also tend to incur higher transaction costs such as wider bid-offer spreads. In addition, there is a credit risk on equity swaps. The sums involved can be quite considerable, more than is typical for traditional fixed-floating interest rate swaps. Partly for this reason many equity swaps employ quarterly or monthly rather than semi-annual payments, and maturities also tend to be shorter than is the case with interest rate swaps.

Banks can manage credit risk by asking for initial margin and reserving the right to ask for additional collateral in defined circumstances. Legal risks can pose further problems. If it is proved that a counterparty is acting *ultra vires* (that is, beyond its legal authority) in entering into the swap agreement in the first place then the contract may be cancelled by the courts.

15.18   CHAPTER SUMMARY

An index futures contract is an agreement made on an organized exchange to exchange cash payments based on the movement in a stock index. Contracts are cash-settled and there is no physical delivery of shares. When a futures position is set up initial margin has to be deposited; the contracts are also regularly marked-to-market. On the last trading day they are closed out against the underlying cash index. The fair value of an index futures is the cash index plus the net cost of carrying a position in the shares that comprise the index. The relationship between the cash and the futures price is called the basis. If the futures price deviates from fair value it may be possible to construct an index arbitrage trade, buying the cash market and selling the futures, or vice versa. In practice it is necessary to take into account the effects of transaction costs on the likely profits. Index futures are used for trading purposes and also to hedge positions in shares and to implement asset allocation decisions. Exchanges have also introduced single stock futures. An equity swap is an agreement between two parties to exchange payments on regular future dates, where at least one leg is based on the change in the value of a share or a basket of shares (sometimes plus dividends). The return leg is based on a fixed or floating rate of interest or sometimes another equity index. Investors can use equity swaps to transform the nature of their assets and to gain exposures to changes in share prices without having to buy the actual stock. Equity swap dealers can use offsetting swaps or positions in shares or futures contracts to manage their risks. Because swaps are dealt over-the-counter they can be tailored to meet the needs of clients. However they are illiquid. They also carry credit risk. This can be managed by taking collateral.

16
Fundamentals of Options

16.1 CHAPTER OVERVIEW

This chapter introduces fundamental option concepts. It takes a 'building block' approach and describes the basic option strategies that are applied in different combinations in later chapters. It explains the key 'jargon' expressions used in the options market – call and put; strike price; expiry date; premium; intrinsic and time value; in-, at-, and out-of-the-money; break-even point and so on. These concepts are illustrated with practical examples. The chapter shows the payoff profiles for four basic option strategies – long a call; short a call; long a put; short a put. These are compared with the profits and losses achieved by buying or selling underlying shares. To relate option theory to the 'real world' of the financial markets the chapter also examines key index option and stock option contracts traded on derivatives exchanges. It explains the specification of the contracts, how the premiums are quoted, and how to calculate potential profits and losses. The Appendix describes some common varieties of exotic options.

16.2 DEFINITIONS

Options contracts on commodities such as grain have been around for many years. Options on financial instruments are relatively recent but volume has expanded rapidly since the introduction of contracts on exchanges such as the Chicago Board Options Exchange (CBOE). The buyer of a financial option contract has the right but not the obligation:

- to buy (call option) or to sell (put option);
- an agreed amount of a specified financial asset, called the underlying;
- at a specified price, called the exercise or strike price;
- on or before a specified future date, called the expiry date.

For this right the buyer pays an upfront fee called the **premium** to the writer of the option. This is the most money the buyer can ever lose on the deal. On the other hand the writer of an option can face virtually unlimited losses (unless a hedge is put in place). This is because it is the buyer who decides whether to exercise or take up the option.

Exchange-traded options are standardized, but their settlement is guaranteed by the clearing house associated with the exchange. Over-the-counter (OTC) option contracts are agreed directly between two parties, one of which is normally a bank or securities trading house. As a result the contracts can be customized to meet the needs of specific clients. However they cannot be freely traded and they do not carry the guarantee of a clearing house. For this reason there is potential default risk on OTC options – the risk that the counterparty may fail to fulfil its obligations. As discussed in previous chapters, at the time of writing there is increased concern about credit risk on OTC derivatives generally in the wake of shocks such as the collapse of the giant investment bank Lehman Brothers in September 2008.

16.2.1 Types of Options

There are two main varieties of option contract.

- **Call Option.** The right but not the obligation to buy the underlying asset at the strike price.
- **Put Option.** The right but not the obligation to sell the underlying asset at the strike price.

A so-called **American-style** option can be exercised on or before expiry. A **European-style** option can only be exercised on the expiry date of the contract. In fact these labels are historical and have nothing to do with where options are actually dealt. Most options traded on exchanges around the world are American-style. OTC options, regardless of where they are created, are often European-style. Because an American option confers additional rights, it is worth at least the same as the equivalent European contract.

Bermudan Options

For those who like the flexibility of early exercise but who do not wish to pay the full cost of an American option, the market has created alternative contracts known as Bermudan options. These can be exercised on specific dates up to expiry, such as one business day a week.

In practice relatively few options are ever exercised. A trader who has bought an exchange-traded option can simply sell it back through the exchange if it becomes more valuable, rather than actually exercising the contract. Options are bought and sold as assets in their own right and many traders simply make profits on the difference between the purchase and the sale price. And in any event the majority of options expire worthless.

16.3   BASIC OPTION TRADING STRATEGIES

The following sections explore the return and risk characteristics of the four basic option trading strategies.

- long call;
- short call;
- long put;
- short put.

This section begins with a call option. The details of the contract are specified in Table 16.1.

Table 16.1   Call option contract

Type of option:	American-style call
Underlying share:	XYZ
Number of shares:	100
Exercise price:	$ 100 per share
Expiry date:	One year from today
Current share price:	$ 100
Option premium:	$ 10 per share

The buyer of the option has the right but not the obligation to buy 100 XYZ shares at a fixed strike price of $100 each on or before the expiry date in one year. For this right the buyer has to pay an upfront premium of $10 per share to the writer of the contract. In this example the strike price and the current share price are exactly the same. This is known as an **at-the-money** (ATM) option.

Intrinsic Value

An American option that is at-the-money has zero intrinsic value. Intrinsic value is the value (if any) that can be realized by immediately exercising an option contract. It is either zero or positive because the buyer of an option is never obliged to exercise and to make a loss through exercise.

If the underlying share was currently trading at (say) $120 then the $100 strike call would be **in-the-money** (ITM) and would have $20 intrinsic value per share. The holder of the call could exercise the right to buy the share at the strike price of $100 and immediately re-sell the stock on the cash market at $120. Ignoring funding and transaction costs, the value realized would be $20 per share. On the other hand if the underlying was currently trading at $80 then the $100 strike call would be **out-of-the-money** (OTM) with zero intrinsic value. The share price would have to rise by more than $20 before the contract would be worth exercising.

16.3.1 Intrinsic and Time Value

The option in Table 16.1 is at-the-money in relation to the spot price of the underlying. It has zero intrinsic value. The premium is charged by the writer simply because there is time remaining to expiry. The share price may increase over this period, resulting in a profit for the holder of the call (who has the right to buy the stock at a fixed price) and a loss for the writer (who is required to deliver the stock at that fixed price if the option is exercised). In the meantime, also, the holder of the call can gain by depositing the strike price and earning interest.

- **Intrinsic Value.** This measures any money that can be released by exercising an option. In the case of a European option this can only be done at expiry. An American contract can also be exercised early.
- **Time Value.** This measures the value of an option over and above its intrinsic value. Even an out-of-the-money option (with zero intrinsic value) will have some time value if there is time remaining until expiry, assuming the price of the underlying asset can fluctuate.
- **Total Option Value.** This equals intrinsic value plus time value. At expiry the time value is zero.

16.4 LONG CALL: EXPIRY PAYOFF PROFILE

A useful way to look at an option strategy is in terms of its profit or loss profile at expiry, net of the initial premium paid. At expiry there is a simple decision for the buyer of an option to make – either the contract is exercised or it is discarded as worthless. Put another way, an option at expiry has positive intrinsic value if it expires in-the-money; it has zero

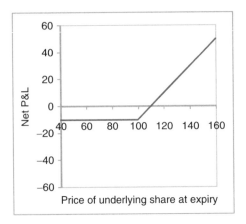

Figure 16.1 Expiry payoff profile for a long call.

intrinsic value if it expires out-of-the-money or at-the-money. It has no time value because it has expired.

Suppose a trader buys the at-the-money call in Table 16.1. The premium paid to the writer is $10 per share. The strike is $100 per share. This is a **long call** position. It profits from a rise in the value of the underlying share. To keep things simple the following analysis ignores transaction and funding costs, including the fact that the premium is paid upfront whereas the decision on whether to exercise the option is taken at expiry. Figure 16.1 illustrates the payoff (per share) for different levels of the underlying asset at expiry.

At expiry the owner of the call option will only exercise the contract when the underlying price is above the strike price. For example, if the share is trading at $90 at expiry then the holder of the call will not take up the right to buy the share at a fixed price of $100: it could be purchased more cheaply in the cash market. If the option is not exercised the loss is the initial $10 premium. However if the underlying share is worth more than $100 in the cash market then it makes sense to exercise the call. It has intrinsic value.

Break-even Point

The break-even point on the long call is reached when the share is trading at $110. At that level the $10 initial premium is exactly offset by the $10 intrinsic value of the long call. The call confers the right to buy a share at $100 that is worth $110 in the cash market and $10 could be realized by exercising the option.

16.4.1 Downside and Upside

In the jargon of the markets a long call position has **limited downside risk** but **unlimited upside**. In other words, the maximum loss is restricted to the initial premium paid, because there is no obligation to exercise a contract that expires out-of-the-money. On the other hand there is no limit to the profit that the buyer of a call option can make. The underlying share price could (in theory) rise to any level and the holder of the call has the right to buy the share at the fixed strike price.

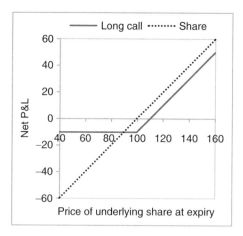

Figure 16.2   Long call versus a long position in the underlying share.

16.4.2 Long Call and Cash Position Compared

Buying a call probably seems like a very attractive proposition (limited risk, unlimited return). However the initial premium acts as something of a dead weight on the profitability of the position. For example, rather than buying the above at-the-money call, the trader could simply buy the underlying share in the cash market at $ 100. Then if the share price rose to $ 110 the trader would make a $ 10 profit, while because of the initial premium paid the option position would simply break even. Figure 16.2 compares the profit and loss profile of the long call against a position in the underlying share purchased in the cash market at $ 100.

One factor which Figure 16.2 ignores is that the initial outlay on the long call is much less than the cost of buying the actual share. This means that the option position has the benefit of **leverage**. For example, if the share price doubled the call would be worth $ 100 intrinsic value per share. This would produce a very large percentage return on the initial $ 10 premium paid to buy the option.

16.5   SHORT CALL: EXPIRY PAYOFF PROFILE

This section looks at the $ 100 strike call in Table 16.1 from the perspective of the writer (seller) of the contract. The initial premium received is $ 10 per share. This is the most money the writer can ever make out of the deal. If the option expires out-of-the-money the buyer will not exercise the contract and the premium is a profit for the writer. However if it expires in-the-money the buyer will exercise and has the right to purchase shares at $ 100 each which have a higher value in the cash market.

Figure 16.3 shows the payoff profile of a short or sold call option at expiry. This is sometimes called a **naked short option** position because it is unhedged. If the buyer of the call exercises the contract the writer has to buy shares in the cash market at their current value and deliver the shares at a fixed price of $ 100 each. In practice, writers of call options normally hedge their risks, sometimes through offsetting options positions, sometimes by purchasing the underlying asset. A naked short call is dangerous because it has limited upside (limited to the initial premium received) and potentially unlimited downside.

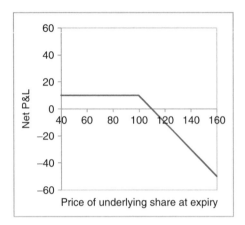

Figure 16.3 Expiry payoff profile for a short call.

Some option contracts are **cash settled** rather than through the physical delivery of the underlying asset. In this case the writer of the contract pays any intrinsic value over to the buyer at expiry. For example, if the strike of a call option is $ 100 and the underlying stock is worth $ 120 at expiry the writer will pay $ 20 to the buyer of the call. If the stock is worth (say) $ 80 at expiry the writer will pay out nothing.

16.6 LONG PUT: EXPIRY PAYOFF PROFILE

This section explores the position of the buyer of a put option i.e. a **long put**. The contract is specified in Table 16.2. In this contract the strike is $ 100. The buyer of the put has the right (but not the obligation) to sell 100 XYZ shares at $ 100 each. The premium is $ 10 per share. A long put is a 'bear' position: it makes money when the price of the underlying falls. However the maximum loss is the premium paid to the writer of the contract at the outset.

The contract in Table 16.2 is an at-the-money put option since the spot price is the same as the strike price. The contract has zero intrinsic value – there is no profit to be made through immediate exercise. If the underlying share price was, for example, $ 90 rather than $ 100 then a put with a strike of $ 100 would have $ 10 intrinsic value since the holder of the put could immediately exercise the option and sell for $ 100 each shares that are only worth $ 90 in the cash market. The holder of the put could buy the shares for $ 90, exercise the option and 'put' the stock on the writer of the option for $ 100, making a $ 10 profit. Of course if an option is already in-the-money when it is purchased this will be reflected in a higher premium cost.

Table 16.2 Put option contract

Type of option:	American-style put
Underlying share:	XYZ
Number of shares:	100
Exercise price:	$ 100 per share
Expiry date:	One year from today
Current share price:	$ 100
Option premium:	$ 10 per share

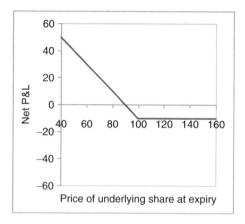

Figure 16.4   Expiry payoff profile for a long put.

Figure 16.4 shows the profit and loss profile of the above long put at expiry, net of the initial premium paid, on a per share basis. If the underlying is trading *below* the $ 100 strike price at expiry it makes sense to exercise the option – it has positive intrinsic value. The break-even point is reached when the stock is trading at $ 90. Then the $ 10 profit from exercising the put cancels out the $ 10 premium. If the underlying is trading *above* the $ 100 strike at expiry the option expires worthless and the loss on the long put is the $ 10 premium.

16.6.1   Long Put Versus Shorting the Stock

A long put is a bear position, but it is far less risky than shorting the underlying stock. The potential losses to a short seller are theoretically unlimited since the 'short' has to buy the shares back and return them to the original owner at the prevailing market price – which might be far above the sale price. Figure 16.5 compares the payoff on the $ 100 strike long put with a position in the underlying stock sold short at $ 100.

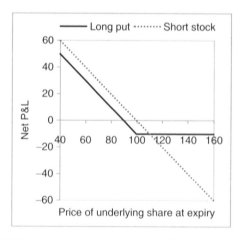

Figure 16.5   Long put versus a short position in the underlying.

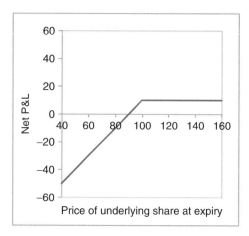

Figure 16.6   Expiry payoff profile for a short put.

16.7   SHORT PUT: EXPIRY PAYOFF PROFILE

Figure 16.6 shows the payoff profile at expiry of the put option in Table 16.2, this time from the writer's perspective. The strike is $ 100 per share.

The maximum profit for the writer of the put option (per share) is the premium of $ 10 and the maximum loss is $ 90. If the share price closes at or above the strike at expiry the holder of the option will not exercise the contract and the writer has made a $ 10 profit. On the other hand if the share price is below $ 100 the holder of the put will exercise the contract. The break-even point occurs when the share is trading at $ 90. At that level the writer of the put will be sold a share for $ 100 which is only worth $ 90 in the cash market, making a $ 10 loss which is offset by the initial premium. Below $ 90 the position shows a net loss.

Figure 16.6 shows the payoff profile of a 'naked' short put option, that is, without a hedge in place. Given the risks on such a position normally the writer will hedge the risks by trading other option contracts or by shorting the underlying – which will show a profit if the share price falls to offset the losses on the put.

16.8   SUMMARY: INTRINSIC AND TIME VALUE

- The intrinsic value of an American call is zero or the price of the underlying asset minus the strike, whichever is the greater.
- The intrinsic value of an American put is zero or the strike minus the price of the underlying asset, whichever is the greater.
- Strictly speaking the strike of a European option should be compared with the *forward price* of the underlying at expiry since the option can only be exercised (and the strike price paid) at expiry. In practice many people ignore this factor and calculate intrinsic value on a European option using the spot price. In the case of shorter-dated options the difference may not be very great.
- An option either has positive or zero intrinsic value. Intrinsic value by definition is never negative – the holder of an option cannot be forced to exercise the option and make a loss on exercise.
- Intrinsic value can only be realized before expiry through exercising an option in the case of an American contract. However the current value of an option will reflect any intrinsic value it may have.

Table 16.3   Summary of key options strategies

Strategy	Premium	Characteristic
Buy call	Pay	Right to buy the underlying at the strike price
Write call	Receive	Obligation to deliver the underlying if exercised
Buy put	Pay	Right to sell the underlying at the strike price
Write put	Receive	Obligation to take delivery of the underlying if exercised

- Even if an option has no intrinsic value, if there is any time remaining until expiration and the share price can fluctuate, the option will have time value.
- From the perspective of the option writer, time value reflects the risk involved in having to deliver a share (short call) or take delivery of a share (short put) at a fixed price.
- All other things being equal, the longer the time to the expiry of an option the higher its time value. A long-dated option provides more profit opportunities for the holder than a short-dated option.
- The premium of an option consists of intrinsic value (if any) plus time value. To put it another way, subtracting the intrinsic value from the premium calculates the time value component.

Finally, for this section, Table 16.3 summarizes the characteristics of four basic option strategies considered so far. The next sections explore a variety of stock and index option contracts traded on major exchanges.

16.9   CBOE STOCK OPTIONS

Calls and puts on the shares of individual companies can be freely bought and sold on exchanges such as the Chicago Board Options Exchange® (CBOE®), LIFFE, and Eurex. Table 16.4 shows the prices of trades in IBM stock options on the CBOE on 2 September 2008. The underlying IBM stock was trading at $122.28 when the data was taken.

The premiums in Table 16.4 are quoted in dollars per share, although the contract size is actually based on 100 shares. This is the normal lot size on US listed stock option contracts. The CBOE stock options are American-style and can generally be exercised on any business day before expiration. Exercise results in the physical delivery of the underlying stock. The following bullet points take some examples from the table.

- The September $120 strike call is in-the-money. The premium is $4. Intrinsic value is $2.28 so the time value is $1.72.
- By contrast the September $125 strike call is out-of-the-money and the premium of $1.10 is entirely time value.
- The October $125 strike call is also out-of-the-money but it is more expensive than the September $125 call. It has greater time value because there is more time to expiry and therefore a greater chance that the underlying stock price will increase and that the option will move in-the-money.

Table 16.4   IBM stock option prices on the CBOE

Expiry	Strike ($)	Call premium ($)	Put premium ($)
20 September 2008	120	4.00	1.20
20 September 2008	125	1.10	3.30
18 October 2008	120	6.00	3.10
18 October 2008	125	3.60	5.08

Source: Chicago Board Options Exchange, reproduced with permission.

- The $ 125 strike puts are in-the-money because they confer the right to sell IBM shares above the current spot price of $ 122.28.
- The $ 120 strike puts are out-of-the-money, but the October series is more expensive than the September series because the contracts have more time value – there is more chance that the share price will fall below the strike by October compared to September.

16.9.1 Early Exercise

As discussed further in Chapter 17, In practice it rarely makes sense to early exercise an American-style option. Only the intrinsic value is earned, and the option is killed off in the process. Instead, the contract can be sold at the current market premium, which will include the intrinsic value plus also any remaining time value. The main exception occurs when the underlying stock has a dividend forthcoming. In this case it can sometimes make sense to early exercise a call to buy the stock and secure the dividend payment.

16.10   CME S&P 500 INDEX OPTIONS

The specification for the CME option on the S&P 500 is set out in Table 16.5. The underlying here is an S&P 500 futures contract. As always, the clearing house acts as an intermediary between buyers and sellers. The S&P 500 contracts are American-style and can be exercised on any business day. If the owner of an option exercises a contract, a seller of options is randomly assigned for exercise:

- if it is a call the seller will acquire a short position in the futures at the strike price of the option;
- if it is a put the seller will acquire a long position in the futures at the strike price of the option.

16.10.1 Premium

Premiums on the S&P options are quoted in **index points**. The dollar value of a premium is the quoted price times $ 250. Table 16.6 shows a selection of closing prices for the September 2008 expiry S&P 500 index options. This data was taken on 2 September 2008.

Table 16.5   CME options on S&P 500 index futures

Underlying:	One S&P 500 stock index futures contract
Index point value:	$ 250 per full index point
Expiry months:	March, June, September, December, plus serial months
Regular tick size (value):	0.1 index points ($ 25)

Source: Chicago Mercantile Exchange.

Table 16.6   CME options on S&P 500 futures closing prices on 2 September 2008

Strike	Call premium	Put premium
1265	29.40	17.90
1270	26.50	20.00
1275	23.70	22.20
1280	21.00	24.50
1285	18.40	26.90

Source: Chicago Mercantile Exchange.

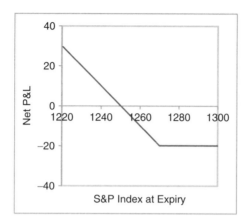

Figure 16.7   Expiry payoff profile of S&P 500 put.

On the day the data in Table 16.6 was taken the underlying September futures contract closed at 1276.50. This information can be used to interpret the option premiums in the table.

- **September 1265 Calls.** These are in-the-money relative to the September futures price. Intrinsic value is 11.50 points and so time value is $29.40 - 11.50 = 17.9$ points. This amounts to $\$4475$ per contract.
- **September 1285 Calls.** These are out-of-the-money and the 18.40 points premium is all time value. In dollar terms the premium is $\$4600$ per contract.
- **September 1270 puts.** These are out-of-the-money and the 20 points premium is all time value. In dollar terms the premium is $\$5000$ per contract.

Figure 16.7 shows the expiry payoff profile of a long position in the September 1270 strike puts. The profits and losses are shown per contract in index points. The break-even point (ignoring transaction costs) is the strike minus the 20 point premium, which equals 1250 index points. This is on the assumption that the contract is retained until the expiry of the options and of the underlying futures in the third week of the contract month.

16.11   STOCK OPTIONS ON LIFFE

Table 16.7 shows closing prices for a selection of calls and puts on BP taken on 2 September 2008. The contracts expire on the third Friday of the contract month. Quotations are in British pence per share, to the nearest 0.5. The interval between strikes is set according to a scale determined by the exchange. It introduces new exercise prices as the underlying share price

Table 16.7   BP stock option closing prices on LIFFE on 2 September 2008

Expiry month	Strike (pence)	Call premium (pence)	Put premium (pence)
Sep 2008	500	20.00	7.00
Sep 2008	520	9.00	16.25
Oct 2008	500	28.25	13.25
Oct 2008	520	17.00	22.00

Source: LIFFE.

rises and falls. The lot size for stock options on LIFFE is normally 1000 shares per contract, although it is 100 for some securities. The contracts are American-style and are physically exercised. When a long call is exercised the holder takes delivery of shares and pays the strike. When a long put is exercised the holder delivers stock and is paid the strike.

The closing price of the underlying BP stock was 511.50 pence on the day the data in Table 16.7 was taken (i.e. GBP 5.115 per share). The following bullet points take some examples from the table.

- The 500 strike September calls are trading at 20 pence per share (a total of GBP 200 on the contract, which is based on 1000 shares). The calls are in-the-money because the underlying is trading at 511.50. They have 11.5 pence intrinsic value and 8.5 pence time value.
- The 520 strike September calls are out-of-the-money and the 9 pence premium is all time value.
- The 520 strike October calls are also out-of-the-money but have a longer time to expiry (45 days) than the September calls (17 days) and so have greater time value.
- The 500 strike puts (the right to sell at 500) are out-of-the-money given that the underlying is trading above that level at 511.50. They have zero intrinsic value. The 520 strike puts are in-the-money.

16.12   FT-SE 100 INDEX OPTIONS

The contract specification for the LIFFE FT-SE 100 index option (European-style exercise) is set out in Table 16.8. Call and put prices are quoted in index points, with a tick size (minimum price movement) of 0.5 index points. The value of a full index point is GBP 10, the same value as for the FT-SE 100 index futures contract.

Quoting premiums in index points makes it easy to carry out break-even calculations. For example, suppose a 5650 strike FT-SE 100 call costs 82 index points. This is GBP 820 per contract in sterling terms. Figure 16.8 shows the expiry payoff profile of a long

Table 16.8   LIFFE FT-SE 100 index options European-style exercise

Point value:	GBP 10 per full index point
Expiry months:	March, June, September, December plus additional months
Tick size (value):	0.5 index points (GBP 5)
Quotation:	Index points
Expiry:	Third Friday in the contract month

Source: LIFFE.

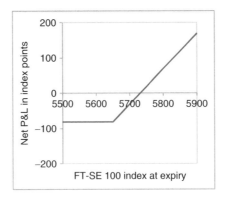

Figure 16.8   Expiry payoff profile of long FT-SE 100 index call.

position in this option. The underlying index has to be trading above 5732 (the strike plus the premium) for the strategy to break even. In practice transaction costs must also be taken into account.

When the FT-SE 100 options expire any open contracts are cash settled against the value of the underlying index. If contracts expire in-the-money a trader with a long position in an option receives the intrinsic value in cash at GBP 10 per point. Otherwise the contracts expire worthless and the holder has lost the premium.

16.13   CHAPTER SUMMARY

An option confers the right but not the obligation to buy or sell an underlying asset at a fixed price (the strike price) on or before a fixed date (the expiry date). A call option is the right to buy the underlying, and a put is the right to sell the underlying. European options can only be exercised at expiry. American options can also be exercised early. The maximum loss for a buyer is the premium, but the maximum profit can be far greater. Writing options is risky because the maximum profit is the initial premium received whereas the maximum loss can be unlimited. Traders can manage this risk by trading in the underlying assets. An option premium has two components: time value, and intrinsic value. Intrinsic value is never negative. For a call intrinsic value is zero or the price of the underlying minus the strike, whichever is the greater. For a put intrinsic value is zero or the strike minus the price of the underlying, whichever is the greater. An option that has intrinsic value is in-the-money. If the strike is the same as that of the underlying asset an option is at-the-money. If the option could only be exercised at a loss it is out-of-the-money (although it will not be exercised in this circumstance). The buyer of a call breaks even at expiry when the underlying trades at the strike plus the premium (plus transaction costs). The buyer of a put breaks even at expiry when the underlying trades at the strike minus the premium (minus transaction costs). Options contracts on stock market indices such as the S&P 500 and on individual shares are traded on derivatives exchanges.

APPENDIX: EXOTIC OPTIONS

The term 'exotic option' is a rather loose one, but it is conventionally used to describe later generation options whose terms differ in some way from the standard terms of a vanilla call or put option. This Appendix describes briefly some of the key structures used in the markets.

Asian or Average Price Options

The payoff from an average price call is the maximum of zero and the average price of the underlying during the life of the option minus the strike. The payoff from an average price put is the maximum of zero and the strike minus the average price of the underlying. Asian options are generally less expensive than conventional options since averaging prices over a period of time has the effect of lowering volatility. The more frequently the averaging is carried out the greater this effect, so that daily averaging reduces volatility more than weekly or monthly averaging. For the same reason geometric averaging reduces volatility more than arithmetic averaging.

A variant on the structure is the **average strike** option. Here the price of the underlying over some period of time is averaged out and the strike price is set to that average. The payout of an average strike call is zero or the difference between the price of the underlying at exercise and the strike, whichever is the greater.

Barrier Options

The payoff from a barrier option depends on whether the price of the underlying reaches a certain level during a specified period of time or during the whole life of the option. Barriers are either **knock-in** or **knock-out** options. A knock-in comes into existence only if the underlying price hits a barrier (sometimes called the instrike). A knock-out ceases to exist if the underlying price reaches a barrier (sometimes called the outstrike). Sometimes the buyer receives a pre-set rebate if the option is knocked out or fails to be knocked in. With call options there are four possibilities:

- **Down-and-in call.** Comes into existence if the stock price falls to hit the barrier.
- **Up-and-in call.** Comes into existence if the stock price rises to hit the barrier.
- **Down-and-out call.** Ceases to exist if the stock price falls to hit the barrier.
- **Up-and-out call.** Ceases to exist if the stock price rises to hit the barrier.

The same possibilities exist with puts. For example, an up-and-out put ceases to exist if the stock price rises and hits a barrier above the current spot price. It will be less expensive than a standard put option and when used to protect against falls in the value of a share will provide cheaper protection than a vanilla option. However the 'insurance' will cease to exist if the stock price rises to hit the barrier or outstrike.

Bermudan Options

In an American option the holder can exercise at any time during the life of the option. With a Bermudan option the holder may only exercise at agreed times during the life of the option. Bermudan options provide more flexibility than European options because of the possibility of early exercise but are normally cheaper than standard American-style options.

Binary (Digital) Options

Binary options pay out a fixed amount or nothing at all. For example, a **cash-or-nothing** call pays out a fixed amount of cash if the underlying is above the strike at expiry, otherwise it expires worthless. Another variant is the **asset-or-nothing** call. This pays out the value of the underlying asset if it expires in-the-money, otherwise it pays nothing.

Chooser (Preference) Options

With a chooser or 'U-choose' option the holder can choose whether the option is a call or a put at a specified point in time. Normally the call or put will have the same time to expiry and strike price although more complex structures have been assembled where this is not the case. A trader or investor might buy chooser options when he or she believes that the underlying asset will be subject to price volatility but is uncertain whether the price will go up or down.

Compound Options

These are options on options. There are four main types:

- a call on a call;
- a put on a call;
- a call on a put;
- a put on a put.

In the case of a call on a call the buyer has to pay a premium upfront for the option to buy a call option. If the holder exercises that option he or she receives the underlying call and pays in return a further premium. The underlying call will normally have standard terms: it will be an American or European-style option with a fixed expiry date and a fixed exercise price.

Exchange Options

Exchange options are options to exchange two assets – for example, one stock for another, or one foreign currency for another. Effectively a convertible bond is an exchange option since the holder has the right but not the obligation to exchange a bond for equity or (sometimes) for another type of debt.

Forward Start Options

Forward start options are paid for now but start at some future date. Normally it is agreed that the strike will be set at-the-money on the start date.

Cliquet

A cliquet or ratchet option consists of a standard at-the-money option followed by a strip of forward start options whose strike will be set at-the-money on the forward start date. For example, a cliquet option might consist of a one-year at-the-money spot start call option followed by strip of two forward start at-the-money call options each with one year to expiry. Suppose the underlying spot price at the outset is $100. If at the end of year one the underlying is trading at $110 the holder makes $10 on the one-year spot start call. The strike for the next option in the strip is set at-the-money at $110. If at the end of year two the underlying is trading at $115 the holder makes a further $5 profit. The strike for the final call in the strip is set at $115. If at the end of year three the underlying is back trading at $100 the final option expires worthless. However the holder has locked in the interim $15 gains.

Ladder Options

Ladders are similar to cliquets in that the holder can lock in profits made during the life of the contract. At expiry a **fixed strike** ladder call pays the difference between the highest of a series of threshold prices or 'rungs' reached by the underlying and the strike, or zero if no rung is reached.

In a **floating strike ladder** option the initial strike is reset whenever the underlying price hits a prescribed 'rung' in the ladder rather than (as is the case with a cliquet) on specific dates. For example, consider a ladder call with the initial strike set at $ 100 and rungs set at $ 10 intervals above that level. If the underlying hits $ 110 at any point the strike is reset to $ 110 and the $ 10 profit is locked in. If the underlying subsequently reaches $ 120 a further gain of $ 10 is achieved and the strike is again reset, this time to $ 120.

Lookback Options

The payoff from a lookback option depends on the maximum or minimum price of the underlying asset during the life of the option. In a **floating strike** lookback call the strike is the minimum price achieved by the underlying during the life of the option. Its payoff is the extent to which the asset price at expiry exceeds that strike. It is a way of buying the underlying at the lowest price it trades at during the life of the option. In a floating strike lookback put the strike price is the maximum price of the underlying during the life of the option. Its payoff is the extent to which that strike price exceeds the asset price at expiry. A lookback put is effectively a way of selling the underlying at the highest price it achieves during the life of the option.

The payoff from a **fixed strike** lookback call option at expiry is the extent to which the highest price achieved by the underlying over the life of the option exceeds the strike. Lookback options are normally more expensive than conventional call and put options.

Multi-asset Options

The payoff from a multi-asset option depends on the values of two or more underlying assets. A simple example is a basket option whose payoff is typically determined by the weighted average value of a portfolio of underlying assets. Another example is a **best of** call whose payoff depends on the highest price achieved by two or more underlying assets. By contrast the payoff on a spread or **outperformance** option depends on the difference between the prices of two assets.

Quanto Options

A quanto is an option based on a variable quantity of an underlying asset. An example is a call option based on the performance of a basket of UK shares that is payable in US dollars. The payoff from the option depends on the sterling value of the basket, which is a variable, and also on the GBP/USD exchange rate which introduces a further variable. The writer of the option is faced with a problem in managing a hedge for the FX exposure because the sterling value of the basket is a variable quantity.

Shout Option

These are similar to cliquets and ladders except that the strike is reset by the holder rather than at predetermined times or price levels. For example, if the initial strike is $ 100 and the asset price reaches $ 120 the holder can 'shout' and lock in a gain of $ 20. The strike will be reset at $ 120. The total gain at expiration will be $ 20 plus any intrinsic value on a call with a strike set at $ 120.

17

Option Valuation Models

17.1 CHAPTER OVERVIEW

Later chapters use the standard option pricing model originally developed by Black, Scholes, and Merton. They explore the practical applications of the model in pricing options and strategies, and its sensitivities as measured by the so-called 'Greeks': delta, gamma, theta, vega, and rho. The current chapter provides a more detailed insight into how options are priced, and may be skipped over by readers who are more concerned with applications. At the same time it is not intended to cover the more complex mathematics of option pricing. The chapter shows that an option pricing model has to meet certain constraints, and moves on to demonstrate a key result, the **put-call parity** relationship. A simple option valuation model is developed using a one-step and then a three-step binomial tree, with the volatility of the underlying incorporated into the model. As more and more steps are added to the tree the option value converges on that calculated by the famous Black-Scholes option pricing model. The Black-Scholes equation is presented in a manner that can easily be set up in a spreadsheet. Finally, the chapter looks at some of the simplifying assumptions made by the model, the circumstances in which they tend to break down, and how option traders compensate for these problems in practice. The Appendix shows how to calculate the volatility of an asset based on its historical returns.

17.2 FUNDAMENTAL PRINCIPLES: EUROPEAN OPTIONS

Until the 1970s there was no generally agreed method to price options. Valuations were sometimes based on little more than sentiment. In this situation a trader who was bullish about a share might tend to value calls more highly than someone who was bearish about its prospects. Conversely, the bull would tend to regard the puts as virtually worthless, while the bear would be an avid buyer. Some practitioners used a set of 'rules of thumb' – for example, pricing at-the-money options as a set percentage of the spot price of the underlying. Some used their 'feel' for the market and traded on prices that were remarkably close to Black-Scholes values.

A useful first step in understanding how option models work is to consider the fundamental relationship that must hold between the value of an option before expiry and the price of the underlying. The following sections explore this relationship by testing a series of propositions applied to European-style options on shares which do not pay dividends. The discussion then considers the effects of dividends and the value of American options.

Statement 1

A call can never be worth more than the underlying share.

If this statement were not true arbitrage profits could be generated. For example, suppose a trader could buy a share at $120 and sell a call on the stock at a higher premium, say at $121. The trader owns the share so is fully protected if the call is ever exercised. This would produce a risk-free profit.

Statement 2

A European call on a share that does not pay dividends has a minimum value which is either zero or the difference between the spot price of the underlying and the present value of the strike, whichever is the greater.

The 'zero' part if this statement is clear enough, because it should not be possible to buy a call for less than nothing even if it is deeply out-of-the-money! To see why the next part of the statement must be true, consider an in-the-money European call with a strike of $110. The spot price of the underlying share is $120 and the stock does not pay dividends. The option has one year to expiry and interest rates are 10% p.a. on a simple interest basis. Statement two says that the following equation holds.

$$\text{Minimum Call Value} = \$120 - \frac{\$110}{1.1} = \$20$$

To test this proposition suppose the call can be purchased for less than $20, say for $10. Then an arbitrage strategy can be constructed as follows.

- Short the underlying stock for $120.
- Buy the $110 strike call for a premium of $10.
- Deposit the remaining $120 − $10 = $110 for one year at 10% interest.

The deposit will be worth $121 when it matures in one year, which is more than it will ever cost to buy the underlying stock to close out the short position. For example, if the share price is above $110 at expiry the call can be exercised and the share purchased at $110, making an overall $11 profit on the arbitrage strategy. If the stock can be bought in the market for *less* than $110 the call will expire worthless but the overall profit is even higher.

This 'long call/short stock' strategy always has a positive payout, so clearly something is wrong. The problem lies with the assumed $10 premium. If the call premium is $20 or above there are circumstances when the strategy produces zero or negative payouts. Therefore the call must be worth at least $20, the difference between the spot price of the stock and the present value of the strike price.

Statement 3

There is a fixed relationship known as **put-call parity** between the value of European calls and puts on the same underlying that have the same strike and expiry date. For European options on a non-dividend paying share put-call parity states that:

Put Value + Share Value = Call Value + Present Value of the Strike Price

---

To test the formula, compare a call and a put on a particular stock both struck at $ 110 and both with one year to expiry. The spot value of the underlying share is $ 120. The call is worth $ 25. The one-year interest rate (expressed with simple interest) is 10 % so the present value of the $ 110 strike price on the call and the put is $ 100. What is the value of the put option? To help answer this question consider two portfolios A and B:

- Portfolio A consists of a long put option on one share struck at $ 110 plus one share;
- Portfolio B consists of a long call option on one share struck at $ 110 plus a one-year deposit of $ 100.

The two portfolios have the same value at the expiry of the options for any given price level of the stock. For example, if the stock price in one year is $ 90 then portfolio A is worth $ 110: $ 20 intrinsic value on the long put plus $ 90 for the share. Meantime B is also worth $ 110: zero for the long call plus $ 110 on the matured deposit. If the stock price in one year is $ 130 then portfolio A is worth $ 130: zero for the long put plus $ 130 for the share. Portfolio B is also worth $ 130: $ 20 intrinsic value on the long call plus $ 110 on the matured deposit.

Since A and B have the same payoff in all circumstances it follows that they should have the same value today. The current value of portfolio B today is $ 25 for the call plus the $ 100 deposit, a total of $ 125. This implies that portfolio A is also worth $ 125 today. Since the spot price of the share is $ 120 the value of the put option today must be $ 5. This is the result predicted by the put-call parity formula:

$$\$ 5 + \$ 120 = \$ 25 + \$ 100$$

17.3 SYNTHETIC FORWARDS AND FUTURES

The put-call parity formula applies with European options where the call and the put have the same strike price and expiry date and are on the same underlying. For a non-dividend stock if the strike is also set at the *forward price* of the underlying for the expiry date of the options then the present value of the strike will equal the spot price of the underlying. To take the example in the previous section, suppose the spot price of the share is $ 120 and the one-year interest rate is 10 %. The stock does not pay dividends. Then:

$$\text{Forward Price} = \$ 120 \times 1.1 = \$ 132$$

Clearly if the strike of a call and a put both with one year to expiry is set at $ 132 the present value of the strike at a 10 % discount rate is $ 120, the same as the spot price of the share. The put-call parity formula for a non-dividend paying stock says that:

$$\text{Put Value} + \text{Share Value} = \text{Call Value} + \text{Present Value of the Strike Price}$$

If the share value is the same as the PV of the strike price these two items cancel out in the formula, which then says that the call and the put will have the same value. This is a very useful result. It shows that if a trader buys a European call and writes a European put on the same underlying and with the same expiry both struck at the forward price for the expiry of the options then the combination has zero net premium. In fact it is a **synthetic**

long forward position. If the underlying is trading above the strike at expiry the trader will exercise the long call. If it is trading below the strike the short put will be exercised. Either way, the trader will end up with a long position in the underlying at expiry at the strike of the two options. Traders often use this relationship to construct arbitrage trades or to build forwards out of pairs of options.

Note that when a share pays dividends the put-call parity formula can be modified by subtracting the present value of the expected dividends over the life of the option from the spot price of the underlying asset.

17.4   AMERICAN OPTIONS AND EARLY EXERCISE

Because it confers additional rights it follows that an American option can never be worth *less* than a European option. However it is not necessarily *more* valuable.

Statement 4

It never pays to exercise an American call on a non-dividend paying share early. Therefore it has the same value as the equivalent European style option (with same strike and so on).

If an in-the-money American call is exercised early the value realized is just its intrinsic value, the difference between the spot price of the share and the strike. However the call can be sold in the market for its intrinsic value *plus* time value. Early exercise would simply 'kill off' the time value component. And since the underlying stock does not pay any dividends no income will be lost as a result of failing to exercise the option to acquire the share. Since an American call on a non-dividend share should not be exercised early, it should be worth exactly the same as a European call. However if the stock *does* pay dividends the value of capturing a forthcoming dividend can sometimes exceed the loss of time value. Since there are circumstances in which it is profitable to exercise an American call on a dividend-paying stock early it is worth more than a European call.

On the other hand it *can* be profitable to exercise an in-the-money American put option early even when the share does not pay dividends. To take an extreme case, suppose a trader owns a one-year put with a strike of $ 110. The underlying share price is close to zero with low volatility. Since the share price cannot be negative there is very little scope for further profit from the put option, and the cash received from early exercise could be invested immediately rather than at expiry. The interest earned is likely to exceed any additional profit the put could generate. Since there are sometimes advantages to early exercise it follows that American puts are more valuable than European puts.

17.4.1   Put-Call Parity and American Options

Put-call parity applies only to European options. For American options on the same underlying with the same strike and expiry it is possible only to state certain inequalities. For example for a non-dividend paying share:

$$\text{Call Value} - \text{Put Value} \leq \text{Share Value} - \text{Present Value of the Strike Price}$$

The inequality is introduced here because the value of an American put on a non-dividend paying share can be *greater* than that of a European-style put, since there are times when it is profitable to exercise the contract early.

17.5 BINOMIAL TREES

Previous sections developed constraints on how an option model has to work, and discussed the fundamental put-call parity relationship. A useful next move in understanding how the Black-Scholes option pricing model operates is to construct what is known as a **binomial tree**. This section builds a one-step tree and uses it to price a European call on an underlying share. The tree is based on the assumption that the underlying is currently trading at $100 and can only move up by a factor of 1.25 and down by a factor of 0.75 over one time period. This is illustrated in Figure 17.1. For example, $125 is $100 times the 'upmove factor' of 1.25.

Suppose a trader sells an at-the money call on the stock. The call expires at the end of one time period. The goal is to establish a fair value for the call today (at time zero) on a per share basis. Call this fair value C. It is clear that at time one the short call is either worth $25 or zero – either it has $25 intrinsic value or it expires worthless. This is illustrated in Figure 17.2.

The value of C at time zero can be established by looking at what it would cost the trader to hedge a short position in the call. Suppose the interest rate for the period of the option is 10% with simple interest. The trader creates the following hedge portfolio at time zero:

• sell a call and receive the premium C;

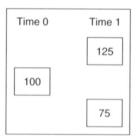

Figure 17.1   One-step share binomial tree.

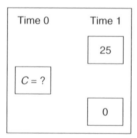

Figure 17.2   Value of at-the-money call per share.

- buy Δ (delta) underlying shares costing $\$100 \times \Delta$;
- fund the share purchase partly through the premium C and by borrowing the remainder B at 10%.

The following simultaneous equations are to be satisfied at time one:

$$(\Delta \times 125) - (B \times 1.1) = 25$$

$$(\Delta \times 75) - (B \times 1.1) = 0$$

The first equation takes the case where the share price at expiry is $\$125$ and the trader has to pay out $\$25$ intrinsic value on the short call. It says that for the trader to break even this $\$25$ must be covered by the value of the Δ shares in the hedge portfolio less the principal and interest on the loan. The second equation takes the case where the share price at expiry is $\$75$ and the short call has zero intrinsic value. For the trader to break even in this case the value of the Δ shares in the hedge portfolio less the principal and interest on the loan should equal zero. Combining the two equations produces the following:

$$(\Delta \times 125) - (\Delta \times 75) = 25$$

Therefore $\Delta = 0.5$. This is the option delta, otherwise known as the **hedge ratio**. It means that if a trader writes a call on a certain number of shares he or she will have to buy half that number of shares to neutralize the exposure to movements in the underlying stock price. This is called a delta hedge and the resulting position is called a **delta-neutral** position. Note that the option delta can be calculated directly as follows:

$$\Delta = \frac{C_u - C_d}{S_u - S_d}$$

where:
$\quad C_u = $ value of the call if the share price goes up
$\quad C_d = $ value of the call if the share price goes down
$\quad S_u = $ value of the share when it moves up
$\quad S_d = $ value of the share when it moves down

In this example:

$$\Delta = \frac{25 - 0}{125 - 75} = 0.5$$

Since a value for delta has been calculated this can be inserted into either one of the simultaneous equations to calculate the amount borrowed at time zero. Using the second of the equations:

$$(\Delta \times 75) - (B \times 1.1) = 0$$

$$(0.5 \times 75) - (B \times 1.1) = 0$$

$$B = 34.09$$

The final step is as follows. For the trader to break even at time zero the cost of buying the delta shares in the hedge portfolio must be met from the amount borrowed B plus the amount charged for the call C. In this case delta is 0.5 and B is 34.09. So C must be $\$15.91$ per share.

$$C + B = \Delta \times \text{ Spot Price of Share}$$

$$C + 34.09 = 0.5 \times 100$$

$$C = 15.91$$

17.5.1 Call Value Formula

The calculation can be simplified by using some algebra that encapsulates the steps worked through above. Let:

$$p = \frac{(1+r) - d}{u - d}$$

where:

$r =$ simple interest rate for the period as a decimal (here 0.1)

$d =$ the factor that moves the share price down from its spot price in the binomial tree (here 0.75)

$u =$ the factor that moves the share price up from its spot price in the binomial tree (here 1.25)

In this example:

$$p = \frac{1.1 - 0.75}{1.25 - 0.75} = 0.7$$

The call value per share C is given by the following equation:

$$C = \frac{(p \times C_u) + [(1 - p) \times C_d]}{1 + r}$$

where:

$C_u =$ value of the call at time one if the share price rises

$C_d =$ value of the call at time one if the share price falls

In the example:

$$C = \frac{(0.7 \times 25) + (0.3 \times 0)}{1.1} = 15.91$$

This is actually a type of **weighted average payout** calculation, but based on the idea that the risk on the option can be fully hedged. Under this special assumption the 'probability' of the stock rising to $\$125$ at expiry and the intrinsic value of the call being $\$25$ is 0.7 or 70%. The probability of the stock falling to $\$75$ and the intrinsic value being zero is 30%. The average of the two payouts weighted by the 'probability' of achieving each payout is discounted back one period at a 10 % simple interest rate to calculate the value of the call at time zero.

These pseudo-probabilities apply in a so-called **risk-neutral** world in which the risk on the option can be exactly matched by creating a delta hedge portfolio. They are not to be confused with an analyst's subjective estimate of what the stock price is likely to be in the future. Note that the 'expected' share price at time one in the above example is not $ 100, but the forward price, which is $ 100 × 1.1 = $ 110. Intuitively, this explains why the 'probability' of the stock reaching $ 125 (70 %) is greater than the 'probability' of it reaching $ 75 (30 %).

17.6   EXPANDING THE TREE

Of course the binomial tree developed in the last section is highly simplistic. Firstly, it assumes that the share price can only move up to $ 125 and down to $ 75 over one time period. In reality the price will tend to move up or down by much smaller steps, and then take a series of further steps. Secondly, the factors u and d that moved the share price from its spot level were simply invented for the purposes of illustration. It would be helpful to apply factors that derive from the *volatility* of the underlying share. Intuitively, the more volatile the share, all other things being equal, the more the share price is likely to deviate from its current level, and the more expensive the option should be.

To show how these problems can be tackled this section constructs a three-step binomial and uses it to price a European call on a non-dividend paying stock. The details of the share and the option are as follows:

- Underlying cash price $S = 300$
- Exercise price $E = 250$
- Risk-free rate $r = 10\%$ p.a. continuously compounded
- Time to maturity $t = 0.25$ years
- Volatility $\sigma = 40\%$

The Appendix at the end of this chapter shows how volatility can be estimated from historical data.

17.6.1   Incorporating Volatility

To construct a tree that matches the volatility of the underlying share the factors u and d can be calculated using values proposed by Cox, Ross, and Rubenstein:

$$u = e^{\sigma \sqrt{t/n}}$$

$$d = \frac{1}{u}$$

where:

$e =$ the base of natural logarithms (approximately 2.71828)
$\sigma =$ volatility, the annualized standard deviation of returns on the share (here 0.4)
$t =$ time to option expiry in years (here 0.25)
$n =$ number of steps in the binomial tree (here 3)

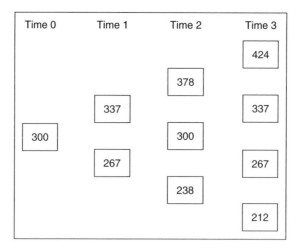

Figure 17.3   Three-step share binomial tree.

In this example:

$$u = e^{0.4\sqrt{0.25/3}} = 1.1224$$

$$d = \frac{1}{1.1224} = 0.8909$$

The total life of the option (0.25 years) is being cut into three equal binomial periods here. Figure 17.3 shows how the values for u and d are used to construct the binomial tree. For example, the first 'up move' value of 337 at time one is the initial spot price of 300 times u. The 'down move' value 267 is the spot price times d. If the stock reaches 267 at time one it can either move back up to 300 at time two (calculated by multiplying 267 by u) or fall further to 238. And so on.

17.6.2   Constructing the Call Value Tree

The next step is to construct a tree that represents the values of the 250 strike call in response to changes in the value of the underlying share. It is easy to fill in the values at the end nodes – at expiry the value of the call is its intrinsic value. This is illustrated in Figure 17.4. For example, at the top right of the share tree in Figure 17.4 the stock is worth 424. In that case the 250 strike call is worth 174.

In Figure 17.4 C is the call value at the outset. C_u is the value if the share takes one step up; C_{uu} if the share takes two steps up. C_d is the call value if the share takes one step down; C_{dd} if the share takes two steps down. C_{ud} is the value of the call if the share takes one step up and then a step down (it is the same as the value if the share takes a step down and then back up).

At each step the call can be evaluated exactly as if it were a one-step binomial as shown in the previous section. Firstly, calculate the 'probability' numbers p and $1 - p$ from the up and the down-move factors u and d. The calculation (this time using a continuously

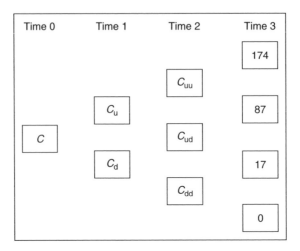

Figure 17.4 Call option three-step binomial tree.

compounded interest rate) is as follows:

$$p = \frac{e^{0.1 \times 0.25/3} - 0.8909}{1.1224 - 0.8909} = 0.5074$$

$$1 - p = 0.4926$$

Then, to take just one example from the call option tree, C_{uu} is the present value of the sum of:

- the call value if it takes a further step up (174) times the 'probability' that this will occur (50.74 %);
- the call value if it takes a further step down (87) times the 'probability' that this will occur (49.26 %).

In an equation:

$$C_{uu} = [(174 \times 0.5074) + (87 \times 0.4926)] \times e^{-0.1 \times 0.25/3} = 130$$

17.6.3   The Complete Call Value Tree

The complete tree is set out in Figure 17.5. The value of the call today with 0.25 years to expiry is roughly 61. Note that the option is a European call without dividends. If it was an American put it would be essential to check at any node in the tree that the option is not worth less than its intrinsic value. This is because an American put may sometimes be exercised early and should therefore never trade at less than intrinsic value.

17.7   BLACK-SCHOLES MODEL

As the number of binomial steps is increased the call value will converge on the result produced by the famous **Black-Scholes** model. The model was developed by Black, Scholes,

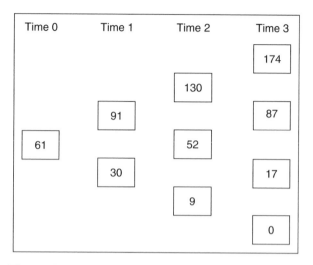

Figure 17.5 Completed call option three-step binomial tree.

and Merton in the 1970s and is a vital tool in modern finance. For European options with
no dividends Black-Scholes gives the following values:

$$C = [S \times N(d_1)] - [E \times e^{-rt} \times N(d_2)]$$
$$P = [E \times e^{-rt} \times N(-d_2)] - [S \times N(-d_1)]$$

where:

$$d_1 = \frac{\ln(S/E) + (r \times t) + (\sigma^2 \times t/2)}{\sigma \times \sqrt{t}}$$
$$d_2 = d_1 - (\sigma \times \sqrt{t})$$

C = call value

P = put value

S = spot price of the underlying

E = strike price of the option

$N(d)$ = cumulative normal density function. The Excel function to use is NORMSDIST()

$\ln(x)$ = natural logarithm of x to base e. The Excel function to use is LN()

σ = volatility p.a. of the underlying asset (as a decimal)

t = time to expiry of the option (in years)

r = continuously compounded interest rate p.a. (as a decimal)

$e \approx 2.71828$, the base of natural logarithms. The Excel function to calculate e^x is EXP(x)

The formula for a call says that the call value C is the spot price (S) minus the present value of the strike (E), where S and E are weighted by the risk factors $N(d_1)$ and $N(d_2)$. Like the binomial approach, the formula is based on the assumption that options can be delta-hedged in a riskless manner by trading in the underlying and by borrowing and lending funds at the risk-free rate. It assumes that the returns on the underlying asset follow a normal distribution. Under such specific assumptions, the factor $N(d_2)$ measures the probability that the call will expire in-the-money and be exercised. The factor $N(d_1)$ is the option delta, the hedge ratio. Generally, the function $N(d)$ calculates the area to the left of d under a normal distribution curve with mean 0 and variance 1. That is, it calculates the probability that a variable with a standard normal distribution will be less than d.

17.7.1 Example

In a previous example a three-step binomial was constructed to price a European call with the following data:

- Underlying cash price $S = 300$
- Exercise price $E = 250$
- Risk-free rate $r = 10\%$ p.a. (0.1 as a decimal)
- Time to maturity $t = 0.25$ years
- Volatility $\sigma = 40\%$ p.a. (0.4 as a decimal)

The Black-Scholes formula gives the following value:

$$C = [300 \times 0.8721] - [250 \times e^{-0.1 \times 0.25} \times 0.8255] = 60.36$$

where:

$$d_1 = \frac{\ln(300/250) + (0.1 \times 0.25) + (0.4^2 \times 0.25/2)}{0.4 \times \sqrt{0.25}} = 1.1366$$

$$d_2 = 1.1366 - (0.4 \times \sqrt{0.25}) = 0.9366$$

$$N(d_1) = 0.8721$$

$$N(d_2) = 0.8255$$

The risk-neutral probability of exercise in this case is 82.55%, since the option is quite deeply in-the-money.

17.7.2 Black-Scholes with Dividends

The model can be adjusted to price European options on assets paying dividends. The following version assumes that dividends are paid out in a continuous stream and is commonly used to price index options. If q is the continuous dividend yield then:

$$C = [S \times e^{-qt} \times N(d_1)] - [E \times e^{-rt} \times N(d_2)]$$

where:

$$d_1 = \frac{\ln(S/E) + [(r - q) \times t] + (\sigma^2 \times t/2)}{\sigma \times \sqrt{t}}$$

$$d_2 = d_1 - (\sigma \times \sqrt{t})$$

In the case of an individual share it is not quite realistic to assume that dividends are paid in a constant stream. One common approach is to use Black-Scholes but to replace the spot price with the spot price minus the present value of the expected dividends over the life of the option. These are discounted at the risk-free rate.

17.8 BLACK-SCHOLES ASSUMPTIONS

The model makes some simplifying assumptions about the world which have a tendency to break down in extreme market conditions. These include the following:

- That the returns on the underlying asset follow a normal distribution, the famous bell curve. Many analysts believe there is a pronounced skew or 'negative tail' in the actual returns on equities, meaning that there is a bigger chance of significant losses than is built into the shape of the standard bell curve. Other assets such as currencies may exhibit positive *and* negative tails.
- That the returns on the underlying follow a continuous random walk in which the last price movement bears no relationship to the next price movement and in which prices are not subject to sudden 'jumps'. This may be a realistic assumption in a normal market but not in a market crash.
- That it is possible to delta hedge option positions by buying and selling the underlying without transaction costs and without liquidity constraints. In the real world option traders do face transaction costs and liquidity problems, and will not readjust their delta hedges on a continuous basis.
- That the volatility of the underlying is known and remains constant throughout the life of the option. In a market crash, however, experience suggests that panic sets in and volatility can increase sharply.

In practice option traders can compensate for the limitations of the model by adjusting the volatility at which they sell options. For example, if the underlying is not particularly liquid and is hard to trade it will be difficult to manage the risks on a short option position. To compensate, the trader will increase the price of the options such that the **implied volatility** is greater than the actual historical volatility of the underlying (where implied volatility is the volatility assumption built into an actual option premium). Otherwise, traders can work with more complex models which relax the key Black-Scholes assumptions e.g. by allowing changes in volatility.

17.9 CHAPTER SUMMARY

An option pricing model has to meet certain constraints. A European call is worth the maximum of zero and the difference between the spot price of the underlying and the present value of the strike. An American call on a share that does not pay dividends should never be exercised early and therefore is worth the same as a European call. It can sometimes make sense to exercise an American put option early so it can be worth more than a European put. One of the most fundamental results in options is the put-call parity relationship for European contracts. This says that the combination of a long call and a short put on an asset both struck at the forward price can replicate a long forward position in the asset. A long put and a short call can replicate a short forward position. Put-call parity does not hold for American options. A simple European option pricing model can be constructed using the binomial tree methodology. The first step is to generate a tree that represents the movements in the underlying. The intrinsic value of the option at expiry is then calculated. By 'working backwards' along the tree the value of the option today can be calculated. As more steps are added to the tree the result converges on the option value calculated by the Black-Scholes model. Black-Scholes can easily be set up on an Excel spreadsheet and adapted for assets that pay dividends. In practice the assumptions made by the model may not work very effectively in extreme markets. Traders can compensate for this by adjusting the implied volatility they use to price and trade options. Implied volatility is the volatility assumption built into an actual option premium. It is based on forecasts of future events and not just on history.

APPENDIX: MEASURING HISTORIC VOLATILITY

In the options market historic volatility is commonly measured as the standard deviation of the returns on the underlying asset over some historical period of time. It is normally annualized. The percentage returns are calculated by taking the natural logarithms of the price relatives rather than simple percentage price changes. The Excel function that calculates the natural log of a number is LN(). It is the inverse of the EXP() function. Using natural logs has very useful consequences. For example, suppose that a share is trading at 500 and the price rises to 510. The **price relative** is the new share price divided by the old price:

$$\frac{510}{500} = 1.02$$

The simple percentage price change is:

$$\frac{510}{500} - 1 = 2\%$$

But suppose then that the share price falls back again to 500. The simple percentage fall in price is:

$$\frac{500}{510} - 1 = -1.96\%$$

The problem is that these simple percentage changes cannot be added together. If the share price starts at 500 and ends at 500 then the overall change in the share price is actually zero, not 0.04%. Using natural logarithms cures this problem:

$$\ln\left(\frac{510}{500}\right) + \ln\left(\frac{500}{510}\right) = 0$$

Table 17.1 illustrates the calculation of historic volatility using natural logarithms. The price of the underlying security starts at 500 on day zero. Column (2) shows the closing price of the stock over the next 10 trading days (covering two calendar weeks). Column (3)

Table 17.1 First stages in calculation of historic volatility

(1) Day	(2) Price	(3) Price change	(4) Deviation	(5) Deviation^2
0	500			
1	508	1.59 %	1.37 %	0.02 %
2	492	−3.20 %	−3.42 %	0.12 %
3	498	1.21 %	0.99 %	0.01 %
4	489	−1.82 %	−2.04 %	0.04 %
5	502	2.62 %	2.41 %	0.06 %
6	507	0.99 %	0.77 %	0.01 %
7	500	−1.39 %	−1.61 %	0.03 %
8	502	0.40 %	0.18 %	0.00 %
9	499	−0.60 %	−0.82 %	0.01 %
10	511	2.38 %	2.16 %	0.05 %
	Average =	0.22 %	Sum =	0.33 %

calculates the natural logarithm of the price relatives. For example, the percentage change in the share price between day 0 and day 1 is calculated as:

$$\ln\left(\frac{508}{500}\right) = 1.59\,\%$$

The average daily percentage change in the share price is 0.22 %. Column (4) calculates the extent to which each daily percentage price change deviates from the average. For instance, 1.59 % is 1.37 % above the average. Column (5) squares the deviations.

Sample variance is a statistical measure of the extent to which a set of observations in a sample diverges from the average value. Table 17.1 has 10 observations based on the change in the share price over two calendar weeks. The sample variance is calculated as follows:

$$\text{Variance } \sigma^2 = \frac{\text{Sum of Squared Deviations}}{\text{Number of Observations} - 1}$$

$$\text{Variance } \sigma^2 = \frac{0.33\,\%}{10 - 1} = \frac{0.0033}{9} = 0.000367 = 0.0367\,\%$$

The reason for dividing by one less than the number of observations is simply to adjust for the fact that the calculation is based on a sample of price changes (and a relatively small sample at that). Volatility is defined as the standard deviation of the returns on the share. It is the square root of the variance:

$$\text{Standard Deviation } \sigma = \sqrt{\text{Variance}} = \sqrt{0.000367} = 0.0192 = 1.92\,\%$$

Here 1.92 % is the **daily volatility** of the returns on the share. It was based on the average daily percentage price change over a series of trading days. Volatility is normally expressed on an annualized basis in the options market. If there are 252 trading days in the year then the annualized volatility is the daily volatility times the square root of 252:

$$\text{Annual Volatility} = 1.92\,\% \times \sqrt{252} = 30.4\,\%$$

Intuitively, the 'square root rule' used here to annualize volatility is based on the idea that short-term fluctuations in the prices of securities tend to smooth out to some extent over a longer period of time. Annual volatility is therefore far less than daily volatility times the number of trading days in the year. Note that this may be a reasonable assumption to make in normal market conditions when shares are following something close to a 'random walk' and there is no statistical relationship between the previous movement in the share price and the next movement. In extreme circumstances such as stock market crashes these conditions may well not apply.

18

Option Pricing and Risks

18.1 CHAPTER OVERVIEW

This chapter reviews the main inputs to pricing an option using the Black-Scholes model and considers how changes in the inputs affect the outputs. The model itself is described in Chapter 17. This chapter focuses on the sensitivity of the option value to changes in the key input assumptions – the price of the underlying; the time to expiry; volatility; and the cost of carrying a hedge position in the underlying. It explores the so-called option 'Greeks': delta, gamma, theta, vega, and rho. The chapter looks at how traders can use these measures to manage the risks on option positions by trading in the underlying, and the circumstances when hedges are more or less efficient. The body of the chapter looks at how traders manage 'delta exposures': potential losses on option positions that arise from changes in the value of the underlying. This is explored in more detail in an Appendix, with a description of how the gamma exposure on an option position can be hedged.

18.2 INTRINSIC AND TIME VALUE BEHAVIOUR

The value of an option consists of intrinsic value plus time value. For a call, intrinsic value is the maximum of zero and the price of the underlying minus the strike. For a put, it is the maximum of zero and the strike minus the price of the underlying. Other things being equal, the time value of an option tends to be greater:

- the longer the time remaining until expiry;
- the greater the volatility of the underlying asset.

The more time to expiry, the greater the opportunity for the option to be exercised profitably. Equally, the more volatile the underlying share, the greater the chance or probability of a substantial change in the price of the underlying. With an out-of-the-money call, volatility increases the probability that the price of the underlying will rise above the strike. It also increases the risk of a *fall* in the share price, but the holder of a call is not forced to exercise the option if this happens. This represents an opportunity for the buyer of the option and a risk for the writer of the contract. Time value reflects the value of that opportunity and that risk.

Inputs to the Black-Scholes Model

According to the model (adapted for a share that pays dividends) the value of an option is determined by:

- the exercise or strike price of the option;
- the price of the underlying asset;

- the time to expiry of the option;
- the volatility of the underlying;
- the net cost of carrying a position in the underlying.

Figure 18.1 shows (dotted line) the fair value of a $ 100 strike call for different price levels of the underlying asset. The other inputs to the pricing model have been kept constant, including volatility and time to expiry. The graph also shows (solid line) the intrinsic value of the call. The difference between the solid line and the dotted line represents time value.

When the call is deeply out-of-the-money then it has zero intrinsic value, but also very little time value. The underlying has to rise above the strike to expire in-the-money. The probability of that happening is relatively small. On the other hand the probability is not zero, and has to be paid for through time value.

The graph in Figure 18.1 also shows that as the share price increases towards the strike (other inputs to the model remaining constant) the time value of the option also rises. The chance of the option expiring in-the-money is increasing. Time value peaks when the call option is at-the-money, when the price of the underlying and the strike are equal.

As the option moves *into* the money, the total option value continues to increase as it acquires more and more intrinsic value. However the time value component steadily declines. Buying a deeply in-the-money call is rather like buying the underlying. Time value for an in-the-money option primarily represents the additional amount an investor is prepared to pay, over and above the intrinsic value, for the privilege of owning an option with limited downside risk. Unlike holding the actual asset, the loss is limited to the premium. The more in-the-money the option is, however, the smaller the time value – there is less chance that the 'disaster insurance' that the option provides will actually be required.

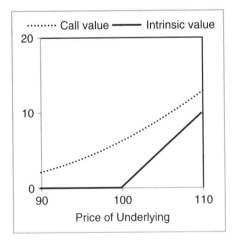

Figure 18.1   Relationship between call value and underlying price.

18.2.1 Probability of Exercise

Although it is something of a simplification, capital market practitioners sometimes think of the value of a European-style option in terms of probability of exercise. With an out-of-the-money call the probability of the option being exercised is low. The probability of an at-the-money call being exercised is around 50 %. If a call is very deeply in-the-money then the probability of it being exercised and being turned into a long position in the underlying asset approaches 100 %.

18.3 VOLATILITY ASSUMPTION AND OPTION PRICING

According to the Black-Scholes model the value of an option is determined by the five factors described in the previous section. The only real difficulty with this is the volatility assumption. The asset price and the carry cost can be obtained from market information screens. The time to expiry and the strike are written into the option contract. The main problem is how to estimate the volatility of the underlying asset. A reasonable starting point is to look at its historical price behaviour over some period of time. Other things being equal, the more variable the price, the greater the risk to the writer of the option, the greater the opportunity to the buyer, the higher the time value of the option.

Historic Volatility

Historical volatility is measured as the standard deviation of the percentage returns on the underlying asset around the average return for a given historical time period. (The calculation is illustrated in the Appendix to Chapter 17.) It is sensible to base the calculation on percentage returns rather than the absolute changes in the asset price because it makes it possible to compare volatility on assets that are trading at different price levels. Standard deviation is the most common statistical measure of dispersion around a mean or average value.

A major problem with measuring historic volatility lies in deciding *which* historical time period to choose. Should an analyst look at the price behaviour of the stock over the last few months, or the last few years? Is the recent historical period atypical in some way? Was it a period of relative calm or extreme turbulence? Should more recent price changes be given a greater weight in the calculation of historical volatility?

An even more fundamental problem is that the expected payout from an option (and hence the initial premium the writer of the contract should charge) is *not* based on the historical volatility of the underlying asset but on its volatility over the life of the contract. Unfortunately, in the absence of a crystal ball, it is not possible to observe future volatility levels directly. What a trader *can* do is to make a forecast of volatility, taking into account what has happened in the past, but also building in estimates of what is likely to happen up to the expiry of an option. In some cases a trader may decide that the underlying asset is likely to go through a period of extreme turbulence, exhibiting more volatility than the average value calculated from historical experience. In other cases the trader may take the view that the asset price will settle down after a recent period of uncertainty.

Rather than using historical volatility to calculate an option fair value, traders often take the actual price at which an option is trading in the market and calculate the volatility assumption that is implied in that price, using a model such as Black-Scholes. This **implied**

volatility can then be compared against historical experience and future volatility forecasts. If the trader believes that the underlying is likely to be more volatile than the level built into the option prices being quoted in the market then it makes sense to buy options. They are cheap relative to the expected payout. If the trader believes the market is over-estimating the level of future volatility on a given asset then the appropriate trade is to write option contracts. The initial premium received will exceed the expected payout. To put it another way, if a trader sells options using a high volatility assumption and then volatility forecasts calm down in the market then (other inputs to the pricing model remaining more or less equal) the trader will be able to buy the contracts back at a cheaper price.

18.4 DELTA (Δ OR δ)

As well as calculating the fair value of an option, Black-Scholes tells us about the sensitivity of the option value to changes in the inputs to the model. This is what delta, gamma, theta, vega, and rho measure. These so-called option **Greeks** are essential to the management of risk in an options position. Delta is the most significant measure and is integral to the way in which the Black-Scholes model prices an option. It can be defined as follows.

Delta

Delta measures the change in the option price for a small change in the price of the underlying asset, assuming all other inputs to the model are held constant. It is often expressed as a ratio or a percentage. For example, if a bought call option has a delta of 0.50 or 50 % this means that if the price of the underlying increases (decreases) by one tick the option value will increase (decrease) by 0.5 ticks. A tick is the minimum allowed price movement in a financial asset, such as one cent.

Traders often give the delta of an option position a positive or a negative value. The sign tells us about the directional exposure of the position to changes in the price of the underlying.

- **Long Call: Positive Delta.** The option position increases (decreases) in value if the price of the underlying increases (decreases).
- **Short Call: Negative Delta.** The position loses value as the price of the underlying increases – the option becomes more expensive to buy back to close out the position. If the underlying falls in price the position gains in value because the option becomes cheaper to buy back. In this sense shorting a call is like a short position in the underlying; hence the negative delta.
- **Long Put: Negative Delta.** The option position increases (decreases) in value as the price of the underlying falls (rises).
- **Short Put: Positive Delta.** The position increases in value as the price of the underlying rises (the option becomes cheaper to buy back to close out the position) and falls in value if the underlying falls. In this sense shorting a put is like a long position in the underlying. Hence the positive delta.

The sign shows whether the position is a 'bull' or a 'bear' position. Positive delta means that the position makes money if the price of the underlying rises. Negative delta means the position makes money if the price of the underlying falls. For example, suppose that a trader buys a put option with a delta of -0.50 or $-50\,\%$. Then:

- If the underlying price falls by one tick the value of the long put position increases by half a tick;
- if the underlying price rises by one tick the value of long put position falls by half a tick.

18.5   DELTA BEHAVIOUR

For a standard or 'vanilla' call the value of delta lies between zero and one (0 % and 100 %). A deeply out-of-the-money long call has a delta approaching zero: it is highly insensitive to a small change in the underlying. As the option approaches the at-the-money point its delta increases until it reaches approximately 0.50 or 50 %. The option transmits around half of the price change in the underlying asset. As the call moves increasingly in-the-money (ITM) delta moves toward a limit of one or 100 %. The option moves tick for tick with the underlying stock. An ITM option increasingly comes to resemble a position in the underlying security. A bought ITM call resembles a long position in the underlying. A bought ITM put resembles a short position in the underlying.

18.5.1   Delta as the Slope on the Option Price Curve

Figure 18.2 shows the price curve for a $ 100 strike call in relation to different prices of the underlying. It also shows the **slope** or tangent on the price curve when the option is at-the-money. This is delta. It is approximately 0.5: for a one tick move in the underlying the option moves in value by around half a tick. The slope of the curve approaches zero when the call is deeply out-of-the-money; the option is insensitive to small changes in the price of the underlying. The slope of the curve approaches one when the call is deeply in-the-money. It behaves like a long position in the underlying asset and for small changes in the price of the underlying its value moves in step.

18.5.2   Delta as the Hedge Ratio

Delta is not only valuable as a sensitivity measure. It is used by option traders to hedge the risks on their trading books. For example, suppose a trader has written calls on 10,000 shares, each with a delta of 0.50. The position delta is negative because the trader has sold calls. If the share price rises sharply the options would become more valuable. This would be a *loss* for the trader: it would cost more to repurchase the calls than the sale price.

A useful way to look at this is to calculate a **position delta**. The trader has sold calls on 10,000 shares. For a small movement in the underlying share price the calls will move by

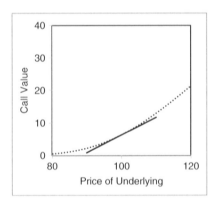

Figure 18.2   Delta as the slope on the option price curve.

half as much as the shares. Therefore:

$$\text{Position Delta} = -10.000 \times 0.50 = -5000 \text{ shares}$$

This means that (for small movements in the price of the underlying) the trader has the same market exposure as a short position in 5000 shares. If the share price rises by (say) one cent the loss would be the same. To hedge this risk the trader can buy 5000 of the underlying shares. The delta of each purchased share is plus one (it moves fully in line with itself), so the net position delta is now zero. Any losses on the short options position resulting from a small move in the underlying share price would be offset by profits on the long position in the stock. For example, suppose the underlying share price rises by one cent. Then the trader will lose $50 on the calls:

$$\text{Loss on Calls} = -10.000 \times 0.50 \times \$0.01 = -\$50$$

In this scenario the calls have increased in value by $50, and if the trader closes the short option position by buying the calls back it would cost $50 more than the premium at which they were sold. However the 5000 shares purchased to delta hedge the position will have increased in value by a total of $50:

$$\text{Gain on Shares} = 5000 \times \$0.01 = \$50$$

Option portfolios hedged in this way so they are not exposed to small movements in the price of the underlying security are said to be **delta neutral** or delta hedged.

18.6   GAMMA (Γ OR γ)

Gamma measures the **change in delta** for a small change in the price of the underlying asset. Figure 18.2 shows that delta (the slope of the option price curve) is not a constant. It depends on which point on the curve is taken. Delta is really only a reliable measure of the change in the value of an option for *small* changes in the underlying price. It assumes a linear relationship between the underlying price and the value of the option. If the price of the underlying moves by a substantial amount then the actual option price change will be different from that predicted by delta. Delta is the analogue of the duration measure discussed in Chapter 5 when exploring the relationship between the price of a bond and current market interest rates. Like duration, delta is not a constant.

Gamma as Convexity

Gamma (convexity) measures the rate of change of delta. It is a measure of the curvature in the relationship between the value of an option and the price of the underlying. The greater the amount of curvature, the more rapidly delta (the slope or tangent on the option price curve) will change.

18.6.1 Gamma Risk

Because option professionals use delta to manage the risk on their books, they are exposed to changes in their position delta. In the delta hedge example in the previous section the trader sells calls on 10,000 shares with a delta of 0.50. The position delta is therefore −5000 shares. In other words, for small movements in the share price the profit and loss on the short option position will behave rather as if the trader is short 5000 shares – not 10,000, because the calls move half as much in price terms as the underlying shares.

To delta hedge this position the trader buys 5000 shares in the underlying. The hedge will work well for small movements in the underlying share price. The problem is that if the share price rises sharply the short call position will actually lose more money than predicted by the delta measure. This is the effect of gamma or convexity, the curvature in the option price graph. The 5000 shares purchased to hedge the risk will not match the losses on the options because the profit and loss profile on 5000 shares in the delta hedge is always linear.

18.6.2 Sensitivity of the Delta Hedge

An option trader tends to think of the gamma problem in terms of the change in the delta, and the possibility that the delta hedge may have to be adjusted. In the above example the trader sells calls on 10,000 shares with a delta of 0.50, or in share equivalent terms −5000 shares. The trader hedges the delta risk (the exposure to small movements in the underlying price) by buying 5000 shares in the underlying. Suppose that shortly after the calls are sold and delta hedged the share price rises sharply, to the extent that the option delta moves to 0.60. In that case the position delta on the calls is equivalent to being short 6000 shares rather than 5000. It is more risky than before.

Now the trader has a tough decision to make. The first possibility is to leave things as they are (with only 5000 shares in the hedge portfolio) and hope that the stock price falls back again. However then the overall position will be badly under-hedged if the share price keeps rising – i.e. the losses on the calls will greatly outweigh the offsetting profits on the 5000 shares in the delta hedge. Alternatively, the trader can readjust the delta hedge by buying an additional 1000 shares. But then if the share price falls back again the trader will have too many shares in the delta hedge and will no longer be delta neutral but delta positive (with a bull position on the underlying which will lose money if the share price falls further). The trader can sell some or all of the additional 1000 shares. However this will crystallize a loss on the hedge portfolio (buy at a high price, sell at a low price).

18.7 READJUSTING THE DELTA HEDGE

The last example illustrates a key problem with option trading. Normally traders do not sell large quantities of 'naked' options. It would be too dangerous. Instead, writers of options can manage their exposures to directional changes in the underlying share price by trading the underlying stock. The risk is that if the underlying is more volatile than predicted then the delta hedge will have to be readjusted at frequent intervals, realizing trading losses on the shares used in the hedge. The trick is to assess the *volatility* of the underlying properly and price this into the premium charged for the options. In that case an option writer should be able to readjust the delta hedge from time to time and still retain some of the initial premium as a profit.

Of course in practice a trader will not rebalance the delta hedge every time the underlying price moves; transaction costs would quickly eat away at any profits that might be made. A key skill in being an option trader lies in deciding what constitutes an exceptional movement in the price of the underlying that should be covered to guard against unacceptable losses. In practice, also, many of the delta risks in an option book will tend to cancel out. For example, a short call is a negative delta position, but a short put is a positive delta position. If the underlying rises or falls by a small amount the profits and losses will offset each other to some extent. Normally it is the residual delta risk in the trading book that is covered by trading in the underlying asset.

18.7.1   Position Gamma

Gamma is the change in delta for a small change in the underlying price. It can be measured in a number of different ways. Perhaps the most useful way is to show it in share equivalent terms. In the above example the trader sells calls on 10,000 shares with a delta of 0.50 or -5000 shares. If the gamma of the option is (say) 0.01 this means that for a one cent rise in the underlying price the delta will move to $0.5 + 0.01 = 0.51$. The profit and loss on the option position now behaves as if the trader is short 5100 shares rather than 5000. So:

$$\text{Position Gamma} = -10.000 \times 0.01 = -100 \text{ Shares}$$

Assuming the trader bought 5000 shares at the outset to hedge the delta risk, the gamma measure tells the trader that he or she has to buy a further 100 shares to rebalance the hedge if the underlying rises by one cent.

18.8   GAMMA BEHAVIOUR

The graph in Figure 18.3 shows the relationship between the delta of a $\$100$ strike call and the price of the underlying. There are three months to expiry. The delta changes most rapidly when the option is around the at-the-money level, in this case $\$100$. Here the delta is most sensitive to changes in the price of the underlying, i.e. the gamma is at its highest. Generally, options tend to be at their most sensitive when they are at-the-money. It is the 'pivot' point.

By contrast the change in delta (the gamma) is relatively low when the calls are at out-of-the-money or in-the-money. A deeply OTM call has a delta close to zero. It is unlikely to be exercised and therefore has very little sensitivity to small changes in the price of the underlying. Furthermore, the delta is more or less anchored at close to zero and the value is unlikely to change very much unless there is a sharp change in the price of the underlying. A deeply ITM call has a delta close to one. It is highly likely to be exercised and behaves rather like a position in the underlying share. The delta is close to one and the value is more or less anchored at that level. It would take a sharp fall in the price of the underlying to affect the situation.

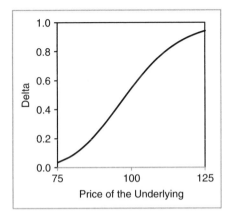

Figure 18.3   Delta curve for $ 100 strike call with three months to expiry.

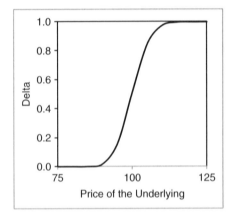

Figure 18.4   Delta curve for $ 100 strike call with five days to expiry.

18.8.1   Gamma and Expiry

Figure 18.4 shows the relationship between the price of the underlying and the delta of the above $ 100 strike call, but this time when the option only has *five days* rather than three months remaining to expiry. It shows that the gamma has increased if the option is at-the-money, but reduced if it is OTM or ITM. To simplify somewhat, with so little time to expiry it is highly likely that the call will not be exercised if it is OTM and that it will be exercised if it is ITM. The deltas are zero and one respectively, and it would take a major change in the price of the underlying to change that situation. Meantime there is much uncertainty about the eventual fate of the option if it is still ATM with only five days remaining until maturity.

The phenomenon of rising gamma on ATM options as they approach expiry matters particularly to a trader who is short options. This is because the more gamma in the position the more unstable a delta hedge is liable to be. As demonstrated before, when a trader is short options and keeps adjusting the delta hedge by dealing in the underlying shares, this can crystallize a series of trading losses. If the share price rises the writer of a call has to add more shares to the hedge portfolio to restore delta neutrality. Then if the stock price falls back again the trader has to sell some or all of those additional shares at a lower price (and at a loss).

Mathematically speaking, delta is the first derivative of the pricing model with respect to small changes in the price of the underlying. Gamma is the second derivative.

18.9   THETA (Θ)

Theta measures the change in the value of an option as time elapses, other inputs to the pricing model remaining the same. To illustrate the concept, Figure 18.5 shows the changing value of a three-month ATM call with a strike of $ 100 as the option approaches expiry. All the other inputs to the pricing model have been kept constant: the strike, the price of the underlying, the volatility assumption, and the carry cost.

Figure 18.5 shows that the option loses time value as it approaches expiry. With less time remaining there is less chance that the option will expire in-the-money. Theta measures the rate of decay in the time value of an option. It is the slope or the tangent at any given point on the curve. The option in Figure 18.5 is at-the-money throughout, and ATM options (especially short-dated ones) tend to have relatively high theta values.

18.9.1   Measuring Theta

Theta is negative for long calls and puts – the position loses value every day. For opposite reasons theta is positive on short option positions. Every day that elapses (other inputs to the pricing model remaining constant) the options tend to lose value. This is good news for a trader with a short position, because the contracts are cheaper to buy back to close out the position.

Figure 18.5 also shows that the rate of time decay on the ATM call *accelerates* as time goes by. With zero days elapsed (three months to expiry) the call in this example has a theta of roughly −$ 0.04. This means that if a further day goes by the call will lose about four

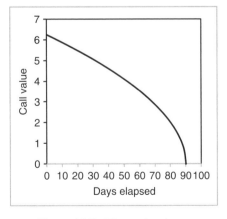

Figure 18.5   Time value decay.

cents in value, assuming that all the other inputs to the pricing model remain constant. The theta with 80 days elapsed (10 days to expiry) is roughly −$0.1. If a further day elapses at that stage the call will lose about 10 cents in value, other things being equal. These numbers are per share. If the options are on (say) 10,000 shares the values are increased in proportion.

18.10   VEGA

The value of an option is also sensitive to the assumption made about the volatility of the underlying. This sensitivity is measured by vega. Vega is the change in the option value for (typically) a 1 % change in the assumed volatility of the underlying, other inputs to the pricing model remaining constant. Buying an option is sometimes known as a long volatility or **long vega** position. If the volatility assumption used to price the option increases the contract will become more valuable. This applies to both call and put options.

Conversely, a trader who is short options hopes for declining volatility, because the options will become cheaper to repurchase. (Vega is not in fact a Greek letter; some people use the Greek letter **kappa** instead.)

Figure 18.6 shows the value of a $100 strike ATM three-month call for different volatility assumptions. As volatility increases the value of the option increases in a more or less linear fashion. The vega of this particular option is about $0.74. This means that for a 1 % change in volatility (all other inputs to the pricing model remaining constant) the option will increase or decrease in value by about 74 cents. As with the theta value in the previous section, this is on a per share basis. Vega is the slope on the line in Figure 18.6 showing the relationship between volatility and option value.

18.11   RHO (p) AND SUMMARY OF GREEKS

The final 'Greek' considered here is rho. Rho measures the change in an option's price (all other inputs to the model remaining constant) for a given change in interest rates, typically 0.01 % or 1 %. Figure 18.7 shows the value of a $100 strike ATM call as interest rates

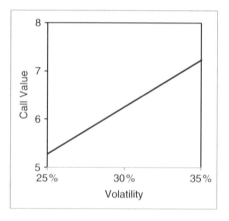

Figure 18.6   Option value against volatility.

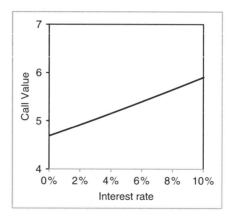

Figure 18.7   Option value against interest rates.

rise. It is a linear relationship and rho is the slope of the line in the graph. In this particular example rho is $0.27. This means that for a 1% increase in the interest rate the call option value (all other inputs remaining constant) increases by 27 cents. Again this is on a per share basis and has to be increased in proportion to the number of shares in the option contract.

18.11.1   Rho on Call Options

The option pricing model assumes that when an option is written a riskless hedge can be put in place using the delta measure. In the case of a call option, delta tells the writer how many of the underlying shares to buy to cover the exposure. The model assumes, in effect, that this is funded through borrowing, offset by any dividend income received on the shares. All other things being equal, when interest rates rise the value of call options also tends to rise. The writers of calls pass on their higher funding costs to the buyers.

18.11.2   Rho on Put Options

On the other hand if interest rates rise the value of put options will fall. Writers of put options are exposed to falls rather than rises in the price of the underlying share. To hedge this delta exposure they can run short positions in the underlying. As interest rates rise they will earn more money by investing the cash received from selling the shares short and can afford to pass the benefits on to the buyers of the puts.

18.11.3   Dividends

The version of the Black-Scholes model adapted for continuous dividend-paying stocks discussed in Chapter 17 prices options using the *net cost* of carrying a hedge position in the underlying – funding cost minus dividend yield. If a dealer sells a call he or she can hedge the delta risk (the directional exposure to rises in the share price) by buying the underlying shares. All other things being equal, the higher the rate of dividends earned on the shares

Table 18.1 Signs of the 'Greeks' for basic option strategies

Strategy	Position delta	Position gamma	Position theta	Position vega	Position rho
Long call	Positive	Positive	Negative	Positive	Positive
Short call	Negative	Negative	Positive	Negative	Negative
Long put	Negative	Positive	Negative	Positive	Negative
Short put	Positive	Negative	Positive	Negative	Positive

carried in the delta hedge, the lower the price the dealer can charge for selling the options. Matters work in reverse for the writer of a put. The seller of a put can delta hedge by borrowing and shorting the underlying shares. He or she will have to pass over dividends on the shares to the lender. The higher the dividends the more this will cost and (all other things being equal) the more the dealer will have to charge for selling the put.

18.11.4 Summary on Greeks

Table 18.1 summarizes the 'signs' of the Greeks for four basic options strategies. For example, a long call has positive delta (it profits from a rise in the share price). It has positive gamma or convexity, which means that the profits accelerate in a more than linear fashion if the price of the underlying rises sharply. If the underlying price falls sharply the losses decelerate because the most money that can ever be lost is the initial premium paid. The position is negative theta because of the time value decay effect. It is positive vega and rho because the call will become more valuable if volatility increases or interest rates rise.

18.12 CHAPTER SUMMARY

According to the Black-Scholes model the value of a European option is determined by the strike price, the price of the underlying, the time to expiry, the assumed volatility of the returns on the underlying asset, and the cost of carrying a hedge position in the underlying. The first two factors determine whether the option has any intrinsic value. They also help to determine the time value of an option. An option that is out-of-the-money is a 'lower probability bet' than one that is at-the-money, and will tend to have less time value. Other things being equal, the time value of an option is highest when it is at-the-money. The change in the value of an option for a small change in the price of the underlying is measured by delta. Delta is the slope or tangent on the option price curve. It is also the hedge ratio, the number the trader uses to decide how much of the underlying he or she should trade to manage the risk on an option position. Delta is not a constant and can be especially unstable when an option is at-the-money and approaching expiry. The 'Greek' that measures the rate of change of delta is gamma. It is possible to gamma hedge a short option position by buying options, especially short-dated at-the-money options. The change in the value of an option as time elapses is measured by theta. It is negative for bought option contracts. Vega measures the change in the value of an option (all other factors remaining constant) for a given change in volatility. It is positive for bought calls and puts. Rho measures the sensitivity of the option value to a change in interest rates. It is positive for long calls and negative for long puts.

APPENDIX: DELTA AND GAMMA HEDGING

The main section of the chapter considered how traders can buy and sell the underlying security to hedge the delta risk on an option position. This Appendix looks at a more detailed example of a delta hedge, and also explores how the gamma risk on an options position might be hedged. In the following example a trader is short calls on 500,000 shares. The following information is available to price the options:

- Spot price of underlying = 650 cents
- Strike price of calls = 651 cents
- Time to expiry = 12 days
- Interest rate = 5.75 % p.a.
- Share dividend yield = 1.74 % p.a.
- Implied volatility = 25 % p.a.

The implied volatility is derived from the price of option contracts traded openly in the market on the same underlying. With the above values the Black-Scholes model (adapted for a dividend-paying share) gives a value for the options of 11.68 cents per share. On 500,000 shares this values the total option position at $58,400. The call delta derived from the model is 0.507. Therefore:

$$\text{Position Delta} = -500,000 \times 0.507 = -253,500 \text{ shares}$$

Delta is negative here because the trader has sold calls; if the underlying share price rises the calls will become more expensive to buy back to close the position. A delta negative position is rather like being short the underlying. To delta hedge the trader can buy 253,500 shares. For small movements in the share price the profits and losses on the options and the shares in the delta hedge will balance out.

Larger Movement in the Underlying Price

But what happens if the share price rise is more substantial? For a 10 cent rise in the share price the options, according to the Black-Scholes model, would cost 17.41 cents per share or $87,050 in total to buy back. Therefore:

$$\text{P\&L on Calls} = \$58,400 - \$87,050 = -\$28,650$$

$$\text{P\&L on Delta Hedge} = 253,500 \text{ shares} \times \$0.1 = \$25,350$$

$$\text{Net P\&L} = \$25,350 - \$28,650 = -\$3300$$

The net loss is due to the effects of gamma. Delta only holds good for small changes in the price of the underlying. The short calls have actually lost more money for a 10 cent rise in the underlying share price than expected if we simply extrapolated from the option delta. The delta on the short option position was 0.507. For a 10 cent rise in the price of the underlying share this delta figure predicts the following loss on the options position:

$$\text{Predicted Loss from Delta Value} = -500,000 \times 0.507 \times \$0.1 = -\$25,350$$

The actual loss would be $-\$28,650$. There is a discrepancy here of $3300.

Delta-Gamma Adjustment

Traders sometimes make a simple adjustment to the delta prediction to get a better estimate of the actual movement in the value of the option position for a larger move in the price of the underlying. This is known as the **delta-gamma** adjustment. The gamma of the calls in this example is approximately 0.0135. For a 10 cent rise in the price of the underlying the gamma effect on the profit and loss can be estimated as follows:

$$\frac{10^2}{2} \times 0.0135 = 0.675 \text{ cents per share}$$

This means that the additional loss caused by gamma on top of the delta prediction for a 10 cent rise in the value of the underlying is estimated at approximately 0.675 cents per share. For calls on 500,000 shares this amounts to about $-\$3375$. The delta-gamma adjustment can be a useful rule of thumb, but is liable to become increasingly inaccurate for larger movements in the price of the underlying. In effect it is a simple means of adjusting for the curvature in the relationship between the price of the underlying and the value of the options.

Gamma Hedging

Buying the underlying shares can manage the delta exposure on a short call option position. However, it does not cover the gamma exposure. The option position has a nonlinear relationship with the price of the underlying, while the value of a fixed number of shares in the delta hedge moves in a linear fashion in response to changes in the share price. An alternative hedge might be to buy short-dated call options. These will have positive delta (they increase in value when the underlying price rises) and at the same time a substantial amount of positive gamma.

Suppose the trader in the example who is short the 651 strike calls considers buying the following short-dated ATM calls on the same underlying:

- Strike price = 650 cents.
- Implied volatility = 25 %.
- Time to expiry = three days.

With the spot price of the underlying at 650 cents the Black-Scholes model prices these options at 5.98 cents per share. The delta is 0.51 and the gamma is 0.0271. The gamma on the 12-day 651 strike calls the trader is short is 0.0135 so the trader has to buy fewer of the shorter-dated 650 strike calls to match the gamma risk. The figure in terms of the number of shares in the contract is calculated as follows:

$$500,000 \times \frac{0.0135}{0.0271} = 249,100$$

Unfortunately this will not fully manage the *delta* exposure on the original position:

Position Delta on Short 651 Strike Calls $= -500,000 \times 0.507 = -253,500$ shares

Position Delta on Long 650 Strike Calls $= 249,100 \times 0.51 = 127,041$ shares

To hedge out the residual delta risk the trader can buy approximately 126,500 shares in the underlying.

Remaining Risks on the Gamma Hedge

This combination of buying short-dated calls and buying the underlying will manage the delta and gamma risks on the short call position fairly effectively, unless the movement in the underlying share price is extreme. However it will not cover all of the risks. For example, there is a residual vega or volatility exposure. The vega on the short calls is 0.47. This means that for a 1 % rise in volatility the loss on the options will be 0.47 cents per share, or $ 2350 for calls on 500,000 shares. However the vega on the long calls (extracted from the model) is only 0.24. For a 1 % rise in volatility the profit on these options will be 0.24 cents per share, or $ 598 for calls on 249,100 shares. The net loss for a 1 % rise in volatility would be about $ 1752.

19

Option Strategies

19.1 CHAPTER OVERVIEW

Options can be combined together and with positions in underlying securities to construct a wide variety of trading strategies and risk management solutions. This chapter begins by exploring one of the most fundamental applications of options, hedging against potential losses on a position in an underlying asset using put options. This can be combined with a short call to construct a 'collar' strategy. If the strikes of the put and the call are set at the right level the premiums of the two options cancel out and the strategy becomes a zero cost collar. The next set of strategies considered are spread trades, which are trading rather than risk management applications of options. Some are designed to capitalize on directional movements in the underlying whilst limiting potential losses. Others profit from changes in the volatility assumptions used to price options or from the fact that options tend to lose value as time elapses. There is a focus in all the cases and examples in this chapter on the returns and potential risks of each strategy, how the risks can be managed in practice, and on the market circumstances in which a trader or investor is likely to employ a given strategy.

19.2 HEDGING WITH PUT OPTIONS

A **protective put** strategy combines a long (bought) position in the underlying security with a long (bought) put option. The combination is designed to provide **downside risk protection** – that is, to hedge against short-term falls in the price of the underlying asset. If the put is a physically exercised contract then it can be exercised when the price of the underlying falls below the strike. The underlying security is then sold at the strike price, eliminating any further losses. If the put is cash-settled then any losses incurred on the underlying below the strike price are compensated for through cash payments received from the writer of the contract.

19.2.1 Options versus Futures Hedge

To illustrate the basic strategy this section takes the example of an investor who owns a stock currently trading at $ 100. The investor is concerned about the possibility of short-term falls in the value of the share due to general turbulence in the equity markets. The investor could of course sell the share and deposit the proceeds in the money markets, or switch into another financial asset. However this will incur transaction costs, and may also trigger tax liabilities. In addition, the investor may have built up the shareholding over time and may prefer not to switch simply because of short-term problems. And of course if the investor does make a premature switch there is the danger of incurring an opportunity loss – the loss of profits that would arise if the share price actually increased rather than fell.

The investor could try to hedge the exposure by selling single stock futures or cash-settled equity forward contracts (see Chapter 15). Then if the share price falls the investor will

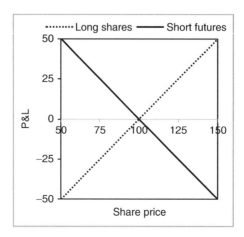

Figure 19.1 Futures hedge.

be compensated in cash through gains on the derivative contracts. The disadvantage of this strategy is that the reverse would hold: profits on the stock would be offset by cash payments the investor would have to make on the futures or forward contracts. Figure 19.1 illustrates the net position resulting from a futures hedge. For simplicity this assumes a perfect hedge and also ignores carry costs, so that the futures are sold at the same as the spot price of the underlying (in this case $ 100).

19.2.2 The Protective Put

The advantage of covering the risks on a long (bought) position in shares with put options rather than with futures is that the investor can achieve 'downside' protection – insurance against losses arising from falls in the share price – whilst at the same time still being able to benefit from rises in the share price. In this above example the investor owns stock trading at $ 100. Suppose this time he or she contacts a dealer and agrees to buy a three-month European put on the stock with a strike of $ 95. The agreed premium is $ 3.5 per share.

Figure 19.2 illustrates the profit and loss on the share and on the put at the expiry of the option. The figures are in dollars and for a range of different prices of the underlying at expiry. Note that in this and subsequent examples matters are simplified by ignoring the effects of the time value of money: in fact the premium would be paid upfront, whereas any payout from exercising the option would occur in three months' time. In addition, all the premiums quoted in this chapter have been rounded to simplify the break-even calculations.

Figure 19.2 shows the profit and loss on the share as a diagonal line cutting through the current share price of $ 100. If the share price rises the investor will make a profit on the stock; otherwise he or she will make a loss. It also shows the bought put option. The maximum loss on the put is the $ 3.5 premium. The contract will only be exercised at expiry if the share price falls below the $ 95 strike. At share price levels below the strike the put is in-the-money. The point at which the put (considered on its own) cuts through the zero profit and loss line is the strike minus the premium, that is at $ 95−$ 3.5 = $ 91.5.

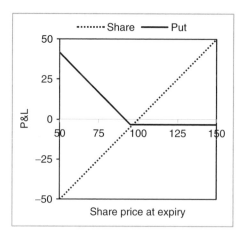

Figure 19.2 Payoff on the underlying share and on the put at expiry.

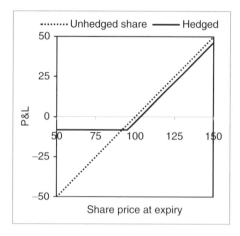

Figure 19.3 Hedge constructed with OTM put option.

Figure 19.3 now shows the *combination* payoff profile of the position in the share and the $95 strike put. For comparison it also shows the profit and loss for an unhedged position in the underlying share.

19.2.3 Maximum Loss with Protective Put

The maximum loss per share on the hedged position at expiry is $8.5. This is the combination of $3.5 premium (which is a sunk cost at expiry and never recovered) plus the difference between the share price which started out at $100 and the $95 strike of the option. The put was initially struck out-of-the-money and the underlying can fall $5 before the protection it affords comes into effect. If the put is physically settled then the investor

will exercise the option and sell the underlying when it is trading below $ 95. In that case
the investor will have lost $ 5 on the share (from the starting level of $ 100) plus the $ 3.5
premium. If the put is cash-settled then losses on the share at price levels below $ 95 will
be compensated in cash by payments received from the writer of the option.

19.2.4 Other Break-even Levels

There are a couple of other reference points that are of interest. What happens if the share
price *rises* and the protection afforded by the put option is not required? The problem here
is that the share price has to rise to $ 103.5 before the initial premium paid for the option
is recovered. This contrasts with the unhedged position, where the position is in profit if
the share price rises above $ 100. Finally, the hedged and unhedged lines in Figure 19.3
meet when the share price is at $ 91.5. This is the point at which both strategies (hedged
and unhedged) lose exactly $ 8.5. In fact this would be a significant level for the investor.
Provided the share price stays above $ 91.5 the investor is actually better off unhedged, i.e.
without buying the put option.

> **Synthetic Call**
>
> Note that the hedged payoff profile in Figure 19.3 resembles that of a bought call on the
> underlying. This is a common feature of options. They can be assembled in many different
> combinations, often replicating (at least in some aspects) other option positions.

19.2.5 Changing the Strike

Buying an out-of-the-money put option to hedge the risk on a share is like buying a cheap
insurance policy – the option is relatively inexpensive, but the protection level is not particularly good. The investor could improve on this by purchasing an *at-the-money* put
struck at the spot price of $ 100. However this would cost more premium. Suppose the
investor has to pay $ 5.5 per share for this ATM contract. Figure 19.4 illustrates the payoff

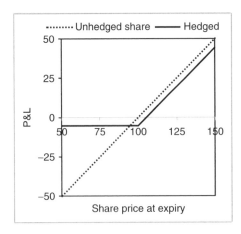

Figure 19.4 Hedge constructed with ATM put option.

profile at expiry, this time on the combined hedged position (long the shares, long the $ 100 strike put).

The maximum loss this time is better at $ 5.5 per share. However if the share price *rises* rather than falls, it would now have to rise to $ 105.5 at the expiry of the put to recover the higher option premium. The figures for the $ 95 strike options were $ 8.5 and $ 103.5 respectively. By purchasing puts that are actually struck in-the-money the investor could further reduce the maximum loss on the combined position (to a level converging on zero) whilst further pushing out the price the share would have to rise to, to break even (to a level converging on infinity). In fact buying a deeply in-the-money put option is really like establishing a short position in the underlying – there is a very high probability that the put will be exercised and the underlying stock sold.

19.3 COVERED CALL WRITING

Options can also be used to generate additional income by selling calls against a holding of securities. This is known as a **covered call** or sometimes a **buy-write** strategy. To illustrate the idea this section takes the same basic circumstances as before: an investor who owns a stock currently trading at $ 100. This time the investor decides to explore selling a three-month out-of-the-money call against this holding at a strike of $ 105. The premium earned is $ 4.5 per share. Figure 19.5 illustrates the profit and loss profile of the long position in the underlying share and the short position in the $ 105 strike call at the expiry of the options.

Since the premium of the short call is $ 4.5 the call payoff profile (considered on its own) will cut through the zero profit and loss line at $ 105 + $ 4.5 = $ 109.5. At that level the investor will lose $ 4.5 on the exercise of the short call, which eliminates the premium initially collected on the option. Now Figure 19.5 illustrates the payoff profile of the *combined* position – long the share, short the $ 105 strike call sold at a premium of $ 4.5 per share. For comparison the original long position in the share is also shown.

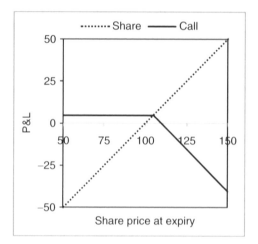

Figure 19.5 Long position in share and short OTM call.

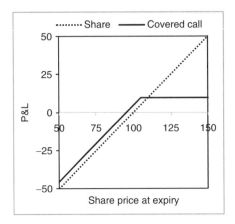

Figure 19.6   Covered call.

19.3.1   Maximum Profit on the Covered Call

The maximum profit is $ 9.5 per share, achieved when the share is trading at $ 105. At $ 105 the short call will not be exercised and the investor retains the $ 4.5 premium. In addition, the investor has made $ 5 on the long position in the underlying. At levels *above* $ 105 the profit flattens. If the short call is physically settled then above $ 105 it will be exercised and the investor will have to deliver the stock and receive the fixed strike of $ 105. If the call is cash-settled then any profit the investor earns on the stock above $ 105 will have to be paid out to the buyer of the call. One advantage of the strategy is that because the investor initially collected $ 4.5 in premium the share price can fall from $ 100 to $ 95.5 before the covered call starts to lose money. Note that the covered call profile in Figure 19.6 resembles that of a synthetic short put option on the underlying security.

Use of Covered Calls

Portfolio managers often sell calls against their holdings in shares to generate additional income for the fund. This can be particularly valuable in a 'flat' market in which it is difficult to make acceptable returns without taking excessive risks. Covered call writing is far less dangerous than selling 'naked' call options. Normally the strike is set out-of-the-money so that the risk of exercise is limited. If the risk of exercise increases then the fund manager can buy the options back and sell calls struck further out-of-the-money.

19.4   COLLARS

In the first protective put strategy considered above the investor bought a $ 95 strike put costing $ 3.5 per share to hedge against potential losses on a position in the underlying. The main drawback of the strategy is the premium. If the share price rises it will have to rise by at least $ 3.5 before the investor starts to break even, net of the premium paid. One alternative is to buy the protective put and also at the same time to sell a call on the stock with the same expiry date. The advantage is that the investor will receive premium on the call to offset the cost of the put.

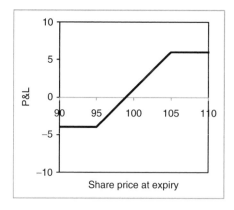

Figure 19.7 Collar strategy.

Suppose the investor buys the $95 strike put costing $3.5 and at the same time sells a $105 strike call and receives premium of $4.5 per share. The combination is usually known as a **collar** strategy. Figure 19.7 shows the combined expiry payoff profile – the net profit and loss on the collar for different levels of the underlying at the expiry of the options. The maximum loss this time is only $4. This is reached at the strike of the long put. However the maximum profit is capped at $6 per share, which is reached at the $105 strike of the short call.

19.4.1 Zero Cost Collar

A zero cost collar is a hedge which involves buying a put and selling a call with the strikes of the options set such that the two premiums exactly cancel out. Suppose as before that the investor buys an $95 strike put against a holding in a share currently worth $100, but this time also sells a call struck further out-of-the-money at $107.5. The premium received for the call is $3.5 per share, which exactly offsets the cost of the put option, so there is zero net premium to pay. The payoff profile of the zero cost collar is illustrated in Figure 19.8.

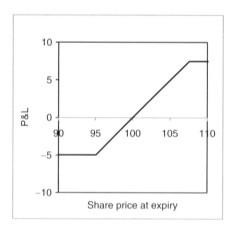

Figure 19.8 Zero cost collar.

The net premium on the two options is zero so the combination strategy payoff profile cuts through the zero profit and loss line at $100. The investor can make $7.5 per share on the underlying before the call is exercised. The investor can lose $5 per share before the protection afforded by the $95 strike put comes into operation. Zero cost collars are popular with investors for the obvious reason that there is no net premium to pay upfront. However there is a potential opportunity cost – if the share price rises above the strike of the short call then the investor's returns are capped and he or she will underperform other investors who do not have the option position in place.

19.5   BULL AND BEAR SPREADS

The previous examples in this chapter explored the use of options to hedge the risk on a position in an underlying asset, or to generate additional returns against a holding in the underlying asset. The remaining strategies consider ways in which call and put options can be assembled in combinations to establish trading positions. These strategies are typically used by traders (and potentially by hedge funds) rather than by traditional buy-side investors such as pension fund managers.

A **bull spread** is an appropriate strategy to put in place when a trader is moderately confident that the underlying will rise in price, but wants to limit the downside risk. As an example, suppose the underlying stock is trading at $100. A trader buys a three-month call struck at $100 on the stock and pays a premium of $6.5 per share. At the same time the trader sells a three-month $105 strike call on the same underlying and charges a premium of $4.5 per share. The expiry payoff profile for the combination strategy is shown in Figure 19.9.

The maximum loss on the bull spread at expiry is the net premium of −$2. The maximum profit is $3 per share. This is achieved when the share price reaches $105. It comprises a profit of $5 on the $100 strike long call, less the net premium. At price levels above $105 any gains on the $100 strike call are exactly offset by losses on the $105 strike short call. Again this analysis ignores the fact that the option premium is paid upfront while any profit

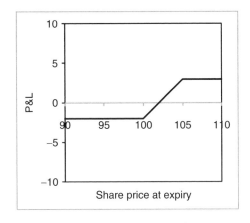

Figure 19.9   Bull spread.

from exercise is achieved at the expiry of the options; properly speaking profits and losses should be adjusted for the time value of money.

> **Use of Bull Spreads**
>
> A bull spread is an appropriate strategy when a trader expects a modest rise in the price of the underlying, since the profits are capped above the strike of the short call. It has certain advantages compared to buying a call on its own. The net premium cost and hence the maximum potential loss are lower, and the level at which the share has to trade at expiry to break even is lower. The position is normally set up with positive delta and fairly neutral values of gamma, theta, and vega.

19.5.1   Bull Spread with Puts

The bull spread just explored can also be assembled by selling an in-the-money put with a strike of $105 and at the same time buying an out-of-the-money put with a strike of $100 to limit the losses in the event that the share price falls sharply. The advantage of setting up the trade in this way is that a positive net premium will be received at the outset. Taking into account the effects of the time value of money fully, however, the maximum profit and maximum loss figures will be identical compared to setting up the strategy with call options.

19.5.2   Bear Spread

A bear spread strategy is useful when a trader is moderately bearish about the underlying. It generates a capped profit when the underlying price falls, but a maximum loss if the price rises.

Figure 19.10 illustrates a bear spread on a stock currently trading at $100. It is constructed by buying a put struck at $100 at a premium of $5.5 per share and selling a put struck at $95 with the same expiry date for a premium of $3.5 per share. The net premium is therefore −$2 per share. If the stock price at expiry is at $100 or above neither option is exercised and the maximum loss is the net premium of −$2. Below $100 the long put has

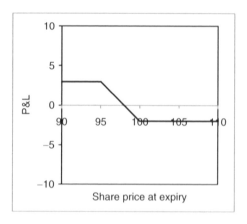

Figure 19.10   Bear spread.

intrinsic value. However the profit on this option is capped at $95 when the strike of the short put is reached. The maximum profit on the bear spread at expiry is therefore $3 per share. The trade can also be assembled by shorting a call struck at $95 and buying a call struck at $100.

19.6   OTHER SPREAD TRADES

The bull and bear spreads examined in the previous section illustrate the payoff at expiry of strategies where options are bought and sold on an equal number of shares. A **ratio spread** is a strategy where this is not the case. For example, Figure 19.11 shows a **put ratio spread**. This has been assembled as a combination of a long in-the-money put struck at $105 and a short out-of-the-money put struck at $95 on double the number of underlying shares. The premium paid on the long put is $8.5 per share. The premium received on the short put is $3.5 per share, or $7 on two shares. The option premiums were calculated as in previous sections using a spot price for the underlying of $100.

If the stock price at expiry is $105 or above neither option is exercised and the loss is the net premium of −$1.5. If the stock price is trading between $105 and $95 the long put is exercised. The maximum profit is $105 − $95 − $1.5 = $8.5. If the stock price is below $95 at expiry the short put position starts to lose money. Unlike the bear spread, however, the profit and loss line does not flatten out. It crosses the zero point again when the underlying stock is trading at $95 − $8.5 = $86.5. The maximum loss is reached when the stock is trading at zero.

Use of Put Ratio Spreads

The above strategy might be appropriate for a trader who is moderately bearish about the underlying but who thinks it unlikely that it will fall below $95. It would also be possible to sell $95 strike puts on three or even more shares for every one share in the long put option position. This would produce a positive initial premium. However it would also greatly increase the downside risk. The losses could be substantial if the underlying stock was trading far below $95 at expiry.

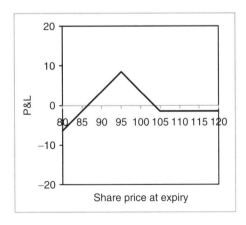

Figure 19.11   Put ratio spread.

19.6.1   Calendar or Time Spread

The final spread trade explored here is known as a **calendar** or time spread. Essentially it is designed to exploit the fact that a shorter-dated option has a faster rate of time value decay – a higher absolute theta value – compared to a longer-dated option on the same underlying. To illustrate the idea, Figure 19.12 shows the time value decay for a three-month and a one-month call on the same underlying stock. Both options are struck at-the-money. The options have been revalued over a period of time assuming that all the other inputs to the pricing model (spot price, volatility, carry cost) remain constant, and that only time elapses. The graph shows that, under this assumption, the shorter-dated call loses time value more quickly than the longer-dated option.

A calendar spread could be assembled to exploit this fact. It would consist of shorting the one-month call and buying the three-month call. As time elapses, other inputs to the pricing model remaining constant, the shorter-dated option will tend to lose value more quickly than the longer-dated option. This would generate a trading profit, because to close out the overall position the short call has to be repurchased and the long call sold back into the market. The more quickly the short call loses value the better, because it can be repurchased at a cheaper price.

At the outset (with zero days elapsed) the theta value on a long position in the three-month call in Figure 19.12 is −$0.036. This means that if one day elapses the loss through time value decay is about 3.6 cents per share, all other inputs to the pricing model remaining constant. However the theta value on a short position in the one-month call is about $0.061. This means that if one day elapses (other inputs to the pricing remaining constant) the gain through time value decay on this option is greater at about 6.1 cents per share. As further days elapse the potential profit from the calendar spread trade can accelerate. This is because the rate of time decay is not linear.

The risk with the calendar spread, of course, is that all the other factors that determine the value of the options may *not* remain constant. In the example the two calls were struck at-the-money in relation to the spot price at the outset, and the deltas would therefore net out – the delta of the short call is negative and that of the long call is positive. As a result,

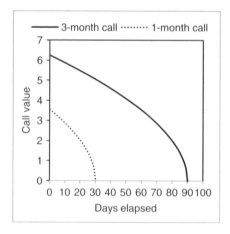

Figure 19.12   Time value decay for calls with different expiry dates.

for small directional movements in the underlying share price the net profit and loss on the overall position will be close to zero: any losses on one option will be compensated for by gains on the other. However the short one-month call has higher gamma than the long three-month call. This means that the delta-neutrality will tend to break down for larger movements in the price of the underlying. If the share price rises sharply, for example, the losses on the short call will exceed the profits on the long call option.

19.7   VOLATILITY REVISITED

Perhaps the key input to the option pricing model is the assumed volatility of the underlying asset. Certainly it is the variable that offers the most scope for disagreement. Historical volatility is calculated statistically as the standard deviation of the past returns on an asset around the historical average return (see the Appendix to Chapter 17 for details). But what time period should be used in the calculation? One approach is to go back many years to incorporate as much information about the behaviour of the asset as possible. But the underlying itself may have changed its characteristics over time.

To take one extreme example, the Finnish company Nokia used to be a conglomerate making a range of unexciting staple goods. Data from that historical period is unlikely to be very relevant to assessing the likely behaviour of the shares today. On the other hand, if too much historical data is excluded and the volatility calculation is based only on recent experience this runs the risk of failing to capture those extreme movements in the price of the underlying that occur very rarely. Some option traders try to resolve this problem by calculating a moving average of the historical volatility of the underlying, which weights its more recent behaviour more heavily than distant events. The logic is that the most recent experience is likely to provide a better indicator of the future.

19.7.1   Implied Volatility

Whatever the methodology, however, there is no getting round the fact that historical volatility is concerned with the past behaviour of the underlying. The outturn profits and losses on an option position will be determined by the actual behaviour of the underlying over the life of the option. One standard approach to this problem is to operate the option pricing model 'in reverse'. Rather than calculating the value of an option from an estimated or assumed volatility, the method involves using the actual premium at which the option is trading in the market and deriving or 'backing out' the volatility assumption that would generate this price using the pricing model. This is called **implied volatility**.

> **Implied Volatility**
>
> Implied volatility is the volatility assumption built into an actual option price. It can be compared with the historical volatility of the underlying or with a forecast of future volatility to decide whether an option is trading 'cheap' or 'dear'.

When implied volatility is calculated from publicly available data, such as the market prices of exchange-traded options, the result at first sight is often a little surprising. It appears that traders tend to use different volatilities to price options on the same underlying that differ only in their strike price or in the time to expiry. For example, out-of-the-money puts on an equity index are often sold at higher implied volatilities compared to at-the-money and in-the-money put options on exactly the same index.

19.7.2   Volatility Smile or Skew

When the calculated implied volatilities are plotted against the strikes of the options the resulting graph is sometimes called a **volatility smile**. In equity index markets it is typically more of a lopsided smile, sometimes called a **volatility skew**. This is illustrated in Figure 19.13.

This is a large subject and detailed treatment is outside the scope of this book, but one possible explanation for this effect is that traders are compensating for imperfections in the standard pricing model by adjusting the volatility assumptions they use to price options. The Black-Scholes model assumes that the returns on shares follow the bell-curve shape of the normal distribution. It appears that there is a greater probability of major falls or crashes in equity markets than is captured by the normal distribution. It may be that traders cover this risk by increasing the premiums they charge for low strike options on equity indices, such as out-of-money puts. It may also be that investors and others bid up the prices of such options (which provide downside insurance) because of their fear of market crashes. In turn, a relatively high premium for an option generates a relatively high value for implied volatility.

A **volatility surface** is a three-dimensional graph which shows the implied volatilities of options on the same underlying for a range of different strike prices and for a range of different expiry dates. Traders and risk managers use the data from volatility smiles and surfaces to pinpoint the correct volatility to use to value options on a given underlying, taking into account the actual strike and expiry date of the options.

19.7.3   Volatility Trades

Implied volatility is a useful concept since it helps traders decide whether the volatility assumptions currently being used by the rest of the market to price options are (in the judgement of the trader) realistic or otherwise. The trader can then 'buy volatility' if it is

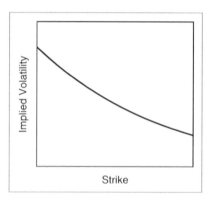

Figure 19.13   Volatility skew.

cheap or 'sell volatility' if it is overpriced. The simplest way to buy volatility is to purchase options (they increase in value as volatility assumptions increase). Selling volatility can be achieved by writing options (for opposite reasons).

In recent years it has also become possible to trade volatility through a range of new products. One such is the **volatility swap**. This is a type of forward contract in which the payoff depends on the difference between a fixed volatility level on a given asset and what the actual realized volatility on the asset turns out to be over the life of the contract. It is also possible now to trade volatility contracts on exchanges.

19.7.4 The Vix Index

The CBOE Volatility Index® (VIX®) was first introduced in 1993. It measures the volatility expectations built into S&P 500 index options with 30 days to expiry. It is calculated now using a range of different strikes and not just at-the-money contracts, to take into account the volatility skew. It uses an explicit formula that derives market expectations of volatility on the S&P 500 directly, rather than extracting or 'backing out' an implied volatility assumption using an option pricing model. The VIX is calculated in real-time throughout the trading day. It is used as the basis for a range of exchange-traded futures and options products that allow traders to speculate on or hedge against changes in volatility levels. The VIX is sometimes called the 'investor fear gauge' because it tends to rise during periods of increased anxiety in the financial markets and steep market falls.

19.8 VOLATILITY TRADING: STRADDLES AND STRANGLES

The case study in the following sections explores a typical volatility trade using combination option strategies known as **straddles** and **strangles**. The underlying is the FT-SE 100 index of leading UK shares. The spot index level is assumed to be 5500 points. Three-month at-the-money options on the index are trading at an implied volatility of 25 %. Suppose that a trader decides that this is excessive and that volatility assumptions are likely to decline in the market. To exploit this forecast the trader sells a straddle. This consists of selling a call and a put on the index with the same strike and expiry date. The chosen strike is at-the-money spot i.e. 5500. At a 25 % volatility the trader is able to sell the call for 300 index points and the put for 250 index points. This is a total of 550 index points. Assuming a value of GBP 10 per index point, the trader earns a total premium of GBP 5500.

Of course the trader could simply sell a call on the FT-SE 100 index outright. This is itself a short volatility position because if volatility expectations decline the call will decline in value and can be repurchased at a cheaper price. The problem is that selling a naked call is also a short delta position: the option will increase in value if the index rises and the trader would lose money as a result. As an alternative the trader could consider selling a put rather than a call option on the index. This is also a short volatility position, but at the same time it is also a long delta position – if the market rises the put will move out of the money and will become cheaper to buy back; if the market falls the put will move into the money and the position will become more expensive to close out.

By selling the straddle the trader starts out with a position that is roughly delta neutral. The negative delta on the short call is balanced by the positive delta on the short put. In practice, this means that if the underlying index rises or falls (by a small amount) then the gains and losses on the put and on the call will cancel out.

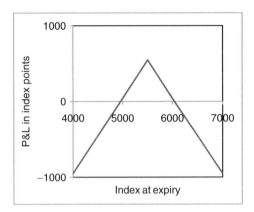

Figure 19.14 Expiry payoff profile for short straddle.

19.8.1 Short Straddle Expiry Payoff

Figure 19.14 shows the payoff profile of the short straddle at expiry for different levels of the underlying index. The maximum profit is achieved when the index remains at 5500 – the trader earns the 550 points total premium and both options expire worthless. There are two break-even points. If the index closes at 6050 the premium initially earned on the options is exactly offset by the 550 point loss on the 5500 strike short call (the put expires worthless). If the index closes at 4950 the premium is exactly offset by the 550 point loss on the 5500 strike short put (the call expires worthless). Since this is a short volatility strategy it is no surprise to find that it generates its maximum profit when the index closes exactly where it started, at a level of 5500.

One fact that Figure 19.14 illustrates clearly is that selling a straddle is a very risky strategy. In theory there is no maximum loss. For this reason many traders would look to close the position by buying back the two options as quickly (and cheaply) as possible. What matters from this perspective therefore is not so much the payoff at expiry but the *current value* of the strategy. This is explored in the next section.

19.9 CURRENT PAYOFF PROFILES

Figure 19.15 shows the current payoff profile of the short 5500 strike call option. This shows the profit and loss on the position in response to *immediate* changes in the underlying index. The assumption is that the call has just been sold for 300 points with three months still remaining to expiry. In other words, the graph shows how changes in the spot price from a starting level of 5500 (all other inputs to the pricing model remaining constant) affect the value of the short call position on the day the option is sold.

If the index rises above 5500 then the call will become more expensive to buy back and the trader would lose money closing the position. In theory the call can keep moving further and further into the money indefinitely, attracting more and more intrinsic value, so there is no limit to the potential loss. On the other hand if the index falls below 5500 the call will move out of the money and the trader could buy it back more cheaply at a profit.

The maximum profit is the 300 point premium the call was initially sold for: the option can never be purchased for less than zero. Selling the call is a short delta position – it is

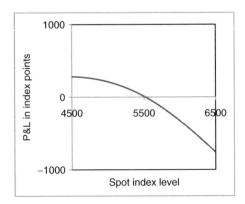

Figure 19.15   Current payoff profile for short call.

rather like being short the underlying. The difference is that while the losses continue to mount when the index rises, the maximum profit on the short call if the index falls is the 300 points initial premium collected.

19.9.1   Short Put Current Payoff Profile

By selling a straddle the trader also sold a put option. Figure 19.16 shows the current profit and loss profile of the three-month 5500 strike put option in response to immediate changes in the underlying index. Again this is taken on the day the put is sold, and assuming that all other inputs to the pricing model remain constant. Selling a put is a positive delta position. It is rather like establishing a long position in the underlying, except that the maximum profit that can be achieved is the premium initially earned (in this example 250 index points).

19.9.2   Short Straddle Current Payoff Profile

Next, the current payoff profile on the short straddle is illustrated in Figure 19.17. This combines the profiles for the call and the put option. The graph shows that for small

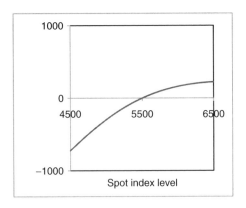

Figure 19.16   Current payoff profile for short put.

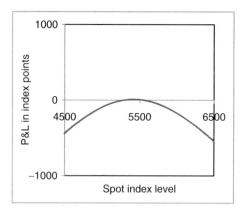

Figure 19.17   Current payoff profile for short straddle.

movements in the underlying index the profits and losses on the two options cancel out. The call has negative delta and the put has positive delta so overall the short straddle is roughly delta-neutral.

If the index rises the call will become more expensive to repurchase (it moves into the money) but the put will become cheaper. The reverse happens if the index falls by a small amount. However the graph also shows that the benefits of delta-neutrality tend to break down for *larger* movements in the index. For example, if the index moves up sharply then the losses on the short call will be considerable (the intrinsic value can increase indefinitely) whereas the maximum profit on the put is the 250 point premium at which the contract was sold.

19.9.3   Position Gamma

The problem here is that while the straddle may be approximately delta-neutral at the outset (the deltas of the call and the put cancel out) it is **gamma negative**. Selling a call is a gamma negative position and so too is selling a put option. The practical consequence of this fact is that if the index rises or falls by more than a small number of points the straddle will no longer be delta-neutral (gamma is a measure of the instability of delta).

The implications are rather unpleasant. If for example the index rises sharply then the short straddle position will become delta negative: effectively the trader is short the market in a rising market. The more the index rises, the more delta negative the position will become. The trader could attempt to restore delta neutrality by buying calls or futures on the index or by buying underlying shares. The danger then is that if the index subsequently falls back sharply the trader will have to sell back some or all of those calls, futures, or shares (which are no longer required) at a loss.

19.10   PROFITS AND RISKS ON STRADDLES

By now it may appear that the short straddle is rather a 'lose-lose' strategy. Certainly it tends to lose money on a current profit and loss basis whether the index rises or falls. In fact two events can generate a trading profit on the short straddle position.

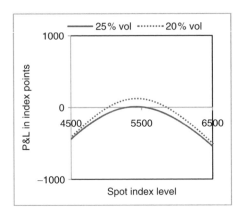

Figure 19.18   Current payoff profile for short straddle at different volatility levels.

- **Declining Volatility.** If market volatility expectations decline then the call and the put in the straddle will lose value and the straddle position can be closed out at a profit. The strategy has negative vega, i.e. it gains from a decline in volatility expectations.
- **Time Decay.** Every day that elapses the options will tend to lose a certain amount of time value (all other things being equal). The strategy has positive theta, i.e. it gains from the lapse of time.

Figure 19.18 shows what happens to the current value of the straddle (still with three months to expiry) for a range of different levels of the underlying index, on the assumption that implied volatility has dropped from 25 % to 20 %. The graph shows that provided the index has not moved appreciably from the starting level of 5500 the two options can be repurchased and the straddle position closed out at a profit.

Even if volatility does *not* decline there is still a chance of making money from the positive theta. As time goes by both the call and the put will lose time value. Provided the underlying index has not moved directionally to any great extent, and volatility has not increased materially, it may still be possible to close out the straddle position at a (modest) profit.

19.10.1   Lowering the Risks: Short Strangle

The losses on the short straddle are potentially unlimited, and it is very exposed to directional changes in the spot price of the underlying. One way to lower this risk is to construct a **short strangle**. This consists of selling a call and a put on the same underlying and with the same expiry date but both struck out-of-the-money. In the example in Figure 19.19 the strikes have been set at 5750 and 5250 respectively. The advantage compared to the short straddle is that the underlying index has to move by a significant degree before the initial premium is lost. The disadvantage is that the premium income is much reduced because the options are struck out-of-the-money. In this example the premium is 330 points compared to 550 points on the short straddle.

19.10.2   Long Volatility Trades

Buying a straddle is a **long volatility** trade. It consists of buying a call and a put on the same underlying with the same expiry date, typically struck at-the-money. It has positive

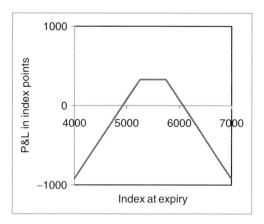

Figure 19.19   Expiry payoff profile for short strangle.

vega, which means that (other things being equal) if the volatility assumptions used to price options on that asset increase both options become more valuable and can be sold at a profit. In addition, the position is positive gamma. This means that although the delta starts off roughly neutral, if the underlying rises the delta will become positive, and if it falls the delta will become negative. This is a comfortable situation to be in: if the underlying rises (falls) the strategy starts to behave like a long (short) position in that asset. Unfortunately a long straddle involves paying premium for the call and the put. It also suffers from time value decay (it has negative theta). Every day that elapses, other inputs to the pricing model remaining constant, the straddle loses time value. At expiry if the underlying is still trading close to the level at the outset most if not all of the initial premium paid will be lost.

Long Straddle Application

A trader may buy a straddle when it seems that the underlying is due to break out of a range but it is not clear what direction the move will take. What the buyer does not want is a dull market with declining volatility.

19.11   CHAPTER SUMMARY

An investor who owns securities and is concerned about losses can buy put options as an insurance or protection device. This limits the potential losses on the securities but at the same time reduces the potential profits because of the cost of the option premium. The more in-the-money the put options are, the better the level of protection they provide, but the more expensive they will be. Investors can generate additional income against their holdings in securities by selling call options. These are normally struck out-of-the-money to reduce the risk of exercise. A collar strategy consists of buying an out-of-the-money put and selling an out-of-the-money call to protect against losses on the underlying while reducing the net premium paid. In addition to their applications in hedging and risk management, options can also be used to implement trading strategies. A spread trade is assembled by buying or selling a combination of options. A bull spread is a strategy that pays a capped profit when the underlying rises, but which suffers a maximum loss if the underlying falls in price. A bear spread pays a capped profit when the underlying falls in price, with a limited loss if the underlying increases in value. Traders can also use options to implement views about volatility. A short straddle is a short volatility position. It consists of selling two options on the same underlying with the same strike and the same expiry date. If volatility declines the straddle can be repurchased at a cheaper price. In addition to historic volatility, which is based on the historical returns on an asset, traders also use a measure called implied volatility. This is the volatility assumption implied in the actual premium quoted for an option. Implied volatility is used by traders as a measure of whether options represent good value or are overpriced (in which case they should be sold). A volatility smile or skew is a graph which plots the implied volatility of options on the same underlying for a range of strike prices. New products are now available which allow traders to bet on or hedge against market volatility expectations on assets such as the S&P 500 index of major US stocks.

20

Additional Option Applications

20.1 CHAPTER OVERVIEW

Previous chapters have looked at option valuation and risk measures as well as key option strategies. In the current chapter these concepts are applied to currency (foreign exchange) and interest rate options as well as to convertible bonds. The chapter explores how currency options can be used to manage foreign exchange exposures. It considers how exchange-traded contracts operate. It outlines how the Black-Scholes option pricing model is commonly adapted to price currency options. The chapter then considers how interest rate options are quoted and traded and how they are used to manage interest rate exposures. Specific products reviewed are caps and 'caplets'; floors and 'floorlets'; interest rate collars; options on short-term interest rate futures; and swaptions, which are options to buy or sell interest rate swaps. Trading and hedging applications of these various products are explored. A summary is provided of hedging or trading strategies (using cash or derivative products) that might be implemented for different interest rate forecasts. Finally, the chapter explains the basic structure and applications of convertible bonds (CBs) including convertible arbitrage trades.

20.2 OTC AND EXCHANGE-TRADED CURRENCY OPTIONS

A currency or FX option is the right but not the obligation:

- to exchange two currencies;
- on the expiry date (on or before the expiry date in the case of an American option);
- at a fixed rate of exchange.

Most currency options are traded over-the-counter (OTC) by dealers, although contracts are also traded on organized exchanges such as LIFFE, the CME, and the Philadelphia Stock Exchange (now part of the NASDAQ OMX group). CME Group is the largest regulated market for FX trading in the world. According to statistics from the Bank for International Settlements, as at December 2007 the notional amount outstanding on OTC currency options globally was $ 12,748 billion. The figure for exchange-traded currency options was $ 132.7 billion.

The CME offers FX futures and options contracts on major currency pairs as well as currencies that are now growing in importance, such as the Chinese renminbi. It also offers European-style as well as American-style options. Settlement on all trades on the exchange is guaranteed by the central counterparty CME Clearing. CME currency options are **options on futures**. This means that if a holder of an American-style call exercises the contract early it becomes a long futures position at the strike price. If the holder of a put exercises, it becomes a short position in the futures. Most FX futures contracts on the CME involve the physical exchange of the two currencies, though a few are cash-settled. Both American and European FX options are automatically exercised at expiry.

The Philadelphia exchange (PHLX) offers **dollar-settled** European-style contracts in a range of major currencies against the US dollar, including the British pound, the Japanese yen, the euro, and the Swiss franc. The premiums are paid in dollars and the contracts are cash-settled in dollars rather than through the physical delivery and receipt of the foreign currency. For example, suppose the spot rate between the euro and the dollar EUR/USD is 1.4150 and a trader buys an October call on PHLX struck at 142 (which means 1.4200 dollars per euro). The premium is 2.17 US cents per euro. The contract size is EUR 10,000 so the total premium payable is as follows:

$$\$ 0.0217 \times 10{,}000 = \$ 217$$

Suppose that when the option expires the exchange rate EUR/USD is 1.4600. The trader can exercise the call or sell it in the market and is paid its intrinsic value in US dollars. In this example the intrinsic value is as follows:

$$(1.4600 - 1.4200) \times 10{,}000 = \$ 400$$

The net profit to the trader is therefore $\$ 400$ minus the premium of $\$ 217$, which amounts to $\$ 183$ on the contract. All sums are paid in cash in US dollars and there is no physical transfer of euros involved.

20.3 HEDGING FX EXPOSURES WITH OPTIONS: CASE STUDY

OTC and exchange-traded currency options can be used by corporates, traders, and investors to hedge FX exposures. This section considers a typical case, that of a US company exporting goods to the UK which is paid in pounds sterling for the goods. The company is due to receive a payment of GBP 100 million in exactly three months' time. The spot rate GBP/USD now is 1.7500. The company could wait three months and sell the pounds at the prevailing spot rate at the time. The problem is that if the pound weakens against the dollar the firm will receive fewer dollars than expected and may lose money on the export transaction.

One alternative for the company is to book a three-month forward contract with a bank to sell the GBP 100 million and receive a fixed amount of US dollars. The problem is that the company is obliged to go through with this deal even if it could obtain a better rate on the spot market in three months' time. In addition if the firm does not receive the pounds for some reason it is still obliged to settle the forward FX contract.

A further alternative for the company is to buy a three-month European sterling put (dollar call) on GBP 100 million. This provides the right but not the obligation to sell GBP 100 million in three months at a fixed exchange rate (the strike price) and to receive in return a fixed amount of US dollars. Suppose the firm buys a sterling put from a bank struck at 1.7300. The premium is three cents per pound sterling, or $\$ 3$ million on GBP 100 million.

20.3.1 Performance of the Hedge

Table 20.1 analyses the hedge and its potential benefits and drawbacks.

- Column (1) shows a range of possible GBP/USD spot rates in three months' time.

Table 20.1   Performance of FX hedge strategy

(1) GBP/USD at expiry	(2) $m Unhedged	(3) $m Hedged	(4) Hedged FX rate
1.5000	150	170	1.7000
1.6000	160	170	1.7000
1.7000	170	170	1.7000
1.8000	180	177	1.7700
1.9000	190	187	1.8700
2.0000	200	197	1.9700

- Column (2) shows the dollar amount the US company would receive from selling GBP 100 million at that rate.
- Column (3) shows the dollar amount the company would receive if it hedged the FX exposure by buying the 1.7300 strike sterling put, netting out the initial $3 million premium.
- Column (4) shows for each spot rate in column (1) the effective rate of exchange achieved if the company hedged the FX exposure by buying the sterling put.

For example, if the GBP/USD spot rate in three months is 1.6000 then the corporate would receive $160 million for the pounds at the spot rate. On the other hand if the firm had bought the 1.7300 strike sterling put to hedge the exposure then the option would be exercised and the corporate would receive $173 million for the pounds. Subtracting the $3 million premium, the net dollar receipt is $170 million. The effective exchange rate achieved through the hedge would be:

$$\frac{\$170 \text{ million}}{\text{GBP } 100 \text{ million}} = 1.7000$$

$$1.7300 - 0.03 = 1.7000$$

To take one other example, if the GBP/USD spot rate in three months is 1.8000 then the dollars received from selling the pounds at that rate would be $180 million. If the corporate had bought the 1.7300 strike sterling put the option would expire worthless, and the firm would sell pounds for dollars at the more favourable spot rate. From the $180 million received must be subtracted the $3 million premium, so the net dollar receipt on the hedged position would be $177 million. The effective exchange rate achieved is therefore GBP/USD 1.7700.

20.3.2   Graph of Hedged and Unhedged Positions

Figure 20.1 graphs the dollar receipts from selling the pounds for a range of GBP/USD spot rates. The dotted line shows the dollars received at the spot rate, with no hedge in place. The solid line shows the dollars received with the put option hedge in place. The lines cross when the spot rate is at $1.7300 - 0.03 = 1.7000$. At that exchange rate the pounds can be sold for $170 million on the spot market. The net amount of dollars received if the put was exercised (net of the premium paid) would also be $170 million. Note that this analysis ignores transaction costs and the fact that the put premium is paid up-front while the proceeds from selling the sterling occurs three months later. To be more exact there should be an adjustment made for the time value of money.

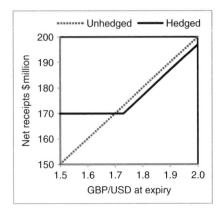

Figure 20.1   Hedged versus unhedged FX exposure.

20.4   PRICING CURRENCY OPTIONS

The Black-Scholes option pricing model was originally written to price equity options. Chapter 17 showed how this is modified for a share or an index that pays a known dividend yield. The inputs to the model are as follows:

- the current price of the underlying;
- the option strike or exercise price;
- the expected volatility of the underlying;
- the risk-free interest rate;
- the dividend yield on the underlying.

This version can be further adapted to price European currency options, and in this guise is commonly known as the Garman-Kohlhagen model. For example, a sterling call (dollar put) is simply the right to buy pounds (the underlying) and to pay in return a fixed price in US dollars. Therefore:

- the spot price of the underlying becomes the GBP/USD spot rate;
- the volatility is the volatility of the spot rate;
- the 'dividend yield' becomes the sterling interest rate, the yield on the currency that would be acquired by the buyer and sold by the writer if the call is exercised;
- the 'risk-free rate' is the dollar interest rate.

Because the model prices European options the valuation is actually based on the *forward* exchange rate between the two currencies at expiry. As shown in Chapter 3, the forward FX rate depends on the spot rate and also on the interest rates in the two currencies, which is why the model requires values for these variables.

20.4.1   Example

This example prices a sterling call (dollar put) with the following input data:

- Spot GBP/USD rate (S) = 175 cents per pound

- Exercise style: European
- USD rate ('risk-free rate') = 3 % p.a.
- GBP interest rate ('dividend yield') = 5.5 % p.a.
- GBP/USD volatility = 10 % p.a.
- Exercise price (E) = 175 cents per pound
- Time to expiry = 0.25 years.

Interest rates are quoted here on a continuously compounded basis. With these inputs the model calculates the following values:

$N(d_1) = 0.4602$

$N(d_2) = 0.4404$

$S \times N(d_1) \times e^{-0.055 \times 0.25} = 79.43$

$E \times N(d_2) \times e^{-0.03 \times 0.25} = 76.49$

The value of the call $C = 79.43 - 76.49 = 2.94$ cents per pound

Although the option is at-the-money in relation to the spot rate, in fact it is actually slightly out-of-the-money in relation to the GBP/USD forward rate. As discussed above, the forward rate is the real reference point to determine the 'moneyness' of a European-style option since it can only be exercised at expiry. The three-month GBP/USD forward rate in this example is lower than 1.7500 (the pound will buy fewer dollars for forward delivery compared to spot delivery) because sterling is the higher yield currency. This means that in relation to the (lower) forward rate a call with an exercise price of 175 cents is actually struck slightly out-of-the-money.

20.5   INTEREST RATE OPTIONS

Interest rate options provide investors, traders, and borrowers with a flexible means of managing interest rate risks and exposures. Since the 1960s central banks and governments around the world have gradually relaxed or abolished controls on currency exchange rates. As a result the short-term rate of interest (especially the repo rate) has become their main weapon against inflation, and from time to time also a means of strengthening or weakening the national currency. This has led, amongst other factors, to increased volatility in interest rates and the need for sophisticated tools to manage interest rate risks and exposures.

FRA and Futures Hedge

A corporate borrower concerned about rising interest rates can buy a forward rate agreement (FRA) or sell interest rate futures (see Chapter 11). However there is a potential drawback. If interest rates fall the borrower has to make a compensation payment to the seller of the FRA, or variation margin payments on the futures contracts. Of course this will be offset by lower interest costs on the borrower's underlying loans, but it will nevertheless suffer an 'opportunity loss'. Net of the payments made on the FRA or futures, its effective borrowing cost will be higher than if it did not have the hedge in place.

20.5.1 Hedging with Interest Rate Options

An alternative strategy for a corporate borrower is to hedge interest rate exposures by buying over-the-counter or exchange-traded interest rate options. An OTC interest rate call option is essentially an option to buy an FRA.

- If at the expiry of the option the LIBOR rate for the period covered by the contract is above the contract rate (the strike price or rate) the corporate will exercise the call.
- It will then receive a cash compensation payment from the writer of the call. The payment is calculated in the same way as it would be for a standard FRA contract.
- If LIBOR is equal to or lower than the strike rate then the option contract expires worthless and no further payment is due to the writer.

Since the buyer of the option has the privilege of exercising the contract in favourable circumstances or otherwise allowing it to expire worthless, the buyer will have to pay an upfront premium to the writer of the contract.

Interest Rate Puts

An investor concerned about falling interest rates can buy an OTC interest rate put. This is effectively the right but not the obligation to sell an FRA to the counterparty (normally a bank). The put will be exercised at expiry if the cash LIBOR rate for the period covered by the contract is set below the strike rate. The investor then holds a sold FRA contract which is cash-settled – that is, a cash compensation payment is received from the counterparty. If at expiry the LIBOR rate is equal to or above the strike rate the put is left to expire worthless and the investor has lost only the initial premium paid.

20.6 EXCHANGE-TRADED INTEREST RATE OPTIONS

Borrowers and investors can also use exchange-traded interest rate options to manage their interest rate risks and exposures:

- the buyer of a put has the right but not the obligation to sell an interest rate futures contract;
- the buyer of a call has the right but not the obligation to buy an interest rate futures contract.

Interest rate futures are quoted in terms of 100 minus the interest rate for the period of time covered by the contract. For this reason, as discussed in Chapter 11, they work in the opposite way to FRAs which are quoted in interest rate terms.

- A borrower concerned about rising interest rates can sell interest rate futures or buy interest rate put options (the right but not the obligation to sell interest rate futures).
- An investor concerned about falling interest rates can buy interest rate futures or buy interest rate call options (the right but not the obligation to buy interest rate futures).

20.6.1 CME Eurodollar Options

Table 20.2 shows settlement or closing prices for December expiry Eurodollar options on the Chicago Mercantile Exchange as at mid-September 2008. The underlying is a three-month

Table 20.2   CME Eurodollar option prices

Strike	Call Premium	Put Premium
9675	0.4375	0.1050
9700	0.2525	0.1675
9725	0.1325	0.2975

Source: Chicago Mercantile Exchange.

Eurodollar futures contract with a notional value of $\$1$ million. As in the case of the underlying futures contract, one basis point represents $0.01\% \times \$1$ million $\times 90/360 = \$25$. The strikes are quoted in terms of 100 minus the implied interest rate for the period covered by the underlying futures contract.

To take one example from the table:

- the 9725 call represents the right to buy the underlying Eurodollar futures contract at a strike price of 9725;
- this implies an interest rate for the three-month period starting in mid-December of 2.75 % per annum;
- the premium cost in dollars per contract is 13.25 basis points $\times \$25 = \$331.25$.

Suppose a trader buys one December 9725 call and retains the position until the expiry of the contract. At that point the three-month Eurodollar interest rate is in fact fixed at 2.5 % per annum. The underlying futures will close at 9750. The trader has the right to buy the futures at 9725. The net profit per call option is calculated as follows:

$$\text{Profit on Exercise} = 25 \text{ points} \times \$25 = \$625$$

$$\text{Net Profit} = \$625 - \$331.25 = \$293.75$$

Looked at another way, the option contract represents an option to invest a notional $\$1$ million at a fixed interest rate of 2.75 % p.a. for the three-month period starting in December. The premium is 0.1325 % p.a. If the LIBOR rate for the period in fact is set at 2.5 % p.a. then the net profit on the option is:

$$\$1 \text{ million} \times (0.0275 - 0.025 - 0.001325) \times \frac{90}{360} = \$293.75$$

20.6.2   CME Eurodollar Put Options

Table 20.2 also shows premiums for December put options. To take one example from the table:

- the 9700 put confers the right to sell a December Eurodollar futures contract at a strike price of 9700;
- this implies an interest rate of 3 % p.a. for the three-month period starting in mid-December.
- the premium on this option per contract is 16.75 basis points $\times \$25 = \$418.75$.

Suppose a trader buys one December put contract and pays 16.75 points premium. If in mid-December the LIBOR rate for the three-month period covered by the contract is set above 3 % p.a. then the underlying futures will close below 9700. The trader will then make a profit from exercising the put and selling the futures at the strike of 9700. To calculate the net profit the initial premium paid has to be deducted from this figure. Ignoring funding and transaction costs, the break-even point is reached when the LIBOR rate is set at 3.1675 % p.a. In that case the futures contract will close at 96.8325 and the trader will recover the 16.75 points in premium paid at the outset.

Of course in practice Eurodollar option contracts need not be retained until expiry or even exercised in order to realize their intrinsic value. They are financial assets in their own right and can be freely traded on the exchange. The value of an option position will respond to changes in the input factors such as the current market price of the underlying interest rate futures contract, the remaining time to expiry, and the volatility of the underlying future interest rate.

20.6.3 LIFFE EURIBOR Options

These contracts are options on three-month EURIBOR futures. The underlying futures contracts have a notional value of EUR 1 million and are quoted as 100 minus the implied rate of interest for the contract period. The LIFFE EURIBOR options are American-style contracts and can be exercised on any business day up to the last trading day. If the holder of a bought call or put option decides to exercise a contract they are assigned a long or short position in the futures contract for the associated delivery month at the strike price. The option premium is not paid in full at the time of purchase. Instead an initial margin is paid and the option position is marked-to-market on a daily basis, and as a result variation margin is either paid or received.

20.7 CAPS, FLOORS, AND COLLARS

A cap is a series of European over-the-counter interest rate call options covering different forward time periods each with the same strike price. Each option is individually exercised or otherwise left to expire.

A Cap as Strip of FRAs

In effect a cap is a series or 'strip' of call options on forward rate agreements. Borrowers can use the product to 'cap' or set a limit on their cost of borrowing over the life of the contract, while still being able to take advantage of falls in interest rates (since they are not obliged to exercise any of the options in the cap).

The cap premium is simply the sum of the premiums of the individual interest rate options that make up the structure. The individual options are sometimes known as **caplets**. Prices on caps are often quoted as a simple percentage of the contract notional amount. This can be paid upfront or 'amortized' over the life of the contract, that is, paid in instalments.

20.7.1 Interest Rate Floors

A **floor** is a series of European over-the-counter interest rate put options each written at the same strike rate. It is a strip of puts on forward rate agreements. An investor can buy a floor to establish a minimum rate of return on money market investments. If the market interest rate for a given time period turns out to be below the strike then the investor will exercise the put which covers that period and receive a cash payment to compensate for the lower reinvestment rate on his or her underlying investments. In return, the investor has to pay a premium for the floor in a lump sum or in instalments.

20.7.2   Interest Rate Collars

A borrower can enter into an interest rate collar strategy by:

- buying an interest rate cap;
- selling an interest rate floor.

This strategy establishes both a maximum and a minimum rate of interest. If interest rates rise above the strike of the cap the borrower will exercise the interest rate calls in the cap and receive compensation payments. If interest rates fall below the strike of the floor, the interest rate puts will be exercised and the borrower will have to make compensation payments to the buyer of the floor.

20.8   INTEREST RATE CAP: CASE STUDY

To illustrate how caps are used in practice this section takes the case of a UK company which has to renew a GBP 100 million loan in six months. The loan will be for three years with semi-annual payments and the rate is likely to be set by the lending bank at LIBOR + 75 basis points. The company's financial officer is concerned about the effects of possible interest rate rises on the profitability of the company, and decides to explore three possible strategies to cope with this problem.

1. Renew the loan in six months at LIBOR + 75 and do not hedge the interest rate risk.
2. Renew the loan as above, but also enter today into a three-year interest rate swap starting in six months paying fixed and receiving floating. The fixed rate on an appropriate forward start three-year sterling swap would be 7.25 % semi-annual against six-month LIBOR.
3. Renew the loan as above, but also buy an interest rate cap on LIBOR covering the payment periods on the loan. A cap with a strike of 7.25 % would cost 1.20 % of the notional principal, payable upfront. Alternatively, the premium can be paid in six semi-annual instalments to match the payment dates of the underlying loan, at a cost of 0.23 % of the notional principal per period or 0.46 % per annum.

The finance director decides to explore a number of scenarios for interest rates and to consider how each strategy would perform.

20.8.1   Scenario A: LIBOR is 6.5 % Over the Life of the Loan

1. The cost of borrowing unhedged is LIBOR + 0.75 % = 7.25 % p.a.
2. The cost of borrowing with the swap in place is fixed at 6.50 % + 0.75 % + 7.25 % − 6.5 % = 8 % p.a.
3. The cost of borrowing with the cap in place is 6.5 % + 0.75 % + 0.46 % = 7.71 % p.a. In this scenario LIBOR is below the strike of the cap so the options in the cap will not be exercised and therefore no payment is due. However the cap costs 0.46 % p.a. in premium.

Table 20.3 Interest rate hedge strategy

LIBOR over life of loan	Unhedged LIBOR + spread	Swapped at 7.25 %	Capped at 7.25 % premium 0.46 % p.a.
5.5 %	6.25 %	8 %	6.71 %
6.5 %	7.25 %	8 %	7.71 %
7.5 %	8.25 %	8 %	8.46 %
8.5 %	9.25 %	8 %	8.46 %

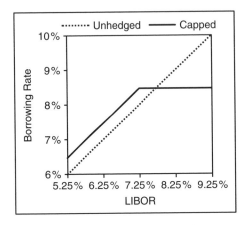

Figure 20.2 Unhedged versus capped exposure.

20.8.2 Scenario B: LIBOR is 7.5 % Over the Life of the Loan

1. The cost of borrowing unhedged is LIBOR + 0.75 % = 8.25 % p.a.
2. The cost of borrowing with the swap in place is fixed at 7.5 % + 0.75 % + 7.25 % − 7.5 % = 8 % p.a.
3. The cost of borrowing with the cap in place is 7.5 % + 0.75 % − 0.25 % + 0.46 % = 8.46 % p.a. LIBOR is above the 7.25 % strike of the cap so the options in the cap will be exercised. The corporate receives 0.25 % per annum (the difference between LIBOR and the strike). The annual premium cost is 0.46 %.

Table 20.3 shows how the three strategies perform under a wider range of different interest rate scenarios. Figure 20.2 compares the unhedged exposure to interest rates with the position with the cap in place.

20.8.3 Interpreting the Results

Notice that with the benefit of hindsight the capped strategy is second best to one of the other two strategies:

- if interest rates fall then the best strategy is to be unhedged;
- if LIBOR rises sharply then the best strategy is to have locked into a fixed borrowing cost via the swap.

The problem is that the finance officer does not know in advance the direction interest rates will take. The cap strategy offers 'something of both worlds'. If LIBOR falls then the options in the cap will simply not be exercised and the corporate is still able to take advantage of falling interest rates (which is not the case if the liability is swapped into a fixed rate). If LIBOR rises the corporate has established a maximum cost of funding (which is not the case if the interest rate exposure is left unhedged). The main disadvantage of the cap strategy is the cost of the premium. This could be offset by selling a floor (a strip of interest rate puts) which will also establish a minimum cost of borrowing.

20.9 PRICING CAPS AND FLOORS: BLACK MODEL

Interest rate options can be priced using a variant of the Black-Scholes model developed by Black in 1976. In the Black version adapted for interest rate options the underlying is a forward interest rate and the volatility is the volatility of the forward interest rate. The fair value C of a European call is given by the equation:

$$C = [F \times N(d_1) - E \times N(d_2)] \times e^{-r_m t_m}$$

where:

F = forward interest rate
E = strike price
e = the base of natural logarithms (approximately 2.71828)
r_m = risk-free rate (continuously compounded) to the maturity of the caplet
t_m = time to maturity of the caplet (in years)
σ = annual volatility of the forward interest rate
$N()$ = cumulative normal function
t_e = time to expiry of the caplet (in years)
$\ln$ = natural logarithm of a number to base e

$$d_1 = \frac{\ln(F/E) + (\sigma^2 \times t_e/2)}{\sigma\sqrt{t_e}}$$

$$d_2 = d_1 - \sigma\sqrt{t_e}$$

The value P of the corresponding put option is given by the equation:

$$P = [E \times N(-d_2) - F \times N(-d_1)] \times e^{-r_m t_m}$$

20.9.1 Caplet Valuation Using the Black Model: Example

The task is to value a cap written on six-month dollar LIBOR. The strike is 6 % p.a. and the nominal is $ 10 million. The first option or 'caplet' in the strip covers a six-month forward period of time (182 days) starting in six months (183 days). The forward rate for this period is 6 % p.a. The expiry date of the first caplet is therefore in 183 days. The relevant dates for this caplet are illustrated in Figure 20.3.

The Black model assumes that the expected LIBOR rate for the forward period will have an average value of $F = 6\%$ and a standard deviation given by the volatility of that rate.

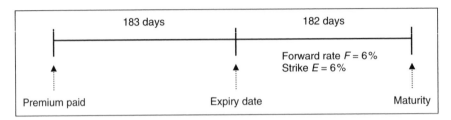

Figure 20.3   Caplet payment dates.

The expected payout of the caplet (made in arrears, 182 days after the option expiry date) is F weighted by $N(d_1)$ minus E weighted by $N(d_2)$. This is then discounted back one year to establish the option premium. In this example:

- Forward rate $(F) = 6\%$ p.a. (actual/360 day-count)
- Exercise price $(E) = 6\%$ p.a. (actual/360 day-count)
- 1-year risk-free rate $(r_m) = 5.43\%$ p.a. (continuously compounded)
- Time to caplet expiry $(t_e) = 183$ days $= 0.5014$ years
- Volatility of $F(\sigma) = 10\%$ p.a.

With these inputs the Black model calculates the following values:

$d_1 = 0.0354$

$d_2 = -0.0354$

$N(d_1) = 0.5141$

$N(d_2) = 0.4859$

$$\text{Expected Payout at Caplet Maturity} = F \times N(d_1) - E \times N(d_2) = 0.1695\%$$
$$\text{Present Value} = 0.1695\% \times e^{-0.0543 \times 1} = 0.1605\%$$

This establishes a value C for the first caplet, which covers a six-month (182-day) period starting in six months. It is shown here on the same basis as the forward rate and the strike, as an annualized rate of interest quoted using an actual/360 day-count. In dollar terms on a notional of \$ 10 million the caplet premium would cost:

$$\$ 10 \text{ million} \times 0.001605 \times \frac{182}{360} = \$ 8114$$

Valuing the whole cap is simply a matter of pricing the remaining interest rate caplets and summing the premiums.

20.9.2   Valuing Floors

Interest rate put options or 'floorlets' can be priced using the equation for P given above, or alternatively by put-call parity. This key result tells us that if C is the value of a

European-style call then the value P of a European put with the same terms (strike, expiration date and so on) is given by the following equation:

$$P = C - [(F - E) \times e^{-r_m t_m}]$$

This formula means that the value of the put equals the call value minus the present value of the difference between the forward rate and the strike price. If the strike E of the call and the put are both set at the fair forward rate F then the present value of F minus E is zero. In that case the call and put will have the same value. The value of a floor is simply the sum of the values of the constituent floorlets.

20.9.3   Issues with the Black Model

The Black model in its original form has some features that are open to criticism. It assumes that forward interest rates are variable with mean value F and standard deviation σ, whereas in practice short-term interest rates do not tend to move very far from their average values. This phenomenon is known as 'mean reversion'.

Traders can cope with this problem by adjusting the volatility assumption (often using different volatilities for each individual caplet in a cap) or by using more complex pricing models. The same sort of problem occurs when pricing bond options, particularly options on Treasury bonds, which do not deviate very significantly from their face value and in fact tend to 'pull' towards their face value with reducing volatility as they approach maturity.

20.10   SWAPTIONS

A swaption is an option on a swap. A buyer has the right but not the obligation to enter into an interest rate swap with a given maturity and fixed rate of interest. The difference between a swaption and a cap or a floor is that the swaption can only be exercised once. A European cap or a floor is a strip of interest rate options each of which may or may not be exercised on its expiration date.

Swaption Types

In a **payer** swaption if the contract is exercised the buyer pays the fixed rate and receives in return the floating rate on an interest rate swap. In a **receiver** swaption if the contract is exercised the buyer pays floating and receives fixed on an interest rate swap.

A payer swaption might be purchased by a corporate or a bank concerned that interest rates will rise, but which does not want to lock into a rate of interest immediately by entering a standard interest rate swap. In that case it could not take advantage of any falls in interest rates until the swap matures. A receiver swaption might be purchased by an institutional investor or a bank concerned that investment rates will fall but which does not want to lock into a fixed return immediately by receiving fixed and paying floating on a swap. In each case the swaption provides flexibility. In return for the initial premium, the buyer has the right but not the obligation to enter into the underlying swap contract.

20.10.1 Swaption Valuation Using the Black Model

To illustrate the method this sub-section takes the case of a European payer swaption with the following details:

- Strike $(E) = 6\%$ p.a. (semi-annual, actual/actual)
- Fair swap rate $(F) = 6\%$ p.a. (semi-annual, actual/actual)
- Volatility of the swap rate $= 15\%$ p.a.
- Expiry $= 1$ year
- Notional principal $= \$100$ million

The underlying swap starts in one year and has a tenor (maturity) of two years with semi-annual payments. The yield curve is flat at 6% p.a. semi-annual. Figure 20.4 illustrates the relevant dates for the swaption and the underlying swap contract.

The swaption is to be priced on its purchase date, with one year to expiration. The values in this case are:

$$F = E = 0.06 \text{ (semi-annual)}$$

$$\sigma = 0.15$$

$$t_e = 1 \text{ year}$$

$$N(d_1) = 0.5299$$

$$N(d_2) = 0.4701$$

$$F \times N(d_1) - E \times N(d_2) = 0.3587\% \text{ (the expected payout)}$$

The expected payout value as an interest rate is then applied to the notional principal $\$100$ million (divided by two since the swap is semi-annual) on each of the four swap payment dates to calculate a dollar value:

$$\text{Expected Payout per Period} = \$100 \text{ million} \times \frac{0.003587}{2} = \$179,350$$

The dollar payouts are then present valued and summed, as shown in Table 20.4. The discount rate applied in each instance is 6% on a semi-annual basis. Note that the first payment due on the swap occurs in 1.5 years or three semi-annual periods from the purchase

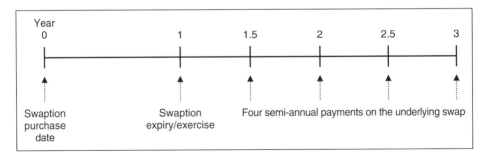

Figure 20.4 Swaption payment dates.

Table 20.4 Swaption expected payouts and present values

Payment date (years)	Expected payout ($)	PV at 6 % ($)
1.5	179,350	164,131
2	179,350	159,350
2.5	179,350	154,709
3	179,350	150,203
	Net Present Value =	628,393

date of the swaption (0.5 years after its exercise date). The final payment is due three years or six semi-annual periods from the purchase date of the swaption. The premium value of the swaption on its purchase date is approximately $ 628,400 or about 0.6284 % of the notional.

20.11   INTEREST RATE STRATEGIES

Table 20.5 sets out some possible strategies that a trader or hedger who expects interest rates to rise or fall might wish to consider. Note that these strategies do not all have the same risk/return characteristics. For example, the maximum loss on buying an interest rate cap is the premium. The maximum loss on selling an interest rate floor (unhedged) can be much greater.

Table 20.5 Interest rate strategies

Market view	Possible strategy
Rising interest rates	• Short bonds or money market paper
	• Sell Treasury bill or bond futures
	• Buy forward rate agreements
	• Sell interest rate futures
	• Pay fixed, receive floating on a swap
	• Buy caplets (calls on FRAs) or caps
	• Buy exchange-traded interest rate puts
	• Sell floorlets (puts on FRAs) or floors
	• Sell exchange-traded interest rate calls
	• Buy payer swaptions
	• Sell receiver swaptions
Falling interest rates	• Buy bonds or money market paper
	• Buy Treasury bill or bond futures
	• Sell FRAs
	• Buy interest rate futures
	• Pay floating, receive fixed on a swap
	• Buy floorlets (puts on FRAs) or floors
	• Buy exchange-traded interest rate calls
	• Sell caplets (calls on FRAs) or caps
	• Sell exchange-traded interest rate puts
	• Buy receiver swaptions
	• Sell payer swaptions

20.12 CONVERTIBLE BONDS

A convertible bond (also known as a 'convert' or a CB) is a bond that can be converted into (normally) a fixed amount of common stock or ordinary shares, at the choice of the investor. The shares are those of the issuer of the bond. Often conversion can take place over most of the life of the bond. The number of shares it can be converted into is called the **conversion ratio**. The current value of those shares is called the **parity** or conversion value of the CB. Some CBs have been issued in which the conversion ratio is adjusted in defined circumstances.

A CB has embedded within it a call option on the underlying shares, which will increase in value if the share price performs well. The option is embedded in the sense that it cannot be split off and traded separately from the convertible bond. It can only be exercised through conversion. When a CB is first issued the investors do not pay a premium to the issuer for the embedded option. Instead, they receive a lower coupon rate on the CB than they would on a standard or straight bond from the same issuer i.e. one without the conversion feature. The first cousin of the convertible is the **exchangeable bond**. This is exchangeable for shares of a company other than the issuer of the bond.

20.12.1 Investors in Convertible Bonds

Buyers of CBs tend to fall into two main categories. The first consists of hedge funds and traders searching for arbitrage and relative value opportunities. Section 20.15 below describes a classic CB arbitrage trade. The second category are the more traditional or 'outright' investors. These include fund managers who are seeking to generate additional returns by taking an equity exposure but who also wish to ensure that the value of the capital invested in the fund is not placed at undue risk. Convertibles offer clear advantages for the more risk-averse investors.

- **Capital protection.** There is no obligation to convert a CB. If the share performs badly a CB can always be retained as a bond, earning a regular coupon and with the par value repayable at maturity. On a day-to-day basis, even if the value of the embedded call has collapsed, a CB will not trade below its value considered purely as a straight bond. This is sometimes called the **bond floor**.
- **Upside potential.** On the other hand, if the share performs well then the investor in a CB can convert into a predetermined quantity of shares at a favourable price. In the jargon of the markets, a CB offers upside potential (because of the embedded call option) but also downside protection (because of the bond floor.)
- **Income enhancement (versus equity).** The coupon rate on the CB may be higher than the dividends an investor could receive if he or she bought the underlying shares, at least for a period of time. If so, the investor will earn an enhanced income until conversion. However, if the embedded call is particularly attractive this may not be the case. Some CBs pay no interest at all.
- **Higher ranking than equity.** CBs are higher ranking than straight equity (ordinary shares or common stock). A company must make interest and principal payments to bond investors before the common stockholders are paid anything.
- **Equity-like bond.** Professional investors managing fixed-income funds can face restrictions on purchasing common stock. The advantage of a CB is that it is structured as a bond although it has an equity-linked return. If the share price rises the convertible will also increase in value.

20.12.2   Issuers of Convertible Bonds

Historically CB issuance tended to be dominated by high-growth companies with lower credit ratings, especially in the technology and biotechnology sectors. In recent times there have been periods when more highly-rated issuers have been attracted to CB issuance to satisfy an increased appetite among investors for equity-linked bonds.

A lower-rated corporate may find it difficult to obtain an acceptable price for selling its shares. The stock may be perceived by investors as too risky. On the other hand, if it issued straight bonds the coupon rate demanded by investors may be too high. Or there may be no takers at all. If so, the company may find that it can raise capital more effectively by tapping the convertible bond market. A CB provides investors with a good measure of capital protection in the shape of the bond floor, whilst offering the prospects of attractive returns if share price performs well. In addition, if the issue is keenly priced, it will attract hedge funds and other traders seeking to construct arbitrage strategies. In summary, CBs can provide a useful source of capital for companies. There are a number of potential advantages for the issuer compared to selling shares or regular straight bonds.

- **Cheaper debt.** Because investors have an option to convert into shares, the coupon paid by the issuer of a CB will be less than the company has to pay on a regular or straight bond (without the conversion feature). In addition, issuance costs are usually lower and it is not normally essential to obtain a credit rating.
- **Selling equity at a premium.** The conversion price of a CB is what it would cost an investor to acquire a share by purchasing and then converting the bond. When a CB is issued the conversion price is set at a premium compared to the price of the share in the cash market. In bull markets the premium can be 50 % and more. Investors accept this because they believe there is a good chance that the share price will rise by at least this percentage over the life of the bond. For the issuer this is equivalent to selling shares substantially above the level of the share price at issue (assuming the bonds are converted).
- **Tax deductibility.** Usually companies can offset interest payments against tax, but not dividends. A corporate that issues a CB can benefit from this so-called **tax shield** until such time as the investors decide to convert and the company issues them with shares.
- **Weaker credits.** The CB market can help lower credit-rated corporates tap the capital markets. In such cases the share price is often highly volatile which increases the potential from the embedded call and can make the CB attractive to hedge funds.

20.13   CB MEASURES OF VALUE

To explore some valuation issues, this section considers a CB which was issued some time ago at par, and now has five years remaining until maturity. The details are as follows.

- Issuer: XYZ Inc.
- Par or nominal value = $ 100
- Conversion ratio = 20 (the bond is convertible into 20 XYZ shares)
- Coupon rate = 5 % p.a.
- Conversion style: at maturity.

When the CB was first issued the coupon rate was set below that for a straight bond without the conversion feature. However, investors were prepared to buy the CB because of the value of the embedded call option. At issue, typically somewhere around 75 % of the value of a CB consists in bond value and the rest is option value.

This example is based on pricing the CB not at issue, but some time later with five years remaining to maturity. Suppose that the required return for straight debt of this credit rating is now 5 % p.a., exactly the same as the coupon rate on the CB. This means that the bond value of the CB is now exactly par, i.e. $ 100. The CB should not trade below its bond value (bond floor) since this represents the value in today's money of the future interest and principal cash flows. Whether the CB is worth *more* than $ 100 depends on the current XYZ share price. Suppose that the cash price of the share is now $ 6. This is used to calculate the bond's parity or conversion value.

$$\text{Parity Value Now} = \$6 \times 20 \text{ shares} = \$120$$

Parity measures the equity value of the CB. In other words, it measures the current value of the package of shares into which the bond can be converted. Just as a CB should not trade below its bond value, it should not be possible to purchase a CB for less than its parity value, assuming that immediate conversion is permitted. The reason is the possibility of arbitrage. If a trader could buy the bond for less than $ 120 and immediately convert into shares worth $ 120 the trader would make a risk-free profit. Market forces should prevent this from happening and a CB should trade for at least its parity value. Parity is related to the modern concept of intrinsic value. The CB should not trade below its parity value in the same way that an American-style call option should not trade below its intrinsic value.

Does this mean that the CB should *only* trade at its parity value? No, for at least two reasons. Firstly, unlike an investment in the underlying shares, the CB offers capital protection in the shape of the bond floor. Secondly, the CB still has five years to maturity and there is a good chance that the share price will increase over that time, which would drive the value of the CB up further. The CB contains an embedded call on 20 XYZ shares with five years to expiry, which has significant time value. The amount that investors are prepared to pay over the parity value of a CB is called **conversion premium** or premium-over-parity. Suppose the XYZ share price is currently $ 6 so that the parity value of the CB is $ 120. If the CB is trading for (say) $ 150 in the market then its conversion premium is calculated as follows:

$$\text{Conversion Premium} = \$150 - \$120 = \$30$$

$$\text{Percentage Conversion Premium} = \frac{\$30}{\$120} \times 100 = 25\%$$

$$\text{Conversion Premium per Share} = \frac{\$30}{20 \text{ shares}} = \$1.5$$

If an investor buys the CB for $ 150 and immediately converts, then the cost of buying the equity through this method is $ 7.5 per share. This is $ 1.5 or 25 % more than it would cost to buy the share in the cash market. It also means that the share price has to rise by at least 25 % before it would make sense for the investor to convert the bonds into shares. Note that the expression 'conversion premium' does not mean quite the same thing as the modern term 'option premium' though it is related, as shown in the next section.

20.14   CONVERSION PREMIUM AND PARITY

Figure 20.5 illustrates the basic relationship between bond value, parity, and conversion premium for the CB from the last section. The bond value (bond floor) is assumed to be $100 and there are now five years to maturity. The CB has been priced assuming a 30% volatility for the underlying shares and assuming that they pay no dividends. Since the CB has a 5% coupon this means that an investor has an income advantage in holding the bond.

In Figure 20.5 parity is shown as a diagonal line. Since the CB is always convertible into exactly 20 shares the relationship between the share price and parity is perfectly linear. If the share price is very low at (say) $1, then the parity value is $20. At an underlying share price of $10 parity is $200. The bond floor is shown as a horizontal line: the bond value of the CB is taken to be $100 whatever the current share price is taken to be. The total CB value is a dotted line.

The difference between the total CB value and the parity value at a given share price is the conversion premium. There are two main factors that determine the conversion premium for this bond, and which predominates depends on where the share price is trading.

1. **Bond floor.** At very low share prices the value of the CB reverts to its bond floor. It is extremely unlikely that it will ever be converted and the value of the embedded call option is almost zero. It is deeply out-of-the-money. At this level the conversion premium is largely determined by the fact that the holder of the CB is not obliged to convert and has the comfort of being able to retain the security as a pure bond investment. If the investor owned shares instead, then the value of those shares would be sliding down the diagonal parity line.
2. **Embedded Call.** At very high share prices the value of the CB converges on its parity value. The CB starts to trade like a package of 20 shares since it is almost 100% certain that it will be converted. There is very little uncertainty about the eventual outcome. The embedded call is deeply in-the-money and (as is the case with such options) the time value component is very low.

20.14.1   Other Factors Affecting CB Value

It is often said that a 'CB is just a bond with an option'. This is a good enough definition when explaining the basic structure of the instrument, but it can be a little misleading in

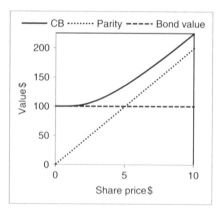

Figure 20.5   Share price and CB value.

practice and needs a few words of qualification. Firstly, a CB can normally be converted over a period of time and not just at maturity. The pricing methodology has to take into account the fact that it should not trade at less than its parity value, otherwise arbitrage opportunities would be created.

Secondly, when a CB is converted the issuing company normally creates new shares. This has the effect of diluting the value of the equity. Thirdly, the graph in Figure 20.5 assumes that the bond floor is unaffected by changes in the share price. In practice this is unlikely. A CB is issued by a company and is convertible into the shares of the same company. If the share price collapses the bond floor may also drop because of fears that the company may default on its debt. In assessing the value of the CB it is necessary to make some assumptions about the relationship between movements in the stock price and the value of the bond floor.

Finally, many CBs incorporate complex early redemption features which affect valuation. For example, the issuer may have the option to 'call' the bond back early at par or just above if it is trading above a certain trigger level for a period of time. By putting out a call or early retirement notice the issuer can then force issuers to convert. It can then sell new convertible bonds at a conversion price set above the current share price level. Some CBs incorporate a number of different early retirement features. In some cases the investor is able to 'put' the bond back to the issuer for cash in defined circumstances.

20.15   CONVERTIBLE ARBITRAGE

Traders and hedge funds often see convertible bonds as a cheap way of 'buying volatility'. This happens when the implied volatility on the embedded call option is relatively low. One way to exploit this situation is to buy the CB and sell exchange-traded or OTC options on the same underlying stock, assuming that these contracts are trading at higher implied volatility levels on the market. In effect this involves simultaneously buying 'cheap' options and selling more expensive options on the same underlying stock. However this is not a perfect arbitrage, because the value of the CB is affected by a range of factors and not just movements in the underlying share price. For example, if the credit rating of the issuer is cut this will lower the bond floor and hence the overall CB value.

The 'classic' convertible arbitrage trade involves buying a CB and shorting the underlying stock in the correct proportion. Take the example of the CB from the previous section, which is convertible into 20 XYZ shares. Suppose the underlying stock is trading at $5 and the CB has a delta of 0.75. Then (in response to small movements in the share price) the CB will behave like a long position in 15 underlying shares. In the classic arbitrage trade this is then matched by shorting 15 XYZ shares. Buying a CB involves acquiring an embedded call on the underlying stock. This is a positive delta position. Shorting the stock balances this out because it is a negative delta position. This means that (for small movements in the stock price) the profits and losses will cancel out. The overall position is delta neutral.

For example, suppose a trader buys $100 par value of the above CB. The current XYZ stock price is $5 and the delta of the CB is 0.75. The trader shorts 15 shares. The underlying share price then rises by $0.01 without any other changes that will affect the value of the CB (such as a change in volatility). Then the profit on the CB and the loss on the short stock position will be as follows:

$$\text{Profit on CB} = \$0.01 \times 0.75 \times 20 \text{ shares} = \$0.15$$

$$\text{Loss on Shares} = \$0.01 \times -15 \text{ shares} = -\$0.15$$

However if the stock price increases sharply the profits on the CB will exceed the losses on the short stock position, because the CB benefits from the positive gamma in the embedded call option. Conversely, because of positive gamma, if the stock price falls sharply the gains on the short stock position will exceed the losses on the CB. For example, if the stock price rises by $\$2$ then (other things being equal) the delta value predicts a rise of $\$30$ in the CB value.

$$\text{Profit on CB Predicted by Delta} = \$2 \times 0.75 \times 20 \text{ shares} = \$30$$

To keep matters simple the CB in this case is priced as a combination of a straight bond worth $\$100$ and a European call on 20 XYZ shares. This method suggests that a $\$2$ rise in the stock price will actually generate an increase in the CB value of about $\$33$. The extra $\$3$ is produced by the gamma effect. Meantime the loss on the 15 shares in the delta hedge (for a $\$2$ rise in the stock price) will be only $\$30$. Figure 20.6 shows the theoretical profits on the arbitrage trade for different levels of the underlying stock price, assuming all other inputs to the pricing of the CB remain constant.

The 'classic' CB arbitrage trade is positive gamma, as shown in Figure 20.6. It is also positive vega. This means that it will tend to make a profit if volatility expectations on the underlying stock rise in the market. This will increase the value of the embedded call in the CB. (It may also depress the price of the underlying stock.) The classic CB arbitrage trade as normally constructed is not actually a pure arbitrage position. This is because a number of risks remain:

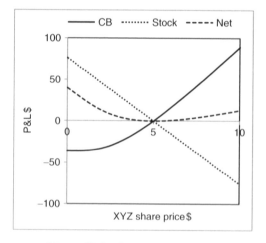

Figure 20.6   Convertible arbitrage.

- If volatility expectations fall the CB will tend to lose value. Meantime there may be little effect on the underlying share price, or it may even rise in value, which will generate losses on the short stock position.
- If the issuer's credit rating is cut this will lower the bond value of the CB (although this may also be accompanied by a fall in the underlying share price which would generate profits on the short stock position). This credit risk could be contained by buying protection through a credit default swap, though at a cost.
- The CB may be fairly illiquid which increases transaction costs and also the risk that it may be difficult and expensive to unwind the arbitrage trade in an hurry.
- Borrowing the stock to create the short position incurs fees, and it may be difficult to arrange in some circumstances.

In addition, the CB may have 'call' features incorporated such that it can be retired early by the issuer. This puts a cap on the profit that can be achieved on a long position in the bond.

20.16   CHAPTER SUMMARY

A currency or FX option is an option to exchange two currencies at a fixed exchange rate. The right to buy one currency is at the same time the right to sell the counter-currency. FX options are traded over-the-counter by dealers or on organized exchanges. Settlement and delivery on exchange-traded contracts is guaranteed by the clearing house. FX options can be used to hedge currency exposures. For example, a US company due to receive a fixed amount of pounds can buy a sterling put (dollar call) which is the right to exchange the pounds for dollars at a fixed rate. If the company can obtain a better rate in the spot market the option need not be exercised. Because the option provides flexibility the buyer has to pay premium to the writer. FX options are often priced by an adaptation of Black-Scholes. The key inputs are the spot exchange rate, the volatility of the exchange rate, and the interest rates in the two currencies.

An OTC interest rate option is essentially an option to buy or sell a forward rate agreement. An exchange-traded interest rate option is an option to buy or sell an interest rate futures contract. An interest rate cap is composed of a series or strip of individual interest rate options each of which may or may not be exercised. It can be used to establish a maximum borrowing cost, but at the expense of paying a premium. An interest rate floor is used to establish a minimum investment rate. A borrower who buys a cap and sells a floor has an interest rate collar. This establishes a maximum and a minimum cost of borrowing. If the strikes of the cap and floor are set appropriately the premium due from the floor will offset the premium payable on the cap and there is zero net premium to pay on the collar. A swaption is an option to enter into an underlying interest rate swap, either as the payer or the receiver of the fixed rate. It can be exercised only once. Interest rate options can be priced using the Black model. It is relatively simple to work with but tends to overstate the extent to which interest rates diverge from their average value. Traders can cope with this by adjusting their volatility assumptions or by using more complex pricing models.

A convertible bond or CB is convertible into a pre-determined number of shares at the option of the holder of the bond. CBs are often considered as a combination of a straight bond and an embedded call on the underlying stock, although in practice they often include early retirement features which complicates their valuation. Traditional investors are attracted to CBs by the fact that they can be retained as a bond, with the par value repayable at maturity, but can also be converted into stock if the underlying share performs well. Traders and hedge funds use CBs as a source of cheap options and also to construct arbitrage trades. The classic CB arbitrage trade consists of buying a CB and shorting the underlying stock. The trade generates profits if the stock price moves more than expected and/or volatility rises. However it can lose money if volatility declines and/or the creditworthiness of the issuer worsens. It also incurs transaction costs and sometimes can be difficult to unwind in a hurry.

Glossary of Financial Terms

Accounts payable
Invoiced amounts owed by a business to its suppliers. In UK accounting known as creditors. Included amongst current liabilities in the company's balance sheet.

Accounts receivable
Invoiced amounts owed to a business. In UK accounting known as debtors. Included amongst current assets in the company's balance sheet.

Accreting swap
A swap in which the principal increases in each time period.

Accruals accounting
A fundamental principle in accounting. Revenues and costs are recorded in the income statement in the period in which they are earned or incurred rather than when cash is actually received or paid.

Accrued interest
Interest on a bond or swap or other financial instrument that has accrued but has not yet been paid out.

Actuary
A specialist in financial mathematics and statistics responsible for estimating the future claims on insurance companies and pension schemes. Firms of consulting actuaries are also used by the trustees of pension funds to help evaluate the performance of asset managers and to help allocate investment management mandates.

Aftermarket
Dealings in a security after it has been launched in the primary market (the market for new issues).

Agency cross
When a broker acts as an agent for both the buyer and the seller in a share transaction.

Agent
Someone authorized to transact business on behalf of a client.

AGM
Annual general meeting.

Alpha
A share or portfolio with returns that exceed its required return adjusted for beta (i.e. its risk-adjusted return) is said to have positive alpha. See: Beta; Capital asset pricing model.

Alternative Investment Market (AIM)
A UK market for issuing and trading shares operated by the London Stock Exchange. It is designed for smaller companies and imposes lower regulatory costs and reporting requirements compared to a full official listing.

American depository receipt (ADR)
A receipt issued in the US by a bank against shares in a foreign company held in custody for investors. ADRs are priced in dollars and settlement procedures are the same as those for a US security. ADRs may trade over-the-counter or on an exchange such as the NYSE.

American option
An option which can be exercised on or before expiry.

Amortization
The repayment of the principal on a loan in instalments over a period of time rather than all at the maturity of the loan. Alternatively, writing off an intangible asset such as goodwill from the balance sheet of a company through a series of charges to the income statement.

Amortizing swap
A swap in which the principal is reduced in each time period.

Analyst
A specialist with expertise in a particular economy, market, or class of securities who advises investors, traders, and salespeople.

Arbitrage
Buying and selling in different marketplaces and making risk-free profits from the disparity between market prices. Sometimes used in a looser sense to include trades that are not strictly risk-free but which take advantage of pricing differences and anomalies.

Asian or Asiatic option
Another name for an average price option.

Asset allocation
The process in portfolio management of deciding how to allocate funds between broad classes of assets (shares, bonds etc.) and different sectors and geographical locations (US, Asia Pacific etc.).

Asset-backed commercial paper
Commercial paper secured on assets such as accounts receivable (debtors).

Asset-backed securities
Bonds backed by a pool of assets such as mortgages and credit card loans. The cash flows from the assets are used to repay the bond holders.

Assets
A company's assets consist of tangible fixed assets such as plant and machinery, current assets such as inventory and cash, and intangible assets such as goodwill. Financial assets held by investors include cash, shares, and bonds.

Assignment
Formal notification from an exchange that the writer of a call (put) option must deliver (take delivery of) the underlying security at the exercise price. Alternatively, the process of transferring ownership of a contract such as a loan from one of the original parties to an acceptable replacement counterparty.

At-best order
An order to a broker to buy or sell a security or derivative contract at the best price available on the market.

At-the-money option
An option whose exercise price is equal to the current market price of the underlying. It has no intrinsic value.

Average price (or rate) option
In a fixed strike contract the payout is based on the difference between the strike and the average price of the underlying during the life of the option. In a floating strike contract the strike is based on the average price of the underlying during the life of the option and the payout is based on the difference between this value and the price of the underlying at expiry.

Back office
The part of a securities operation that settles the trades carried out by the dealers and brokers who work in the 'front-office'.

Backwardation ('normal backwardation')
When the actual futures price of a commodity is less than the expected future spot price. See: Contango.

Balance sheet
The accounting statement that lists a company's assets and its liabilities and share capital. It is drawn up at a specific point in time, such as at the end of the company's financial year.

Balloon or balloon payment
A final payment instalment on a loan that is much greater than the previous payments.

Bancassurance
A business strategy in which a bank also provides products such as life assurance and pension plans.

Bankers' Acceptance (BA)
A negotiable short-term debt security issued by a company typically to finance an international trade deal. Payment on the bill is guaranteed by a bank and the goods involved in the trade deal also serve as collateral. BAs trade at a discount to their face value.

Bank for International Settlements (BIS)
The BIS is based in Basle and is often called the 'central banks' central bank' although most of its activities in this area have been taken over by the International Monetary Fund (IMF). The BIS acts to promote international co-operation in financial matters.

Bank of England

The central bank for the UK. Its Monetary Policy Committee sets UK interest rates to achieve price stability (low inflation). Its responsibilities for banking regulation have been transferred to the Financial Services Authority (FSA) and its responsibility for issuing UK Treasury bills and bonds has been transferred to the Debt Management Office (DMO), a separate agency of the UK Government.

Barrier option

An option that either comes into existence or ceases to exist when the underlying asset reaches a threshold or barrier level. For example, an up-and-out put ceases to exist if the underlying rises to hit a knock-out or barrier level (also known as the out-strike) during the life of the option.

Basis

The relationship between the cash (spot) price of an asset and its forward or futures price. When the forward price of a share is above the cash price the basis is negative. This represents the negative cost of carrying a position in the stock to deliver on the future date. (The funding rate is higher than the dividends earned.) When the forward price is below the cash the basis is positive.

Basis point

In the money and bond markets one basis point equals 0.01 %.

Basis risk

Specifically, the risk that arises because futures prices do not exactly track changes in the underlying asset, because of changes in the basis. More generally, used to mean the risk that results from potential changes in the relationship or 'basis' between two market factors. For example, a bank that funds itself via commercial paper and lends at a spread over LIBOR may be said to have a basis risk. The relationship between commercial paper rates and LIBOR is not a constant.

Basis swap

A swap in which both legs are based on floating interest rates but each is calculated on a different basis. For instance, one leg might be based on the rate on commercial paper and the other on LIBOR.

Basket option

An option whose payoff depends on the performance of a basket of assets. To price the option the dealer has to make an assumption about the correlation between the price movements of the constituent assets. Normally the assets will not be perfectly correlated and due to the offsetting movements in their prices the volatility of the basket will be less than the simple weighted average of the volatilities of the constituent assets.

BBA

British Bankers' Association. The BBA publishes LIBOR rates each business day for a range of currencies.

Bear

A bear is someone who thinks that a security or sector or market will fall in price. A bear market is one in which traders and investors are feeling negative and prices are falling or static.

Bear spread
A combination option strategy which pays a limited profit if the underlying asset falls in value but which only suffers a limited loss if the underlying rises in value.

Bearer security
A security for which the owner of the certificate has full title. There is no register of ownership.

Benchmark bond
A liquid government bond with a round maturity such as 10 years. Its price is actively followed in the market.

Bermudan option
An option that can be exercised on specific dates up to expiry, such as one day per week.

Beta
A measure of the systematic or undiversifiable risk of a security or portfolio. Securities with betas higher than one are more risky than the market as a whole, and their required returns are higher.

Bid
The price a dealer is prepared to pay to buy a security. In the money markets, the interest rate a dealer will pay to borrow funds.

Bid/offer (or bid/ask) spread
The difference between the price a dealer will pay for buying and for selling a security. In the money markets, the difference between the interest rate a dealer pays for borrowing and for lending funds.

Big figure
In the FX markets, the first decimal places of a currency rate quotation.

Binomial tree
A set of prices developed from the current price of the underlying asset such that at any 'node' in the tree the asset can either move up or move down in price by a set amount. Used to price standard and exotic options and instruments such as convertible bonds.

Black model
A variant on the Black-Scholes model, used to price options on forwards and futures.

Black-Scholes
The European option pricing model developed by Black, Scholes, and Merton in the 1970s. Refinements of the model still form the basis of many option trading systems used today.

Block trade
The sale or purchase of a large number of shares.

Blue chip
A top-name company whose shares may be considered to provide a consistent return.

Bond

A debt security issued by a company (corporate), a sovereign state, and its agencies, or by a supranational body such as the World Bank. A straight or plain vanilla bond pays fixed amounts of interest – known as coupons – on regular dates. The par or redemption value of the bond is repaid when the bond matures. Non-straight bonds have different features – for example, there may be no maturity date; or a variable coupon.

Bond option

An option on a bond.

Bond ratings

Ratings of the credit risk on bonds issued by agencies such as Moody's and Standard and Poor's. The ratings establish a ranking system such that on average defaults on higher-rated bonds are less common than those on lower-rated securities. See also: Credit risk.

Book value of equity

The assets of a company less its liabilities. A company's book value may be very different to its market value. See: Market capitalization.

Bookbuilding

The process used by the managers of a new issue to assess demand for the securities, set the issue price, and sign up investors.

Bootstrapping

Deriving zero coupon or spot rates from the yields on liquid coupon bonds trading at par or from the par swap curve.

Bottom fishing

Buying shares when the price has fallen to low levels, expecting the price to rise again.

Bottom-up

A style of portfolio management which is based on building a portfolio from the 'bottom up' based on individual stock selections. See: Top-down.

Boutique

A financial services firm that concentrates on a limited range of specialized activities.

Brady bonds

Bonds issued in the 1990s as part of a scheme to reschedule the debt of Latin American countries. They were issued in US dollars and US Treasuries were used as collateral to guarantee some or all of the payments. They were named after Nicholas Brady, the former US Treasury Secretary.

Break

A rapid and sharp decline in the price of a security or commodity.

Broken date

In the money markets, a non-standard term for a deal (e.g. 50 days).

Broker

A person or firm paid a fee or commission to act as an agent in arranging purchases or sales of securities or arranging contracts.

BTP
Treasury bond issued by the Italian government.

Bull
Someone who thinks that a particular security or the whole market will increase in price. A bull market is one in which traders and investors are feeling positive and prices are rising.

Bull spread
A combination option strategy which pays a limited profit if the underlying asset rises in value but which only suffers a limited loss if the underlying falls in value.

Bund
Treasury bond issued by the Federal German government.

Buy side
An analyst or fund manager working for an investment management firm is said to operate on the 'buy side'. An analyst or salesperson working for a securities house and providing investment ideas to fund managers is said to operate on the 'sell side'.

Cable
The sterling–dollar exchange rate. So-called because deals used to be transacted through a trans-Atlantic cable.

CAC 40
An index of the top 40 French shares. Also used as a basis for index futures contracts.

Calendar or time spread
A combination option strategy that involves buying and selling options with different expiry dates to exploit differences in the rates of time decay.

Call feature
A feature of many corporate bonds that gives the issuer (the borrower) the right to redeem the bonds before maturity. The call price may be at par or slightly above par, depending on the terms of the issue.

Call money
A deposit or loan that is repayable on demand.

Call option
The right but not the obligation to buy the underlying asset at a fixed strike price.

Capital
Financial capital is wealth used to create further wealth. It is provided by governments, corporates, and households and used by governments, corporates, and supranational agencies such as the World Bank. Banks intermediate between suppliers and users of capital. The same word is also used to mean the different sources of funds available to a business, such as common stock (equity capital) and loans and bonds (debt capital).

Capital adequacy
A system under which banks are obliged to maintain a required ratio of capital in proportion to assets such as loans. Assets are weighted according to their risk. Capital includes common stock and preferred stock. The system is designed to help prevent banks from over-extending themselves.

Capital asset pricing model (CAPM)
A model used to establish the required return on a security or a portfolio of securities given the level of risk. According to CAPM the required return on a security is the risk-free rate (the return on Treasuries) plus the market risk premium (the additional return on a diversified market portfolio of securities over and above the risk-free rate) adjusted by the beta factor for the security. See: Beta; Equity risk premium.

Caplet
One component of an interest rate cap.

Capped floating rate note (FRN)
A floating rate note in which the rate of interest cannot exceed a given level.

Cash-and-carry arbitrage
Arbitraging between the cash and the futures market.

Cash flow waterfall
The system of payments in a CDO structure. The tranches are paid in sequence out of the cash flows from the collateral, from the highest to the lowest ranking, with the equity tranche paid last. See: Collateralized debt obligation.

Cash security
Term used to mean the underlying asset rather than a derivative of that asset. An IBM share is a cash security whereas an option on an IBM share is a derivative. A cash market is one is which the underlying assets are traded rather than derivatives.

Cash settlement
Settling a contract in cash rather than through the physical delivery of an asset or commodity. For instance, if an option contract is exercised and cash settled then the writer of the option pays the holder the intrinsic value in cash. The underlying asset is not exchanged.

Cat bond
Catastrophe bond. Pays a high coupon but investors risk losing principal if the losses to insurers on certain 'catastrophic' events such as hurricanes exceed certain levels.

Certificate of Deposit (CD)
A negotiable money market instrument issued by a commercial bank. A CD promises to pay the face value plus a fixed rate of interest at maturity, normally one year or less from issue. Longer-dated CDs may pay interest in a number of instalments.

Chicago Board Options Exchange (CBOE)
The major options exchange founded in 1973.

Chicago Board of Trade (CBOT)
Started as a commodity market in the nineteenth century and has now developed major financial futures contracts such as contracts on US Treasury bonds. Now merged with the CME.

Chicago Mercantile Exchange (CME)
The other Chicago futures and options exchange. Also known as the 'Merc'. Now merged with the CBOT.

Chooser option

The buyer can decide at a pre-set time whether it is a call option or a put option. Also known as U-Choose, as-you-like, call-or-put options. It produces a similar payoff to a straddle but is generally cheaper. See: Straddle.

Circuit breaker

In response to the 1987 crash the NYSE instituted measures called circuit breakers to reduce market volatility and increase investor confidence. Trading stops when the market moves through a trigger level.

Clean price

The price of a bond excluding interest that has accrued since the last coupon date. See: Dirty price.

Clearing house

The organization that registers, matches, monitors, and guarantees settlement on trades made on a futures and options exchange. More generally, an organization that settles trades between financial institutions.

Clearing member

Not all members of a futures and options exchange are clearing members. All trades must be eventually settled through a clearing member which deals directly with the clearing house.

Clearstream

Provides a range of post-trading services to the securities industry including settlement and custody. A wholly owned subsidiary of Deutsche Börse AG.

Cliquet (ratchet) option

An option in which the strike is reset at specific dates according to the spot price of the underlying on that date, locking in any interim gains.

Collared floating rate note

A floating rate note with a minimum and a maximum coupon rate.

Collateral

Cash or securities pledged against the performance of some obligation. A trader wishing to buy or sell futures contracts on an exchange has to put up collateral. If the trader loses money on the trade but is unable to pay, the clearing house has the right to discharge the trader's obligations from the collateral.

Collateralized debt obligation (CDO)

A debt security issued by a special purpose vehicle (SPV). The CDO is repaid from the cash flows generated by a portfolio of assets such as bonds or loans, also known as the collateral. Normally different classes or tranches of CDOs are issued with different risk and return characteristics. Depending on the nature of the underlying assets in the pool a CDO may be called a Collateralized Loan Obligation (CLO) or a Collateralized Bond Obligation (CBO). See: SPV.

Commercial bank

A bank that makes loans e.g. to corporations and governments. The loans may be funded through the money markets rather than through a retail banking business.

Commercial paper (CP)
Short-term unsecured debt securities issued by companies and banks. USCP is commercial paper issued in the US domestic market by US or by foreign companies, at a discount to face value. Euro-commercial paper is issued in international markets and trades on a yield basis.

Commission
The fee charged by a broker to a customer for completing a purchase or sale.

Commodity
A physical item such as oil, gold, or grain. Commodities are traded for spot and also for future delivery. There also exist options to buy and sell commodities.

Common stock
Securities which provide a share in the net income of a business, after payments have been made to the debt holders and on any preferred stock. Common stockholders have a residual claim on the firm's assets in the event of liquidation. They normally have voting rights. Known in the UK as ordinary shares.

Compound option
An option on an option. For example, a call on a put is the right but not the obligation to buy a put option at a fixed premium.

Contagion risk
The risk that problems in a bank or a region may spread to other parts of the local or international financial system.

Contango
When the futures price of a commodity is higher than the expected future spot price. See: Backwardation.

Contract size
A unit of trading on a futures and options exchange. For example, the 30-year Treasury bond futures contract traded on the CBOT is for $ 100,000 par value of US Treasury bonds.

Conversion premium
A term used in the convertible bond market. It measures how much more expensive it is to buy shares by buying and immediately converting a convertible bond compared to buying the shares in the cash market.

Conversion (price) factor
A factor used when bonds are delivered against bond futures contracts which adjusts the invoiced amount according to the coupon and maturity date of the bond that is actually delivered.

Conversion ratio
The number of shares a convertible bond can be converted into.

Convertible bond
A bond that is convertible (at the option of the holder) into a fixed amount of (normally) common stock of the issuing company.

Convexity
A measure of the curvature in the relationship between the price of a bond and market interest rates. The change in duration.

Cost of capital
The rate of return that a business has to pay to providers of capital. The rate will depend on the riskiness of the business.

Cost of carry
The difference between the cost of financing a position in a security and the income received on the security. A trader borrowing money to buy a security will earn positive carry if the income (interest or dividends) exceeds the funding cost. Otherwise the carry is negative.

Counterparty
The other party to a trade or contract.

Counterparty risk
The risk that a trading counterparty may fail to fulfil its obligations e.g. it fails to deliver securities on the agreed trade settlement date.

Coupon
The interest amount payable on a bond.

Coupon rate
The annual rate of interest on a bond. Semi-annual bonds pay the interest in two instalments each year.

Covenants
Legal restrictions placed on a borrower to protect the interests of lenders.

Covered bond
A bond normally issued by a financial institution that is backed by a pool of assets such as mortgages but which also remains on the balance sheet of the issuer. This means that unlike securitization deals involving a special purpose vehicle the bond investors have a claim on the issuer in the event of default and not just on the asset pool.

Covered warrant
A warrant on shares or on baskets of shares in other companies issued by a bank or securities house. A type of tradable option. See: Warrant.

Credit default swap (CDS)
A contract in which a protection buyer pays a periodic premium ('spread') to a protection seller. If a credit event such as bankruptcy occurs affecting the reference entity specified in the contract the protection buyer receives a payment from the protection seller. The reference entity can be a corporation, or a financial institution, or a sovereign state. If a credit event occurs some CDS are settled by the protection buyer delivering a debt asset of the reference entity and receiving the par value from the protection seller. Others are settled in cash.

Credit derivative
A derivative whose payoff depends on the creditworthiness of a specific organization or a set of organizations.

Credit enhancement
Method used to enhance credit quality. For example, in a securitization the creation of subordinated tranches which suffer the first losses arising from default in the asset pool allows the senior tranche to achieve a top credit rating. See: Securitization.

Credit rating
An issuer credit rating is an assessment of the likelihood that a borrower or issuer of securities will make timely payments on its financial obligations. The ratings agencies also rate specific debt issues.

Credit risk
The risk of default or non-payment on a loan or bond or a contractual agreement such as a swap.

Credit spread
The additional return on a bond or a loan over some benchmark rate, dependent on the creditworthiness of the borrower. Often it is expressed as a number of basis points over LIBOR or the yield on a government bond.

Credit spread derivative
A contract whose payoff depends on the difference between the actual spread on two assets in the future and a spread agreed in the contract. The spread could be over LIBOR or a Treasury bond or some other benchmark.

Creditors
UK accounting term. See: Accounts payable.

Cross-currency swap
An interest rate swap in which the payment legs are made in two different currencies. The principals are normally exchanged at the outset and re-exchanged at maturity.

Cum-dividend (cd)
The buyer of a cum-dividend security is entitled to the next dividend payment.

Cum-warrant
A bond with a warrant still attached. See: Warrant.

Currency option
The right but not the obligation to exchange one currency for another at a fixed exchange rate – the strike or exercise rate. Also known as an FX option.

Currency overlay
A strategy used in investment management to divorce decisions made on buying foreign assets from decisions on currency exposures. The fund manager can hedge the currency risk or take additional currency exposure.

Currency risk
The risk of losses resulting from movements in currency exchange rates.

Currency translation risk
The risk that results from translating foreign currency earnings back into its home currency when the consolidated accounts of a company with international operations are prepared.

Current assets
Short-term assets in a company's balance sheet including cash, accounts receivable, and inventory.

Current liabilities
Short-term liabilities in a company's balance sheet including accounts payable and short-term bank loans.

Current ratio
Current assets divided by current liabilities. A measure of how easily a company can meet its most pressing short-term obligations from cash held and from other short-term assets – such as accounts receivable and inventory – that can be quickly turned into cash.

Current yield
The coupon on a fixed-rate bond divided by its clean price. Also known as running or flat or interest yield.

Custodian
A bank or institution that holds securities for safe-keeping and handles administrative arrangements such as collecting coupons and dividends.

DAX
An index of the 30 largest and most actively traded shares traded on the Frankfurt Stock Exchange weighted by market capitalization. It is a total return index – dividends on the shares are assumed to be reinvested. Most equity indices do not take into account income from dividend reinvestment in their calculation.

Day-count
The calendar convention applied to a quoted interest rate or yield.

Dealing spread
The difference between a trader's bid and offer (ask) price.

Debentures
In the US, bonds that are not secured by specific assets but are a general claim on the assets of the issuer. By contrast, in the UK debentures are normally secured on property assets.

Debt
Money owed to creditors or lenders or holders of debt securities.

Debt security
A tradable security such as a bond or Treasury bill or commercial paper that represents a loan made to the issuer.

Debtors
UK accounting term. See: Accounts receivable.

Deliverable obligation
A debt asset that can be delivered by the protection buyer to the protection seller in a credit default swap.

Delivery

The process of delivering assets. In derivatives markets some futures and options contracts involve the physical delivery of the underlying asset. For example, a buyer of bond futures receives physical bonds if he or she has not sold the contracts before the delivery month. See also: Settlement of differences.

Delivery month

The month when a futures contract expires and delivery or final cash settlement takes place. The most common months are March, June, September, and December.

Delta

Measures the change in the value of an option for a small change in the value of the underlying asset. Option traders use delta to hedge their books – it tells them how much of the underlying they need to buy or sell to protect against (small) changes in the price of the underlying.

Delta neutral

An option position that is delta hedged and therefore protected against small changes in the price of the underlying asset.

Depository receipt

A title to shares in a foreign company held by a bank and issued in local currency. Dividends are normally paid in local currency. See also: American depository receipts.

Depreciation

The process of writing off the purchase price of a physical asset through a series of charges to the income statement.

Derivative

An instrument such as an option whose value depends on the value of an underlying asset such as a share or a bond. A derivatives market is a market in which derivative securities are traded.

Digital option

Also known as a binary option. The payoff from the option is a fixed sum.

Dilution

The reduction in earnings per share caused by the creation of new shares in a company.

Dirty price

The total present value of a bond. Clean price plus accrued interest. See also: Clean price.

Discount factor

The present value of $1 at the spot or zero coupon rate for a specific time period, used to discount cash flows due at that period.

Discount rate

Generally, the rate used to discount future cash flows to a present value. Also, in the US money markets, the rate charged to banks when they borrow directly from the Federal Reserve through the discount window.

Discount security

A security such as a Treasury Bill that pays no interest but trades below its face or nominal value.

Disintermediation
The process of cutting out an intermediary. Disintermediation occurs, for example, when companies issue bonds to raise capital directly from the market rather than borrowing from a commercial bank.

Diversification
Buying a portfolio of assets to reduce risk and take advantage of a range of investment opportunities.

Dividend
The payment per share a company makes to its shareholders. On common stock it varies with the profitability of the firm. On preferred stock it is normally fixed.

Dividend cover
Earnings per share divided by dividend per share. It measures the extent to which the dividend payment is 'covered' by earnings. See: Dividend payout ratio.

Dividend discount model
A model used to value a share by discounting expected future dividend payments.

Dividend payout ratio
Dividend per share divided by earnings per share. The proportion of a company's earnings paid out in dividends. The reciprocal of dividend cover.

Domestic corporate bond
A bond issued by a company in its home market and in its home currency. Normally subject to regulation by government authorities.

Dow Jones Industrial Average (DJIA)
Price-weighted index based on 30 leading US companies traded on the New York Stock Exchange. It is adjusted for events such as stock splits.

Downside risk
The risk of making a loss on a trading position or an investment.

Dual currency bond
A bond that pays interest in one currency but which is denominated in another currency.

Due Diligence
A legal requirement that advisors, brokers, and underwriters must meet to ensure that the statements made by a company are accurate and complete. The purpose is to ensure the public has full and accurate information in transactions such as IPOs. Also used in mergers and acquisitions to mean the work a company and its advisors has to do to ensure that they have accurate and complete information about a potential target.

Duration
A measure of the value-weighted average life of a bond's cash flows and of its sensitivity to changes in interest rates. See also: Macaulay's duration and Modified duration.

Duration matching
Matching the duration of assets with those of liabilities.

Earnings per share (EPS)
Net income attributable to the common stockholders divided by the common stock in issue.

Earnings yield
The reciprocal of the price/earnings ratio.

EBIT
Earnings before Interest and Tax. Often used to mean a company's operating profit before exceptional items such as restructuring charges. A measure of a company's earning capability from its ongoing business activities.

EBITDA
Earnings before interest, tax, depreciation, and amortization.

Economic value-added (EVA)
A measure of whether or not a company achieves returns on invested capital above its cost of capital.

Efficient market theory
The theory that share prices reflect currently available information and fully discount expected future cash flows.

Eligible bill or paper
A bill that can be used as collateral by a bank to raise funds from the central bank.

Embedded option
An option that is incorporated into a security or financial product and which cannot be traded separately. For example, there is an embedded call option in a convertible bond. The option can only be 'exercised' through conversion.

Emerging markets
Developing countries with fledgling capital markets. Banks make loans to emerging markets nations and also assist them in issuing bonds and other debt securities.

Equity
Primarily common stock. A common stockholder is a part-owner of the business, receives dividend payments if the company makes a profit, and/or participates in the growth in the value of the company. Preferred stock may also be classified as a form of equity although it (normally) pays a fixed dividend and as such behaves more like debt. In accounting terms, equity equals balance sheet assets less total liabilities.

Equity collar
A strategy that involves buying out-of-the-money put options and selling out-of-the-money calls to protect against losses on the underlying asset whilst at the same time reducing (or eliminating) the net premium due. The disadvantage is that profits on the underlying asset are capped.

Equity risk premium
The additional return required by investors to hold a diversified portfolio of shares above the risk-free rate (the return on Treasuries). See also: Capital asset pricing model.

Equity swap
An agreement between two parties to make regular exchanges of payments where at least one payment leg is based on the value of a share or a basket of shares.

Equity tranche
In a securitization, the class of securities that takes the first loss if assets in the underlying portfolio suffer from default.

ESOP
Employee share option plan.

Eurex
The merged German-Swiss derivatives exchange. Contracts are traded electronically rather than on a physical trading floor.

EURIBOR
Reference rate set in Brussels for interbank lending in euros, the European common currency. Its rival is euro-LIBOR, set in London by the British Bankers' Association.

Eurobond
A bond denominated in a currency other than the currency of the country in which it is issued, and marketed to international investors normally via a syndicate of underwriting banks. Now commonly known as an international bond.

Euroclear
Brussels-based provider of settlement services for bonds and equities.

Euro-commercial paper (ECP)
Short-term unsecured bearer notes issued by major corporations in international markets.

Eurocurrency
A currency held on account outside the domestic market and outside the direct control of its regulatory authorities.

Eurocurrency deposit
Eurocurrency placed on deposit with a bank. The largest market is for Eurodollar deposits.

Eurodollar
A dollar held on deposit outside the US.

Eurodollar futures
A futures contract traded on the Chicago Mercantile Exchange based on the interest rate on a notional three-month Eurodollar deposit for a future time period. The price of the contract is taken as an indication of the market's consensus expectations on future interest rates.

European Investment Bank (EIB)
The body formed by member states of the European Union to provide capital for regional development projects.

European option
An option that can only be exercised at expiry.

Exchange
A market in which securities are traded. Some exchanges use open outcry trading. Others use only electronic trading methods.

Exchange delivery settlement price (EDSP)
The price used to settle a futures contract on the delivery day.

Exchangeable bond
A bond that is exchangeable (at the option of the holder) for a fixed number of shares of a company other than the issuer of the bond.

Exchange-traded contract
A derivative contract traded on an exchange rather than on an over-the-counter basis.

Ex-dividend (xd)
The buyer of a security trading xd is not entitled to the next dividend. It goes to the seller.

Exercise
The action taken by the holder of a call (put) option when he or she takes up the option to buy (sell) the underlying.

Exercise or strike price
The price at which the holder of a call (put) option takes up the right to buy (sell) the underlying asset.

Exotic option
An option that is not a standard call or put e.g. a barrier or an average price or a binary option.

Expiry or expiration date
The last day of a contract.

Ex-rights (xr)
The buyer of a share trading ex-rights is not entitled to any rights to subscribe to new shares. See also: Rights issue.

Face value
The par value of a debt security such as a bond or a Treasury Bill. Normally the face value is repaid at maturity.

Fair value
The theoretical value of a financial asset, often established using a pricing model.

Fannie Mae (FNMA)
Federal National Mortgage Association. Set up as a private corporation sponsored by the US government to facilitate home lending in the US. It raises funds through the bond markets and buys mortgages from banks and other financial institutions. In September 2008 FNMA was taken under government control after major losses on sub-prime mortgages.

Federal funds (Fed funds)
Funds placed on deposit with the Federal Reserve by US banks. A bank that has excess reserves can lend via the 'Fed funds' market to another bank that is temporarily short of funds. The bulk of lending is for overnight maturity, on an uncollateralized basis, although longer-term loans are also contracted. The Federal Reserve sets a target rate for the Fed funds rate and uses this to implement its monetary policy.

Federal Open Market Committee (FOMC)
The committee of the US Federal Reserve that sets interest rates and issues instructions on open market operations conducted by the Federal Reserve Bank of New York.

Federal Reserve
The US central bank. Actually a system consisting of 12 regional Federal Reserve Banks, the Federal Reserve Board and the Federal Open Markets Committee.

Fedwire
An interbank payments system in the US.

Fill-or-kill (FOK)
A type of order on an exchange which is either executed at the stipulated price or cancelled.

Financial future
An exchange-traded contract in which a commitment is made to deliver or take delivery of a financial asset on a future date or between a range of dates at a fixed price. In some contracts no physical delivery actually takes place and the contracts are settled in cash.

Financial institution or financial intermediary
A generic name for banks, investment management institutions, securities houses, brokers, insurance companies etc.

Financial Services Authority (FSA)
The combined regulatory body in the UK that regulates the banking system, the securities industry, investment management, personal financial services, and insurance.

Financial Statements
Accounts prepared by companies, comprising a balance sheet, income statement (profit and loss account), cash flow statement, related notes, and other statements required by regulation.

Fixed interest or income security
Literally, a security that pays a fixed income on a regular basis until maturity. Often though it is used as a generic term for bonds.

Fixed price offer
In a UK new share issue, when the new shares are offered to the public at a fixed price rather than in a tender (auction).

Fixed re-offer price
An expression used in bond issues. The syndicate of underwriters re-offer the bonds at the same price to the market until the securities are all sold, when the syndicate breaks.

Flat price
Clean price.

Flex options
Exchange-traded options that have some flexibility as to their terms e.g. the strike price can be non-standard.

Floating rate
A rate of interest such as LIBOR that varies over time.

Floating rate certificate of deposit
A CD with a coupon that resets periodically according to a benchmark rate such as LIBOR.

Floating rate note (FRN)
A bond whose coupon is linked to current market interest rates. The coupon resets e.g. every three months according to a benchmark rate such as LIBOR.

Floor broker
On a US exchange, someone who buys and sells securities on the floor of an exchange on behalf of clients.

Foreign bond
A bond issued by a foreign borrower in another country's domestic market.

Foreign exchange risk
The risk of losses resulting from changes in foreign exchange rates.

Forex
Foreign exchange.

Forward contract
An agreement to buy or sell a security or commodity or currency at an agreed price for delivery at some date in the future. A forward contract is a legally binding agreement made directly between two parties and is not traded on an exchange.

Forward exchange rate
The rate to exchange two currencies on a date later than spot.

Forward interest rate (forward-forward rate)
The rate of interest that applies between two dates in the future. The forward yield curve is constructed using such rates.

Forward rate agreement (FRA)
A contract between two parties to make compensation payments based on the difference between a contractual interest rate for a forward time period and the actual market rate for that period.

Forward start option
An option that starts on a future date.

Forward start swap
A swap that starts on a date later than spot.

Freddie Mac (FHLMC)
Federal Home Loan Mortgage Corporation. US body set up to facilitate mortgage lending. It issues bonds backed by pools of mortgage loans. It was taken under US government control in September 2008.

Front running
When a trader creates a position on the trading book in anticipation of a large deal which may move the market.

FT-SE 100 Index
An index of the top 100 UK shares weighted by market capitalization.

Fully Diluted Earnings per Share
A calculation carried out by companies to warn shareholders of potential deterioration of earnings per share in the future as a result of new shares being issued due to the exercise of convertible bonds, warrants, or options. The calculation reworks the earnings per share figure for the current year on the basis that the dilution had already occurred.

Fundamental analysis
An analysis of the fair value of a share based on an assessment of the prospects of the company, its balance sheet, forecast earnings growth etc. The work of an investment analyst in a bank or broking operation or in a fund management business.

Funded pension scheme
A pension scheme in which the regular payments are used to buy assets such as shares and bonds.

Fungible
Two securities or contracts are said to be fungible when they can be considered as identical and directly interchangeable.

Futures contract
An agreement transacted through an organized exchange to buy or sell a security or commodity at an agreed price for delivery at some date in the future. Futures contracts can be freely traded on the exchange. Some contracts such as index futures are cash settled and no actual physical delivery takes place.

Futures option
An option to buy or sell a futures contract.

Gamma
The change in an option's delta for a small change in the price of the underlying asset. Gamma measures how quickly delta changes and therefore how unstable a trader's delta hedge is likely to be. See: Delta.

Gilt or gilt-edged security
A bond issued by the UK Government.

Glass-Steagall Act 1933
US law (now repealed) preventing commercial banks from underwriting new issues or dealing in securities.

Global bond
A bond issued simultaneously in major markets around the world.

Going Concern
One of the fundamental accounting concepts. It is assumed that a company will continue in operational existence for the foreseeable future.

Goodwill
The price paid for a business over and above the value of its physical assets. This may be amortized over a period of time. See: Amortization.

Government securities
Bills, notes, and bonds issued by governments.

Greeks
The market's name for the option sensitivity measures: delta, gamma, theta, vega, and rho.

Greenshoe option

A means of stabilizing a new issue. The manager of the issue takes a short position in the stock which is covered by an option to acquire additional shares from the company. If the share price after the issue rises above the exercise price of the option, the manager can close the position by exercising the option. If the share price falls below the exercise price, the manager will let the option lapse and close the position by buying shares in the market. This will create additional demand for the shares and act as a stabilizing mechanism.

Grey market

Trading in securities before they are issued.

Growth investment

A style of equity investment that favours growth shares.

Growth share or stock

Shares in a company whose earnings are expected to grow rapidly. The shares often trade on a high price/earnings ratio.

Haircut

When bonds are pledged as collateral against a loan the lender will normally apply a 'haircut' and lend less than their current market value. This is to protect against falls in the value of the collateral.

Hedge fund

Originally meant a 'long-short' fund which takes both long and short positions in securities. In this sense the fund may be relatively low risk since much of the risk is hedged out. It is now also used though to mean funds that take highly leveraged or speculative positions e.g. on currencies or interest rates or equity markets or market volatility.

Hedge ratio

The calculation of how much of the hedge instrument has to be traded to cover the risk on the asset to be hedged. For example, the number of futures contracts that have to be bought or sold to hedge an exposure on a share or a bond.

Hedging

Protecting against potential losses. For example, a borrower can buy a forward rate agreement as a hedge and will receive compensation payments if interest rates rise.

Herstatt risk

The risk in an FX transaction that payment is made to a counterparty which then fails to make the return payment in the other currency. Named after a German bank that failed in 1974.

High-yield bonds

Bonds with a credit rating lower than the Standard and Poor's BBB − rating but which pay a higher yield. They are sometimes called speculative or 'junk bonds'.

Historic volatility

The standard deviation of the historical returns on a security over a period of time, such as three months.

Holding company

A company which controls one or more subsidiary companies in which it owns shares.

Holding period return
The annualized return on an investment that is held over some specified time horizon.

Hypothekenbank
A German mortgage bank.

Implied repo rate
The repo or funding rate implied in an actual bond forward or futures price.

Implied volatility
The volatility assumption implied in an actual option price.

Index
A figure representing the changing value of a basket of securities, such as a stockmarket index. The index is set at some arbitrary value such as 1000 on the base date. Indices such as the UK FT-SE 100 are weighted by the market capitalization of the constituent companies.

Index arbitrage
Arbitrage trade assembled by simultaneously buying and selling shares and index futures.

Index credit default swap
A CDS which is based on an index representing a basket of names rather than a single reference entity.

Index fund or index tracker
A fund that seeks to track or match the performance of a market index.

Index futures
A financial futures contract based on a market index. The contracts are cash settled.

Index option
An option on a market index such as the S&P 500.

Initial margin
A trader on a futures and options exchange has to deposit initial margin as a performance deposit. This can be cash or (by agreement with the broker) some other acceptable collateral such as Treasury bills.

Initial public offer (IPO)
An offer to the public to buy shares in a company for the first time. Originally a US expression but it has become universal.

Insider trading
Trading on price-sensitive information not yet in the public domain. It is illegal in the US and Europe and in most countries now.

Institutional investor
A firm such as a pension fund investing money on behalf of other people. In the financial markets sometimes known as 'the buy side'.

Instrument
A share or a bond or some other negotiable security.

Intangible asset
A non-physical asset on a company's balance sheet, such as goodwill.

Interbank market
Dealings in the capital markets between banks. The bulk of foreign exchange deals, for example, are interbank.

Interest cover
A measure of a company's ability to meet its interest bill. Often calculated as operating profit divided by gross interest expenses.

Interest rate cap, floor, collar
A cap is an option product typically sold to borrowers, which places a limit or 'cap' on their cost of borrowing. If the interest rate for a given time period covered by the cap is above the strike then the cap buyer will receive a compensation payment from the seller. A floor establishes a minimum interest rate level and may be sold to investors. A collar establishes both a minimum and a maximum interest rate.

Interest rate future
An exchange-traded contract based on the interest rate for a period of time starting in the future. The listed equivalent of the forward rate agreement. See: Eurodollar futures.

Interest rate margin
The difference between a bank's lending rate and its funding rate.

Interest rate option
An option based on an interest rate.

Interest rate swap
An agreement between two parties to exchange regular cash flows on regular dates for a specified time period. Normally one payment is based on a fixed interest rate and the return payment is based on a floating or variable rate, usually LIBOR. The rates are applied to the notional principal to calculate the payments.

Interest yield
See: Current yield.

Interim dividend
A dividend paid part of the way through a company's financial year.

Internal rate of return
The annualized return on a set of cash flows assuming that interim cash flows are reinvested or borrowed at a constant rate. The method used to calculate the yield-to-maturity of a bond.

International Capital Market Association (ICMA)
The self-regulatory organization and trade association representing financial institutions operating in the international capital markets.

International Swaps and Derivatives Association (ISDA)
A trade association for dealers in over-the-counter derivatives such as swaps, caps, floors, collars, and swaptions. The ISDA Master Agreement is widely used as the legal basis for swaps.

In-the-money option
An option that has positive intrinsic value. In the case of a call, when the strike is below the current price of the underlying. In the case of a put, when the strike is above the current price of the underlying.

Intrinsic value
The value that could be released from an option by immediate exercise. In the case of an American call it is the maximum of zero and the spot price of the underlying minus the strike. In the case of an American put it is the maximum of zero and the strike less the spot price of the underlying. Intrinsic value is either zero or positive.

Investment bank
Originally referred to a bank that underwrites and deals in securities such as bonds and shares. Now mainly used to mean a bank that operates in the capital markets, issuing and trading securities and derivatives, and which also advises on mergers, acquisitions, and privatizations. Many investment banking operations now are divisions of larger financial services groups. For example, JP Morgan Investment Bank is part of JP Morgan Chase & Co.

Investment grade bonds
Bonds that are rated BBB- and above by Standard & Poor's. Some investing institutions are only allowed to buy investment grade paper.

Investment manager
An individual or institution managing funds on behalf of clients. Also known as a fund or asset or portfolio manager.

Investment trust
The UK name for a closed-ended investment fund structured as a limited company whose shares are listed and traded on an exchange.

Issue price
The price at which a new security is issued including fees paid to underwriters and selling agents.

Issuer warrant
Warrant (long-dated option) issued by a company on its own shares, which trades in the form of a security.

Junk bond
Below investment grade bond trading at a high yield.

Knock-out or knock-in level
The level of the underlying at which a barrier option ceases to exist or comes into existence. Sometimes known as the out-strike and the in-strike. See: Barrier option.

Ladder option
An option which locks in intervening profits during its life. Whenever the underlying hits a 'rung' or threshold price level the gains to that point cannot then be lost.

Lead manager
The bank or group of banks which takes the lead in arranging a syndicated loan or an issue of new securities and which takes the largest share of the fees. Also known as the bookrunner.

Leasing
Where a bank or other financial institution buys equipment and leases it to the end-user for a period of time. Often there is a tax advantage to a leasing deal.

Lender of last resort
Traditionally the role of the central bank. If it fears systemic risk it may stand ready to lend to an ailing financial institution when no one else will.

Leverage (US) or Gearing (UK)
The proportion of debt to equity in a company's capital structure. In a trading or investment situation leverage refers to generating higher returns through a strategy that requires a relatively small outlay of capital. For example, an at-the-money call option will cost a fraction of the underlying share price, and the potential returns are very high if the share price rises sharply.

Leveraged buy-out (LBO)
When a company or subsidiary is bought funded mainly by debt.

Liabilities
Money owed by a company to its creditors, bondholders, and other providers of debt such as banks. A company's assets less its liabilities – its net assets – belong to its shareholders.

LIBID
London Interbank Bid Rate. The rate top banks pay for taking in deposits in the London market.

LIBOR
London Interbank Offered Rate. It is an average based on data provided by a panel of major banks on offer (lending) rates for short-term interbank funds available in the London market. LIBOR is compiled by the British Bankers' Association in conjunction with Reuters and released shortly after 11:00 a.m. London time. There is a separate LIBOR rate for each currency listed by the BBA and for a range of maturities.

LIBOR OIS Spread
The difference between three-month LIBOR and the overnight index swap (OIS) rate. See: Overnight index swap.

LIFFE
The London International Financial Futures and Options Exchange. Part of the NYSE Euronext Group.

Limited liability
If a limited liability company goes into liquidation the shareholders can only lose their initial stake; their personal assets are not at risk.

Limit order
An order from a client to buy or to sell a security or a futures or options contract where the client specifies a maximum purchase price or minimum sale price.

Limit price move
Some exchanges only allow price moves within certain limits in the course of a day. Trading is stopped if the limit is broken. This is intended to give the market time for reflection.

Liquidation
Winding up a company. It may be voluntary or imposed by creditors.

Liquidity
There is a liquid market in a security if it is easy to find a buyer or seller without having to increase or lower the price to a great extent.

Liquidity preference theory
The theory that other things being equal investors prefer short-dated investments and have to be offered a higher return to buy longer-dated investments.

Liquidity ratio
A balance sheet ratio that measures how easily a company could pay off its short-term liabilities. See: Current ratio.

Liquidity risk
The risk that trading in a security or a currency or other asset dries up and either prices cannot be found, or are subject to sharp fluctuations. Also used in retail and commercial banking to mean the risk that arises from funding on a short-term basis and lending on a longer-term basis.

Listing
A listed company is one whose shares are quoted and traded on a recognized major market such as the NYSE. Listed companies have to provide a substantial amount of information on a regular basis about their trading and financial position. Normally a company selling shares in an IPO will also seek a listing on an exchange or exchanges.

London Stock Exchange (LSE)
The stock exchange for UK shares and gilts and also shares in foreign countries. Traditionally a quote-driven market based on market makers, it has also introduced an electronic order-matching system.

Long position or long
The position of a trader who has bought securities or futures or options contracts.

Lookback option
An option whose payoff is based on the maximum or minimum price of the underlying during the life of the option.

Macaulay's duration
The weighted average time to maturity of a bond's cash flows. The weight assigned to a cash flow is its present value as a proportion of the total present value (dirty price) of the bond.

Management buy-out (MBO)
When the existing management team buys a company or a subsidiary usually with the financial assistance of banks and/or private equity funds.

Mandatorily convertible or exchangeable bond
A bond that must be converted into or exchanged for shares on or before a certain date. See: Convertible bond; Exchangeable bond.

Margin call
A trader who has bought or sold contracts on a futures and options exchange receives a call to make an additional margin payment (on top of the initial margin deposited) if there is an adverse movement in the value of the contract.

Margin trading
In some markets it is possible to buy shares or other financial assets 'on margin' – that is by putting up a proportion of the purchase price and borrowing the rest from the broker.

Market capitalization or market cap
The value of a company on the stockmarket. It is the current market price of a share times the number of shares on issue. The book value of the equity in the company's balance sheet is often a much lower figure. The stockmarket attempts to value a firm as a going concern. Equity book value is normally based on the historical cost of the assets less depreciation.

Market expectations theory
The theory that holds that the yield curve builds in the market's consensus expectations about future interest rates and bond prices.

Market maker
A trader who makes a market in particular securities by quoting bid and offer (ask) prices. Unlike a broker, who acts purely as an agent matching buyers and sellers, a market maker buys or sells securities on his or her firm's own account and runs a trading book. Also said to operate on a principal as opposed to an agency basis.

Market risk
Also known as price or rate risk. The risk that results from the effects of changes in the market prices of securities or interest or exchange rates.

Mark-to-market
Revaluing investments based on the current market price. For example, if an investor bought bonds for $1 million yesterday and they are now worth $1.1 million today the mark-to-market profit is $100,000. This is a paper or unrealized profit – the profit is only realized if the bonds are actually sold.

Maturity date
The date on which a bond matures and the face or par value is repaid. Also known as the redemption date. Other financial instruments such as interest rate swaps also have fixed maturity dates.

Medium-term note (MTN)
MTNs were originally debt securities with maturities of two or so years and designed to fill the gap between commercial paper and bonds. Now the maturity can be 10 years and more. The main feature of MTNs is the issuance procedure. Borrowers set up an MTN programme and sell notes on a continuing basis rather than on a specific issue date. The notes are often sold via dealers acting as selling agents rather than underwritten.

Merchant bank
The old UK name for investment bank.

Mezzanine capital
A hybrid source of capital that lies somewhere between debt and equity. The term is often used to mean subordinated debt which ranks behind the senior or secured debt for payment, but in front of the equity. There are specialist funds dedicated to making mezzanine finance investments.

Middle office
The part of a trading operation that stands between the traders in the front-office and the back-office staff who settle deals and manage cash payments. In practice responsibilities can vary greatly. They range from helping dealers input trades into an electronic deal capture system, to working out the end-day profits and losses. Many banks feel that it is important that profits and losses are checked by middle office staff rather than by the dealers who created the positions.

Modern portfolio theory
A theory that measures the risk on a security or a portfolio based on the statistical variance of returns. An optimal portfolio is one that maximizes return for a given level of risk.

Modified or adjusted duration
Used to measure the percentage change in the dirty price of a bond for a 1 % change in yield.

Momentum investment
A style of investment that involves riding the market trend in a share or sector until it changes direction.

Monetary Policy Committee (MPC)
The committee of the Bank of England that sets short-term UK interest rates.

Money market
The market for short-term wholesale deposits and loans (up to one year) and for trading short-term negotiable securities such as Treasury bills and commercial paper.

Monte Carlo simulation
A method of establishing the value of a complex financial asset or portfolio by setting up a simulation based on random changes to the variables that determine the value of the asset or portfolio. The average or 'expected' outcome is then calculated.

Mortgage-backed securities (MBS)
Generally, bonds and notes backed by a pool of mortgages. The mortgage payments are earmarked to pay interest and principal on the bonds. In a simple pass-through structure all the investors receive the same pro-rata payments from the mortgage pool. In a collateralized mortgage obligation (CMO) different classes of securities are issued with different payment characteristics. See: Collateralized debt obligations.

MSCI Indices
A family of equity indices maintained by MSCI Barra used as benchmarks by international investors.

Mutual fund
The US term for an investment vehicle managed by a fund management firm in which savers can pool their savings to invest in a diversified portfolio of assets. Shares in the fund are bought and sold from the fund manager or from a broker rather than on a stockmarket.

Naked option
An option position that is not hedged.

Naked short sale
Selling a stock short without first having made arrangements to borrow the stock.

NASDAQ®
The US electronic screen-based share trading market. It is an entirely quote-driven system, based on market makers that buy and sell shares from inventory in transactions with investors and with other dealers.

Nearby month
A futures or options contract with the nearest delivery or expiry date from the date of trading.

Negative convexity
Bonds with embedded call features can exhibit negative convexity. This means that the rise in the bond price for a larger fall in yield is less than the fall in the bond price for the same rise in yield.

Negotiable security or instrument
A security that can be freely traded after it is issued. For example, CDs are negotiable securities whereas term deposits with a bank are not.

Net asset value (NAV)
For a company, equivalent to shareholders' equity. It is balance sheet assets minus liabilities.

Net income
The 'bottom line' figure in a company's income statement. It measures the profit from trading activities over a given period attributable to the shareholders. Often a proportion is paid out as dividends and the rest is reinvested in the business.

Net present value (NPV)
The sum of a set of present values.

New issue
A new issue of shares or bonds or other debt securities.

New York Stock Exchange (NYSE)
The largest stock exchange in the world by market capitalization. Floor brokers act on behalf of clients, transacting buy and sell orders for a commission fee. The role of the specialists is to manage the order-matching process. They can also act as a market maker if a broker is unable to match a trade.

Nikkei 225
An index based on the price-weighted average of 225 shares traded on the Tokyo Stock Exchange. The Nikkei 300 is weighted by market capitalization.

Nil paid
An expression used in connection with rights issues. The holder of rights can sell them to another investor 'nil paid' and the buyer will then have to pay the rights price to the issuing company to receive the shares.

Nominal interest rate
The stated or quoted rate of interest or yield on a loan or debt security.

Normal distribution
The classic bell curve whose properties were proved by Gauss. In the Black-Scholes model it is assumed that the returns on shares follow a normal distribution.

Nostro account
From the Latin for 'our'. A bank's payment account held at another bank. See: Vostro account.

Notional principal
The face value of a derivative contract such as a swap.

OAT
French government bond.

Off-balance-sheet
An item that does not appear on the assets or liabilities columns on a company's balance sheet. The item can still give rise to contingent liabilities.

Offer price (ask price)
The price at which a trader is prepared to sell a security. In the money markets, the interest rate a dealer asks for lending funds.

Off-market swap
The fixed rate is different to the current market rate. One party makes a compensating payment to the other.

On-the-run bond
The most recently issued and actively traded US Treasury for a given maturity. The coupon on the bond is close to the current level of interest rates and many investors like to hold the bond.

Open-ended fund
A mutual fund that can continuously take in additional capital from investors and create new shares or units in the fund. Investors buy and sell the shares directly from the fund manager or a broker operating on its behalf rather than on a stock exchange. Traditionally known in the UK as a unit trust.

Open-ended investment company (OEIC)
An investment company listed on a stock exchange that has the flexibility to issue or cancel shares in response to investor demand. The shares trade at a single price.

Open interest
The number of futures or options contracts for a given delivery month that are still open. It is usually shown as the number of open long contracts or equivalently the number of open short contracts (not both combined). Many traders start to close out contracts before the last trading day, reducing the open interest.

Open market operations
The activities of a central bank in the money market designed to influence short-term interest rates and implement monetary policy.

Open outcry market
A physical market in which trades are conducted by dealers calling out prices.

Open position
A long or a short position in securities or other assets which is not yet closed out and which therefore gives rise to market or price risk until it is closed or hedged.

Operating profit or loss
A company's profits and losses arising from its day-to-day business operations.

Option
The right but not the obligation to buy or to sell a given asset at a fixed price (the exercise or strike price) on or before a specified date (the expiry or expiration date).

Order-driven market
A market in which client buy and sell orders are directly matched.

Ordinary share
A stake in the equity of a company, carrying an entitlement to participate in the growth of the business and (normally) voting rights. US: Common stock.

Out-of-the-money option
In the case of a call, when the strike is above the price of the underlying. In the case of a put, when the strike is below the price of the underlying.

Outright forward FX
A forward foreign exchange deal in which two currencies are exchanged for a value date later than spot.

Outright purchase or sale
A sale or purchase of securities by a central bank without time limit, as opposed to temporary sales and purchases via repo.

Overnight index swap (OIS)
A fixed/floating interest rate swap in which the floating leg is linked to a published index of an overnight reference rate. At maturity one party pays to the other the difference between the fixed rate and the geometrical average of the overnight rates over the life of the swap, applied to the notional principal.

Over-the-counter (OTC) transaction
A trade that is agreed directly between two parties rather than through an exchange.

Paid-up capital
The part of a company's issued shares that has been paid for by shareholders.

Par
The face or nominal value of a bond or bill, normally repaid at maturity. Bonds are quoted as a percentage of par.

Par bond
A bond that is trading at par.

Parallel curve shift
When the yield curve shifts up or down in parallel i.e. the yield change is the same at all maturities. A 'twist' in the curve happens when there are non-parallel movements.

Parity
An expression used in the convertible bond market. It measures the equity value of a convertible bond. It is the bond's conversion ratio (the number of shares it converts into) times the current market share price.

Par swap
An interest rate swap in which the present value of the fixed and the floating legs are equal.

Participating preferred stock
Preferred stock that pays an additional amount on top of the fixed dividend depending on the level of profits.

Partly-paid Share
The shareholder is liable to pay an additional sum of money when the outstanding amount is called by the company.

Pass-through security
A security backed by underlying loans such as mortgages. The cash flows from the loans are passed through on a pro-rata basis to make the principal and interest payments to the bondholders. See: Collateralized debt obligation.

Payback period
How long it takes to recover the initial negative cash flows on an investment. The traditional payback measure does not discount cash flows and hence ignores the effects of time value of money.

Perpetual bond
A bond with no fixed maturity date. Coupons are paid in perpetuity.

Perpetual floating rate note
A floating rate note with no maturity date.

Pfandbriefe
A bond issued by one of the German mortgage banks and backed by mortgage loans and loans to local government authorities. It is a type of covered bond. See: Covered bond.

Physical delivery
The process of delivering the underlying asset specified in a contract. Some derivative contracts involve physical delivery of the underlying at a pre-agreed price. In other cases the contracts are 'cash settled' and one party pays the difference between the contract price and the price of the underlying in the spot market on the date the contract is settled.

Plain vanilla
The most standard form of a financial instrument, such as a straight coupon-paying bond with a fixed maturity.

Political risk
The risk of losses in financial markets that result from exceptional activities by governments e.g. halting foreign exchange trading in the national currency, or imposing special taxes.

Portfolio insurance
A hedging technique much maligned (probably unjustly) in the aftermath of the 1987 stock market crash. It involves dynamically adjusting a hedge against losses on the market as the market moves by e.g. trading index futures.

Portfolio management
Also known as fund or asset or investment management. Managing money for individual and institutional investors such as pension funds by assembling a diversified portfolio of assets. The assets may include shares, bonds, cash, money market securities, property etc.

Portfolio trading
Buying and selling whole portfolios of shares.

Position
A trader or investor who has bought securities has a long position. Someone who has sold short has a short position. A trader with an open position is exposed to market risk unless it is hedged or closed out.

Preferred stock (UK: preference share)
Preferred stock normally pays a fixed dividend and does not carry voting rights. However the dividend must be paid before the common stockholders (ordinary shareholders) receive a dividend. It ranks ahead of common stock for payment if the company goes into liquidation.

Premium
In the options market the premium is the price of an option – the sum which the buyer pays to the seller for the rights granted by the contract. On other occasions the word is used when an asset is trading above some reference level – for example, a bond trading above par is said to be trading 'at a premium to' its face value.

Present value
The discounted value of a future cash flow or cash flows.

Price/book ratio
The market capitalization of a company as a ratio of the book value of the equity (i.e. its net assets).

Price/earnings ratio
The most commonly used measure of relative value in the equity market. It is the current market price of a share divided by the historic or prospective earnings per share.

Primary dealer
A large financial institution that participates in the auctions of new government securities and which buys and sells stock in the secondary market. In the UK known as Gilt-Edged Market Makers (GEMMs).

Primary market
When a security is first issued it is said to be launched in the primary market. See also: Secondary market.

Prime rate (US)
The base rate of interest on dollar loans to companies posted by the largest banks in the US.

Private equity
A business or fund that takes equity stakes in unlisted companies or companies listed on smaller exchanges, often participating in management buy-outs (MBOs) and spin-offs from corporate restructurings. Normally this is with a view to selling the stake at a later date through a trade sale or an initial public offering.

Private placement
When new securities are placed directly with large institutional investors rather than through a public offer.

Privatization
When an operation in public ownership is turned into a company in the private sector through a share offer or trade sale.

Profit
A company's gross profit is revenues minus the direct costs of running the business. Subtracting sales and general expenses calculates operating profit. Net income is the 'bottom line' profit figure taking into account non-operating items. It is attributable to the equity holders. Normally a proportion is paid out in dividends and the rest is reinvested in the business.

Profit and Loss Account (UK)
A statement showing a company's income and expenditure over a period of time, usually one year. Part of the financial statements of the company. In the US called the Income Statement.

Project finance
Complex financing deals involving construction and engineering projects, often employing a mixture of sources of finance and sometimes with government involvement.

Prospectus
A document prepared by a company issuing securities to the public.

Protective put
Buying a put option to protect against losses on an asset.

Provisions
Liabilities where the company is uncertain as to the amount or timing of the expected future costs. For example, if a company is subject to a law suit, it may provide now for the expected loss.

Proxy hedge
A hedge that involves using a related financial instrument that is to some extent correlated with changes in the value of the underlying asset to be hedged. For example, a trader who has sold options on a basket of shares may buy liquid futures contracts on a market index expecting that profits and losses on the shares and the futures will offset. There is a risk that the correlation between the two may turn out to be lower than anticipated.

Prudence
A fundamental accounting concept. Accounts must be prepared on a prudent basis. Revenue must never be shown in the accounts until the cash realization of the revenue is reasonably certain. Costs arising as a result of past actions should be provided for immediately, even if the cash will not be paid over until the future.

Pull-to-par
The movement in a bond price towards its par or face value as it approaches maturity.

Put-call parity
A fixed relationship between the fair value of European call and put options. It shows that a long or short forward position can be assembled from a combination of call and put options on the underlying with the same expiry date (when the strikes are set at the forward price).

Put feature
A feature of some bonds that allows the investor to sell the bonds back to the issuer before the maturity date.

Put option
The right but not the obligation to sell the underlying at a fixed strike or exercise price.

Quanto option
An option in which the payoff depends on an underlying denominated in one currency (such as the UK FT-SE 100 index) but is paid in another currency (such as the US dollar).

Quick ratio
Current assets minus inventory as a ratio of current liabilities. A measure of how easily a company can pay off its most pressing debts with cash and other assets that can quickly be turned into cash. Also known as the acid test or acid ratio.

Quote-driven market
A market in which market makers (traders) quote bid and offer prices for securities.

Rainbow option
An option whose payoff depends on two or more underlyings. For example, an option based on the best performing of two equity indices over the time to expiry.

Ranking (Subordination)
Some securities rank ahead of others in terms of entitlement to payments. Holders of senior secured debt must be paid before other bond holders are paid. Preferred stock ranks ahead of common stock.

Ratings agency
Agencies such as Moody's and Standard and Poor's and Fitch which rate the default risk on corporate and sovereign debt.

Real interest rate or yield
An interest rate or rate of return on an investment excluding inflation.

Recovery rate
A measure of what can be recovered on a loan or a bond that defaults e.g. 40 cents in the dollar.

Recovery share
An unloved share trading at a low price that is deemed to be ripe for recovery.

Redemption
When the redemption value of a security is re-paid to the investors.

Red Herring
US term for the initial prospectus in a new share issue, published before the issue price has been set. In the UK sometimes called a pathfinder prospectus.

Reference entity
The corporation or other organization on which protection is bought and sold in a credit default swap.

Registered securities
Shares or bonds whose ownership is recorded in a central register. The opposite is a bearer security for which the physical certificate is the only title of ownership.

Registrar
A bank or other institution employed by a company to maintain the share register.

Reinvestment risk
The risk that arises with coupon bonds that coupons cannot in practice be reinvested at a constant rate. Hence the actual return may be higher or lower than the yield-to-maturity at which it was originally bought.

Repo
Short for sale and repurchase agreement. In a repo a debt security is sold for cash with an agreement that it will be repurchased on a specified future date at the same price. The original holder of the security borrows money using the security as collateral and will pay interest on the loan at a reduced borrowing rate. The other party is effectively borrowing the security for the term of the repo, perhaps to maintain a short position. Nowadays central banks lend money to commercial banks using the repo structure and the rate at which a central bank will lend against collateral has become a key money market rate.

Repo rate
The rate of interest charged by the lender of funds in a repo. Also used to mean the rate of interest for repo transactions between a central bank and commercial banks.

Reserve assets
Funds that commercial banks must have in cash or on deposit with the central bank in proportion to the deposits they take in.

Reset or refix date
The date when a floating rate on a swap is refixed for the next payment period.

Retained earnings
Company profits not paid out in dividends and added to the equity in the balance sheet.

Return on capital
Profit as a proportion of the capital employed in the business (debt plus equity).

Return on equity
Net income attributable to the common stockholders as a proportion of shareholders' equity.

Return on total assets (ROTA)
Net income as a proportion of total assets.

Reverse FRN
A special kind of floating rate note. The coupon rate moves inversely with current market interest rates. They are extremely sensitive to changes in interest rates.

Rho
The sensitivity of an option value to a change in interest rates, usually a one basis point change.

Rights issue
'Rights' is short for pre-emption rights. An offer to existing shareholders to buy new shares at a discount to the current market price. A shareholder can take up the rights or sell them on. See also: Ex-rights.

Risk management
Monitoring, evaluating, and hedging against potential losses caused by changes in asset prices, interest rates, currency exchange rates etc. Investment banks and securities houses normally have a risk management function that provides an independent assessment of the risk on trading positions.

Rollover
In listed derivatives, rolling a position over from one expiry or delivery month to a later month.

Running yield
See: Current yield.

Samurai bond
A bond denominated in yen issued in the Japanese domestic market by a foreign issuer.

Savings and loan association (SLA)
US financial institution that takes in deposits and makes housing loans. Similar to the UK building societies.

Secondary market
A market to buy and sell securities already launched through the primary market. See: Primary market.

Securities and Exchange Commission (SEC)
Federal agency responsible for regulating the securities industry in the US.

Securitization
The process of creating asset-backed securities by packaging up future cash flows such as the interest and principal repayments due on loans. Bonds are sold to investors which are backed by the underlying cash flows.

Security
The generic name for a negotiable (tradable) instrument such as a share, bond, or bill.

Seed Capital
Equity funding injected in the early stages of a start up venture where the product, process, or service is in its conceptual or developmental phase.

Sell-side
Analysts and salespeople and traders working for investment banks and securities houses who provide investment ideas and execute trades for fund managers (the buy-side).

Senior tranche
Normally the safest class of securities in a securitization deal, which only suffers losses if the level of default in the underlying portfolio is substantial. Sometimes a 'super senior' tranche is created which ranks above the senior tranche.

Series
An expression used in derivatives exchanges. Option contracts on the same underlying with the same strike and expiry.

SETS
Stock Exchange Trading System. The electronic order-driven system for trading securities run by the London Stock Exchange.

Settlement date
The date when a security is transferred and cash is paid for it. Depending on the market, settlement may be the day after the deal is agreed or a week or more later. The expression '$T + n$' means that settlement is made n business days after the trade date.

Settlement of difference
With some derivatives contracts there is no physical delivery. The difference between the contract price and the price of the underlying is settled in cash.

Settlement price
The price used by a clearing house to mark-to-market a derivatives contract. Often an average of the last trades at the end of the trading day.

Short position, short sale, short
Someone who has sold a cash security he or she does not own. Or someone who has sold futures or options without yet having bought contracts to close the position.

Sinking fund
When the issuer sets aside funds to redeem a bond issue or (more commonly) retires a certain amount of the issue each year.

Sovereign
Used in the capital markets to mean a government borrower as opposed to a corporate.

Sovereign risk
The risk that a sovereign borrower might default on a loan or a bond issue.

SPAN
Standard Portfolio Analysis of Risk. A system developed on the CME to calculate margins on portfolios of derivatives contracts.

Sparkassen
German savings banks.

Specialist member
A member firm of the New York Stock Exchange that manages the order matching process on a trading post.

Special purpose vehicle (SPV)
A tax-exempt trust company specially set up to implement a securitization. The SPV issues bonds and buys the title to the ownership of the cash flows that will repay the bonds. It manages the payments to the bondholders.

Spot foreign exchange rate
The rate for exchanging two currencies in (for major currency pairs) two business days.

Spot interest rate or yield
Zero coupon interest rate or yield.

Spot price
The price of a security for spot delivery. Also known as the 'cash price' although the actual settlement and delivery may actually take place a day or so after the trade is agreed.

Spread
The difference between two prices or rates. For example, a dealer charges a spread – the difference between his or her bid and offer price. A commercial bank lends money at a margin or spread over its funding rate. The extra yield or return on a corporate bond over the yield on safe government debt is known as a credit spread since it reflects the additional default risk.

Spread trade
Simultaneously buying and selling to take advantage of anticipated changes in the price difference between two securities or derivatives contracts.

Stabilization
The process of supporting the price of a new issue of securities by means of the management group of the issue buying the relevant bonds or shares in the market place for a limited period of time in the after market.

Stag
An trader speculating on a new share issue.

Stamp duty
A government tax on share dealings.

S&P 500
Standard and Poor's 500. An index of 500 top shares traded on the NYSE and on NASDAQ.

Stock dividend
When an investor takes a dividend in the form of new shares rather than cash.

Stock exchange or market
An organized and regulated market for trading securities. It can be a physical market located on a trading floor, or based on screens and telephones, or a purely electronic market.

Stock index
An index that tracks the changing price of a typical portfolio of shares. In the US key indices include the Dow Jones Industrial Average and the S&P 500. The most commonly quoted index in the UK is the FT-SE 100.

Stock index futures
A futures contract based on an index such as the S&P 500 or the FT-SE 100. These are 'settlement of differences' contracts – there is no physical delivery of shares. On the main S&P 500 futures contract each index point is worth $250.

Stock lending
Holders of shares can make extra money by lending the shares to a borrower for a fee. The lender demands collateral to ensure that the shares are returned.

Stock split
When a company thinks its share price is too unwieldy it can issue a number of new shares to replace each existing share. Also known as a bonus or capitalization issue in the UK. A stock split differs from a rights or other new equity issue in that the company is not raising new capital.

Stop-loss order
An order to a broker to close out a position and limit the losses whenever a given price level is reached.

Stop-profit order
An order to a broker to close out a position and take the profits to date whenever a given price level is reached.

Straddle
A combined option strategy that involves simultaneously selling a call and a put (short straddle) or buying a call and a put (long straddle) on the same underlying with the same strike and the same time to expiration.

Straight bond
A bond that pays fixed coupons on fixed dates and has a fixed maturity date. A 'plain vanilla' bond, without non-standard features such as a variable coupon or the right to convert into shares.

Strangle
Like a straddle except the options used in the strategy have different strikes. See: Straddle.

Strike price
Another term for the exercise price of an option.

Stripping and strips
Also known as coupon stripping. Separating the principal and the interest payments on a coupon bond and selling off the parts as zero coupon bonds. The resulting zeros may be known as 'strips'.

Structured note
A security usually assembled using derivatives that has non-standard features e.g. the payments are linked to a commodity price or an equity market, or the difference between interest rates in two currencies, or the change in the creditworthiness of a particular company.

Swap
A binding contract between two parties agreeing to exchange payments on specified future dates over an agreed time period, where the amount that each has to pay is calculated on a different basis. See: Cross-currency swap; Equity swap; Interest rate swap.

Swap curve
A yield curve based on the fixed rates on standard par interest rate swaps. It can be bootstrapped to generate spot rates. See: Bootstrapping; Yield curve.

Swaption
An option to enter into an interest rate swap. A payer swaption is an option to pay fixed and receive floating. A receiver swaption is an option to receive the fixed and pay floating. Also now used to mean an option to enter into a credit default swap.

SWIFT
Society for Worldwide Interbank Financial Telecommunications. The interbank secure messaging system based in Belgium.

Syndicate
A group of investment banks combining to underwrite and distribute a new issue of securities; or a group of commercial banks combining to create a syndicated loan.

Syndicated loan
A loan made to a corporation or a government by a syndicate of lending banks. Members of the syndicate may allocate a proportion of the deal to a number of 'participating' banks.

Synthetic securitization
A securitization deal in which the underlying assets consist in a portfolio of credit default swaps rather than actual loans or bonds.

Systematic risk
Undiversifiable or market risk.

Systemic risk
The risk that an event such as a bank failure might have a domino effect on the rest of the financial system.

Takeover
Acquiring control of a corporation, called a target, by share purchase or exchange, either hostile or friendly.

Tangible Assets
Fixed assets that are physical and can be touched, such as land, cars, and plant.

Technical analysis
Analysing the pattern of price movements of an asset to predict future price changes. In the UK also known as chartism.

TED spread
Treasury/Eurodollar spread. The difference between the three-month dollar LIBOR rate and the return on three-month US Treasury bills.

Tender
In the UK sometimes used to mean an auction of securities.

Tenor
Time to maturity.

Term deposit or loan
A deposit or loan with a specific maturity.

Term repo
A repo with longer than overnight maturity.

Term structure of interest rates
Spot rates in a given currency for a range of maturities.

Theta
The change in the value of an option as time elapses.

Tick size
In theory, the minimum price move allowed in a price quotation. In practice half and even quarter ticks have been introduced on some exchanges.

Tick value
The value of each one tick movement in the quoted price on the whole contract size.

Time value
The difference between an option's premium and its intrinsic value. Time value is related to time to expiry and the probability that the option will make money for its owner (lose money for the seller) and is calculated by models such as Black-Scholes. If an option has no intrinsic value then all the premium is time value.

Time value of money
The basis of discounted cash flow valuation. If interest rates are positive then money today is worth more than money in the future because it can be invested. Money due to be received in the future is therefore worth less today.

Top-down
A style of portfolio management based on firstly making top-level decisions about which classes of assets and which markets to invest in, and only later picking individual securities. See: Bottom-up.

Touch
The highest bid and the lowest offer price for a security.

Trader
An individual or an employee of a financial institution who buys and sells securities and runs trading positions.

Trade fail
When something goes wrong in the settlement of a trade e.g. the payment instructions are not carried out properly.

Tranche
From the French word for 'slice'. In a securitization different tranches of bonds are often sold with different risk/return characteristics to appeal to specific investor groups. See: Securitization.

Treasury bill (T-Bill)
A short-term negotiable debt security issued and fully backed by a government.

Treasury bond
A longer-term debt security issued and fully backed by a government. US Treasury bonds have maturities over 10 years when issued. Treasury notes have maturities between one and 10 years.

Triple witching hour
US expression for the day when stock and index options and index futures all expire.

Two-way quotation
A dealer's bid (buy) and offer (ask or sell) price. The difference between the two is the dealer's spread.

Ultra vires
Beyond the legal power. Used when an organization or individual enters into a transaction which they are not legally entitled to conduct.

Underlying
The asset (such as a share or bond) that underlies a derivative product. The value of the derivative is based on the value of the underlying.

Underwriting
The underwriters of a new issue of securities effectively guarantee that the securities will be fully taken up at the issue price. If they cannot find buyers the securities are left with the underwriters. In a larger issue there will be a syndicate of underwriters.

Underwriting risk
The risk that the underwriters will lose money if they are unable to sell securities for more than the price they have guaranteed the issuer.

Underwriting syndicate
In a new issue of shares or bonds a group of banks and securities firms may form a syndicate to pool the risk and ensure the successful distribution of the issue.

Universal bank
A banking group that offers a wide variety of products and services globally, including investment and commercial banking. It may also have a retail banking operation, a fund management business, and an insurance subsidiary. Sometimes a large banking group that offers a wide range of services but which is focused on one region (e.g. Europe) is called a regional bank.

Upside potential
Potential for profits.

Value at Risk (VAR)
A statistical estimate of the maximum loss that can be made on a portfolio of assets to a certain confidence level and over a given time period. For example, if a portfolio of securities is currently worth $ 1 million and the one-week VAR at the 99 % confidence level is $ 50,000 this means that there is only a 1 % chance that losses on the portfolio over the course of one week will exceed $ 50,000.

Value investment
A style of investment that favours relatively 'cheap' shares (with low price/earnings ratios) that are reckoned to be undervalued.

Variation margin
Additional margin paid or received when a derivatives contract is marked-to-market and there is a margin call from the clearing house.

Venture capital
Sometimes used now as a synonym for private equity. More often it means taking a stake in a start-up company or a business in an early growth phase. The venture capitalist often takes a substantial proportion of the equity and plays a 'hands on' role advising management on the development of the business. See: Private equity.

VIX Index
The CBOE Volatility Index® (VIX®) measures the volatility expectations built into S&P 500 index options with 30 days to expiry. The VIX is sometimes called the 'investor fear gauge' because it tends to rise during periods of increased anxiety in the financial markets and steep market falls.

Voice broker
A broker who relays current market bid and offer prices to subscribing clients via a voice-based system rather than electronically.

Volatility
A key component in option pricing. A measure of the variability of the returns on the underlying security. This can be based on historic evidence or future projections. The more volatile the returns on a security the more expensive a standard option on that security will be – the holder of the option has more chance of making money, the seller has more chance of losing money. See: Historic volatility; Implied volatility.

Volatility smile
A graph showing the implied volatilities of options on the same underlying for a range of strike prices. It is used to pinpoint the correct volatility to use to price or revalue options. In- at- and out-of-the-money options often trade on different implied volatilities in the market. In practice the graph may be a skew rather than a smile.

Volatility surface
A three-dimensional graph showing the implied volatilities of options on the same underlying for a range of different strike prices and expiration dates.

Volume weighted average price (VWAP)
The average price at which a share was traded during a given time period, such as one day. Each trading price is weighted by the number of shares traded at that price. Dealers and fund managers use VWAP as a benchmark to see whether or not they have traded close to the market level.

Vostro account
From the Latin for 'your'. A payment account maintained by a bank on behalf of another bank. See: Nostro account.

Warrant
A long-dated option in the form of a security that can be freely traded, often on a stock exchange. Issuer warrants are issued by a company on its own shares. Covered warrants are sold by banks and securities houses and are based on another company's shares or on baskets of shares. They may be call or put warrants. Covered warrants are often cash-settled i.e. the intrinsic value of the option is settled in cash and no physical shares are ever delivered.

Weighted average cost of capital (WACC)
Most companies are funded through a mixture of equity and debt capital. WACC is usually calculated as the cost of debt times the proportion of debt in the business, plus the cost of equity times the proportion of equity in the business. It is used as a discount rate to establish the present value of a firm's expected future cash flows, and thereby to establish a value for the whole company.

Withholding tax
Tax deducted at source on the payment of dividends or interest.

Working capital
Current assets minus current liabilities.

World Bank
Provides financial and technical help to developing countries around the world.

Writer
The seller of an option.

Yankee bond
A US dollar bond issued inside the US domestic market by a non-US issuer.

Yield
The return on an investment, taking into account the amount invested and the expected future cash flows.

Yield curve
A graph showing the yields on a given class of bonds (e.g. US Treasuries) against time to maturity. A positive or upward-sloping curve occurs when rates on shorter maturity bonds are lower than those on longer maturity bonds. A negative or inverse or downward-sloping curve occurs when short-term yields are higher.

Yield-to-call
The internal rate of return on a bond assuming that it is held to the first call date and is then called.

Yield-to-maturity
The return earned on a bond if it is bought at the current market price and held until maturity with coupons reinvested at a constant rate. The bond's internal rate of return.

Zero cost collar
A collar strategy on which there is zero net premium to pay. The premiums on the calls and puts cancel out.

Zero coupon bond
A bond which does not pay a coupon and which trades at a discount to its par or face value. At maturity the holder is repaid the face value.

Zero coupon rate (spot rate)
The rate of interest that applies to a specific future date. Specialists in fixed income markets use zero coupon rates to discount cash flows and price instruments because no reinvestment assumptions need be made.

Index

Index compiled by Indexing Specialists (UK) Ltd